# Population and Development in the 21st Century - Between the Anthropocene and Anthropocentrism

*Edited by Parfait M. Eloundou-Enyegue*

Published in London, United Kingdom

Population and Development in the 21st Century - Between the Anthropocene and Anthropocentrism
http://dx.doi.org/10.5772/intechopen.1001522
Edited by Parfait M. Eloundou-Enyegue

Contributors
Agnès Adjamagbo, Aja M. Sutton, Anne E. Calvès, Anton Kolotusha, Chenoa Flippen, Christopher S. Awinia, Claude Mbarga, Concepció Patxot, Deborah J. Milly, Emilio Parrado, Emily Klancher Merchant, Eugeny Banin, Gemma Abio, Gervais Beninguisse, Guadalupe Souto, Hamish Robertson, Huaqing Wang, Imad Rherrad, Irina Kalabikhina, Lesego Selotlegeng-Mbe, Louis G. Tassinary, Michel Tenikue, Natalia Loukachevitch, Nick Nicholas, Parfait M. Eloundou-Enyegue, Samantha Friedman, Sandra Florian, Sarah Giroux, Siaka Cissé, Thalia Tom, Zack W. Almquist, Zhuang Han



First published in London, United Kingdom, 2024 by IntechOpen
IntechOpen is the global imprint of INTECHOPEN LIMITED, registered in England and Wales, registration number: 11086078, 167-169 Great Portland Street, London, W1W 5PF, United Kingdom

British Library Cataloguing-in-Publication Data
A catalogue record for this book is available from the British Library

Additional hard and PDF copies can be obtained from orders@intechopen.com

Population and Development in the 21st Century - Between the Anthropocene and Anthropocentrism
Edited by Parfait M. Eloundou-Enyegue
p. cm.
Print ISBN 978-1-83769-724-3
Online ISBN 978-1-83769-723-6
eBook (PDF) ISBN 978-1-83769-725-0

For EU product safety concerns:
IN TECH d.o.o., Prolaz Marije Krucifikse Kozulić 3, 51000 Rijeka, Croatia,
info@intechopen.com or visit our website at intechopen.com.

# Meet the editor

Parfait Eloundou-Enyegue, Ph.D., is a Professor of Global Development at the Brooks School of Policy, Cornell University, New York. His scholarly interests are in population and development. He has lectured in multiple countries in North America, Africa, and Asia. Between 2007 and 2017, with support from the Hewlett Foundation, he led a network to build demographic capacity in Africa. He has consulted with the United Nations, the World Bank, and the United States Agency for International Development (USAID). He has served on multiple scientific and advisory boards and was a member of a team of scientists nominated by the UN's Secretary General Panel to draft the first quadrennial report on Sustainable Development Goals. He currently chairs the review board at the Institut National d'Etudes Démographiques (France) and is a coordinating author on the United Nations' Global Environment Outlook (GEo7).

# Contents

# Preface

## The Anthropocene: How Demography May Change the World

The premise of this book is that demography can profoundly mark the 21st century. The mark need not be indelibly deterministic. As even the boldest prospective will concede, "demography is not destiny" and yet, several signs point to the dawn of a demographic epoch. One of these ushering signs is the looming end of world population growth. According to recent projections by the United Nations, the world's population will peak at around 10.4 billion during the 2080s, when it will stabilize before eventually declining. This decline has already begun for many. As of 2022, two thirds of people in the world lived in a country or area where fertility rates were below replacement; more than 60 countries were projected to decrease by 1 per cent or more between 2022 and 2050.[1]

This historical reversal matters. For one, it changes the direction of population worry from "bomb to bust" in a world where the structure of families and the economics of childbearing are pushing fertility ever lower, fueling a second demographic transition. The question is whether this "bust" will quell the socioeconomic and environmental fears once stoked by rapid population growth. Would it be powerful enough to stop the ecological harm predicted under the Anthropocene? Will it narrow the income gaps between rich and poor? Or instead, would it raise new concerns about the workforce or the elderly, for instance? More broadly, how will societies respond to the demographic forces driving or following the upcoming population bust, whether these forces relate to immigration and fertility declines or to aging and changes in family life?

The book's first section explores these responses. It covers a range of domains from inequality and immigration to aging and health. To begin with global inequality, the first three chapters in the volume address the new conventional wisdom of "partial convergence" in which inequality would decrease between countries but increase within many countries. Chapter 1 by Eloundou-Enyegue explores the population and inequality in the 21st century. In Chapter 2, Han et al. undertake a similar analysis but focus on countries of the global South where they find a demographically induced divergence: Because national fertility transitions in this sub-region varied in timing and impact, they widened the economic divide across countries. Along with internal inequalities between the rich and poor, these results portend future economic divergence in the global South. Chapter 3 examines inequality within the United States, a country where income inequality has been increasing over the last three decades. According to Friedman and Tom, this inequality is increasingly crystallized by residential segregation along education lines, suggesting a need to heed the intersection between class and spatial mobility. How both mobilities are modulated by education will determine whether school becomes the greater "equalizer" or the greater "divider."

[1] United Nations (2022). *World Populations Prospects* 2022. https://population.un.org/wpp/; last consulted in November 2023.

Immigration, another key issue, is also reaching a historical milestone. It is now the sole driver of population growth in high-income countries,[2] with potentially far-reaching effects on the economy, politics, and culture. Robertson and Nicholas explore a variety of institutional and socioeconomic responses to immigration into Australia in Chapter 4, including effects on the work force and on social care. In Chapter 5, Florian et al. focus on cultural dimensions and women's employment, concluding that consequences ultimately depend on patterns of women's incorporation in the labor force. As was true for inequality, demographic forces are found to be salient but not deterministic. How immigration changes global culture and politics depends on laws and policies governing the integration of migrants. Global immigration can be turned into a positive force if, as the UN prescribed, "[both sending and receiving] countries across the world take steps to facilitate orderly, safe, regular and responsible migration."[3] Selotlegeng Mbe completes this analysis with a perspective from African countries in Chapter 6. This chapter advances the debates on the consequences of international migration by paying attention to specific migrations across the Mediterranean and the unique challenge of addressing these consequences for youth in the context of Africa's youth bulge.

Aging is another major trend. According to UN statistics, the global population aged 65 and older will grow from 10 per cent in 2022 to 16 per cent in 2050. This will force many countries to quickly adapt their health care and social security systems. At the front end of the age spectrum, the world has cut the rates of infant and child mortality by nearly half over the last two decades.[4] Beninguisse and Mbarga explore these gains across eighteen sub-Saharan countries in Chapter 7. They find gains in the aggregate but substantial variation across rural/urban or socioeconomic groups. Looking at the same broad region in Chapter 8, Cisse and Rherrad also find substantial gains in maternal health, under the effect of diffusion, modernization, and education. Together, these reports paint a happy story of health improvements across the life cycle. Yet these gains, and the resulting aging of national populations, also bring a trail of social needs to address urgently. More importantly, the Covid-19 pandemic, pollution-induced mortality, and new deaths of despair in some industrial nations are pushing scholars to revisit earlier optimism about a global mortality and epidemiological transition that would continue unabated.

## An Anthropocentric Perspective: How the World Will Change Demography

Clearly, the tide of demographic change is upon us. It may not lift all boats, but it can profoundly transform societies across the world. Indeed, the reverse is also plausible. As the world turns, it can spin the field of demography in new directions, reshuffling its central debates, its theories, and its methods. Just as demography can mark the century, the century can return the favor by tilting demographic research in new directions. With this in mind, the book's second section complements its first by

[2] See United Nations (2022); op cit. For high-income countries between 2000 and 2020, the contribution of international migration to population growth (net inflow of 80.5 million) exceeded the balance of births over deaths (66.2 million).

[3] United Nations (2022); op. cit.

[4] Between 2000 and 2020, infant mortality fell by 45% (from 53 to 29 per thousand) while under-5 mortality fell by 49% (from 76 to 39). (World Development Indicators https://databank.worldbank.org/source/world-development-indicators, Last accessed, November 2023)

turning the "population–society" link on its head, looking now at how broad societal changes can affect future demographic research.

**Research themes**: Insofar as research priorities are socially defined, future research themes in demography will reflect changes in the global order, readership, or authorship. Thirty years ago, Watkins wondered how a feminist lens would affect the coverage and practice of demographic research.[5] The same can be asked of the effects of a transnational, racial, or class lens. Or, simply of the effects of a change in global culture, itself shaped in part by new demographic realities.

For instance, the global fall in fertility and mortality is reshaping the lives of women. In pre-transitional societies where fertility was high and life expectancy low, the normative life course of women was heavily structured around childbearing and childrearing activities. Today, a larger window of time is opening for paid employment, and this calls for more research on women's work. As Calves and Adjamagbo note in Chapter 9, answering this call requires new data and methods, but researchers can already build creatively on existing data and on prior conceptual advances in taxonomy.

Aging will also likely emerge as a major research theme, especially in high-income societies where elder care becomes a pressing need. This need can be met by foreign workers, but the administrative and socio-political viability of this solution requires careful assessments. As Milly's case study of Japan in Chapter 10 shows, even a question seemingly as simple as estimating the number of care workers is not easily answered without careful attention to definitional issues or to the perspectives of prospective users.

Beyond women's work and elder care, another emerging topic is the demographic responses to environmental change. Students of the Anthropocene worry about human activity wrecking the environment, but the converse, more anthropocentric stance is to worry back about how environmental pressures affect human communities. In debating these effects, contemporary demographers can draw upon Kingsley Davis's generic proposition of a multiphasic response. In this case, responses could range from adaptation and mitigation to relocation. More broadly, and as Chapter 11 by Awinia reminds the reader, the study of demographic responses to environmental change can be seen as a niche topic within social demography or, more specifically, the study of demographic responses to societal transformations and shocks. The difference in this case is the focus on *emerging* shocks from artificial intelligence, globalization, automation, or changes in the global economic order.

**Demographic theory**: Societal changes can also affect theory. Insofar as dominant theories reflect the dominant culture, any major shift in academic or global culture may force a corresponding shift in theory. Pollak and Watkins (1993)[6] once saw demographic theory as being driven "imperialistically" by microeconomics and its tenets of rational choice and methodological individualism. This paradigm has often

5 Watkins, SC (1993). If all we knew about women was what we read in Demography, what would we know? *Demography*, 30(4), 551–577

6 Watkins, SC and R. Pollak. 1993. "Cultural and Economic Approaches to Fertility: Proper Marriage or Mésalliance?»." *Population and Development Review* 19(3):467–95.

obscured the role of context and social structures. Fortunately, contextual analyses are now commonplace in demography, but they must be accompanied by contextual theories that specify relevant dimensions of context and their mechanisms. Interestingly, methodological individualism also overlooks biology, focusing instead on personal socioeconomic attributes. Merchant ably covers this topic in Chapter 12 in her review of the growing use of biomarkers in demographic studies. While rejecting biological determinism, she reviews how interactions between genetic and environmental factors combine to shape individual outcomes, including health and education.

**Demographic methods**: Finally, societal change can upend the ways research is done. Computer technology and statistical advances are supplying scientists with new tools to collect, merge, share, and analyze new or big data. These tools are bound to expand the scope, depth, and robustness of empirical analyses. In terms of scope, omnibus and merged surveys make it possible to broaden the list of topics and predictors. Big data are revolutionizing demographic research by accelerating the pace of data collection, broadening the range of topics, and expanding the audience of readers. As Wang and Tassinary illustrate in Chapter 13 in their thorough review of digital information from administrative sources and from mobile devices, these data can expand human health research, especially if their reliability is carefully monitored. Beyond releasing quantitative information in real time, the use of mobile devices also allows scraping of online text information, and its triangulation with quantitative data. Indeed, as Kalabikhina et al. show in Chapter 14, clever uses of text data do blur the frontier between qualitative and quantitative data. In a related vein, the growing use of longitudinal data is helping refine the analysis of people's life courses by yielding detailed person-year data, while multi-country surveys such as the Demographic and Health Surveys can power comparative studies. The rich multi-country and historical comparisons attempted in this volume by Mbarga and Beninguisse or by Cisse and Rherrad permit remarkable gains in breadth and historical depth that would have been hard to envision just three decades ago. In addition to historical depth, demographers can also achieve sociological depth when they leverage large datasets in detailed analyses of smaller sub-populations. As Aja M. Sutton and Zack W. Almquist further demonstrate in Chapter 15, such sub-area/sub-population estimation can be accomplished via advances in statistical analysis and computing power.

In the final chapter Gemma Abio, Concepció Patxot and Guadalupe Souto presents selected applications of NTA data to show its potential to study the generational economy, including both the demographic dividend—how aging affects economic growth—and the effects of aging on the welfare system.

Overall, demographers will increasingly be able to tell highly nuanced and disaggregated stories by building on data that are "mile-wide and mile-deep," that is, data that combine contextual breadth with historical and sociological depth. At the same time, the increased ability to drill down raises worries about "decimal-point demography" in which the detail overwhelms and obscures the big picture. This is a worry shared by other social sciences, but demography may have a comparative advantage here. On the one hand, the demographic perspective has long valued disaggregated analysis (by age and sex in the case of population pyramids). On the other hand, core demographic methods exist to aggregate the details from individual sub-populations to see the entire picture. Life tables, for instance, are designed to aggregate age-specific information into a national picture. Lexis diagrams likewise aggregate the unique features of multiple cohorts to understand change at the national level. Most broadly, methods of demographic decomposition offer a practical tool for moving from aggregate national trends to the individual experiences of various sub-populations. Several contributions in this volume (Han et al.; Cisse and Rherrad; Beninguisse and Mbarga) offer a glimpse of that potential of connecting micro-demographic behaviors to macro-demographic outcomes of interest.

Economists often refer to theirs as the "dismal science." Founders of sociology sought to crown it the mother of all social sciences, in light of its broad content. In a sense, demography could lay claim to either of these crowns: It has occasionally been reduced to Malthusian doom; and its breadth has occasionally been extended to be about "life and death and everything in between." Yet perhaps the unique crown that demography could earn in the 21st century might be as the "integrative science." As data and technological advances continue to permit detailed analyses of subpopulations, demography can become uniquely positioned to collate these disaggregated stories into the global history of the 21st century.

**Parfait M. Eloundou-Enyegue**
Professor,
Cornell University,
Ithaca, NY, USA

Section 1

# The Anthropocene: How Demography May Change the World

Chapter 1

# Population and Inequality in the Twenty-First Century: Will Dividends Divide the World?

*Parfait M. Eloundou-Enyegue*


## Abstract

This chapter explores the potential role of demographic change on global inequality, at a time of great concern and uncertainty over future prospects. It fills a gap in a "population-development" literature that has extensively studied the links between population and economic growth but neglected implications for inequality. It extends theories of demographic dividends and uneven transitions to predict that current demographic transitions will reduce inequality between, but widen inequality within, countries. The hypothesis is tested in part with decomposition methods that explore the role of global demographic transitions over the last half century. The approach is then used to extrapolate expected trends over the next half century, based on current demographic projections. Further insights are generated by analyzing socioeconomic differences in fertility across low and middle-fertility countries. The findings support the hypothesis of a mixed effect on global inequality.


**Keywords:** population, inequality, dividends, division of world, demographic change

## 1. Introduction

Every new century inspires its share of prophecies, and the twenty-first century was no different. Indeed, as the dawn of a new Millennium, it fed even bolder predictions about the near future: the "Internet of Things" would revolutionize production and consumption processes; it would transform data and work environments, and it would accelerate geographic and spatial exploration, perhaps with the first human colonies settling on Mars. The long list of predictions extended far beyond the economy into the world of culture and politics. Huntington [1] thus anticipated a clash of major civilizations, while Fukuyama [2] envisioned an "end of history" in which liberal democracy would spread far and wide, ultimately emerging as the pinnacle of progress in governance. Many analysts foresaw the end of a unipolar world dominated by the US [3].

In many of these predictions, technology was the driving force, the core engine of a high-tech future that would transform global society. Yet some of the push was also expected to originate from social and demographic forces, as several influential population processes were poised to reach historic milestones. Immigration was emerging as the leading source of population growth in Western Europe, fueling worries about a "great replacement" [4]. The size of world population was swelling to an all-time high that would define the Anthropocene, a time when human activity and wanton consumerism wreak serious damage to the environment [5]. After this peak, world population would begin to decline, in another historic moment that would also mark the century [3]. The aging of world population, coupled with automation would transform the nature of work [6]. Together, these forecasts stoked a larger and emerging debate about population and development in the twenty-first century.

Our chapter advances this debate. It does so in two ways. First, it compares this new debate to past debates on population and development (P-D debates hereafter). Second, it takes a distributional perspective. The idea is to go beyond average outcomes to explore inequality. At issue is how population inequality affects economic inequality. In the process, the chapter addresses pressing questions about global economic inequality: Will the current century bring the world closer together or split it apart? Will it accelerate the "big time divergence" claimed by Pritchett [7] or will it flatten the world as envisioned by Freedman [8]?

We predict a partial convergence in which economic inequality both rises and declines. It will decline between countries but rise within. The resulting involution will gradually concentrate the bulk of global inequality within, rather than between, countries. By the century's end, nations will have become less important than social class in defining a person's position on the global totem pole. Both facets of this hybrid trend, we argue, stem in part from demographic forces. In particular, global fertility transitions will turn out to be a major spur, operating both as a unifying and a dividing influence. They unify the world by closing the gap between countries, as the global South catches up demographically with the global North and reaps related dividends. As **Figure 1** shows, major world regions have completed their fertility transitions in a staggered fashion, starting with Europe and continuing with East Asia, Latin America, South Asia, the Middle East and North Africa, and ultimately sub-Saharan Africa. On the other hand, these fertility transitions will also divide countries of the global South. Just as fertility transitions unfold in top-down fashion across nations, they also unfold from top-to-bottom income groups within nations. For this reason, the early stages of

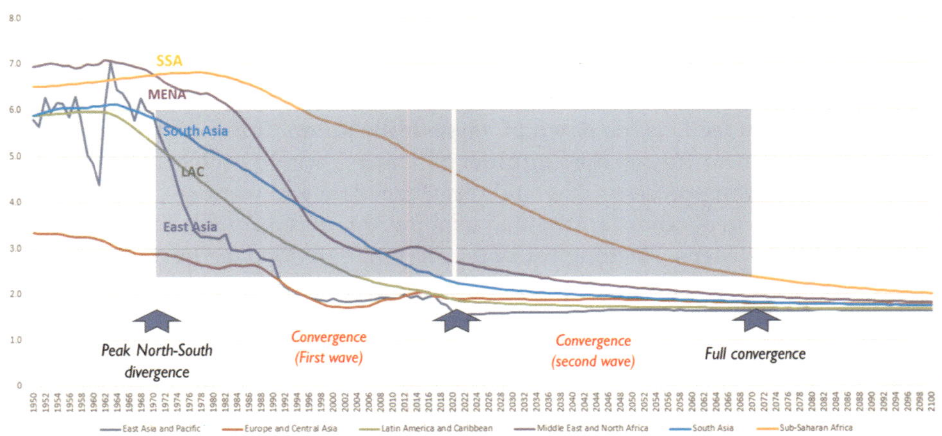


**Figure 1.**
*Recent and projected levels of fertility, for all major world regions, excluding the high-income groups (1950–2100). Source: based on 2022 Revision of World Population Prospects (https://population.un.org/wpp/), last consulted in January 2024.*

demographic transitions will widen economic inequality within countries in the global South. In sum, we hypothesize that the demographic dividends in the global South will divide the world in interesting ways, raising inequality within countries but reducing the overall inequality between countries:

We test this hypothesis of partial convergence with two sets of complementary data. To explore inequality between countries (BCI hereafter), we analyze national statistics compiled by the World Bank [9]. The World Bank [9] curates a comprehensive online database containing over 1500 indicators of development for all the world's nations and territories. The data needed for our analyses was available for 130 countries covering 92% of the global population. This database now spans over six decades (from 1960 to today), making it possible to assess contemporary trends. Our study period covers the century from 1970 to 2070, i.e., from the completion of fertility transitions in the global North till their projected completion in sub-Saharan Africa (**Figure 1**). Within this century, the year 2020 stands as a strategic mid-point. From that median line, one can analyze the first half of the study period (1970–2020) and build on findings to project trends in the second half (2020–2070).

To explore inequality within countries (WCI hereafter), we use survey data from the United States Agency for International Development (USAID). The USAID's Demographic and Health Surveys program [10] likewise offers a rich online data platform to support international studies of fertility. It stores and compiles data from household surveys fielded across high and medium fertility nations over the last three decades. We use these data to examine fertility inequality among countries that fielded a DHS survey since 2015.[1] Specifically, we analyze the differentials in total fertility rates between families in the top versus bottom quintiles. These survey data support micro-analyses that complement the macro-analyses based on World Bank statistics.

The rest of the chapter flows as follows: first is a background review of the recent evolution in P-D debates. The next three sections focus each on a separate aspect of inequality, whether dynamic, cross-national, or internal aspects. Section III thus examines how the GDP rankings of various countries evolved in the half century from 1970 to 2020. Section IV explores BCI and the contribution of demographic transitions. Section V explores how fertility transitions are shaping WCI. The chapter closes with a summary of findings and speculation about the future.

## 2. Population and development: classic vs twenty-first-century debates

The recent P-D debate unfolded into three historical phases that differ in substance and scale (**Table 1**). Its first and classic phase evinced a strong focus on aggregate outcomes, mostly national rates of population and economic growth [11, 12]. Ideologically, it pitted free-market advocates against Malthusians worried about the

[1] These countries (61 in total) include Afghanistan, Albania, Angola, Armenia, Azerbaijan, Bangladesh, Benin, Bolivia, Brazil, Burkina Faso, Burundi, Cambodia, Cameroon, Central African Republic, Chad, Colombia, Comoros, Congo, Congo Democratic Republic, Cote d'Ivoire, Dominican Republic, Egypt, Ethiopia, Gabon, Gambia, Ghana, Guatemala, Guinea, Haiti, India, Indonesia, Jordan, Kazakhstan, Kenya, Liberia, Madagascar, Malawi, Maldives, Mali, Mauritania, Mozambique, Myanmar, Nepal, Niger, Nigeria, Pakistan, Papua New Guinea, Peru, Philippines, Rwanda, Senegal, Sierra Leone, South Africa, Tajikistan, Tanzania, Timor-Leste, Togo, Turkmenistan, Uganda, Zambia, and Zimbabwe.

| | Phase 1 | Phase II | Phase III |
|---|---|---|---|
| Time period | Pre 1990s | 1990–2000 | >2000 |
| Label | Classic | Post Cairo | Millennium |
| Analytical level | Macro | Micro | Meso |
| Key population variables | Population growth | Demographic events and reproductive health | Age structure/ cohort |
| Key economic variables | GDP growth | Individual and family wellbeing | Demographic dividends |
| Tone | Worry | Hands off | Middle ground |
| Analytical methods | Cross-country regression | Microregression, causal analysis | Decomposition methods |

*Source: author.*

**Table 1.**
*Three historical phases in the recent debate on population and development.*

"population bomb" and its fallout on scarcity, conflicts, and epidemics [13]. Empirically, it relied on evidence from historical or cross-country regressions, despite caveats on the reliability of these methods [14].

The second phase in this debate grew out of the 1994 Cairo's International Conference on Population and Development. This post-Cairo phase moved the debate from a macro- to a micro-level scale, with the policy paradigm shifting away from national targets and to individual reproductive experiences. It spawned a wave of micro-level research that was empirically more detailed and rigorous, thanks in part to large data and statistical tools that were becoming increasingly accessible [15–17]. Yet this new P-D equation had two weaknesses of its own: its left-hand side downplayed structural influences and its deep interaction with individual factors. Such individual focus runs counter to current social science theory [18, 19]; and its right-hand side downplayed national impacts, running counter to the United Nations' agendas of Millennium and Sustainable Development Goals [20].

A third perspective was thus essential to stay relevant in the era of Millenium Development while keeping the spirit of Cairo. The challenge was to reconcile micro and national perspectives, i.e., to craft a people-centered approach that also remains attentive to national goals. The solution was found in meso-level studies using subregions, social classes, cohorts, or age groups as units of analysis. Studies in this "Millennium" phase of the P-D debate meet both criteria of macro-relevance and micro-detail. They do so with analytical strategies that explain national trends by aggregating the more detailed information from constituent subpopulations [21].

Beyond scale and substance, the P-D debate evolved in tone, with the strident opposition between Malthusians and Cornucopians softening to concede that "demography is not destiny [22, 23]:" in other words, innate demographic features such as sex or race do not seal one's fate, as they leave room for individual agency and structural effects. Yet this rejection of determinism does not imply irrelevance. Rather, it merely accepts the reality of overdetermination: no single factor, including demographics, can fully account for the entire variation in human experience. Population does matter, but in nuanced ways that consider contextual variation, intersectionality, cumulation, and momentum.

The principle of contextual variation means that demographic influences vary over time and space.[2] The intersectionality principle acknowledges the complex interactions between multiple facets of individual identity. The principle of cumulation means that small but persistent annual differences between groups will end up building large gaps over time. Finally, the momentum principle means that the effects of demography gather strength over time, and they can persist even after the initial push wanes. Compared to economic and social phenomena, demographic influences are less volatile. An economic bust can quickly follow a boom, but demographic processes are less prone to wild swings and rollbacks; they are more likely to show momentum and remanence.

## 3. Population trends and the global order

### 3.1 Theory

This section explores the dynamic dimension of inequality. Will there be a major turnover in world order during this century, or will the current economic rankings of countries persist? The theory is unclear. According to dependency theory, no reshuffling is forthcoming precisely because the "development project" is set to maintain the exploitation of poor countries by rich ones [18]. Rich countries stay on top, and inequalities can in fact widen. Modernization theories paint a less gloomy picture: the global order may not change, but inequalities can shrink. Today's poor countries slowly catch up, thanks to modern technology, improved governance, and international aid but also thanks to demographic processes. "Opportunistic" theories of development are even bolder in their outlook. Unlike dependency or modernization theories, they see turnovers as possible: drastic changes in the global resource environment can create unique openings that lower-income countries can exploit to overtake leading nations. The key question here is whether fertility transitions can support such a quantum leap in the development of poor nations.

### 3.2 Extent of global mobility

To assess economic mobility, we rank all countries by GDP per capita, grouping them into five quintiles. By comparing each country's rankings/quintile positions between 1970 and 2020, one can thus monitor jumps in rankings, distinguishing between nominal, real, and major jumps. Nominal jumps are small but sufficient to move a country to the next quintile, simply because the country stood near the cutoff line in 1970. Such jumps are artifactual and not statistically meaningful. Jumps become more meaningful when a country overtakes at least 26 nations, i.e., the number of countries in a quintile. They are even more meaningful and labeled "major" if they move a country across more than one quintile.

Global mobility is gauged by the frequency of real and major jumps. If these jumps turn out to be frequent, a case can be made for opportunistic theory. If they are rare, then the evidence is consistent with Marxist theories that posit a continued subjugation of countries from the global South [18].

The evidence on mobility is summarized in **Table 2**. The diagonal on this matrix indicates immobility, i.e., the countries staying within the same quintile between 1970

[2] For instance, how family size affects children's schooling varies systematically with contextual features such as the structure of families, the costs of children, gender equality, and levels of state subsidization [24].

and 2020. Cells above the diagonal capture upward mobility, and those below the diagonal capture downward mobility. Cells close to the diagonal capture single-quintile jumps; those farther away capture multiple-quintile jumps. Off-diagonal countries are marked with an asterisk, the number of asterisks reflecting the real number of quintiles jumped. In theory, the number of countries above the diagonal should be the same as the percentage below, since we assume a zero-sum hierarchy where ascending countries replace other countries.

The matrix suggests three main findings. First, the turnover in world rankings was substantial, at least in nominal terms. Belying expectations from dependency theory, cross-quintile mobility was common, as it was experienced by more than one-third (39%) of all nations. Yet many of these jumps were only nominal, i.e., they occurred only because the country was very close to the cutoff line. Real jumps—countries moving at least 26 spots—represent only about 15% (19/130) of all cases. Major jumps were even less common, with only 4% of countries moving by more than one quintile. Countries making major leaps forward included China (from 5th to 2nd quintile), South Korea (from 4th to 2nd quintile), and Botswana (from 5th to 3rd quintile). The

| Country's global position | | As of 1970 | | | | | |
|---|---|---|---|---|---|---|---|
| | | Top quintile (Q1) | Second quintile (Q2) | Third quintile (Q3) | Fourth quintile (Q4) | Bottom quintile (Q5) | Total |
| As of 2020 | Q1 | 20 (76.9%) | Japan, Hong Kong, Austria, Greenland, Singapore*, Ireland* | | | | 26 |
| | Q2 | Fr. Polynesia, Bahamas, Kuwait*, Italy, N. Caledonia, Andorra | 13 (50.0%) | Malaysia, Seychelles, Costa Rica, Oman, St Kitts and Nevis* | Korea** | China*** | 26 |
| | Q3 | | Suriname, Jamaica, South Africa*, Peru, Argentina, Mexico, Cuba | 14 (53.8%) | Paraguay, Equatorial Guinea*, Thailand*, St Vincent* | Botswana** | 26 |
| | Q4 | | | Senegal*, Nicaragua, Iran*, Algeria, Tunisia | 15 (57.7%) | Myanmar*, Cambodia, India, Kenya, Bangladesh, Indonesia* | 26 |
| | Q5 | | | Zambia** Zimbabwe** | Madagascar, Afghanistan, DRC*, Syria*, Pakistan, Kiribati | 18 (69.2%) | 26 |

*Source: author's calculations, based on GDP statistics from World Development Indicators (https://databank.worldbank.org/source/world-development-indicators), last accessed in January 2024.*
** denotes countries that jumped one quintile by overtaking at least 26 nations.*
***, and *** denote countries that jumped two or three quintiles, respectively.*

**Table 2.**
*Global mobility matrix for world countries, 1970 to 2000.*

two countries that fell back the most were Zambia and Zimbabwe (both from 3rd to 5th quintile).

As a second observation, the jumps were least frequent at the tails of the distribution, i.e., countries that were either very rich or very poor in 1970: most of the reshuffling took place around the middle, not at the extremes of the distribution. The percentages of countries staying in place were 77% at the top and 69% at the bottom, against smaller percentages (58%, 54%, and 50%, respectively) in the middle quintiles. This relative immobility of the poorest and richest nations should nuance the optimistic conclusions derived from overall mobility data. While the overall mobility data support the optimism from opportunistic theory, a focus at the top or bottom of the GDP distribution shows less mobility. It thus supports dependency theory, especially since very few jumps exceeded one quintile.

### 3.3 Role of population in global mobility

Given the above reshuffling of GDP rankings between 1970 and 2020, the question is whether population was a factor. To answer this question, we first looked at the statistical correlation between fertility declines and economic mobility, allowing for a 5-year lag. We found only a very modest correlation, with the changes in fertility rankings explaining only 1% of the variance in the change in GDP rankings (**Figure 2**). Even if this correlation had been large, it still would be insufficient proof of a causal effect. Given this small and possibly spurious correlation, a causal or single story may not explain the economic trajectories of all nations during that period. A case-by-case analysis is warranted. The chart shows four types of countries, including countries that (a) progressed on both the fertility and the economic fronts (China), (b) progressed on neither front (the DRC), (c) progressed on the economic but not the fertility front (Equatorial Guinea), and (d) regressed economically despite progress on the fertility front (Syria). Again, countries are best studied on a case-by-case basis.

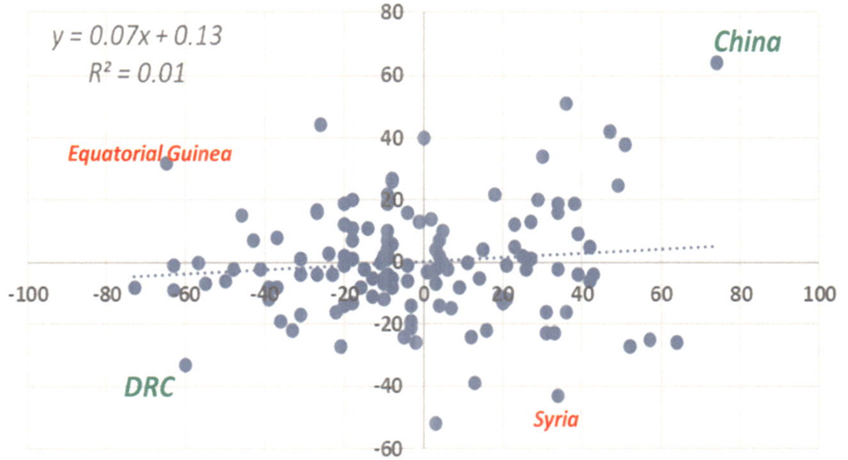


**Figure 2.**
*Correlation between national gains in fertility rankings and gains in GDP rankings (1970–2020). Source: author's calculations, based on GDP data from World Development Indicators (https://databank.worldbank.org/source/world-development-indicators), last access, January 2024.*

We thus complement the correlation analysis with decomposition methods. The specific method used estimates how much a country's GDP gains between 1970 and 2020 is explainable by changes in the age dependency of the national population. The general idea is to express a country's GDP per capita as a product of its labor productivity, employment levels, and age structure.[3] Any change in per capita GDP can therefore be traced to changes in these three components. We pay special attention to the contribution of changing age structure, which captures the so-called dividend from fertility transitions. We can then assert whether these dividends played a major role in fostering the mobility of nations.

The results show substantial boosts among the Asian Tigers, with South Korea in particular growing its GDP nearly sixteen-fold from 1965 to 1981 [9]. In the process, the country vaulted over many countries, moving from the bottom to the second quintile by the turn of the century. Past studies to estimate the contribution of demographic dividends to this economic growth have generated estimates ranging anywhere from 1/3 to 1/5 [25, 26]. Dividends also fueled Botswana's remarkable economic progress during that period. The country's GDP grew by 140% between 1990 and 2020, and 22% of this growth reflected favorable changes in the country's age dependency [26].

## 4. Population and "between-country" inequality

The previous sections analyzed trends in rankings, i.e., the relation positions of world countries and how much these positions changed over time. As a complement, this section explores absolute gaps. More than rankings, absolute gaps capture the full extent of inequality and its trends. In theory, world economies could change in isomorphic ways that preserve the rank order of nations but increase or reduce their absolute gaps. For this reason, absolute inequalities are also worth monitoring. The question in this section is about contemporary trends in inequality, a topic of spirited debate. So spirited, ideological, and partisan the debate that prominent scholars deemed it "silly," with one side steadfast in claiming "big time divergence," and another just as unequivocally seeing a "flattening world" [27]. The two sides eventually reconciled under a consensus view that inequality was both waning and widening, depending on whether one looks between or within countries [20]. This section focuses on BCI, and the role of demographic forces in the process.

### 4.1 Theory

Dividend theory can explain why fertility transitions would reduce BCI. According to this theory, sustained declines in national fertility tend to lower rates of age

---

[3] The standard formula of GDP per capita (GDP/Pop) can be transformed as (GDP/A) *(A/Pop) or even in greater detail as (GDP/E) *(E/A)*(A/Pop), where E represents the employed population and A is the adult population. More simply GDP /Pop = $\pi^*\varepsilon^*\alpha$ where the first term ($\pi$) represents labor productivity, the second term ($\varepsilon$) captures the rate of employment and the third ($\alpha$) captures the age structure. In this framework, any change in GPD per capita during two periods is a sum of changes in productivity, employment, and age dependency. Specifically, $\Delta(GDP) = \Delta\pi(\overline{\varepsilon\alpha}) + \Delta\varepsilon(\overline{\pi\alpha}) + \Delta\alpha(\overline{\pi\varepsilon})$. When statistics on these three parameters are available, one can easily decompose the GDP change in terms of these three substantive influences.

dependency in ways that create a temporary window of opportunity for saving and investing in economic growth [28]. If fertility declines occur in poor countries, as is the case now, the corollary effect at the global level will be an economic convergence: as today's low-income nations finally join the global fertility transition, the resulting economic dividends will narrow the income gap with richer nations. In other words, demographic convergence begets economic convergence.

This corollary theory remains untested for conceptual and methodological reasons: conceptually, as long as the P-D debate remained limited to its "growth-growth" dimension, concerns about inequality were obscured. This framing has fortunately broadened on both the population and the development sides of the equation. Analyses increasingly extend beyond population growth to include age structure [28]. They likewise cover multiple goals of sustainable development, such as schooling, gender, insecurity, or inequality. Our chapter embraces this broader framing. Rather than linking population and economic growth, it studies the link between demographic and economic inequality.

### 4.2 Trends in "between-country" inequality

Our empirical analyses begin by reviewing trends in GDP inequality between countries. We explore four complementary indices of inequality, including the Gini, the Theil index, the Mean Logarithmic Deviation (MLD), and the coefficient of variation. We focus on the MLD index which is more easily decomposable. The MLD computes as

$$MLD_t = \sum p_{jt} * ln\left(\frac{1}{i_{jt}}\right) \tag{1}$$

Where j and t index countries and time respectively; $(p_j)$ is a country's share of the world population, and $i_j$ is the national income ratio, i.e., its income per capita relative to the world's average.

Using data from the *World Bank Development Indicator* database [9], we extract country information on population size, labor force participation, age structure, and gross national income per capita (GDP). We chose the Atlas variant of GDP because of data availability. The data for this variant covered 121 countries, including 44 in Asia, 52 in Latin America, and 25 in Africa over the five decades. The results in **Figure 3** clearly show a historical decline in GDP inequality between countries. To be sure, one can see qualitative differences in the initial levels and the magnitude of the decline: depending on metric, the decline ranged from a low of 17% (Gini coefficient) to a high of 44% (Mean Log Deviation). Yet all metrics show a clear decline, which becomes steeper and steadier after the turn of the century. While the trend oscillated before the 1990s, the decline became monotonic after the year 2000.

## 5. Population and "between-country" inequality

We used a decomposition analysis to explore how population trends affected between-country inequality. Building on Eq. (1), and further noting that a country's GDP per capita is a function of labor force productivity $(\pi_j)$ and population age structure $(\alpha_j)$, one can decompose the change in MLD between two time periods as

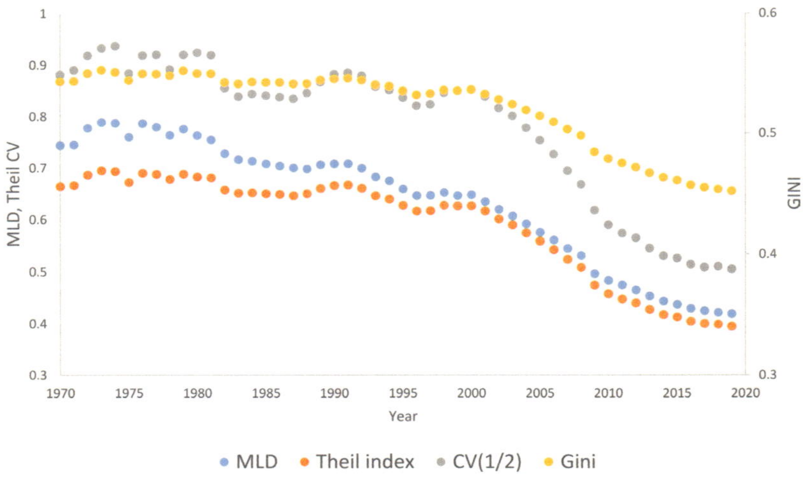


**Figure 3.**
*Global GDP inequality between countries (1970–2019). Source: author's calculations, based on GDP data from World Development Indicators (https://databank.worldbank.org/source/world-development-indicators), last access, January 2024.*

$$\Delta MLD \cong [\sum(\bar{i}_j - \overline{\ln(i_j)}) * \Delta p_j] + [\sum(\overline{p_j i_j} - \bar{p}_j) * \Delta \ln(\alpha_j)] + [\sum(\overline{p_j i_j} - \bar{p}_j) * \Delta \ln(\pi_j)] \quad (2)$$

***Pop size effect*** | ***age structure effect*** | ***Productivity effect***

where barred values represent averages, and Δ marks change between two time periods. For instance, when studying change in global inequality between 1980 and 1990, $\bar{i}_j = (i_{j(1980)} + i_{j(1990)})/2$, and $\Delta p = p_{1990} - p_{1980}$.

**Table 3** shows the findings from this decomposition. It shows what percentage of the 1970–2020 decline in BCI comes from the countries' relative changes in the population size, age structure, and productivity. The table lists the results for the entire period (last column) but also for each decade, from 1970 to 2020.

For the full period, the relative changes in productivity accounted for 86% of the total convergence: countries grew economically similar because their labor productivity became more similar, perhaps the result of a worldwide expansion of education and diffusion of technology. However, demography was also a factor. Countries became more similar in age structure, and this demographic convergence accounted for 19% of the GDP convergence. Of the two population factors, age structure was the most influential. Changes in the relative size of population did in fact exacerbate rather than reduce inequality. This is because lower-income nations were growing faster, thus steadily accounting for a growing share of the world population. The fact that age structure, not population size, is the more influential factor underscores the limitations of the classic P-D debate and its narrow focus on population growth.

A detailed analysis by decade shows that the global trend in age dependency has consistently worked to reduce inequality. In the first decade, when global inequality was rising, they slowed that rise. In subsequent periods, when global inequality was declining, they accelerated that trend, especially during the 1990s and the most recent

| | Time period | | | | | |
|---|---|---|---|---|---|---|
| **Inequality outcomes** | **1970–1980** | **1980–1990** | **1990–2000** | **2000–2010** | **2010–2019** | **1970–2019** |
| Total change in MLD | 0.019179 | −0.055 | −0.06042 | −0.16469 | −0.06403 | −0.32496 |
| Percent change in MLD due to changes in | | | | | | |
| Population size | −20% | 12% | −1% | −9% | −18% | −7% |
| Age structure | −5% | 24% | 33% | 12% | 31% | 19% |
| Productivity | 128% | 64% | 68% | 95% | 88% | 86% |

*Source: author's calculations, based on GDP statistics from World Development Indicators (https://databank.worldbank.org/source/world-development-indicators), last accessed in January 2024.*
**Some of the percentages do not add up to 100%, due to rounding error.*

**Table 3.**
*Relative contributions of economic and demographic factors to the global convergence in GDP per capita observed between 1970 and 2019 [29].*

| | Time period | | | | | |
|---|---|---|---|---|---|---|
| **Inequality outcomes** | **1970–1980** | **1980–1990** | **1990–2000** | **2000–2010** | **2010–2019** | **1970–2019** |
| Total change in MLD | 0.019179 | −0.055 | −0.06042 | −0.16469 | −0.06403 | −0.32496 |
| Percent change in MLD due to changes from | | | | | | |
| Global North | 268% | −72% | −86% | −7% | −34% | 14% |
| East Asia | −299% | 124% | 163% | 55% | 38% | 16% |
| South East Asia | −70% | 18% | 25% | 13% | 22% | 2% |
| Latin America and Carribbean | 49% | −4% | −7% | 0% | −2% | 7% |
| South Asia | 32% | 61% | 63% | 42% | 107% | 61% |
| Middle East and North Africa | 79% | 10% | −9% | −2% | −9% | 14% |
| Sub-Saharan Africa | 45% | −38% | −50% | −3% | −23% | −14% |

*Source: author's calculations, based on GDP statistics from World Development Indicators (https://databank.worldbank.org/source/world-development-indicators), last accessed in January 2024.*

**Table 4.**
*Decomposition results for the relative contributions of various world regions to the global convergence in GDP per capita observed between 1970 and 2019.*

decade (2010–2019). The relative growth in population size did worsen inequality throughout the study period. However, the first two decades were an exception, with the results for 1980–1990 at a time when China was implementing its one-child policy.

One can probe deeper into the drivers of this GDP convergence by looking at the contributions of different world regions (**Table 4**). As in **Table 3**, one can review the full study period or focus on individual decades. The results suggest the following: first, the largest contributions (61%) came from South Asia, followed by East Asia (16%) and the Global North and the Middle East and North Africa (MENA) region (14% each). Over time, East Asia and South Asia stood out as the world leaders in reducing global inequality in GDP, with the first of these regions dominating in the first three decades and the second taking over since. Asia's contribution comes from a mix of slowing population growth and rising productivity (results not shown). So far, sub-Saharan Africa is the only world region that has not contributed to this global economic convergence. The next half century will be interesting in that regard. As Africa completes its demographic transition and if the region reaps substantial dividends, it can become a leading driver of global convergence. Already, over the last three decades, several African countries have advanced their transition, reaping substantial dividends. During the 1990–2020 period, a dozen of African countries at least doubled their GDP, based in part on harnessing dividends. Leading countries on that list (**Table 5**) include Kenya, Morocco, Namibia, Tunisia, Eswatini, Botswana, Rwanda, Cabo Verde, and Lesotho. In all of these countries, changes in age structure accounted for anywhere from 14% to 28% of the entire economic growth registered.

## 6. Population and "within-country" inequality

Global inequality combines the inequalities found between and within nations. While BCIs may reduce inequality across nations, it is also essential to pay attention to inequalities within countries because these WCI are essential to fair and inclusive societies, and to individual sense of relative deprivation. From an individual perspective, and despite the reach of globalization, the ability to keep up with one's immediate neighbors remains the ultimate yardstick of accomplishment. We specifically focus attention on the possible role of fertility transitions in fostering economic inequality within nations.

### 6.1 Theory

Why would fertility transitions affect WCI? One answer comes from dilution theory. According to this theory, parents with large progenies must split their time and material resources among multiple siblings, and this reduces the endowments per child [30]. For this reason, a society in which poor families bear more children than richer families do will breed resource inequality among children. This resource inequality in childhood later fuels income inequality when children become adults. For the same reason, fertility transitions that unfold in top-down fashion should widen economic inequality, especially if these fertility changes occur alongside adverse changes in family structure [31]. Altogether, if higher-income groups are first to adopt new reproductive behavior that deepens the per capita endowments of children, the early phases of fertility transitions will foster economic inequality. This divergence could wane during the late phases of fertility transitions when fertility begins to fall among low-income groups. Yet it could also persist if rich families actively leverage their past position to restrict the poor's social mobility.

### 6.2 Trends in within-country inequality

Recent studies have shown a sharp rise in WCI in most industrial nations [32]. These internal inequalities have been less studied in the global South where poverty remained the primary worry. Yet this region may be facing similar or even steeper rises in inequality. A recent review of national statistics on inequality shows that Africa is now home to 8 of the top 10 most inequal (and 11 of the top 20) countries in the world [9]. Given this rising inequality, given concurrent fertility transitions, and

*DOI: http://dx.doi.org/10.5772/intechopen.1005263*

| | GNI per person | | Period change | | Decomposition results: % of growth linked to change in | | | |
|---|---|---|---|---|---|---|---|---|
| | 1990 | 2020 | Nominal | Relative | Labor productivity | Employment | Labor force participation | Age dependency |
| Sudan | 999 | 642 | *−357* | *−36%* | 101% | 12% | 9% | −21% |
| Niger | 336 | 549 | ***213*** | ***63%*** | 123% | 2% | −18% | −7% |
| Somalia | 133 | 424 | ***291*** | ***219%*** | 104% | −1% | 1% | −4% |
| The Gambia | 306 | 743 | ***437*** | ***143%*** | 104% | −3% | −1% | −1% |
| Mali | 288 | 833 | ***545*** | ***189%*** | 105% | −5% | −3% | 2% |
| Nigeria | 556 | 2003 | ***1446*** | ***260%*** | 115% | −5% | −12% | 3% |
| Tanzania | 192 | 1052 | ***860*** | ***448%*** | 99% | 1% | −3% | 3% |
| Angola | 777 | 1776 | ***998*** | ***128%*** | 104% | −6% | −2% | 4% |
| Malawi | 183 | 586 | ***402*** | ***220%*** | 100% | −1% | −3% | 4% |
| Chad | 267 | 634 | ***367*** | ***138%*** | 125% | −1% | −28% | 4% |
| Mauritius | 2429 | 10,228 | *7799* | *321%* | 97% | 2% | −4% | 5% |
| Guinea | 407 | 963 | ***556*** | ***136%*** | 101% | −2% | −4% | 6% |
| Uganda | 325 | 799 | ***474*** | ***146%*** | 100% | −1% | −4% | 6% |
| Cote d'Ivoire | 776 | 2280 | ***1504*** | ***194%*** | 110% | 1% | −18% | 6% |
| Benin | 367 | 1278 | ***912*** | ***249%*** | 95% | 0% | −2% | 7% |
| Equatorial Guinea | 263 | 5803 | ***5540*** | ***2106%*** | 96% | −1% | −3% | 7% |
| Zambia | 434 | 1163 | ***729*** | ***168%*** | 96% | 5% | −9% | 8% |
| Ghana | 396 | 2313 | ***1917*** | ***484%*** | 99% | 1% | −9% | 8% |
| Sierra Leone | 186 | 509 | ***323*** | ***174%*** | 109% | −2% | −16% | 8% |
| Guinea-Bissau | 224 | 761 | ***537*** | ***240%*** | 94% | 0% | −2% | 8% |
| Egypt, Arab Rep. | 756 | 3004 | ***2249*** | ***298%*** | 100% | 2% | −11% | 9% |
| Burkina Faso | 332 | 773 | ***441*** | ***133%*** | 128% | −3% | −34% | 9% |

| | GNI per person | | Period change | | Decomposition results: % of growth linked to change in | | | |
|---|---|---|---|---|---|---|---|---|
| | 1990 | 2020 | Nominal | Relative | Labor productivity | Employment | Labor force participation | Age dependency |
| Ethiopia | 257 | 893 | *636* | *248%* | 91% | 0% | 0% | 10% |
| Congo, Rep. | 927 | 1815 | *889* | *96%* | 102% | −6% | −7% | 10% |
| Mauritania | 729 | 1669 | *940* | *129%* | 107% | −2% | −17% | 12% |
| Togo | 402 | 921 | *520* | *129%* | 92% | 0% | −4% | 13% |
| Kenya | 373 | 1835 | *1462* | *392%* | 88% | −2% | 0% | 14% |
| Morocco | 1167 | 3069 | *1902* | *163%* | 99% | 3% | −20% | 16% |
| Namibia | 1993 | 4555 | *2561* | *128%* | 77% | −1% | 7% | 17% |
| Tunisia | 1413 | 3305 | *1891* | *134%* | 90% | −1% | −6% | 17% |
| Senegal | 923 | 1430 | *507* | *55%* | 110% | 5% | −33% | 18% |
| Eswatini | 1294 | 3393 | *2099* | *162%* | 96% | −6% | −11% | 20% |
| Cameroon | 966 | 1520 | *554* | *57%* | 91% | 10% | −23% | 21% |
| Botswana | 2724 | 6504 | *3780* | *139%* | 81% | −6% | 3% | 22% |
| Rwanda | 348 | 774 | *426* | *123%* | 87% | −1% | −8% | 22% |
| Zimbabwe | 864 | 1140 | *276* | *32%* | 75% | 1% | 0% | 24% |
| Madagascar | 308 | 469 | *161* | *52%* | 77% | 7% | −8% | 24% |
| South Africa | 3130 | 6012 | *2883* | *92%* | 97% | 2% | −25% | 25% |
| Cabo Verde | 898 | 3058 | *2160* | *241%* | 90% | −4% | −13% | 26% |
| Lesotho | 546 | 1211 | *665* | *122%* | 69% | 24% | −22% | 28% |
| Gabon | 4820 | 7030 | *2209* | *46%* | 93% | −15% | −10% | 31% |
| Comoros | 979 | 1410 | *431* | *44%* | 72% | −13% | 6% | 35% |
| Algeria | 2366 | 3571 | *1205* | *51%* | 24% | 60% | −24% | 39% |
| Central African Republic | 481 | 508 | *27* | *6%* | 84% | −13% | −19% | 49% |

| | GNI per person | | Period change | | Decomposition results: % of growth linked to change in | | | |
|---|---|---|---|---|---|---|---|---|
| | 1990 | 2020 | Nominal | Relative | Labor productivity | Employment | Labor force participation | Age dependency |
| Burundi | 218 | 231 | *12* | *6%* | 257% | −2% | −264% | 109% |
| Congo, Dem. Rep. | na | 557 | *na* | *na* | na | na | na | na |
| Eritrea | na | na | *na* | *na* | na | na | na | na |
| Liberia | na | 602 | *na* | *na* | na | na | na | na |
| Libya | na | 7739 | *na* | *na* | na | na | na | na |
| Mozambique | na | 467 | *na* | *na* | na | na | na | na |
| Sao Tome and Principe | na | 2094 | *na* | *na* | na | na | na | na |
| South Sudan | na | na | *na* | *na* | na | na | na | na |
| Seychelles | 5033 | 13,767 | *8734* | *174%* | na | na | na | na |

*Source: author's calculations, based on GDP data from World Development Indicators* (https://databank.worldbank.org/source/world-development-indicators)*, last access, January 2024.*
*Numbers in these columns represent, respectively, the numerical change (rounded values) in the GDP per capita and the percent change in GDP per capita between 1990 and 2020.*

**Table 5.**
*Decomposition of recent economic growth among African nations (1990–2020).*

given expectations from dilution theory, it is reasonable to consider how these transitions might affect WCI.

### 6.3 Role of population in within-country inequality

Dilution is compelling as a theory, but its empirical evidence is elusive. To prove dilution, it is not enough to show a negative correlation between sib size and children's outcomes because such correlation may merely reflect endogeneity in the reproductive choices of families. For this reason, it is useful to complement correlation with a decomposition analysis to show how changes in the resource inequality of children derive from a mix of economic, social, and demographic factors. Key factors are likely to include inequalities in (a) families' incomes, (b) the share of income devoted to children, (c) the number of children, and (d) access to public subsidies. Unfortunately, the detailed data needed for this analysis was not readily available. Nonetheless, we draw tentative inferences by monitoring fertility inequality. Economic inequality will widen in the course of a fertility transition if it is accompanied by rising levels of fertility inequality, especially if the country's income inequality is also rising.

To assess this theory, we first explore how fertility inequality evolves during a fertility transition. One can explore this link from a historical perspective, by following individual countries over time. One can also explore it from a comparative perspective, by comparing countries at successive stages of their transitions. Results from a historical perspective (results not shown but see [33]) confirm the inverse U pattern expected in theory. Fertility inequality grows after the onset of a fertility transition, and it gradually recedes as the country completes its transition.

**Figure 4** shows the results from a comparative perspective, based on recent DHS data. Specifically, we use information for all 61 countries that fielded DHS surveys in/after 2015. For each country, we compute the differences in the birth rate of the bottom versus the top SES quintile. The numbers thus indicate the difference in average birth rates between families in the bottom versus top SES quintiles. The results show that all the numbers are positive: on average, poorer families always have a higher fertility rate than richer families do; the difference averages almost 2.5, and it ranges from a low of 0.1 (Armenia 2016) to a high of 4.5 children (Angola 2015). Importantly, the data show an inverse U pattern; inequality peaks in the initial stages of fertility transitions when the top SES group begins to innovate demographically and to separate itself from the rest. There is of course some variation around this inverse U curve, but the average pattern is strong: taken alone, the stage in fertility transition

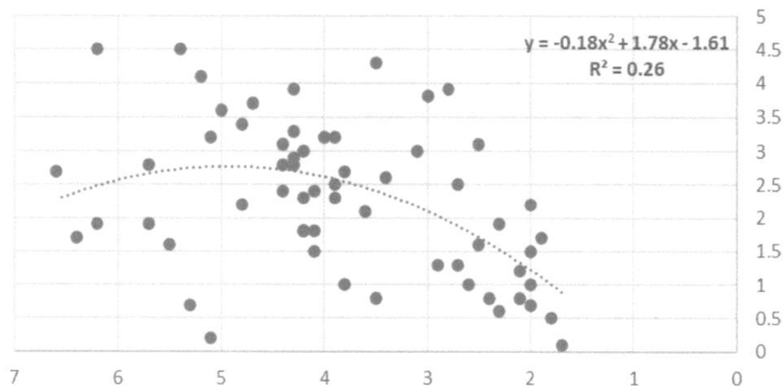


**Figure 4.**
*Fertility gap between top and bottom SES quintile over the course of fertility transitions. Source: author's calculations, based on DHS data (https://www.statcompiler.com/fr/), last access, January 2024.*

explains a quarter of all variation in the fertility inequalities across all study countries. This initial divergence in birth rates is expected to fuel the resource inequality among children and, ultimately, the economic inequality in the next generation. Resource inequality among children will widen most severely if inequality in parental income also grows during that period and if public support is weak or weakening.

## 7. Conclusion

The central question raised in this chapter is whether demographic dividends will unite or divide the world, i.e., whether they will reduce or raise global income inequality. Our analysis of recent data shows mixed influences. Current fertility transitions in the global South are pushing global income inequality in two different directions: they narrow the inequality between countries but raise the inequalities within nations.

Looking across nations, fertility transitions have typically unfolded from the top down, beginning in higher-income regions before spreading to other regions. By 1970, countries of the global North had completed their transitions. Since then, lower-income nations have begun to catch up demographically. As they reap the dividends from these demographic transitions, they catch up economically as well, closing the GDP gap between rich and poor nations. Over the last half century, the between-country inequality in GDP per capita fell anywhere from 17% to 44%, depending on the inequality metric used. A decomposition analysis shows that much of this cross-national convergence in GPD (86%) was due to convergence in labor productivity. Yet, population was a notable factor. Further, changes in age structure, rather than population size, were the bigger population factor.

Looking within nations, fertility transitions also unfold from the top down. Such a pattern is expected to raise economic inequality within countries during the early stages of the transition, insofar as large sib size dilutes the resources available to individual children. The effects of this dilution on economic inequality also depend on the patterns of parental and public investment in children. Because we lack detailed information on these patterns of families' resource allocation, we did not directly estimate the contribution of fertility transitions to resource inequality. Nonetheless, the partial evidence mustered is consistent with the expectation of rising income inequality during the preliminary stages of fertility transitions.

In sum, contemporary fertility transitions have both "dividend" and "divider" effects. The "dividend" effect is fueling an economic convergence of world countries driven in part by fertility transitions in the global South. The "divider" effect also derives from the top-down pattern in which transitions begin, a pattern that initially raises economic inequalities among children. This combination of 'dividend' and 'divider' effects account in part for the double movement in inequality observed during the last half century.

Looking forward, the world is projected to complete its fertility transition by 2070. If these transitions continue to induce the same mix of "dividend" and "divider" effects, the current involution of inequality will continue. The end result would be to flatten the world from a cross-national view but also to fracture it from a national view. This mix of flattening and fracturing will turn the world into a global village in which nations become less important than social class in defining people's standing on the global totem pole. Neither dividends nor divider effects are automatic. Countries harness dividends only if they work to take advantage of their periods of low age dependency by creating employment, encouraging savings, and channeling investments in the most productive sectors. Likewise, divider effects are most severe when fertility transitions occur alongside other demographic and socio-cultural transformations that foster ruthless competition and inequality. Adverse transformations in family structure –notably assortative marriage and greater prevalence of singlehood and divorce among poorer mothers—have occurred in the global North [31]. If these transformations extend to the global South, they will accentuate the fertility transitions and magnify inequality.

## Author details

Parfait M. Eloundou-Enyegue
Cornell University, Ithaca, NY, USA

*Address all correspondence to: pme7@cornell.edu

## References

[1] Huntington SP. The clash of civilizations? Foreign Affairs. 1993; **72**(3):22-49

[2] Fukuyama F. The end of history? The National Interest. 1989;**16**:3-18

[3] Todd E. After the Empire: The Breakdown of the American Order. New York: Columbia University Press; 2003

[4] Camus R. Le Grand Remplacement. Paris, France: David Reinharc; 2011

[5] Crutzen PJ. Geology of mankind. Nature. 2002;**415**:23

[6] Rifkin J. The End of Work: The Decline of the Global Labor Force and the Dawn of the Post-Market Era. Putnam Publishing Group; 1995

[7] Pritchett L. Divergence, big time. Journal of Economic Perspectives. 1997; **11**:3-17

[8] Friedman TL. The World Is Flat. Farrar Straus & Giroux; 2005

[9] World Bank. World Development Indicators Databank. 2023. Available from: https://databank.worldbank.org/source/world-development-indicators [Accessed: September, 2023]

[10] United States Agency for International Development. Demographic and Health Surveys (DHS). Stat Compiler, ORC Macro. 2024. Available from: http://www.statcompiler.com

[11] Ehrlich P. The Population Bomb. 2nd ed. New York: Ballantine; 1971, original 1968

[12] Birdsall N, Kelley A, Sinding S. Population Matters: Demographic Change, Economic Growth, and Poverty in the Developing World. Oxford: Oxford University Press (Oxford); 2001

[13] Lam D. How the world survived the population bomb: Lessons from 50 years of extraordinary demographic history. Demography. 2011;**48**(4):1231-1262

[14] Rodrik D. Why we learn nothing from regressing economic growth on policies [unpublished document]. Cambridge: Kennedy School of Government; 2005

[15] Cassen R, editor. Population and Development: Old Debates, New Conclusions. New Brunswick, NJ: Transaction; 1994

[16] Black SE, Devereux PJ, Salvanes KG. The more the merrier? The effect of family size and birth order on children's education. The Quarterly Journal of Economics. 2005;**120**(2):669-700

[17] Fitzsimons E, Malde B. Empirically probing the quantity-quality model. Journal of Population Economics. 2014; **27**(1):33-68

[18] Haslam P, Shafer J, Beaudet P. Introduction to International Development: Approaches, Actors, Issues, and Practice. 4th ed. Oxford University Press; 2021

[19] Alexander K. Is it family or school? Getting the question right. RSF: The Russell Sage Foundation. Journal of the Social Sciences. 2016;**2**(5):18-33

[20] United Nations (Independent Group of Scientists appointed by the Secretary-General). Global Sustainable Development Report 2019: The Future Is Now – Science for Achieving Sustainable Development. New York: United Nations; 2019

[21] Eloundou-Enyegue PM, Giroux SC. Fertility transitions and schooling: From micro-to macro-level associations. Demography. 2012;**49**(4):1407-1432

[22] Burrows MJ. Conclusion: demography does not have to be destiny. In: Reducing the Risks from Rapid Demographic Change. Report by the Atlantic Council; 2016. pp. 23-23

[23] Temple JB, McDonald P. Is demography destiny? The role of structural and demographic factors in Australia's past and future labour supply. Journal of Population Research. 2008; **25**(1):29-49

[24] Lloyd CB. Investing in the Next Generation: The Implications of High Fertility at the Level of the Family (Research Division Working Papers No. 63). New York: The Population Council; 1994

[25] Mapa DS, Balisacan AM. Quantifying the impact of population on economic growth and poverty: The Philippines in an east Asian context. In: Sevilla LA, editor. Population and Development in the Philippines: The Ties That Bind. Makati City: AIM Policy Center; 2004

[26] Ministry of Economics and Planning, Cameroon (MINEPAT) Transition Démographique et Transformation Structurelle. Unpublished Consultancy Report. 2023

[27] Birdsall N. That silly inequality debate. Finance and Development. 2002; **38**(4):92-94

[28] Bloom D, Canning D, Sevilla J. The Demographic Dividend: A New Perspective on the Economic Consequences of Population Change. Santa Monica (CA): Rand Corporation; 2003

[29] World Bank. World Development Indicators. 2024. Available from: https://databank.worldbank.org/source/world-development-indicators [Accessed: January, 2024]

[30] Blake J. Family Size and Achievement. Berkeley: University of California Press; 1989

[31] McLanahan S. Diverging destinies: How children are faring under the second demographic transition. Demography. 2004;**41**:607-627

[32] Qureshi Z. Rising inequality: A major issue of our time. In: Brookings. 2023. Available from: https://www.brookings.edu/articles/rising-inequality-a-major-issue-of-our-time/

[33] Eloundou-Enyegue PM, Giroux SC, Tenikue M. African transitions and fertility inequality: A demographic Kuznets hypothesis. Population and Development Review. 2017;**43**(S1):59-83

Chapter 2

# Demographic Dividends across the Global South: A Comparison of Africa, Asia, and Latin America (1970–2020)

*Zhuang Han, Claude Mbarga, Michel Tenikue and Sarah Giroux*

**Abstract**

The last half century has seen seismic transformations in the demographic outlook of many countries in sub-Saharan Africa, Asia, and Latin America. Because these transformations have coincided with equally profound economic change, they raise questions about the role of demographic change and its dividends in transforming the developing world. For instance, how much have the differences in onset, patterns, and management of fertility transitions fueled the growing economic divergence now seen across these regions? On the one hand, the four Asian Tigers reportedly leveraged their fertility transition to accelerate economic growth. On the other hand, a few countries in West Africa have yet to initiate their fertility transition, and the list of least-developed nations is increasingly restricted to African and high-fertility nations. In this chapter, we use new decomposition methods to estimate the dividends accrued by individual countries between 1970 and 2020 and to explore how these dividends contributed to the region's economic growth and differentiation. The analysis begins by estimating the size of each country's dividend; then, we consider factors that explain differences across national dividends. Finally, we estimate the percent contribution of this variation in dividends in explaining the cross-country variation in the economic outlook of this world region.

**Keywords:** demographic dividends, inequality, age structure, fertility, global south, economic growth

## 1. Introduction

Over the past fifty years, remarkable demographic transformations have occurred in the global south. These coincided with major economic shifts, prompting inquiries into the role of demographic transitions in reshaping the developing world.

Historically, research on the consequences of demographic change for development initially centered on the relationship between population size and economic progress [1].

In 2003, however, Bloom, Canning, and Sevilla introduced a new perspective focused instead on the role of age structure and the so-called demographic dividend. As birth rates decrease (and before life expectancy increases), countries experience a temporary period of low age dependency, which promotes savings, investment, and economic growth. This dividend argument has gained considerable traction in both academic and policy circles over the past two decades. In research, the number of articles examining dividends on JSTOR rose from 9 in 2002 to 1094 in 2022. In the policy world, a growing number of nation-states have developed "road maps" to harness the demographic dividend [2], and the African Union named 2017 as the year of "Harnessing the Demographic Dividend ... " [3]. However, the concept remains contentious for several reasons.

First, there are questions about whether the demographic dividend is a genuinely novel argument or merely a variation on the standard population growth and development perspective. Is the relationship between age structure and development fundamentally different from the links between total population growth and development? Second, it is challenging to measure the dividend in a compelling way that allows for historical analysis and cross-country comparison. Standard methods (NTA accounting, simulation, DemProj) tend to be data-intensive and more suitable for simulating future scenarios than accounting for past changes. Third, it remains to be seen whether the magnitude of dividends will be similar across all world regions. Current discussions of demographic dividends draw heavily upon data from East Asian countries between 1960 and 2000. In contrast, data from Latin America during the same period indicates that the benefits from demographic transitions did not yield the same level of economic advantages as those observed in East Asia [4].

This paper presents a novel decomposition method that can help address the questions above. Using this method, we examine the magnitude of demographic dividends across the global south over the past 50 years, explore the factors associated with the emergence of these dividends, and assess the extent to which patterns of dividend formation are similar or different across world regions.

## 2. Background

### 2.1 A half century of socio-demographic change

Between 1970 and 2020, the world's population nearly doubled, increasing from 3.7 billion to 7.8 billion. *GNI* per capita rose from $802 in 1970 to $11,040 in 2020, increasing 13-fold during this half-century [5]. However, this increase was accompanied by growing income inequalities between countries and regions, particularly in Latin America and the Caribbean, sub-Saharan Africa, and East and South Asia.[1] **Figure 1** highlights this variation, showing the 3-year-average annual *GNI* per capital Growth Rate over the past 50 years. It also highlights the wide regional variation in the pace of demographic change, as seen in the varying trends in age dependency ratios.

---

[1] Regions here are defined by the World Bank regional coding. Specific details on the country composition of each region can be found in the WDI Online database (WDI Online 2020).

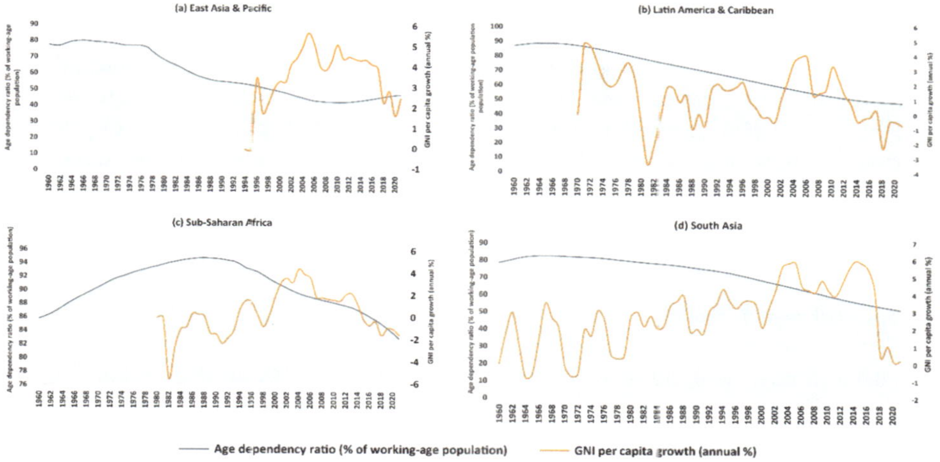


**Figure 1.**
*Demographic and economic evolution in global South between 1960 and 2020. Source: Authors with WDI database.*

## 2.2 Latin America and Caribbean

The socio-demographic landscape of Latin America and the Caribbean has evolved significantly since the 1490s when Europeans first arrived. In the 19th century, migration flows and declining mortality rates triggered a population surge. During the latter half of the 20th century, the total fertility rate (TFR) fell from 5.2 to 1.9, causing the annual population growth rate to decline from 2.5% to 0.8% [6]. **Figure 1b**, utilizing WDI 2022 data from 1970 to 2020, confirms this fertility decline and highlights a reduction in demographic dependency from 88% to 49%. These statistics indicate that the region initiated its demographic transition phase and began to benefit from the demographic dividend after 1980, when the dependency ratio fell below 80%.

Paradoxically, *GNI* per capita growth in the region fell during this time, mainly due to the 1980s debt crisis, which disrupted Western foreign investments and increased poverty and unemployment. Social inequalities, especially among vulnerable groups like the indigent and Afro-descendants, intensified. Additional factors, such as low education levels and urbanization rates, also hindered growth. Despite a reduced dependency ratio (from 71% to 49% between 1990 and 2020), the region failed to effectively harness the demographic dividend during this period [7–9]. While *GNI* tripled from $5969 to $15,243 between 1990 and 2020, it remained slightly below the global average.

## 2.3 Sub-Saharan Africa

Sub-Saharan Africa exhibits the world's highest population growth, with a total fertility rate (TFR) of 4.7 children per woman in 2020, double the global average. The region's population growth rate remained stable from 1970 to 2020, hovering between 2.68% and 2.65% [5]. Age dependency ratios consistently ranked highest, starting at 90% in 1970 and declining to 84% in 2020, peaking at 96% in 1988 (**Figure 1d**). Even today, Sub-Saharan Africa has yet to reach the critical threshold of 80% for the demographic dividend [5, 10, 11].

Despite this unfavorable population structure, the region has seen a gradual but modest increase in gross national income (*GNI*) per capita, with an average annual growth rate of 0.38%. Between 1990 and 2020 (**Figure 1d**), *GNI* per capita grew sevenfold, from $201 to $1500. Numerous studies [10–18] underscore the persistent challenges facing the region, including demographic factors, governance issues, limited educational expansion, low levels of women's empowerment, and unique cultural constraints.

## 2.4 East and South Asia

South and East Asia, home to 23 countries and the world's most populous region, offer compelling examples of economies that achieved significant demographic dividends. The population surged from 1.74 billion in 1970 to 3.63 billion in 2020, representing 46.33% of the global population [2]. Over three decades, the region experienced extraordinary economic progress and generated substantial wealth.

**Figure 1a** and **c** shows the economic and demographic evolution of East Asia & Pacific and South Asia from 1960 to 2020. The data reveal three significant trends in East Asia's population growth: an initial increase from 0.17% to 2.34% (1960–1964), a slight rise from 2.3% to 2.6% (1964–1970), and a gradual decline from 2.6% to 0.4% (1970–2020).

This population change led to a demographic transition characterized by a continuous decrease in demographic dependency (from 79% to 47%), well below the 80% threshold required for capturing the demographic dividend (**Figure 1a**). East Asia entered its window of opportunity for a demographic dividend before 1970, propelling substantial economic growth, with an average annual *GNI* per capita growth rate (in constant $) of approximately 4% between 1970 and 2020, peaking at 6.9% in 2007 and 6.3% in 2010. By 2020, absolute *GNI* per capita had risen from $306 to $11,652, marking a 38-fold increase [5].

South Asia mirrors East Asia's pattern, with a population growth rate declining from 2.31% to 1.02% (1970–2020), slightly higher than East Asia's rate in 2020 [5]. Concurrently, the demographic dependency ratio fell from 82.66% to 51.66% (**Figure 1c**). These trends indicate that South Asia entered its demographic dividend window in the 1970s. The *GNI* per capita growth rate also increased significantly, with *GNI* per capita rising approximately sixteen-fold, from $118 to $1879.

## 2.5 A new argument

In 2003, Bloom, Canning, and Sevilla argued that high-fertility countries face development barriers because the working-age population's earnings are siphoned into supporting a large number of dependents, rather than being saved or invested in ways that would boost economic growth. However, as countries undergo their demographic transitions, fertility decline creates a "window of opportunity" where the share of the working-age population (ages 15–64) is larger than the non-working-age share of the population (ages 0–14 and 65 and older). A country with a large and productive working-age population and a low dependency (or support) ratio is better positioned to spur economic growth and raise living standards. According to Bloom et al. [19], the change in age structure leads to a rise in per capita savings, which they refer to as an accounting effect, or a "mechanical" dividend. They also expected a behavioral effect, stemming from a rise in female labor participation and increased spending on children's schooling [19].

To harness a dividend, fertility declines are a necessary, but not sufficient, condition. The country must additionally have, or build, the essential infrastructure and policies to put its growing workforce to work, such as investing in education and training, improving access to healthcare, and creating an enabling environment for entrepreneurship and job creation [20, 21]. At best, countries can miss the window of opportunity if they do not grow their economies before facing the eventual rise in age dependency stemming from older dependents. At worst, a large, inadequately educated and trained young population can lead to high levels of unemployment and social unrest [22].

Dividend theory thus refocused the population-development debate from its earlier emphasis on population size and high fertility to a focus on age structure. This aspect of demographic change is both theoretically interesting and empirically dynamic. While a country's total population remains relatively stable over time, age structures can shift rapidly depending on the pace of the country's demographic transition.

Yet this thesis is beset by a lack of firm consensus on the evidence, notably whether the dividend is automatic, large, and how it might depend on contextual conditions [23–25].[2] Disparate findings sow theoretical confusion and muddle policy advice to countries hoping to bank on their fertility transitions. A consistent application of robust methodology across various countries and historical periods would foster a better sense of the magnitude and contextual variation in dividends.

### 2.6 Empirical approaches

Scholars have used a range of alternative approaches to estimating the size of dividends, including simulation, DemDiv Model [26], National Transfer Accounting [27, 28], and regression and decomposition-based models [12].

#### *2.6.1 Simulations*

Various simulation models have examined the relationship between population trends and the economy. These models typically investigate how demographic changes influence the economy, using equations based on economic theories and real-world data. For example, studies by Ashraf et al. [29] and Karra et al. [30] explore how decreasing birth rates affect economic growth. Although these models are transparent in their calculations, they can be challenging to use for non-experts and they require large amounts of data [26].

#### *2.6.2 DemDiv model*

The DemDiv model is the most widely and popular used approach for making projections or macro-demographics simulations. It is easy to use and based on widely available data for most countries. It consists of projecting the economic consequences for a country based on population projections and the assumed links between demographic and economic variables. The first draws from the projection work of the

[2] For example, [23–25] work use a model integrating a greater diversity of parameters (the effects of FP policies, endogenous savings, child health, the effects of manufacturing and agriculture, wage distortions, and the effects of women's education on fertility) to try to account for a broad range of policy conditions.

United Nations. The latter comes from scientific research on these links [31]. The DemDiv model comprises a demographic and economic sub-model [31, 32].

#### *2.6.3 National Transfer Accounts*

Another approach for estimating the size of the dividend, the National Transfer Account approach, was developed by Mason and Lee [33]. This method leverages detailed data on earnings, consumption, savings, and economic transfers to build a detailed country profile of the age-specific pattern of economic behavior [34, 35]. With these profiles (and the assumption that these behaviors hold relatively stable), one can gauge how aggregate national outcomes would change as the country's age structure evolves. The wealth and detail on age-specific economic behavior make it possible to examine multiple questions about population-economic relations, including the size of dividends [27, 28].

The NTA approach usefully eschews the narrow assumptions of a universal definition of age structure. Unfortunately, it is highly data-intensive [26]. Not surprisingly, NTA data is not universally available. For instance, files are only available for 21 of sub-Saharan Africa's 46 countries and cover a short historical period. As such, they cannot support detailed cross-country comparisons, even if one ignores the high variability in data quality across countries.

#### *2.6.4 Regression and demographic decomposition*

Dividends are also studied with regression and decomposition-based modeling. This method uses historical time series data to establish statistical relationships between key demographic and economic variables. Researchers have widely employed the regression approach to construct detailed explanations of relationships among key variables [36–39]. The decomposition approach is particularly valuable for assessing the contributions of different key components to economic growth. For instance, using data from 105 countries spanning the 1980–2005 period, Crespo Cuaresma et al. [40], show that changes in educational attainment levels, rather than age structure alone, primarily contributed to the demographic dividend effects.

## 3. Data and methods

### 3.1 Data

We use data from the World Development database on population size, TFR, labor force participation rate, age structure, and gross national income (*GNI*) from 1970 to 2020 [5]. For comparative purposes, we use the Atlas purchasing power parity (PPP) values of the *GNI* to address changing exchange rates.[3] The data is available for 121 countries, with 44 in Asia, 52 in Latin America, and 25 in Africa over the five-decade period (605 data points in total).

[3] The Atlas method facilitates comparison by converting to US dollars using the exchange rates over 3 years, while the PPP method attempts to estimate equal purchasing power among countries. There is no clear rule as to whether one should use the Atlas method vs. PPP.

### 3.2 Methods

We use a decomposition approach to show how the change in the country's *GNI* trends reflects changes in productivity, employment, and age dependency. This accounting uses a mathematical transformation that expresses *GNI* per capita as a product of four conceptually meaningful factors, as follows:

$$GNI \text{ per capita} = (\text{Productivity})^* (\text{Employment})^* (\text{Labor Force Participation})^* (\text{Age Structure}) \quad (1)$$

The is obtained by successively expressing the *GNI* per capita as:

$$\frac{GNI}{P} = \frac{GNI}{A} * \frac{A}{P} = \frac{GNI}{L} * \frac{L}{A} * \frac{A}{P} = \frac{GNI}{E} * \frac{E}{L} * \frac{L}{A} * \frac{A}{P} \quad (2)$$

Where *GNI* is the Gross National Income; *E* is the population employed out of the total labor force (*L*); *A* is the working-age population, and *P* is the total population.

If we rewrite Eq. (2) as $y = pqrs$

$$\begin{aligned}\Delta y &= \overline{p}\Delta(qrs) + \overline{qrs}\Delta p \\ &= \overline{p}\,(\overline{rs}\Delta q + \overline{q}\,\Delta rs) + \overline{qrs}\Delta p \\ &= \overline{p}\,\overline{q}\Delta rs + \overline{p}\,\overline{rs}\,\Delta q + \overline{qrs}\,\Delta p \\ &= \overline{p}\,\overline{q}\,(\overline{r}\Delta s + \overline{s}\,\Delta r) + \overline{p}\,\overline{rs}\,\Delta q + \overline{qrs}\Delta p \\ &= \overline{p}\,\overline{q}\,\overline{r}\,\Delta s + \overline{p}\,\overline{q}\,\overline{s}\,\Delta r + \overline{p}\,\overline{rs}\Delta q + \overline{qrs}\Delta p.\end{aligned} \quad (3)$$

where barred values represent averages, and Δ marks a change between two time periods. For instance, when studying change in x between 1980 and 1990,

$$\overline{\text{x}} = \left(\text{x}_{1980)} + \text{x}_{1990))}\right)/2 \text{ and } \Delta\text{x} = \text{x}_{1990} - \text{x}_{198}. \quad (4)$$

Using the expression above, any historical change in *GNI* per capita ($y = GNI/P$) can be traced to changes in these four components, including the mechanical influence of age structure ($s = A/P$) and the other components represent changes in theoretically important growth factors, including productivity ($p = GNI/E$), rate of employment($q = E/L$), and labor force participation ($r = L/A$). Importantly, demographic dividend theory expects national changes in age structure to affect these drivers through savings and investment in economic development. A decomposition analysis thus helps identify and compare which of these components made the largest contribution to economic growth.

We use the decomposition methods above to estimate the size of each country's dividends. We then use these results in an Ordinary Least Squares (OLS) regression model to better understand the contextual factors shaping the magnitude of dividends across place and time.

## 4. Findings

### 4.1 Age structure and economic growth

We used the decomposition method described above to compute, for each decade from 1970 to 2020, how much a country's change in *GNI* per capita ($y = GNI/P$) was

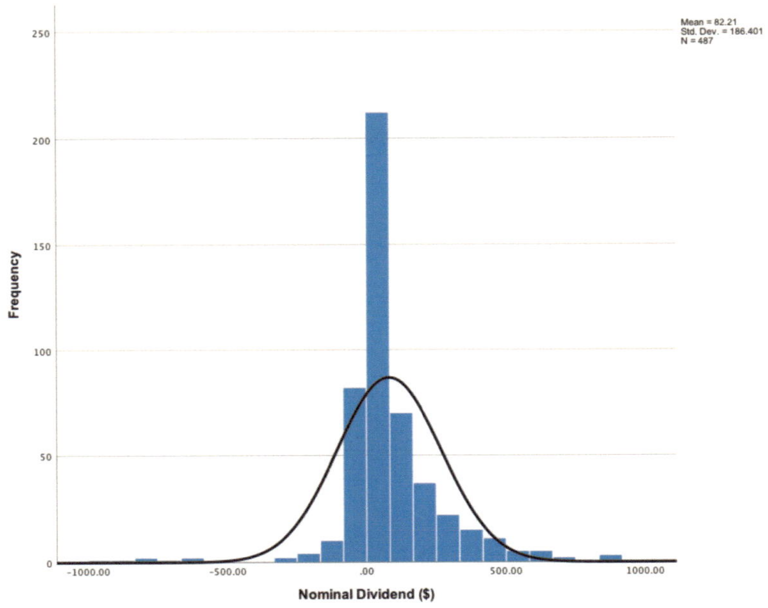


**Figure 2.**
*Size of dividends across the Global South, 1970–2020.*

driven by changes in productivity ($p$), the employment rate ($q$), labor force participation ($r$) and age structure ($s$).

**Figure 2** displays the results from the decomposition analysis, focusing on the role of age structure changes in the economic gains registered over each country period. The mean gain accrued by changes in age structure, which we refer to as the "nominal dividend," was $82, with a slightly lower median of $37. Given that the median gain in *GNI* over each decade period was $396, it appears that, on the whole, the influence of age structure was small but still important. Not surprisingly, the influence of age structure varied significantly over time and across regions, as described in **Table 1**.

## 4.2 Historical variation

**Table 1** summarizes the historical evolution in the magnitude of dividends in the 1970–1980, 1980–1990, 1990–2000, 2000–2010, and 2010–2020 decades.

### *4.2.1 1970–1980*

Between 1970 and 1980, Latin America, Asia, and Africa experienced rapid economic growth, with median growth rates exceeding 200% in all regions. A significant driver of this growth was the surge in commodity prices and export revenues, driven by strong demand and high prices for oil, minerals, agricultural products, and manufactured goods in the global market. These increased export earnings enabled these regions to finance development plans, invest in infrastructure, and expand their industrial sectors [41].

The Median *GNI* gains ranged from $271 in Africa to $538 in Asia, reaching $1424 in Latin America (**Table 1**). The role of age structure and the demographic dividend in

| | | 1970–1980 | | | | 1980–1990 | | | | 1990–2000 | | | |
|---|---|---|---|---|---|---|---|---|---|---|---|---|---|
| | | Nominal change in *GNI*/Capita $ | % change in *GNI*/Capita | % dividend | Nominal dividend | Nominal change in *GNI*/Capita $ | % change in *GNI*/Capita | % dividend | Nominal dividend | Nominal change in *GNI*/Capita $ | % change in *GNI*/Capita | % dividend | Nominal dividend |
| Asia | Mean | $2216 | 380% | 4.0% | $51 | $983 | 45% | 9.4% | $143 | $1121 | 134% | 11% | $143 |
| | Median | $538 | 243% | 2.4% | $20 | $112 | 35% | 5.0% | $62 | $423 | 43% | 8% | $37 |
| | *N* | *17* | | *17* | *17* | *22* | | *22* | *22* | *36* | *36* | *35* | *36* |
| Latin America | Mean | $1396 | 206% | 3.9% | $93 | $276 | 7% | 3.7% | $108 | $2125 | 89% | 2% | $139 |
| | Median | $1424 | 207% | 5.8% | $81 | $32 | 2% | −2.2% | $69 | $1348 | 81% | 7% | $81 |
| | *N* | *22* | | *22* | *22* | *24* | | *19* | *24* | *24* | *24* | *24* | *24* |
| Africa | Mean | $424 | 212% | 0.4% | -$29 | $133 | 5% | −6.3% | $18 | $79 | 2% | 2% | $42 |
| | Median | $271 | 215% | −1.8% | -$6 | $12 | 2% | −0.5% | $1 | -$42 | −15% | −1% | $17 |
| | *N* | *34* | *34* | *34* | *34* | *42* | *42* | *39* | *42* | *45* | *45* | *42* | *44* |
| | | 2000–2010 | | | | 2010–2020 | | | | | | | |
| | | Nominal Change in *GNI*/ Capita $ | % Change in *GNI*/ Capita | % Dividend | Nominal Dividend | Nominal Change in *GNI*/ Capita $ | % Change in *GNI*/ Capita | % Dividend | Nominal Dividend | | | | |
| Asia | Mean | $2626 | 193% | 7% | $180 | $857 | 32% | −1% | $41 | | | | |
| | Median | $2605 | 143% | 8% | $113 | $756 | 22% | −5% | $58 | | | | |
| | *N* | *43* | *43* | *42* | *34* | *44* | *44* | *41* | *39* | | | | |
| Latin America | Mean | $3274 | 111% | 12% | $252 | $1113 | 24% | 4% | $70 | | | | |
| | Median | $2644 | 99% | 7% | $212 | $599 | 23% | 3% | $159 | | | | |
| | *N* | *25* | *25* | *25* | *25* | *24* | *24* | *21* | *23* | | | | |
| AFRICA | Mean | $1504 | 176% | 5% | $79 | -$189 | 15% | 2% | $34 | | | | |
| | Median | $629 | 119% | 3% | $18 | $94 | 8% | 5% | $30 | | | | |
| | *N* | *50* | *50* | *50* | *49* | *50* | *50* | *45* | *52* | | | | |

% Dividend = Percentage of Age Structure's Contribution to Dividend.

Nominal Dividend= Nominal dollars gained from change in age structure.

**Table 1.**
*Regional growth and economic dividends, 1970–2020.*

driving these changes varied across regions. Age structure contributed 2% in Asia, 6% in Latin America and the Caribbean, but had a negative contribution of −2% in sub-Saharan Africa. The poor performance of sub-Saharan Africa can be attributed to its high and rising age dependency (**Figure 1**), in contrast to the other developing regions.

Sub-Saharan Africa's poor performance can be partially understood within the context of the population policies pursued by African states during the post-colonial era, which aimed to encourage population growth due to cultural and social factors favoring larger families [42]. At the time, Africa was considered underpopulated, and the prevailing doctrine promoted population growth, sustaining high fertility rates. This perspective hindered the endorsement of population programs emerging from the initial International Conference on Population and Development in Bucharest in 1974.

In conclusion, from 1970 to 1980, Africa witnessed substantial variations in *GNI* per capita growth across regions. Sub-Saharan Africa's underperformance can be partially attributed to its population policies and the subsequent high and growing age dependency. These findings underscore the complex interplay between demographic factors and economic development, emphasizing the importance of considering regional context in understanding these dynamics.

#### *4.2.2 1980–1990*

During this decade, there was a notable slowdown in economic growth, a phenomenon extensively addressed in the literature. East and South Asia experienced a modest 35% increase, while sub-Saharan Africa and Latin America saw growth rates of just 2%. Several factors contributed to this deceleration. First, the debt crisis in many developing countries hindered their ability to invest in productive sectors, leading to austerity measures and structural adjustment programs imposed by international financial institutions. This resulted in reduced government spending, increased unemployment, and slowed economic activity [43]. Second, declining commodity prices, a significant source of export earnings, had a detrimental impact on these region's economies [44, 45]. Third, political instability, conflicts, and civil wars in various countries disrupted economic activities and discouraged investment. Furthermore, limited technological advancements and access to capital and markets broke economic growth. Collectively, these interconnected factors created an unfavorable environment for sustained economic progress, resulting in diminished growth rates across Asia, Africa, and Latin America during the 1980–1990 period.

However, the impact of significant demographic changes during this period is also evident. The demographic dividend contributed positively to economic growth, primarily in Asia, with a mean and median percent dividend of 9.4% and 5%, respectively. This is largely attributed to the rapidly improving dependency ratios resulting from the population policies aimed at reducing fertility rates across the region. Interventions included contraception access, incentives and disincentives for family size, raising the legal age of marriage, and enhancing female education and empowerment. The impact of these policies varied across countries and regions, depending on factors such as the initial fertility level, policy implementation, and cultural and religious context. For example, China's "One-Child Policy" in 1979 strictly limited family size through a combination of incentives and penalties [46]. India's National Family Welfare Program in the 1960s emphasized voluntary family planning and reproductive health services, including campaigns promoting contraception and the establishment of family planning clinics [47]. Similarly, Thailand's "Contraceptive Revolution" in the 1970s featured a comprehensive family planning program, with free or subsidized contraceptives, education, and expanded access to reproductive health services [48].

In Latin America, demographic dividend contributions were smaller, with a mean positive dividend of 3.7% but a negative median value of −2.2%. This reflects varying fertility trends across the region, with some countries lagging in fertility declines while others were taking action based on the 1974 World Population Plan of Action. The 1984 ICPD in Mexico increased Latin American and Caribbean countries' awareness of fertility's economic impact. Governments in the region began pursuing family planning programs, population education, and women's rights promotion [6, 9, 49, 50].

In sub-Saharan Africa, high dependency ratios (**Figure 1**) led to a mean and median dividend of −6.3% and −0.5%, respectively. During the 1980s, the region experienced persistently high fertility rates alongside limited investments in contraception stemming from cultural norms and the absence of robust population policies. African cultural and social structures favored large families during this time, influencing the desire for high fertility rates. Moreover, inadequate infrastructure and limited availability of contraceptives posed challenges to accessing family planning methods [42]. Insufficient investments in reproductive health and family planning programs further hindered progress in reducing fertility rates.

#### *4.2.3 1990–2000*

In the 1990s, Asia and Latin America experienced rapid growth, with median gains in *GNI* per capita of 43% and 81%, respectively. In contrast, Africa faced a significant economic downturn, with a mean decline in *GNI* per capita of 15%. This decline stemmed from multiple factors. Political instability, including civil wars, ethnic conflicts, and military coups, disrupted economies, destroyed infrastructures, and deterred investment [51, 52]. Some countries struggled due to poor economic policies, such as excessive state control of key sectors, overvalued currencies, heavy reliance on single commodities for exports, and neglect of agriculture [53]. The high debt burden carried by many African nations redirected national budgets toward debt servicing rather than investment or social spending [54].

Additionally, some countries implemented Structural Adjustment Programs, which, though aimed at reducing fiscal imbalances, often led to short-term economic hardship and hindered long-term growth due to social spending cuts [55]. The lack of economic diversification was another challenge, with many African economies heavily reliant on commodities, exposing them to volatile international market prices [56]. Lastly, the HIV/AIDS pandemic in this period had severe social and economic impacts on many African countries, including reduced life expectancy, productivity, and overall economic growth [57].

Favorable demographic conditions yielded significant demographic dividends across Asia and Latin America, with median dividends of 8% and 7%, respectively, in this decade. The 1990s witnessed substantial declines in fertility rates in many countries in these regions. Brazil stands out in Latin America, with its fertility rate plummeting from 6.3 children per woman in the 1960s to an average of 2.3 by the late '90s. This transformation resulted from robust government-sponsored family planning initiatives and increased women's education levels [58].

In Asia, Iran experienced a similarly dramatic shift in fertility trends. The fertility rate dropped from an average of 7 children per woman in 1980 to below the replacement level—about 2.0—by the late 90s. This rapid demographic transition was driven by a nationwide family planning program and improved access to education and employment for women [59].

While Africa faced challenging economic conditions during this period, its demographic outlook was less grim. The median dividend was −2%, meaning that *GNI* losses would have been 2% greater without improvements in age structure. Many Sub-Saharan African countries began experiencing notable fertility declines in the 1990s. Ghana, for instance, saw its fertility rates drop from around 6.4 children per woman in 1988 to 4.2 by 2000, driven by efforts to expand access to family planning services, increase women's education, and gradual urbanization [60]. Rwanda witnessed one of the most rapid fertility declines in the region, with fertility rates declining from approximately 8.2 children per woman in the early 1980s to 4.6 in 2000, thanks to a robust national family planning program and strides in women's education [61].

Yet the demographic picture throughout the region remained varied during this period. During the 1990s, the patterns of fertility transitions across African nations varied significantly, with some countries even observing fertility stalls and reversals, such as in the case of Niger and Mali, where TFR remained about 6 [62]. More dramatically, fertility reversals were observed in some countries, where fertility rates began rising again after an initial decrease, largely due to persisting cultural norms favoring larger families, inadequate access to family planning services, and obstacles in women's education and economic opportunities [63].

### *4.2.4 2000–2010*

The 2000s saw continued growth within Asia and Latin America (with median gains in *GNI* of 143% and 99%, respectively). However, what stood out during this decade was Africa's remarkable economic emergence, with a staggering median *GNI* per capita increase of 119%. This growth was propelled by a surge in commodity prices driven by global demand, particularly from rapidly developing countries like China, which significantly boosted Africa's export revenue [64]. Economic reforms at the national level, including trade liberalization and market deregulation, further accelerated growth by creating a more favorable environment for business and investment [56]. Additionally, the expansion of telecommunications and the booming mobile phone market played a transformative role in driving economic development across the continent [65].

Moreover, **Table 1** underscores the significance of demographic dividends during this period across regions, with mean dividends ranging from 8% in Asia to 7% in Latin America to 3% in Africa. The period was marked by significant global progress in promoting family planning [42], which appeared to contribute to the improvements in age structure observed, especially throughout sub-Saharan Africa. Kenya, for instance, experienced a significant decline in TFR, dropping from 4.9 children per woman in 2000 to 3.9 by 2010, largely due to concerted efforts to expand access to family planning services and education for women [66]. Similarly, in Ethiopia, a robust nationwide family planning program and increased focus on female education resulted in a TFR decrease from 5.9 in 2000 to 4.8 children per woman by 2010 [67]. These instances underscore the impact of dedicated national initiatives and policy changes on fertility transitions.

#### *4.2.5 2010–2020*

From 2010 to 2020, economic growth slowed compared to the 2000s, and regions showed similar patterns, with mean *GNI* gains of 32% in Asia, 24% in Latin America, and 15% in Africa. As the median gains are lower, the growth was concentrated in a few leading countries. Given its significant role as a trading partner and the global demand for commodities, China's economic deceleration had widespread implications [68]. Reduced commodity prices, resulting from the worldwide slowdown, affected resource-rich countries across these regions heavily reliant on commodity exports [69]. Furthermore, political instability, corruption, and governance issues affected economic performance, notably in Latin America and Africa [70]. Conflict and political turmoil stifled economic growth and led to contractions in some countries [69]. Lastly, sluggish productivity growth and weak investment contributed to a slowdown in Asia, particularly in countries that had previously experienced rapid growth, such as India and Indonesia [71].

The role of dividends during this period is especially interesting. Africa had slightly lower median dividends (2%), primarily due to stalls in their fertility decline. For instance, Kenya's TFR remained around 3.9 children per woman from 2010 to 2014, attributed to reduced contraceptive use and changes in marriage patterns [61]. Nigeria also experienced a similar pattern, with the TFR stagnating at about 5.5 children per woman over the same period due to persistent cultural norms favoring large families, and barriers to family planning services [72]. Dividends were smaller in Latin America, where fertility declined from 2.2 to 1.9, and have now turned negative in Asia, where TFR fell from 2.8 to 2.2 in South Asia and 1.9 to 1.5 in East Asia and the Pacific. These smaller and negative dividends stem from the challenges now emerging in many countries of this region.

### 4.3 Drivers of dividends

While the analysis above suggests the role of dividends in shaping economic growth, we also wanted to consider factors that explain variation in the size of national dividends. For this, we conducted a regression (shown in **Table 2**) examining how the size of dividends had varied over time, across regions, and through the stages of the demographic and economic transition.

First, we ask the frequently posed question, "Is Africa Different"? Scholars of Africa's fertility transition have found it to have a tendency to begin later and from a lower threshold of development. Cross-national analyses on the correlates of fertility declines confirm a net "Africa effect" even after adjustment for other development variables such as GDP per capita, education, life expectancy, and urbanization [73]. In terms of dividends, past studies found no reason to preclude a dividend in Africa, and others found early signs or even larger dividends than initially expected. The current thinking is to view African dividends as neither precluded nor inevitable but, as elsewhere, contingent on policy [4, 14, 22, 38, 74, 75].

Model 1, in **Table 1**, presents our findings on regional differences in dividends. Here, we do find evidence of an "Africa" effect. The binary relationship between regions and dividends suggests that countries in Asia and Latin America reap greater benefits compared to those in Africa. Latin America receives the largest sum, which implies that it benefits $101.6 more on average from demographic dividends than African countries.

| | Model 1: region | | Model 2: region, demographic transition | | Model 3: region, demographic transition, economic condition | | Model 4: region, demographic transition, economic condition, historical period | |
|---|---|---|---|---|---|---|---|---|
| **Variable** | **Coeff.** | **Std. error** | **Coeff.** | **Std. error** | **Coeff.** | **Std. error** | **Coeff. std. error** | |
| *Region* | | | | | | | | |
| Asia | 81.4*** | 19.2 | 53.9** | 21.3 | 56.7*** | 20.7 | 50.3** | 20.7 |
| Latin America | 101.6*** | 20.7 | 53.9** | 23.5 | 40.2* | 23.0 | 24.8 | 24.0 |
| Africa | Refer | . | Refer | . | Refer | . | Refer | . |
| *Start of decade TFR* | | | | | | | | |
| TFR <2 | | | −41.0 | 35.7 | −137.5*** | 39.0 | −132.6*** | 40.1 |
| TFR 2–4 | | | 111.9*** | 23.7 | 55.8** | 25.3 | 51.6* | 27.4 |
| TFR 4–6 | | | 41.7* | 21.3 | 18.8 | 21.1 | 22.6 | 21.7 |
| TFR >6 | | | Refer | . | Refer | . | Refer | . |
| Log of start of decade | | | | | | | | |
| *GNI*/capital | | | | | 39.0*** | 7.2 | 51.9*** | 7.5 |
| Starting year | | | | | | | | |
| 2010 | | | | | | | −86.4*** | 30.5 |
| 2000 | | | | | | | 60.2** | 28.0 |
| 1990 | | | | | | | 13.3 | 26.7 |
| 1980 | | | | | | | −8.0 | 27.2 |
| 1970 | | | | | | | Refer | . |
| *Intercept* | 32.9*** | 12.2 | 6.6* | 15.1 | −226.9*** | 45.5 | −305.0*** | 45.8 |
| *Adjusted* $R^2$ | 0.06 | | 0.12 | | 0.17 | | 0.23 | |

*$^{*}p < 0.1$. $^{**}p < 0.05$. $^{***}p < 0.01$.*

**Table 2.**
*Association between contextual factors and size of demographic dividends 1970–2020.*

Model 2 controls for TFR values to account for the stages of demographic transition. In this model, the coefficients for both Asia and Latin America reduced to 53.9 yet remained statistically significant. As we introduced indicators for Gross National Income (*GNI*) and period effect in Models 3 and 4, the magnitude and significance level of the coefficient for Asia stayed constant. This signifies that Asia, on average, gains over $50 more from demographic dividends compared to Africa. Conversely, the coefficient's magnitude and significance level declined for Latin America. Our final model shows no statistically significant difference between Latin America and Africa.

In our analysis, we subdivided the TFR level into four categories that represent the four stages of the demographic transition: pre-transition (TFR above 6), early-transition (TFR between 6 and 4), mid-transition (TFR between 4 and 2), and post-transition (TFR below 2). The coefficients of TFR indicate a curvilinear relationship between demographic dividends and TFR. That is to say, the benefits of demographic dividends increase as countries begin to witness a decline in TFR, peak when countries reach the mid-transition stage, and decrease to a negative value for post-transition countries whose TFR falls below the replacement level. This pattern remains consistent in our subsequent models when controlling economic conditions and period effects. However, the variations in magnitude and significance level suggest that the boundary between the mid-transition and post-transition stages, or the replacement level, is a more precise cutoff.

In the final model, compared to the pre-transition group, the post-transition group incurs an average loss of $132.6, significant at the 0.01 level. The mid-transition group, on the other hand, gains an average of $51.6, significant at the 0.1 level, and the early-transition group shows no significant difference compared to the pre-transition group. These findings add insights to demographic transition theory and provide quantitative cutoffs that facilitate a more comprehensive understanding of the different stages of demographic transition.

Lastly, the regression reveals a statistically significant result for economic conditions, suggesting that countries with more robust economic conditions can profit more from demographic dividends. When the period effect is controlled, only the decades 2000–2010 and 2010–2020 show a statistically significant difference compared to the decade from 1970 to 1980. The findings suggest that countries benefited by an average of $60.2 from the dividends during the decade from 2000 to 2010 and lost an average of $86.4 from the dividends during the decade from 2010 to 2020. This suggests that factors beyond regional differences, TFR transition, and economic conditions can also impact the effect of demographic dividends.

## 5. Conclusion

The past half-century of demographic transitions throughout Africa, Asia, and Latin America have raised important questions about how these changes would shape the economic trajectories between and within regions of the Global South. A quarter-century ago, Bloom et al. [4] argued that the key demographic factor determining this transition would not be population size or fertility rates alone. Instead, they proposed a "new" argument focusing on the role of age structure. With another quarter century of robust data and a novel decomposition method, we confirm the net effects of age structure over and beyond fertility decline.

Using decomposition methods to examine World Bank data from the past half century, we find that a decline in age dependency can significantly boost economic growth, providing new empirical evidence for demographic dividend theory. Yet, this boost is complex and contextually variable. We find a clear pattern or dividend formation that unfolds across the fertility transition. Compared to the pre-transition countries (TFR above 6), mid-transition countries (TFR between 2 and 4) gain the most from their age structure. The post-transition countries (TFR below two or replacement level), on the other hand, suffer a substantive loss from their age structure, indicating the emerging problem of population aging.

We also confirmed that the demographic dividends are experienced unevenly across different geographic regions. At the bivariate level, Africa seems to harness statistically smaller dividends than Latin America and Asia. However, controlling for economic conditions, historical periods, and stages in the demographic transition, Africa is not truly different from Latin America. Asia, on the other hand, remains the leading example of a region where countries have capitalized on their dividends. These findings could indicate an increased inequality within the Global South countries, with sub-Saharan countries left behind. Nevertheless, given that many African countries are still at the earlier stages of the transition, this gives hope that by identifying effective policies, these countries will be able to better leverage their "windows of opportunity" and expand their economies.

## Author details

Zhuang Han[1], Claude Mbarga[2], Michel Tenikue[3] and Sarah Giroux[1]*

1 Department of Global Development, Cornell University, Ithaca, USA

2 Institut de Formation et de Recherche Démographiques (IFORD), Yaounde, Cameroon

3 Luxembourg Institute of Socio-Economic Research (LISER), Porte des Sciences, Esch-sur-Alzette, Luxembourg

*Address all correspondence to: sh104@cornell.edu

## References

[1] Malthus T. An essay on the principle of population. J. Johnson, in St. Paul's Church-Yard. 1798

[2] UNDESA. World Population Prospects. United Nations Department of Economic and Social Affairs, Population Division, Custom Data Acquired Via Website. 2022. Available from: https://population.un.org/wpp/DataQuery/

[3] African Union. 28th AU Summit. African Union. 2017. Available from: https://au.int/en/summit/28

[4] Bloom D, Canning D, Sevilla J. The Demographic Dividend: A New Perspective on the Economic Consequences of Population Change. Santa Monica, CA: Rand Corporation; 2003. Available from: https://books.google.com/books?hl=en&lr=&id=36rNSRG4r7YC&oi=fnd&pg=PR3&dq=demographic+dividend&ots=6Ljka8N3fY&sig=M_dV2ZFcGAK-kit2ZJiidnnK8X0

[5] World Development Indicators. World Development Indicators | DataBank. World Bank: World Development Indicators Databank. 2023. Available from: https://databank.worldbank.org/source/world-development-indicators [Accessed May 19, 2023]

[6] de Cosio MEZ. Changements de fécondité au Mexique et politiques de population. Paris, France: L'Harmattan; 1994

[7] Prebisch R. The Latin American periphery in the global system of capitalism. Revista CEPAL, Naciones Unidas Comisión Económica para América Latina y el Caribe (CEPAL), April. 1981

[8] CEPAL, E. C. for L. A. and the. Estudio Económico de América Latina y el Caribe 1991 = Economic Survey of Latin America and the Caribbean 1991. Economic Commission for Latin America and the Caribbean. 1992. Available from: https://www.cepal.org/en/publications/1030-estudio-economico-america-latina-caribe-1991-economic-survey-latin-america-and

[9] de Cosio MEZ. Démographie, pauvreté et inégalités. 2011; 83

[10] Guengant J-P. Africa's population: History, current status, and projections. In: Africa's Population: In Search of a Demographic Dividend. Cham, Switzerland; 2017. DOI: 10.1007/978-3-319-46889-1_2

[11] Tenikue M., Konan YS, Nyokon CEM, Degnon Dossou FZ. Le dividende démographique en Afrique Premiers signes et estimation par la méthode de décomposition | Population Environment Research Network (PERN). IUSSP; 2017. Available from: https://www.populationenvironmentresearch.org/node/10557

[12] Eloundou-Enyegue P, Giroux S, Tenikue M. African transitions and fertility inequality: A demographic Kuznets hypothesis. Population and Development Review. 2017;**43**(S1):59-83

[13] Eloundou-Enyegue PM, Giroux SC. Fertility transitions and schooling: From micro-to macro-level associations. Demography. 2012;**49**(4):1407-1432

[14] Eloundou-Enyegue PM, Giroux SC. The role of fertility in achieving Africa's schooling MDGs: Early evidence for sub-Saharan Africa. Journal of Children and Poverty. 2013;**19**(1):21-44

[15] Eloundou-Enyegue P, Tenikue M, Konan YS, Nyokon CEM, Degnon Dossou FZ. The demographic dividend in Africa first signs and estimation by the decomposition method. IUSSP; 2018. Available from: https://www.populationenvironmentresearch.org/node/10557

[16] Groth H, May JF. Africa's Population: In Search of a Demographic Dividend. Cham, Switzerland: Springer; 2017

[17] Paris F. Population and sustainable development in sub-Saharan Africa. Population Avenir. 2011;**701**(1):4-8

[18] Eloundou-Enyegue PM, Stokes CS, Cornwell GT. Are there crisis-led fertility declines? Evidence from Central Cameroon. Population Research and Policy Review. 2000;**19**:47-72

[19] Bloom DE, Kuhn M, Prettner K. Africa's prospects for enjoying a demographic dividend. Journal of Demographic Economics. 2017;**83**(1): 63-76

[20] Alary P, Lafaye de Micheaux E. L'économie politique de l'Asie: État des lieux et perspectives de recherche pour l'Asie du Sud-Est. Introduction. Revue de La Régulation. Capitalisme, Institutions, Pouvoirs. 2013:13

[21] CEPII. L'économie mondiale 2020. La Découverte: Cairn.info; 2019. Available from: https://www.cairn.info/l-economie-mondiale-2020–9782348045707.htm

[22] Gribble JN, Bremner J. Achieving a demographic dividend. Population Bulletin. 2012;**67**(2):16

[23] Canning D, Raja S, Yazbeck AS. Africa's Demographic Transition: Dividend or Disaster? Washington, DC: World Bank Publications; 2015

[24] Lam D. How the world survived the population bomb: Lessons from 50 years of extraordinary demographic history. Demography. 2011;**48**(4): 1231-1262

[25] Lutz W, Goldstein JR. Introduction: How to deal with uncertainty in population forecasting? International Statistical Review. 2004;**72**(1):1-4

[26] Beninguisse G, Eloundou-Enyegue PM, Kobiane JF, Yao SK, Tenikue M. 50 questions pour comprendre le Dividende démographique. 2017

[27] CREFAT. Compte nationaux de transfert : Comprendre l'economie generationelle. 2016. Available from: www.ntaccounts.org

[28] Dramani L. Économie générationnelle et dividende démographique: Éléments de diagnostic au Sénégal – Tome 1. Paris, France: L'Harmattan; 2016

[29] Ashraf QH, Weil DN, Wilde J. The effect of fertility reduction on economic growth. Population and Development Review. 2013;**39**(1):97-130

[30] Karra M, Canning D, Wilde J. The effect of fertility decline on economic growth in Africa: A macrosimulation model. Population and Development Review. 2017;**43**:237-263

[31] Moreland S, Madsen EL, Kuang B, Hamilton M, Jurczynska K, Brodish P. Modeling the Demographic Dividend: Technical Guide to the DemDiv Model. 2014. 10.13140/RG.2.1.4162.1607

[32] Diallo I, Maiga M, Moreland S. Modélisation du dividende démographique: Le Model Demdiv. CICES. Dakar, Senegal: USAID; 2015

[33] Lee R, Mason A. Fertility, human capital, and economic growth over the demographic transition. European Journal of Population= Revue Europeenne de Demographie. 2010; **26**(2):159

[34] Measuring and Analysing the Generational Economy: National Transfer Accounts Manual. 2013. Available from: https://www.un.org/en/development/desa/publications/measuring-and-analysing-the-generational-economy.html

[35] Nationen V, editor. Measuring and Analysing the Generational Economy: National Transfer Accounts Manual. New York, NY: United Nations; 2013

[36] Bhattacharya G, Haldar SK. Does demographic dividend yield economic dividend? India, a case study. Economics Bulletin. 2015;**35**(2):1274

[37] Bloom D, Canning D, Fink G, Finlay J. Fertility, the demographic dividend, and economic growth. In: Fourth Annual Research Conference on Population, Reproductive Health, and Economic Development, Cape Town. Santa Monica, CA; 2010

[38] Drummond MP, Thakoor V, Yu S. Africa Rising: Harnessing the Demographic Dividend. Washington, DC: International Monetary Fund; 2014

[39] Misra R. Impact of demographic dividend on economic growth: A study of BRICS and the EU. International Studies. 2015;**52**(1–4):99-117

[40] Crespo Cuaresma J, Lutz W, Sanderson W. Is the demographic dividend an education dividend? Demography. 2014;**51**(1):299-315

[41] UNDESA. UN/DESA Policy Brief #53: Reflection on development policy in the 1970s and 1980s|Department of Economic and Social Affairs (No. 53; World Economic and Social Survey). 2017. Available from: https://www.un.org/development/desa/dpad/publication/policy-brief-53-reflection-on-development-policy-in-the-1970s-and-1980s/

[42] Garenne M. Planning familial et fécondité en Afrique: Évolutions de 1950 à 2010. FERDI. 1950. Available from: https://horizon.documentation.ird.fr/exl-doc/pleins_textes/divers17-08/010070544.pdf

[43] Sims J, Romero J. Latin American debt crisis of the 1980s. Federal Reserve History. 2013;**22**

[44] Emara N, Simutowe A, Jamison T. Commodity price changes and economic growth in developing countries. Journal of Business and Economics. 2015;**6**(10): 1707–1712. Available from: https://ssrn.com/abstract=3812834

[45] Maizels A. The continuing commodity crisis of developing countries. World Development. 1994; **22**(11):1685-1695

[46] Feng W, Gu B, Cai Y. The end of China's one-child policy. Studies in Family Planning. 2016;**47**(1):83-86

[47] Visaria L, Jejeebhoy S, Merrick T. From family planning to reproductive health: Challenges facing India. International Family Planning Perspectives. 1999;**1999**:S44-S49

[48] Knodel J, Debavalya N, Kamnuansilpa P. Thailand's continuing reproductive revolution. International Family Planning Perspectives. 1980; **1980**:84-97

[49] CELADE. Indicadores de pueblos indígenas y afrodescendientes, Santiago

de Chili; disponible à l'adresse. 2013. Available from: http://celade.cepal.org/redatam/PRYESP/SISPPI/

[50] Grinblat JA. L'évolution de la fécondité dans le monde depuis 1965 et ses conséquences. Mondes en développement. 2008;**142**(2):13-22. DOI: 10.3917/med.142.0013

[51] Alesina A, Özler S, Roubini N, Swagel P. Political instability and economic growth. Journal of Economic Growth. 1996;**1**:189-211

[52] Porteous T. L'évolution des conflits en Afrique subsaharienne. Politique Étrangère. 2003;**2003**:307-320

[53] Bates R. Political insecurity and state failure in contemporary Africa. CID Working Paper Series. 2005

[54] Easterly WR. The Elusive Quest for Growth: Economists' Adventures and Misadventures in the Tropics. Cambridge, MA: MIT Press; 2002

[55] Mkandawire PT, Soludo CC. Our Continent, our Future: African Perspectives on Structural Adjustment. Dakar, Senegal: IDRC; 1999

[56] Collier P, O'Connell S. Opportunities and choices. In: Ndulu B, O'Connell S, Bates R, Collier P, Soludo C, editors. The Political Economy of Economic Growth in Africa 1960–2000. Cambridge, UK: Cambridge University Press; 2008

[57] Bell C, Devarajan S, Gersbach H. The long-run economic costs of AIDS: A model with an application to South Africa. The World Bank Economic Review. 2006;**20**(1):55-89

[58] Berquó ES, Cavenaghi SM. Notas sobre os diferenciais educacionais e econômicos da fecundidade no Brasil. In: Revista Brasileira de Estudos de População. Vol. 31. Rio de Janeiro, Brazil: SciELO Brasil; 2014. pp. 471-482

[59] Abbasi-Shavazi MJ, McDonald P, Hosseini-Chavoshi M. The Fertility Transition in Iran. Vol. 75. Dordrect, Netherlands: Springer; 2009

[60] Caldwell JC, Caldwell P. Africa: The new family planning frontier. Studies in Family Planning. 2002;**33**(1): 76-86

[61] Westoff CF, Cross AR. The stall in the fertility transition in Kenya (DHS Analytical Studies No. 9). Article DHS Analytical Studies No. 9. 2006. Available from: https://dhsprogram.com/publications/publication-as9-analytical-studies.cfm

[62] Bongaarts J. The causes of stalling fertility transitions. Studies in Family Planning. 2006;**37**(1):1-16

[63] Garenne ML. Testing for fertility stalls in demographic and health surveys. Population Health Metrics. 2011;**9**(1):1-8

[64] Broadman HG. Africa's Silk Road: China and India's New Economic Frontier. Washington, DC: World Bank Publications; 2006

[65] Aker JC, Mbiti IM. Mobile phones and economic development in Africa. Journal of Economic Perspectives. 2010; **24**(3):207-232

[66] Kenya National Bureau of Statistics, National AIDS Control Council, National AIDS/STD Control Programme, Ministry of Public Health and Sanitation, Kenya Medical Research Institute, National Coordinating Agency for Population and Development, et al. Kenya Demographic and Health Survey 2008–09. 2010. Available from: https://www.dhsprogram.com/publications/publication-fr229-dhs-final-reports.cfm

[67] Agency/Ethiopia CS, International ICF. Ethiopia Demographic and Health Survey 2011. 2012. Available from: https://dhsprogram.com/publications/publication-fr255-dhs-final-reports.cfm

[68] Roach S. Unbalanced: The Codependency of America and China. Amazon.com: Books. 2023. Available from: https://www.amazon.com/Unbalanced-Codependency-America-Stephen-Roach/dp/0300187173 [Accessed: May 19, 2023]

[69] World Bank. World Development Report 2020: Trading for Development in the Age of Global Value Chains. Washington, DC: World Bank; 2020. DOI: 10.1596/978-1-4648-1457-0

[70] 2020 Corruption Perceptions Index —Explore the results. International Transparency. 2021. Transparency.org. Available from: https://www.transparency.org/en/cpi/2020

[71] Bank AD. Asian Development Outlook 2019: Strengthening Disaster Resilience. Metro Manila, Philippines: Asian Development Bank Institute; 2019

[72] Demographic N. Health Survey 2013. National Population Commission (NPC) [Nigeria] and ICF International. Abuja, Nigeria, and Rockville, Maryland, USA: NPC and ICF International; 2019

[73] Bongaarts J. Africa's unique fertility transition. Population and Development Review. 2017;**43**:39-58

[74] Eastwood R, Lipton M. Demographic transition in sub-Saharan Africa: How big will the economic dividend be? Population Studies. 2011;**65**(1):9-35

[75] Karra M, Canning D, Wilde J. A Simulation Model of the Effect of Fertility Reduction on Economic Growth in Africa. Department of Global Health and Population. Boston, MA, USA: Harvard School of Public Health; 2015 Available from: http://economics.usf.edu/pdf/karra%20canning%20wilde

## Chapter 3

# Residential Segregation by Education in the U.S., 2016–2020

*Samantha Friedman and Thalia Tom*


## Abstract

While there is much research on income segregation, we know less about the factors that contribute to the uneven distribution of households across neighborhoods by educational attainment. Although globalization is thought to influence segregation, its association with socioeconomic segregation is debated. Using data from the 2016–2020 American Community Survey, the Globalization and World Cities Research Network, and the MIT Election Data + Science Lab, we investigate the correlates of educational segregation within large core-based statistical areas in the United States, focusing on globalization, income inequality, and political preferences in the 2016 presidential election. Multivariate results reveal that globalization and income inequality are the most significant correlates of educational segregation. Political preferences are only significantly associated with residential dissimilarity between those with a master's degree or higher and those with some college. We discuss the implications of these results for understanding residential inequality on the basis of education in metropolitan America.


**Keywords:** residential segregation, education, globalization, political preferences, metropolitan area

## 1. Introduction

Residential segregation by socioeconomic status is an important topic studied by urban scholars because cities around the world continue to experience significant spatially-based divisions [1–4]. Although globalization is a salient force shaping inequalities in cities [5], the role it plays in influencing socioeconomic residential segregation is subject to debate [6, 7]. Recent research has increasingly suggested that global forces are not solely responsible for the spatial polarization observed in cities, which has motivated researchers to investigate additional factors such as social, cultural, and historical factors [1, 4, 6–8].

Although a substantial body of scholarship examines socioeconomic segregation, it is limited in at least three ways. First, the focus of this research has largely been on income-based residential segregation [3, 9, 10]. Only a handful of studies have investigated residential segregation by educational status [2, 11–13]. Second, much of the research on socioeconomic segregation is largely descriptive in nature [4–8, 14]. An increasing body of literature systematically examines variation in socioeconomic segregation across cities or other geographic areas through empirical analyses [2, 3, 9, 10, 12, 15–17].

Third, little attention has been paid to the association between political preferences and socioeconomic residential segregation, and particularly residential segregation by educational status [15]. In the U.S., the significant growth in animosity between political parties as well as the geographic separation between people of different political parties necessitates an examination of the association between political preferences and educational segregation [18–23]. Examining the association between these factors is particularly important because trends in political polarization have occurred during a period when educational segregation increased [11, 13].

This study's primary objectives are to document residential segregation by educational attainment in metropolitan core-based statistical areas (CBSAs) in the U.S. and examine the factors associated with such segregation, including globalization, income inequality, and political preferences. In doing so, we aim to fill the three gaps in the socioeconomic segregation literature just discussed. First, we document educational segregation in the U.S. Second, we examine the association between globalization and educational segregation in the U.S. Finally, we explore the association between political preferences and residential segregation by educational status, an intersection that has largely been overlooked in the literature.

## 2. Literature review

Although limited research on educational segregation in the U.S. context may reflect the assumption that educational attainment does not contribute much additional variance to existing studies of income segregation, we argue that it is important to assess the extent of educational segregation during a period characterized by the college-for-all ethos [24]. Moreover, trends in educational and economic segregation do not perfectly correspond; the limited research on educational segregation in the U.S. indicates that the level of educational dissimilarity nearly doubled between 1970 and 2000, while economic segregation has not exhibited changes of the same magnitude [11, 13]. Critically, as the U.S. population has grown more educated—37.9% of adults aged 25 and older held at least a bachelor's degree in 2021 [25] compared to 20.3% in 1990 [26], it has also come to reside in increasingly unequally resourced and politically polarized contexts, with consequences for social stratification and the prospects of intergroup cooperation that enhance collective goods [18, 27]. Below, we provide a discussion of how key economic factors, such as globalization and income inequality, as well as political preferences may be associated with variation in educational segregation by reviewing the literature on the correlates of residential segregation by socioeconomic status.

### 2.1 Globalization, income inequality, and socioeconomic residential segregation

Globalization has been the starting point in much of the comparative literature examining residential segregation by socioeconomic status [4, 6, 7]. Sassen [5] advanced a global city thesis with important implications for the study of socio-spatial inequality. According to Sassen [5], cities that are global are characterized as "command points" in the world economy and contain headquarters of multinational, financial and high-order service companies as well as producers of innovation. These industries have largely replaced manufacturing firms. At the same time, global cities function as key markets for products and innovations produced by these high-end firms. The occupational structure present in global cities is a bifurcated one that simultaneously experiences growth in the high- and low-income classes of workers, resulting in "increased asymmetry" or polarization [5]. This economic polarization results in spatial polarization. Sassen [5] compares the gentrification that occurs in global cities to the simultaneous concentration of poverty as evidence of this socio-spatial inequality.

Sassen's [5] global city thesis has been the subject of much empirical testing, but the evidence is mixed as to whether spatial polarization is more present in global cities as compared to cities not demarcated as "global" [1, 4, 6]. For example, Hong Kong and Tokyo are considered to sit atop the world city hierarchy as "alpha+ countries," according to the highly regarded ranking by the Globalization and World Cities Research Network [28]. Yet, they are surprisingly low in their levels of income-based levels of segregation [6]. On the other hand, places like Copenhagen, Budapest, and Tallinn rank lower in the world city hierarchy, but their levels of segregation by social class are much higher than those found in Hong Kong, Tokyo, and Prague [1, 6].

Part of the reason for these contradictory findings likely relates to another important predictor of socioeconomic residential segregation identified in the literature -- income inequality. Studies document a significant, positive relationship between income inequality and socioeconomic segregation [2, 10, 14]. Income inequality is particularly important to examine in the U.S. In 2017, among all G7 countries (i.e., those with the most advanced economies), the U.S. had the highest level of income inequality, as gauged by the Gini coefficient of inequality, with a value of .434 [29]. However, studies that examine the association between income inequality and socioeconomic residential segregation rarely examine globalization [9, 10]. If globalization increases income inequality, as suggested by Sassen [5], the main effect of globalization may be weaker when controlling for income inequality. It remains to be seen whether globalization is associated with segregation by educational status after accounting for the correlation between income inequality and educational segregation.

### 2.2 Political preferences and socioeconomic residential segregation

The findings that globalization does not always lead to high levels of socioeconomic segregation have also led scholars to suggest that global forces, alone, are not responsible for spatial polarization in cities. Other studies find that structural- and institutional-level factors are associated with socioeconomic residential segregation and can modify the effect of globalization [4, 6–8]. The main reason why income-based segregation is lower in some countries compared to others is because of the strong social safety net present in these societies, particularly in Western European countries [1, 4, 7, 8]. Welfare and housing benefits buffer the negative economic impact of social inequality created by globalization that is faced by lower-income groups, thereby reducing residential segregation by socioeconomic status [1, 4]. However, because the safety net is not as strong in the United States as in Western Europe, we expect that other factors could explain the variation in educational segregation.

A factor that has largely been ignored in the socioeconomic segregation literature is political preferences, and we believe this is particularly salient for any contemporary study of residential segregation by educational status. The United States exhibits extraordinarily high levels of political polarization [30], which is perhaps no better encapsulated than by the violent insurrection that roiled the U.S. Capitol on

January 6th, 2021 in an attempt to disrupt the symbolic transfer of power from one administration to the next. In recent decades, scholars have noticed an increase in the geographic separation of people of different political parties [18, 19, 21, 23]. Recent evidence finds a political divide among those with a college degree and those without a college degree; in 2020, 56% of voters with a high school degree or less voted Republican while 56% of those with a college degree voted Democrat [31].

According to the social structural sorting perspective [32], residential segregation reflects an aggregation of the residential preferences and mobility of individuals that depends in part on the information that people have about neighborhoods in their housing search field. In general, when people consider neighborhoods in which to live, they want to share communities with others that share a similar culture and political ideology [33]. While other factors like housing affordability, crime, and school quality are main considerations of movers, similarities in political ideology and cultural values play a role, once accounting for the main factors [34].

If political preferences are related to educational attainment, this begs the question of whether political preferences in the aggregate could be associated with educational segregation. This was found to be the case in Turkey, which is even more politically polarized than the U.S. [15, 30]. Across Turkish provinces, the percentage voting for the liberal political party, which is the political out-group in the society, was positively associated with greater levels of educational segregation across all measures of educational residential segregation [15]. Similar to the U.S., those who voted more liberally tended to be more educated, and areas with greater shares of votes cast towards the outgroup wanted to live among each other, thereby raising educational residential segregation. Across Turkish provinces, the percentage voting for the conservative political party, the party that has been in power, was negatively associated with educational residential segregation [15]. We expect similar findings for the U.S. – the percentage of votes for Clinton in the 2016 election will be positively associated with more educational segregation from 2016 to 2020; the percentage of votes for Trump in the 2016 election will be negatively associated with educational segregation from 2016 to 2020.

## 3. Data and methods

### 3.1 Data and measures

Data come from the 2016–2020 American Community Survey (ACS), the Globalization and World Cities Research Network (GaWC), and the MIT Election Data + Science Lab (MEDSL). We obtain educational attainment counts from the 2016–2020 ACS in order to estimate our primary dependent variable—the dissimilarity index (*D*) or D-score, which captures the evenness with which two groups are distributed across geographic units. These data are among the most recent data available and coincide with the period after the 2016 presidential election but include only one year of the COVID-19 pandemic, making these data ideal for our study. As noted previously, we estimate educational dissimilarity at the census-tract level within metropolitan CBSAs. Consistent with methodological recommendations and prior scholarship, we limit our analyses to metropolitan areas with populations of 500,000 or more [3] and at least 1000 people within each educational attainment category to ensure that we get accurate estimates of segregation [35]. D-scores, which are one of the most commonly used measures of segregation, typically range from a minimum of 0 (indicating no segregation) to a maximum of 1 (indicating complete segregation), but we multiply their values by 100 for ease of interpretation.

Within this context, D-scores may be interpreted as the percentage of individuals within one of two defined social groups who would have to move neighborhoods in order to achieve an even distribution of educational attainment within a particular CBSA. Indices above 60 are classified as high levels of segregation; scores between 30 and 60 are classified as moderate levels of segregation; and scores below 30 are classified as low levels of segregation [36]. Because the dissimilarity index is a pairwise measure of segregation, we obtain estimates for the following educational attainment dyads: 1) bachelor's degree vs. high school diploma; 2) bachelor's degree or higher vs. high school diploma; 3) master's degree or higher vs. high school diploma; and 4) master's degree or higher vs. some college. We focus on these particular categories because we want to evaluate the nature of residential segregation between dyads with high and low levels of education. Additionally, whereas past research has examined dissimilarity between high school and college graduates and between high school diploma and master's degree recipients [11, 13], to our knowledge, limited attention has been paid to the residential sorting patterns of those with some college education.

In order to examine the association between globalization and residential segregation, we include an indicator of whether each CBSA contains a *global city* as defined by the classification of global cities in 2016 by GaWC [28]. Cities with advanced producer services that are integrated with the world city network are identified as *global cities* by this methodology [28]. This classification has been used by many researchers [15, 37, 38].

As discussed above, past research has also implicated income inequality as a robust correlate of residential segregation [10], so we evaluate the association between the Gini index of inequality and educational dissimilarity. The data for the Gini index of inequality at the CBSA level come from the 2016–2020 ACS. The values range from 0 to 1, with 1 indicating high levels of income inequality in the CBSA. We multiply their values by 100 for ease of interpretation and so that the variable is on the same scale as the index of dissimilarity.

To investigate the relationship between educational segregation and political preferences, we use MEDSL data to calculate the percentage of votes cast for Clinton and Trump in the 2016 presidential election within each CBSA. MEDSL data are available at the county level [39]. We aggregated the counts to the CBSA level and calculated the percentages of votes cast for Clinton and Trump. This source of data is beneficial to our study because it allows us to obtain county-level voting data with national coverage. MEDSL has been widely used by scholars in recent research [40–42].

Beyond these key independent variables, we include the following CBSA-level control variables, also obtained from the 2016–2020 ACS data, in our multivariate analyses: 1) percentage with a bachelor's degree (in the models relevant for this population); 2) percentage with a master's degree or higher (in the relevant models); 3) percentage employed in manufacturing; 4) log of the total population of the CBSA; and 5) dummy variables indicating the region where the CBSA is located. Past research indicates that educational attainment and manufacturing employment are salient correlates of socioeconomic segregation [10, 17]. Population size could increase the extent of opportunities for residential sorting by educational attainment and may be positively correlated with educational residential segregation [9, 12, 17]. Alternatively, it may have little to no association with educational residential segregation [15].

### 3.2 Analytical plan

Our analysis proceeds as follows. First, we present descriptive statistics for the dissimilarity index for each educational attainment dyad, and for our key independent and control variables. Then, we report the results from a series of ordinary least squares (OLS) regression analyses that model educational segregation as a function of globalization, income inequality, and political preferences while controlling for other characteristics.

## 4. Results

**Table 1** reports our descriptive results. Across the 108 CBSAs in our analytical dataset, the average level of educational dissimilarity is in the moderate range. The minimum values of the D-scores for all educational dyads fall in the low range of segregation and do not exceed 27. The maximum values fall in the moderate range, generally falling in the middle of the moderate range. The standard deviations for all four sets of dissimilarity scores fall between 4.30 and 5.19, indicating that across the largest metropolitan CBSAs there is similar variation in residential segregation by educational status across the examined dyads. With respect to the D-score values for specific educational dyads, across CBSAs, the average residential segregation between those with a bachelor's degree and those with a high school diploma is 33.9, and the average D-score between those with a bachelor's degree or higher and those with a high school diploma is 36.3, with both scores falling at the lower end of the moderate range. The average D-score between those with at least a master's degree and those with a high school degree is 42.3, and the maximum value for this set of D-scores is the highest at 53.2. The average level of residential segregation between those with at least a master's degree and those with some college education is 33.4.

Our findings that the average levels of residential segregation by educational status are in the moderate range are similar to the findings of Quillian and Lagrange [2] who examine average levels of both educational and income segregation in the largest metropolitan CBSAs in the U.S. using 2006–2010 ACS data. With respect to educational segregation, they find that in the largest 51 CBSAs, the average D-score between those with at least an associate's degree and those with a high school diploma or less is 32.9. They find that dissimilarity scores gauging residential segregation between income groups falling at or below the income percentile and those falling above the income percentile fall in the moderate range of segregation, regardless of the income percentile being examined (see Figure 1b in [2]). Even when they examine specific CBSAs, like New York, their income segregation D-scores are still within the moderate range (see Figure 2b in [2]).

The second part of **Table 1** contains descriptive statistics for our key independent and control variables. With respect to the former, just under half (46.3%) of our 108 CBSAs contain a city categorized as global by the GaWC [28]. The mean Gini index across CBSAs is 46.3, with a range of values between 38.9 and 54.0 and a standard deviation of 2, indicating little variation in the Gini index across these large metropolitan areas. This value aligns with the magnitude of average income inequality reported in previous studies of populous CBSAs [9]. With respect to political preferences, **Table 1** shows that in the 2016 presidential election, on average, 48.40% of the population in our 108 CBSAs voted for Clinton, but values ranged from a minimum of 14.08% to a maximum of 77.07%, which indicates significant CBSA-based variation in

| | Mean | SD | Min | Max |
|---|---|---|---|---|
| **Residential Segregation Scores** Bachelor's Degree/High School | 33.9 | 4.82 | 22.1 | 45.4 |
| Bachelor's Degree or Higher/High School | 36.3 | 5.01 | 23.6 | 47.2 |
| Master's Degree or Higher/High School | 42.3 | 5.19 | 26.8 | 53.2 |
| Master's Degree or Higher/Some College | 33.4 | 4.30 | 22.1 | 43.6 |
| **Key Independent Variables** | | | | |
| Global City | .463 | .501 | 0 | 1 |
| Gini Index of Inequality | 46.3 | 2.00 | 38.9 | 54.0 |
| % of Votes for Clinton | 48.40 | 10.51 | 14.08 | 77.07 |
| % of Votes for Trump | 45.31 | 9.76 | 16.63 | 64.88 |
| **Control Variables** | | | | |
| % with a Bachelor's Degree | 20.87 | 3.88 | 11.38 | 30.08 |
| % with a Master's Degree or Higher | 13.03 | 3.73 | 5.35 | 25.58 |
| % Employed in Manufacturing | 9.86 | 3.60 | 2.87 | 20.44 |
| Log Population | 14.12 | .826 | 13.15 | 16.77 |
| Region: | | | | |
| Northeast | .185 | .39 | 0 | 1 |
| Midwest | .185 | .39 | 0 | 1 |
| South | .407 | .494 | 0 | 1 |
| West | .222 | .418 | 0 | 1 |

*Source: Data come from the 2016–2020 American Community Survey (ACS), the MIT Election Data + Science Lab (MEDSL), and the Globalization and World Cities Research Network (GaWC).*
*Note: Our unit of analysis is at the core-based statistical area (CBSA) level and includes the 108 CBSAs with 500K+ population.*

**Table 1.**
*Descriptive statistics for dependent, key independent, and control variables.*

residents' political preferences. **Table 1** shows that on average, 45.31% of the population voted for Trump, with a similar range of variation; the minimum percentage voting for Trump is 16.63% and the maximum value is 64.88%.

With respect to our control variables, the data in **Table 1** show that across CBSAs an average of 20.87% of the population obtained a bachelor's degree and 13.03% had obtained at least a master's degree. The range of educational attainment across CBSAs reveals that the minimum percentage of the population with a bachelor's degree is 11.38% and with a master's degree is 5.35%; the maximum values, respectively, for these educational categories are 30.08% and 25.58%. **Table 1** reveals that on average, 9.86% of the population is employed in the manufacturing industry. The average log of the total population is 14.12. Finally, the majority of the CBSAs in our analytic sample were located in the South (40.7%), followed by the West (22.2%), the Northeast (18.5%), and the Midwest (18.5%).

**Tables 2** and **3** present the results of our multivariate models examining the factors associated with residential segregation by education. **Table 2** uses the percentage voting for Clinton as the measure for political preferences. **Table 3** uses the percentage voting for Trump. Each table reports coefficients and standard errors from four OLS regression models predicting dissimilarity scores for each of the following educational dyads: 1) bachelor's degree vs. high school diploma; 2) bachelor's degree or higher vs. high school diploma; 3) master's degree or higher vs. high school diploma; and 4) master's degree or higher vs. some college, respectively. Each model includes the key independent variables discussed above and the control variables.

The association between global cities and residential segregation by educational status is significant and positive in all models in **Tables 2** and **3**, with the exception of the models for the educational dyad of those with a master's degree or higher and

| | (1) BA/HS | (2) BA+/HS | (3) MA+/HS | (4) MA+/SC |
|---|---|---|---|---|
| Global City | 2.457* | 2.349* | 2.486* | 1.552 |
| | (1.066) | (1.103) | (1.098) | (0.901) |
| Gini Index of Inequality | 0.720*** | 0.810*** | 0.790*** | 0.689*** |
| | (0.206) | (0.213) | (0.215) | (0.176) |
| % Votes for Clinton | −0.030 | 0.021 | 0.057 | 0.099** |
| | (0.039) | (0.040) | (0.044) | (0.036) |
| % with a Bachelor's Degree | 0.230* | 0.289** | | |
| | (0.103) | (0.106) | | |
| % with a Master's Degree or Higher | | | 0.269* | 0.283** |
| | | | (0.117) | (0.096) |
| % Employed in Manufacturing | 0.083 | 0.111 | 0.121 | 0.147 |
| | (0.112) | (0.116) | (0.119) | (0.098) |
| Log Population | 0.639 | 0.532 | 0.451 | 0.303 |
| | (0.666) | (0.689) | (0.708) | (0.581) |
| Midwest | 5.071*** | 5.015*** | 6.218*** | 4.156*** |
| | (1.180) | (1.220) | (1.289) | (1.058) |
| South | 5.603*** | 5.163*** | 5.903*** | 3.450*** |
| | (0.980) | (1.014) | (1.076) | (0.883) |
| West | 5.233*** | 5.226*** | 6.681*** | 3.149** |
| | (1.087) | (1.124) | (1.197) | (0.983) |
| Constant | −18.113 | −22.087 | −14.258 | −16.274 |
| | (10.965) | (11.341) | (11.326) | (9.297) |
| Observations | 108 | 108 | 108 | 108 |
| R-squared | 0.536 | 0.542 | 0.550 | 0.558 |

*Source: Data come from the 2016–2020 ACS, MEDSL, and GaWC.*
*Notes: Standard errors are in parentheses; *** $p < 0.001$, ** $p < 0.01$, * $p < 0.05$.*
*BA = Bachelor's degree; BA+ = Bachelor's degree or higher; HS = High school diploma; MA+ = Master's degree or higher; SC = Some college education.*

**Table 2.**
*OLS regression models of educational residential segregation for key educational dyads using percent votes for Clinton in the largest CBSAs in the US, 2016–2020.*

| | (1) BA/HS | (2) BA+/HS | (3) MA+/HS | (4) MA+/SC |
|---|---|---|---|---|
| Global City | 2.430* | 2.371* | 2.501* | 1.549 |
| | (1.068) | (1.104) | (1.094) | (0.902) |
| Gini Index of Inequality | 0.696*** | 0.825*** | 0.839*** | 0.783*** |
| | (0.198) | (0.205) | (0.206) | (0.170) |
| % Votes for Trump | 0.034 | −0.026 | −0.077 | −0.111** |
| | (0.043) | (0.044) | (0.049) | (0.041) |
| % with a Bachelor's Degree | 0.243* | 0.278* | | |
| | (0.107) | (0.110) | | |
| % with an Master's Degree or Higher | | | 0.235 | 0.251* |
| | | | (0.123) | (0.101) |
| % Employed in Manufacturing | 0.083 | 0.112 | 0.125 | 0.144 |
| | (0.112) | (0.115) | (0.118) | (0.098) |
| Log Population | 0.632 | 0.528 | 0.419 | 0.311 |
| | (0.664) | (0.687) | (0.705) | (0.581) |
| Midwest | 5.074*** | 5.016*** | 6.152*** | 4.077*** |
| | (1.180) | (1.220) | (1.286) | (1.060) |
| South | 5.601*** | 5.180*** | 5.908*** | 3.396*** |
| | (0.981) | (1.014) | (1.069) | (0.881) |
| West | 5.390*** | 5.108*** | 6.276*** | 2.571* |
| | (1.089) | (1.126) | (1.224) | (1.009) |
| Constant | −20.226 | −20.255 | −9.371 | −10.349 |
| | (11.957) | (12.363) | (12.250) | (10.097) |
| Observations | 108 | 108 | 108 | 108 |
| R-squared | 0.536 | 0.542 | 0.553 | 0.558 |

*Source: Data come from the 2016–2020 ACS, MEDSL, and GaWC.*
*Notes: Standard errors are in parentheses;* $^{***}p < 0.001$, $^{**}p < 0.01$, $^{*}p < 0.05$.
*BA = Bachelor's degree; BA+ = Bachelor's degree or higher; HS = High school diploma; MA+ = Master's degree or higher; SC = Some college education.*

**Table 3.**
*OLS regression models of educational residential segregation for key educational dyads using percent votes for Trump in the largest CBSAs in the US, 2016–2020.*

those with some college (column 4 of **Tables 2** and **3**), even after controlling for the Gini index of inequality. The results in model 1 of **Table 2** indicate that the dissimilarity index between those with a bachelor's degree and those with a high school diploma is 2.457 units higher in CBSAs with a global city than in CBSAs without a global city, controlling for other factors. Similarly, the coefficients for global city in models 2 and 3 of **Table 2** indicate that 1) educational segregation between those with a bachelor's degree or higher and those with a high school diploma is 2.349 units higher in CBSAs with a global city than in those without a global city; and 2) the D-score is 2.486 units higher between those with a master's degree or higher and those with a high school diploma, respectively, controlling for other factors. The results for the global city coefficients in models 1 through 3 of **Table 3** are similar in magnitude and significance as the results in **Table 2**.

The coefficients for the Gini index reveal that the variable is a highly significant and positive correlate of educational dissimilarity across all models in **Tables 2** and **3**, controlling for other factors. Model 1 of **Table 2** demonstrates that a one-unit increase in the Gini index is associated with a .72-unit increase in the D-score between those with a bachelor's degree and those with a high school diploma, controlling for other factors. The magnitude of the association between the Gini index and educational dissimilarity is similar across all educational dyads, and the results are similar in the models that use the votes cast for Trump as the independent variable gauging political preferences (see models 1 to 4 in **Table 3**).

How do political preferences relate to educational segregation? **Tables 2** and **3** show that the percentage of votes cast for Clinton and the percentage of votes cast for Trump, respectively, are only significantly associated with educational dissimilarity between those with a master's degree or higher and those with some college, controlling for other factors. The results in model 4 of **Table 2** indicate that a one percentage-point increase in votes cast for Clinton is associated with a .099-unit-increase in the educational dissimilarity index between those with a master's degree or higher and those with some college. Conversely, model 4 of **Table 3** shows that a one percentage-point increase in Trump votes is associated with a .111-unit decrease in segregation between those with a master's degree or higher and those with some college, controlling for other factors.

Turning to the results of our control variables, we find that the percentage of the population with a bachelor's degree is significantly and positively associated with residential segregation of educational dyads involving those with at least a bachelor's degree (see models 1 and 2 of **Tables 2** and **3**). Similarly, in general, the percentage of the population with at least a master's degree is significantly and positively associated with educational segregation of those with at least a master's degree (see models 3 and 4 of **Table 2**; and model 4 of **Table 3**). Controlling for other factors, the percentage employed in manufacturing and the log of the population size are not significantly associated with residential segregation by educational status, regardless of the educational dyad examined (see **Tables 2** and **3**). Across all educational dyads, educational segregation is significantly higher in the Midwest, South, and West, relative to the Northeast, controlling for other factors (see models 1 through 4 of **Tables 2** and **3**).

## 5. Discussion

This study makes three contributions to the literature on residential segregation. Our first contribution lies in our focus on segregation by educational attainment, which is relatively novel within the U.S. context. To date, the vast majority of research on socioeconomic segregation in the United States has focused on income segregation [10, 43, 44]. While there is a burgeoning line of research on educational segregation in international contexts such as Turkey [15] and South Korea [45], scholarship on this phenomenon in the United States remains limited [2, 11]. This study expands upon past research by examining residential segregation between four educational dyads: 1) bachelor's degree vs. high school diploma; 2) bachelor's degree or higher vs. high school diploma; 3) master's degree or higher vs. high school diploma; and 4) master's degree or higher vs. some college. Our descriptive results reveal moderate levels of bachelor's degree/high school diploma dissimilarity compared to previously reported 2000 county-level indices that fell into the low range of dissimilarity [11]. Per our estimates, over one-third (33.9%) of either bachelor's degree or high school diploma recipients would have to move in order to achieve an even distribution of both groups throughout a CBSA, which is similar to the level found by Quillian and LaGrange [2]. The segregation of all other educational dyads also falls into the moderate range of segregation, although there is variation in the level of segregation depending upon the educational groups compared, thereby moving beyond the one-dyad measure examined by Quillian and LaGrange [2]. Our results are similar to those examining residential segregation by educational status in South Korea [45] and Turkey [15] but differ from those for France, which fall in the low range of segregation [2].

Our second contribution to the literature is our examination of the association between educational segregation and globalization, which has remained absent from much of the U.S.-based literature. We test Sassen's global city thesis [5] by assessing whether globalization is associated with segregation, which has been subject to debate in the existing literature [6, 7]. With the exception of the master's degree or higher/some college educational dyad, we find that educational segregation is significantly higher in CBSAs that contain a global city relative to those that do not have such a city. As Sassen's [5] thesis would suggest, spatial polarization between most educational attainment dyads is greater in places with global cities, which are theorized to have a bifurcated occupational structure. These results echo those in previous comparative and international research on socioeconomic segregation that find globalization to be a force tied to growing inequality [4, 6, 7, 46]. The fact that globalization is not significantly associated with the educational segregation of those with at least a master's degree and those with some college may be because those educational levels are not reflective of the occupational bifurcation that is found between those at further ends of the educational spectrum.

It is notable that the association between globalization and educational residential segregation is significant even after controlling for the Gini index of income inequality. Past research has found income inequality to be a highly significant predictor of residential segregation by income [10, 44]. Our models also show that income inequality is a positive and highly significant predictor of educational dissimilarity, and this result holds across all educational attainment dyads. Globalization, however, also remains significant, suggesting that future research on socioeconomic segregation should include globalization as a correlate.

Our final contribution is our focus on the association between political preferences and segregation. To our knowledge, there is little research examining the relationship between political preferences and residential segregation (for an exception, see [15]). Our results indicate that the percentage of votes cast for Clinton within a given CBSA are positively and significantly associated with segregation between the most highly educated (i.e., those with a master's degree or higher) and one of the least highly educated (i.e., those with some college) groups in our sample. While our results cannot speak to why this association exists, it suggests that specific educational groups value different lifestyles, which plays out in a separation within geographic space.

We envision several fruitful avenues for research to build upon this work in order to elaborate on other aspects of the segregation regime that experts have identified as increasingly important in today's divided cities [1, 6, 7, 47]. More work should be done examining the causal linkages between globalization, income inequality, and educational segregation. How do the relationships form over time? Or does globalization tend to thrive in areas that are already stratified? Characterizing the trends in educational segregation patterns and income segregation would also be a worthy pursuit in order to see how the two aspects of socioeconomic segregation converge and diverge across different metropolitan areas. The fact that political preferences are significantly associated with educational residential segregation for at least one educational dyad necessitates further study of individuals' residential mobility behavior as it relates to their political preferences and their educational level. The social structural sorting perspective is focused on explaining racial and ethnic residential segregation [32]. However, it would be worth examining how people's perceptions of neighborhoods are shaped by their political and educational values and preferences and by other factors like their peer networks and social media. Social distance between political parties, as is already prevalent in the U.S., imperils democracy because it threatens mutual cooperation across parties [18, 22]. More work needs to be done to explore how this social distance is translating into spatial distance and the implications of such residential segregation for our democracy. Moreover, attention should be paid to the association between political preferences and educational segregation for smaller metropolitan and micropolitan areas, which are areas that may be even more politically polarized than larger metropolitan areas.

## 6. Conclusions

Socioeconomic segregation remains a pressing social problem insofar as it reinforces stratification via access to opportunities and the distribution of life chances. This study broadens the traditional focus of scholarship on socioeconomic segregation beyond income to incorporate educational attainment, an understudied component of SES with ramifications for residential sorting. Within the 108 most populous CBSAs in ACS 2016–2020, we find moderate levels of segregation by educational attainment, with the most distance between those with the highest level of education in our sample (i.e., master's degree or higher) and those with the lowest level (i.e., high school diploma). Thus, educational attainment appears to be a salient characteristic shaping the contemporary sorting of households across metropolitan America. Additionally, this analysis contributes to ongoing scholarly debates surrounding the importance of globalization for socioeconomic segregation [6, 7]. Consistent with Sassen's global city thesis [5], among most educational attainment dyads, spatial polarization is most acute in places characterized by globalization. Finally, our consideration of the relationship between residential segregation and voting behavior demonstrates that political preferences may align with educational cleavages in values and lifestyles that manifest in residential separation between those with a master's degree or higher and those with some college. In an era marked by educational expansion and heightened political polarization in the U.S., it is increasingly important for scholars to identify factors shaping residential stratification along these lines.

## Acknowledgements

Support for this research was provided by a grant to the Center for Social and Demographic Analysis at the University at Albany, SUNY from NICHD (R24 HD044943). This work was also supported by a 2014-2015 Fulbright U.S. Scholar Research Fellowship.

*DOI: http://dx.doi.org/10.5772/intechopen.1001900*

## Author details

Samantha Friedman[1*†] and Thalia Tom[2†]

1 Department of Sociology, University at Albany, SUNY, Albany, NY, USA

2 Department of Sociology, University of Southern California, Los Angeles, CA, USA

*Address all correspondence to: samfriedman@albany.edu

†Authors contributed equally to this manuscript

## References

[1] Musterd S, Marcińczak S, van Ham M, Tammaru T. Socioeconomic segregation in European capital cities. Increasing separation between poor and rich. Urban Geography. 2017;**38**(7):1062-1083. DOI: 10.1080/02723638.2016.1228371

[2] Quillian L, Lagrange H. Socioeconomic segregation in large cities in France and the United States. Demography. 2016;**53**(4):1051-1084. DOI: 10.1007/s13524-016-0491-9

[3] Reardon SF, Bischoff K, Owens A, Townsend JB. Has income segregation really increased? Bias and bias correction in sample-based segregation estimates. Demography. 2018;**55**:2129-2160. DOI: 10.1007/s13524-018-0721-4

[4] Tammaru T, Marcinczak S, van Ham M, Musterd S. Socio-Economic Segregation in European Capital Cities: East Meets West. London: Routledge; 2015

[5] Sassen S. The Global City. Princeton, NJ: Princeton University Press; 1991

[6] Maloutas T, Fujita K. Residential Segregation in Comparative Perspective: Making Sense of Contextual Diversity. Burlington, VT: Ashgate Publishing; 2012

[7] Van Kempen R, Murie A. The new divided city: Changing patterns in European cities. Tijdschrift voor Economische en Sociale Geografie. 2009;**100**(4):377-398

[8] Musterd S, Ostendorf W. Urban Segregation and the Welfare State. London: Routledge; 1998

[9] Bischoff K, Reardon SF. Residential segregation by income, 1970-2009. In: Logan JR, editor. Diversity and Disparities. New York: Russell Sage Foundation; 2014. pp. 208-233

[10] Reardon SF, Bischoff K. Income inequality and income segregation. The American Journal of Sociology. 2011;**116**(4):1092-1153. DOI: 10.1086/657114

[11] Domina T. Brain drain and brain gain: Rising educational segregation in the United States, 1940-2000. City and Community. 2006;**5**(4):387-407. DOI: 10.1111/j.1540-6040.2006.00190.x

[12] Florida R, Mellander C. The geography of economic segregation. Social Science. 2018;**7**(8):1-17. DOI: 10.3390/socsci7080123

[13] Massey DS, Rothwell JT, Domina T. The changing bases of segregation in the United States. The Annals of the American Academy of Political and Social Science. 2009;**626**(1):74-90. DOI: 10.1177/0002716209343558

[14] Tammaru T, Marcinczak S, Aunap R, van Ham M, Janssen H. Relationship between income inequality and residential segregation of socioeconomic groups. Regional Studies. 2020;**54**(4):450-461. DOI: 10.1080/00343404.2018.1540035

[15] Friedman S, Kurtulus A, Koç I. Residential segregation by educational status in Turkey, 2013: Examining the association with political preferences. Population, Space and Place. 2022;**28**(3):e2512. DOI: 10.1002/psp.2512

[16] Quick M, Revington N. Exploring the global and local patterns of income segregation in Toronto, Canada: A multilevel multigroup modeling approach. Environment

and Planning B: Urban Analytics and City Science. 2022;**49**(2):637-653. DOI: 10.1177/23998083211021419

[17] Watson T. Inequality and the measurement of residential segregation by income in American neighborhoods. Review of Income and Wealth. 2009;**55**(3):820-844. DOI: 10.1111/j.1475-4991.2009.00346.x

[18] Bishop B. The Big Sort: Why the Clustering of Like-Minded America Is Tearing us Apart. Boston, MA: Houghton Mifflin; 2009

[19] Johnston R, Manley D, Jones K. Spatial polarization of presidential voting in the United States, 1992-2012: The "big Sort" revisited. Annals of the American Association of Geographers. 2016;**106**(5):1047-1062. DOI: 10.1080/24694452.2016.1191991

[20] Iyengar S, Lelkes Y, Levendusky M, Malhotra N, Westwood SJ. The origins and consequences of affective polarization in the United States. Annual Review of Political Science. 2019;**22**:129-146. DOI: 10.1146/annurev-polisci-051117-073034

[21] Kinsella C, McTague C, Raleigh KN. Unmasking geographic polarization and clustering: A micro-scalar analysis of partisan voting behavior. Applied Geography. 2015;**62**:404-419. DOI: 10.1016/j.apgeog.2015.04.022

[22] Mccoy J, Rahman T, Somer M. Polarization and the global crisis of democracy: Common patterns, dynamics, and pernicious consequences for democratic polities. The American Behavioral Scientist. 2018;**62**(1):16-42. DOI: 10.1177/0002764218759576

[23] Walker KE. Political segregation of the Metropolis: Spatial sorting by partisan voting in metropolitan Minneapolis-St Paul. City and Community. 2013;**12**(1):35-55. DOI: 10.1111/cico.12003

[24] Goyette KA. College for some to college for all: Social background, occupational expectations, and educational expectations over time. Social Science Research. 2008;**37**(2):461-484. DOI: 10.1016/j.ssresearch.2008.02.002

[25] U.S. Census Bureau. Census Bureau Releases New Educational Attainment Data. Washingon, D.C.: Census Bureau; 2022 [updated 2022 February 24; cited 2022 May 29]. Available from: https://www.census.gov/newsroom/press-releases/2022/educational-attainment.html#:~:text=The%20percentage%20of%20the%20population,from%2030.4%25%20to%2037.9%25

[26] Social Explorer. Educational Attainment for Population 25 Years and Over [Data Table]. Bronxville (NY): Social Explorer; 1990 [cited 2022 May 29]. Available from: https://www.socialexplorer.com/tables/C1990/R13127294

[27] Enos RD. The Space between us: Social Geography and Politics. Cambridge: Cambridge University Press; 2017

[28] Globalization and World Cities Research Network. The World According to GaWC (Globalization and World Cities Research Network): Classification of Cities [Data Table]. Leicestershire (UK): Loughborough University; 2016 [cited 2021 September 21]. Available from: http://www.lboro.ac.uk/gawc/world2016t.html

[29] Pew Research Center. Most Americans Say there Is Too Much Economic Inequality in the U.S., but Fewer than Half Call it a Top Priority.

Washington, DC: Pew Research Center; 2020 [updated 2020 January 9; cited 2023 January 19]. Available from: https://www.pewresearch.org/social-trends/2020/01/09/trends-in-income-and-wealth-inequality/

[30] Mccoy J, Press B, Somer M, Tuncel O. Reducing Pernicious Polarization: A Comparative Historical Analysis of Depolarization. Washington, DC: Carnegie Endowment for International Peace; 2022 [updated 2022 May 5; cited 2022 May 29] Available from: https://carnegieendowment.org/2022/05/05/reducing-pernicious-polarization-comparative-historical-analysis-of-depolarization-pub-87034

[31] Pew Research Center. Behind Biden's 2020 Victory. Washington, DC: Pew Research Center; 2021 [updated 2021 June 30; cited 2023 January 20]. Available from: https://www.pewresearch.org/politics/2021/06/30/behind-bidens-2020-victory/

[32] Krysan M, Crowder K. Cycle of Segregation: Social Processes and Residential Stratification. New York, NY: Russell Sage Foundation; 2017

[33] Motyl M, Iyer R, Oishi S, Trawalter S, Nosek BA. How ideological migration geographically segregates groups. Journal of Experimental Social Psychology. 2014;**51**:1-14. DOI: 10.1016/j.jesp.2013.10.010

[34] Gimpel JG, Hui IS. Seeking politically compatible neighbors? The role of neighborhood partisan composition in residential sorting. Political Geography. 2015;**48**:130-142. DOI: 10.1016/j.polgeo.2014.11.003

[35] Iceland J, Weinberg DH, Steinmetz E. U.S. Census Bureau, Series CENSR-3,Racial and Ethnic Residential Segregation in the United States: 1980-2000. Washington, DC: U.S. Government Printing Office; 2002 [updated 2002 August; cited 2022 May 29]. Available from: https://www.census.gov/content/dam/Census/library/publications/2002/dec/censr-3.pdf

[36] Massey DS, Denton NA. American Apartheid: Segregation and the Making of the Underclass. Cambridge, MA: Harvard University Press; 1993

[37] Florida R, Mellander C, King K. Winner-take-all cities. In: Glaeser EL, Kourtit K, Nijkamp P, editors. Urban Empires: Cities as Global Rulers in the New Urban World. New York: Routledge; 2020. pp. 40-54

[38] Scholvin S, Breul M, Diez JR. Revisiting gateway cities: Connecting hubs in global networks to their hinterlands. Urban Geography. 2019;**40**(9):1291-1309

[39] MIT Election Data and Science Lab. County Presidential Election Returns 2000-2020 [Data File]. Cambridge (MA): MIT Election Data and Science Lab; 2021 [cited 2021 August 21]. Available from: https://dataverse.harvard.edu/dataset.xhtml?persistentId=doi:10.7910/DVN/VOQCHQ

[40] Kavanagh NM, Goel RR, Venkataramani AS. County-level socioeconomic and political predictors of distancing for COVID-19. American Journal of Preventive Medicine. 2021;**61**(1):13-19. DOI: 10.1016/j.amepre.2021.01.040

[41] Morris DS. Polarization, partisanship, and pandemic: The relationship between county-level support for Donald Trump and the spread of Covid-19 during the spring and summer of 2020. Social Science Quarterly. 2021;**102**(5):2412-2431. DOI: 10.1111/ssqu.13053

[42] Parzuchowski AS, Peters AT, Johnson-Sasso CP, Rydland KJ, Feinglass JM. County-level association of COVID-19 mortality with 2020 United States presidential voting. Public Health. 2021;**198**:114-117. DOI: 10.1016/j.puhe.2021.06.011

[43] Yang R, Jargowsky PA. Suburban development and economic segregation in the 1990s. Journal of Urban Affairs. 2006;**28**(3):253-273. DOI: 10.1111/j.1467-9906.2006.00291.x

[44] Owens A. Inequality in Children's contexts: Income segregation of households with and without children. American Sociological Review. 2016;**81**(3):549-574. DOI: 10.1177/0003122416642430

[45] Lim U, Kim DH. Do birds of a feather flock together? Exploring the geography of educational segregation in Seoul, Korea. Studies Regional Science. 2010;**40**(2):479-494. DOI: 10.2457/srs.40.479

[46] Sassen S. Cities in a World Economy. Thousand Oaks, CA: Pine Forge Press; 2000

[47] Burgers J, Musterd S. Understanding urban inequality: A model based on existing theories and an empirical illustration. International Journal of Urban and Regional Research. 2002;**26**(2):403-413

Chapter 4

# Implications of Migration Dynamics for Aged Care in Australia

*Hamish Robertson and Nick Nicholas*


## Abstract

We examine immigration, population ageing and the aged care workforce, as well as making suggestions for their effects on health, aged and social care including more localised implications. While there is now a push to reopen borders, and while numbers are rising, it is as yet unclear if the 'old order' will resurge or if the situation has changed for the foreseeable future. We draw on data from a variety of official sources in a developmental discussion of the current and likely future effects of labour migration patterns, workforce supply and demand issues in Australia, and the lingering effects of the COVID-19 pandemic. For a variety of reasons, the data used here are emergent and the effects on current and future workforce requirements will be varied at several levels. Australia's ageing population and associated health and social care needs are dynamic in themselves, but they are also situated within a broader international context. There is a need for ongoing monitoring and evaluation of how these factors intersect and likely future scenarios.


**Keywords:** immigration, COVID-19, population ageing, aged care services, workforce

## 1. Introduction

In this chapter we explore some of the intersectional characteristics of Australia's dynamic and changing demography, and association with its immigration and the aged care systems. This is important because the Australian population is ageing, and that process is projected to accelerate in the coming two decades. In addition, the residential aged care sector, in particular, cares for many medically unwell older people, often in their last few years of life. The workforce in this sector has long relied on recent immigrants and their connections to countries of origin (e.g. Nepal and the Philippines) to maintain essential staffing levels. The sector is challenged by low wages and limited career opportunities resulting in high staff turnover [1].

The global pandemic presented by COVID-19 has presented additional challenges to the aged care sector in Australia and elsewhere. Older people suffered much worse in a number of countries including Australia because ageist rhetorics prevailed (the co-morbidity argument for example) and slow or ineffective responses to the pandemic led to many deaths in older cohorts [2, 3]. These were often well above those experienced by other sections of the population. In some places, workers even



IntechOpen

abandoned their residents to their fates, while in others, officials discharged infected people to aged care facilities, spreading the disease to vulnerable residents and patients [4]. In Australia, some aged care workers feared for their own safety in a situation where PPE was not always available, and Federal and state government(s) often seemed to care less about older people and their care providers [5]. Certainly, older people and especially people in residential aged care facilities were (and remained) at greater risk during the pandemic.

A consequence of the last few years has been that the aged care sector is perhaps less stable than before and at a time when the need for both residential and in-community care is rising. Where this is headed and the effectiveness (or lack of it) of the current system is yet to be seen. The Royal Commission into Aged Care had already made more than 100 recommendations for change to the existing aged care system. A number of these (11) applied specifically to the workforce and associated issues and constituted the fourth pillar of the Commission's response [1]. The challenges identified by the Royal Commission included a direct acknowledgement that demand for skilled workers in this sector can only continue to grow, while the supply side lags and working conditions are uncompetitive with other industry sectors.

> *"The gap between supply and demand for aged care workers has widened, even since the royal commission's interim report in 2019. What's more, the shortfall in workers is expected to worsen. The royal commission reported an estimated need for more than 130,000 additional, full-time equivalent workers by 2050—a 70% increase on current levels. In-principle government acceptance of a national registration scheme (recommendation 79) and a minimum Certificate III qualification (recommendation 78), both of which will be initiated through a code of conduct mechanism and national register administered by the Aged Care Quality and Safety Commission, may further exacerbate this gap in the short term."* [6]

A change of government in Australia in 2022 also shifted the prevailing policy and funding environment such that systemic instability is likely for some time to come. A key factor in all of this includes the size, composition and skill of the workforce and the capacity to maintain and develop that workforce in the coming years. The current Aged Care Act [7] is under review, it was amended in late 2022 but a new Act is proposed. Also, aged care providers are adding their perspective to current discussions around the aged care workforce, where those workers may come from and how best to attract and retain them. These are positive indicators, but this problem has a long-established history of concerns, failures and persisting employment issues [8, 9].

## 2. Immigration and the aged care workforce

There is a considerable immigration literature that is well beyond the scope of this chapter to summarise. However, because we are focusing more specifically on aged care in the Australian context, it is important to note that there is, even here, an established and growing research literature. The aim of this research and associated projects is to address key issues around the intersectional nature of Australian immigration patterns, workforce demand, and the experience of those workers. Care work, in particular, has a substantial and growing critical literature since, in many cases, immigration women are paid (often quite poorly) to do care work that they would more usually be providing to their own families [10]. This has become an established characteristic of the growing commodification of aged care work in particular, including the various social, physical and affective dimensions of care work [11, 12].

In the Australian context, the intersectionality of immigration and the aged care sector is comparatively recent as a focus for academic research, even though concerns about funding and delivery long preceded this [13]. The Australian Federal Department of Health and Ageing first published a National Aged Care Workforce Strategy in 2005 illustrating that the issue was gaining attention at the national policy level. This was followed by a more critical examination of the 'crisis in aged care' by Graeme Hugo [14], who published extensively on Australian demography and population ageing more specifically. Fine and Mitchell [15] wrote anticipating labour shortages in this sector, especially as population ageing progressed and the demand for more workers grew. They estimated a need for more than 290,000 workers in the sector by the year 2031. Since then, the availability of an aged care workforce has been a consistent and recurrent concern of government, industry and the community. The emergence of the COVID-19 pandemic made this concern even more acute, as it did internationally. Consequently, we can see that the aged care workforce is both a feature of and also reactive to current and emerging conditions–ranging from immigration policy to ageing trends and workforce policy and funding.

## 3. National level demographic trends

At the international level, we know that skilled migration represents a competitive environment for many of the higher income countries and so Australia has to be able to offer an attractive migration environment [16]. It seems likely that, as with the international student market (which also serviced the aged care sector to some degree) this remains to be clarified. The Brexit scenario in the United Kingdom and associated loss of many international workers may represent an opportunity for Australia but many of the higher skilled NHS workers were from mainland Europe and thus were regional relocations more than transnational migrants. They could more easily work in the United Kingdom and still travel easily back to their countries of origin. For the aged care sector, the workforce demand situation is broader in that workers at all skill levels are required to sustain current and emerging demand [17].

Other issues currently facing Australia include a growing impact from climate change and climate-related disaster events. While these are not affecting major urban areas at present, many regions and regional centres have been acutely affected by bushfires and flooding in recent years and the expectation is that such events will increase in frequency and severity [18]. These affect not only communities themselves but also emergency services, first responders, and acute and social care providers but also aged care facilities which often need to evacuate flood and fire prone areas. The capacity to respond to such events effectively relies to a marked degree on the preparedness, skills and motivation of the workforce and its management team(s). The unique geography of Australia makes for a key consideration in meeting the needs of an ageing population and in successfully recruiting and retaining health and aged care workers for these settings [19].

## 4. Data and methods

In this developmental piece, we draw on data form official sources only. These are, usually, government information sources used because they are accepted by academic and industry users. One of the more obvious limitations with government data sets can be the lag time in the collection, analysis and release of such data. In addition, different data providers may have different approaches to the level of detail in the data they collect as well as in what they release. Likewise, analytical and visualisation methods may vary, although this scenario is improving in the Australian context as public sector providers invest time and effort in the application of data visualisation software to enhance access to their data and its utility for different kinds of audiences. On the spatial side of this equation, there is still some way to go as issues of privacy, and perhaps a lack of familiarity (outside of infirmed users), slow developments here.

Consequently, the data that informs this discussion come from a more than one source and the ultimate storey they present requires interpretation. A second consideration is that the timing of such data releases and the complexities arising from the impact of COVID-19 at the international, national and sub-national levels are far from settled. These types of factors contribute to the developmental nature of our discussion but, also, add to its interest since a variety of audiences have an interest in how the pandemic and its lingering effects intersect with workforce issues and, ultimately, our capacity to service and care for various groups in an ageing population.

## 5. Contemporary population ageing in Australia

Australia's population is ageing and the rate at which it is doing is rising. At the 2021 Census, the total population was just over 25 million people [20]. Of this total, almost 4.4 million were aged 65 years and over or 17.2%. This represented a growth in the older population from the 2016 Census level of 15.8%. While this is not rapid growth across the intercensal period, nonetheless all data and associated projections indicate that population ageing is progressing and will grow much more rapidly from the mid 2020's onwards [21].

This trend has a variety of implications including many more older people living in the community, also more people transitioning to aged care facilities as their health declines, as well as more people dying in any given year (the pandemic appears to be driving some of this shift). The pattern of growth in residential aged care was rapid for some years but that appears to be levelling out to some degree as access to services in the community improves and/or people choose not to transition to residential care unless they are genuinely medically unwell. In the past residential aged care included a higher component of 'nursing home' accommodation and options that afforded home-like living and support. However, this pattern has shifted to include a growing emphasis on home-based supports that can slow the transition to residential aged care, a system which is expensive for government since much of it is privatised due to previous policy commitments and ideological positions.

The point we make here is that this intimate connection between population dynamics, such as population ageing, and the epidemiology of ageing have multiple implications for the workforce, in addition to those they have older people in both community and residential aged care environments. One strategy that needs to be considered mush more seriously than it has in the past, we propose, is both prevention and management of such conditions. If the aim is to prevent harms and suffering to older people, then we need to develop much more of an 'upstream' focus than has been the case previously.

The emergence of the COVID-19 pandemic has also had a major impact on older people, which is the focus of a growing literature of its own. Many examples exist of how older people experienced a disproportionate degree of illness and death from COVID-19, often glossed as largely a consequence of 'pre-existing conditions' [22]. In addition to its immediate effects, it has also raised the spectre of long-COVID-19 sufferers for whom dementia and other conditions will be an important factor [23].

The Centre for Excellence in Population Ageing Research (CEPAR) has recently published updated projections for future patterns of ageing across Australia [24]. At the national level, they estimate that over the two decades 2021–2041 the older population will increase substantially in the 65–84 (grouped) cohorts (42.4%) but even more dramatically in the 85–99 (139.3%) and 100+ grouped cohorts (200.4%). The 85+ cohorts represent perhaps the greatest challenge to existing models of care and associated resource distributions in health and social care more generally. This is in part due to the rising proportion of older women in this grouping, often living with multiple health conditions and various forms of disability [25].

This analysis affirms the need for not only change in aged care policy but corresponding shifts in the aged care workforce, how it is managed and the skills that will be needed. While we have limited space to go into detail here, the *geography* of the ageing population in Australia is also likely to present a challenge in that it is already difficult to supply many regional, rural and remote areas with the workforce they need. This situation is only likely to become more acute unless incentives can be designed to bridge the gap between major metropolitan areas and these others. This brings us back to the need for greater and more effective integration of the health, aged and disability care sectors. Current policy-based silo approaches are already inadequate to address existing problems and it seems very clear they will be even less adequate as the trends discussed here progress and intensify.

A key feature of Australia's population ageing trend is that growth in the older and oldest old cohorts is rising faster that those under 75 years of age. The chart below from Wilson and Temple [24] also illustrates this clearly, as growth in the 85+ cohorts is clearly steepening through to 2041 in two phases, firstly 2021–2031 and then again from 2031 to 2041. This is important because it means that factors such as frailty, support needs and health interventions are already likely to characterise those growing numbers of much older people and the demands their care is likely to place on service providers can only grow (**Table 1**).

In addition, we can say with some confidence that, although the data is developmental, it is very likely that long COVID-19 will make a broad contribution to the intersection of these health and ageing issues and their associated systemic demand. This includes a rise in the average number of deaths in any year, growth in the chronic disease states associated with COVID-19 (including heart and lung problems) and the dementias as small vessel disease and related neurological factors play out [26]. The re-emergence of major infectious disease is a major complicating factor for many of the higher income countries since it complicates accepted trends and compounds the need for more health resources, including skilled workers being available at the point of care.

This complex mix of demographic, epidemiological and systemic factors has implications for the kind of workforce needed in Australia and, consequently, the nature of its immigration programs going into the future. It has implications for educational and skill levels and, consequentially, for pay rates and working conditions. Internal migration must also be considered since there has been an uptick in people relocating to coastal centres, many of which are already ageing (e.g. Port Macquarie and Tweed Heads in New South Wales). These issues are already highly topical in Australia as the Royal Commission into Aged Care [1] illustrated very clearly and

| Age group | 2021 | 2031 | 2041 | No. | % |
|---|---|---|---|---|---|
| 0–14 | 4,750,600 | 4,895,200 | 5,323,900 | 573,300 | 12.1 |
| 15–24 | 3,103,000 | 3,714,200 | 3,864,400 | 761,400 | 24.5 |
| 25–64 | 13,520,700 | 14,561,300 | 16,190,100 | 2,669,400 | 19.7 |
| 65–84 | 3,779,500 | 4,799,400 | 5,381,300 | 1,601,800 | 42.4 |
| 85–99 | 529,000 | 800,300 | 1,265,700 | 736,700 | 139.3 |
| 100+ | 5300 | 10,500 | 15,900 | 10,600 | 200.4 |
| Total | 25,688,100 | 28,780,900 | 32,041,300 | 6,353,200 | |

*Source: Wilson and Temple [24].*

**Table 1.**
*Projected population growth by broad age group, Australia, selected years population change 2021–2041.*

subsequent investigations and research largely support. One thing that is very apparent is that the current competition for labour that has emerged in the not-quite post-COVID-19 environment will have important flow-on effects for the aged care sector.

## 6. Australian immigration patterns

The post-war period brought many immigrants from Europe including countries such as the UK, the Netherlands, Italy, Greece and others. These cohorts have now aged, with limited continuing immigrating from those countries for various reasons, including the rebuilding of European economies in the 1950s and 1960s. Now, as the chart below illustrates, the pattern has shifted yet again. Over the decade from the 2011 to 2021 censuses, England has maintained its position as the major source country but India and China, for example, have grown significantly and quite rapidly. By way of contrast the reader can see that Italy is still a source country but at a much-reduced level than in the post-war period and the trend is downwards over the decade.

These data suggest that the diversity of immigrant cohorts is high but that their correspondence with the previous immigrant groups that are now aged is quite low. In other words, there is a continuing disconnect, specialist services aside, between some ageing cohorts and the workforce available to meet their care needs. To some extent this is inevitable because both migration and aged care are enmeshed in a set of international trends and variables that they cannot control. A consequence of this is that factors such as the cultural diversity of workers and aged care recipients needs to be integral to models of care if that care is to be provided to the best possible standard (**Figure 1**).

The ABS also notes that the major countries of origin vary for each state and territory in Australia. So, in NSW the state with the largest population, Nepal is the largest contributor. For the states of Victoria, Queensland and South Australia, India is the main source country. In Western Australia, that country is the Philippines. Then, Samoa was the highest contributor for Tasmania, Afghanistan were the highest contributors for the Northern Territory and China for the Australian Capital Territory (ACT) respectively. This varied patterning of migration and country of origin by state and territory leads us to look more closely at the migration program itself and its key sub-programs.

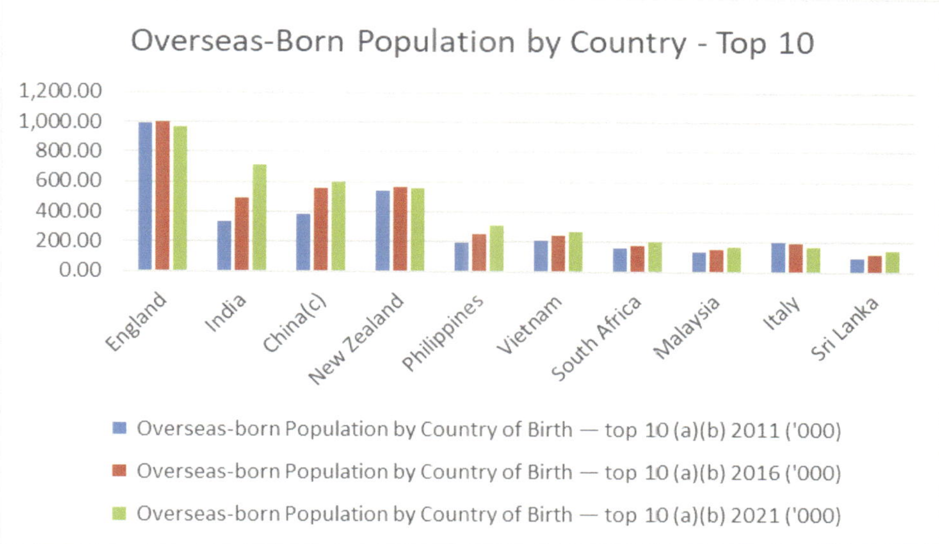


**Figure 1.**
*Overseas-born population by country of birth. Source: ABS, 2021 Census (2021 data are estimates) [20].*

## 7. Australian immigration by migration program

The data in this section is from a 2023 data release by the Australian Department of Home Affairs [26]. The **Table 2** shows the particular dynamic between skilled migration and family migration which shifted during the COVID-19 pandemic. During 2020–2021 in particular we can see that the ratio of skilled migrants to family altered dramatically

| Outcome | Stream | | | | | | |
|---|---|---|---|---|---|---|---|
| **Year** | **Skill** | **Family** | **Child** | **Special eligibility** | **Total** | **% Skill** | **% Family** |
| 2011–2012 | 125,755 | 58,604 | 0 | 639 | 184,998 | 68 | 31.7 |
| 2012–2013 | 128,973 | 60,185 | 0 | 842 | 190,000 | 67.9 | 31.7 |
| 2013–2014 | 128,550 | 31,112 | 0 | 338 | 190,000 | 67.7 | 32.2 |
| 2014–2015 | 127,774 | 61,085 | 0 | 238 | 189,097 | 67.6 | 32.3 |
| 2015–2016 | 128,550 | 57,400 | 3512 | 308 | 189,770 | 69 | 30.8 |
| 2016–2017 | 123,567 | 56,220 | 3400 | 421 | 183,608 | 68.6 | 31.2 |
| 2017–2018 | 111,099 | 47,732 | 3350 | 236 | 162,417 | 69.8 | 30 |
| 2018–2019 | 109,713 | 47,247 | 3248 | 115 | 160,323 | 69.8 | 30.1 |
| 2019–2020 | 95,843 | 41,961 | 2481 | 81 | 140,366 | 69.5 | 30.4 |
| 2020–2021 | 79,620 | 77,372 | 3006 | 54 | 160,052 | **50.7** | **49.3** |
| 2021–2022 | 89,063 | 51,288 | 3006 | 199 | 143,556 | **63.4** | **36.5** |

*Source: Department of Home Affairs, Australian Government [26].*

**Table 2.**
*Immigration program outcomes 2011-2022.*

from a rough split of two-thirds to one-third in preceding years to an almost 50:50 split. In the following year, 2021–2022, this began to shift again but clearly there was a lingering COVID-19 effect. In addition, the overall immigration figure dropped significantly from a total usually much closer to 200,000 people per year to between 140,000 and 160,000 across the 2019–2022 periods. This trend will be interesting to monitor as internal Australian factors develop, such as a new Aged Care Act and reforms to policies, funding and workforce issues. What may also need to be considered is how external factors contribute to the emergent pattern as the health and social care sectors. In the next section we explore available data on some of these issues in more detail.

## 8. Australian arrivals by occupational category over time

The table below shows that the percentage of arrivals in the health and social assistance categories is and remains high compared to many other occupational groupings. However, we can see that as at the end of 2022, the year this data was collated, this percentage had fallen from previous periods.

This illustrates the variability in workforce composition over time in response to both internal and external factors (**Table 3**).

In addition, the gendered nature of this data is also useful in that the health social assistance category is a significant component of the overall immigration pattern. For those who arrived less than 5 years ago, 18.94% of total female arrivals were in this category compared to 6.19% of total male arrivals. The same basic pattern applies also

| | Total (% of industries) | | |
|---|---|---|---|
| **Industry** | **Arrived less than 5 years ago** | **Arrived 5 to 10 years ago** | **Arrived more than 10 plus years ago** |
| Accommodation and food services | 13.74 | 8.16 | 6.83 |
| Administrative and support services | 15.36 | 10.83 | 9.73 |
| Agriculture, forestry and fishing | 1.24 | 0.9 | 0.66 |
| Arts and recreation services | 1.34 | 1.29 | 1.47 |
| Construction | 4.1 | 5.56 | 5.25 |
| Education and training | 5.29 | 5.72 | 6.87 |
| Electricity, gas, water and waste services | 0.38 | 0.57 | 0.7 |
| Financial and insurance services | 3.01 | 4.15 | 4.84 |
| **Health care and social assistance** | **12.23** | **16.19** | **15.3** |
| Information media and telecommunications | 1.43 | 1.58 | 1.6 |
| Manufacturing | 4.35 | 5.14 | 5.4 |
| Mining | 0.43 | 0.97 | 0.98 |
| Other services | 3.31 | 3.59 | 3.39 |
| Professional, scientific and technical services | 11.22 | 10.79 | 9.88 |

| | Total (% of industries) | | |
|---|---|---|---|
| **Industry** | **Arrived less than 5 years ago** | **Arrived 5 to 10 years ago** | **Arrived more than 10 plus years ago** |
| Public administration and safety | 1.79 | 3.06 | 4.56 |
| Rental, hiring and real estate services | 1.46 | 1.64 | 1.65 |
| Retail trade | 8.49 | 7.47 | 7.98 |
| Transport, postal and warehousing | 4.92 | 4.84 | 4.93 |
| Wholesale trade | 3.39 | 3.78 | 3.88 |
| Total | 100 | 100 | 100 |

*Source: Australian Bureau of Statistics [20].*

**Table 3.**
*Immigration by industry sector and time of arrival.*

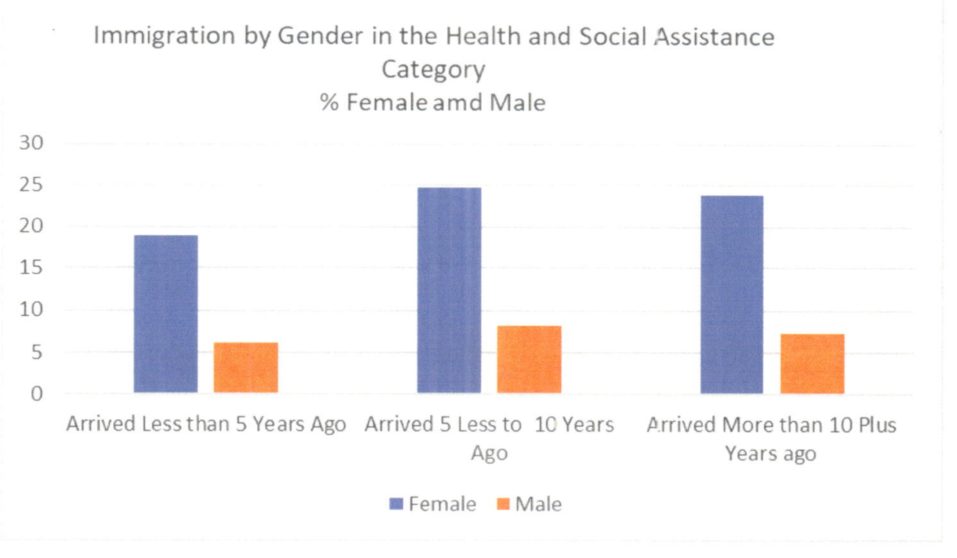


**Figure 2.**
*Immigration by gender in the health and social assistance migration category. Source: Australian Bureau of Statistics [20].*

to those who arrived 5–10 years ago (24.77% female versus 8.2% male) and those who arrived more than a decade ago (23.2% female versus 7.38% male). Thus, this gender skew is persistent over time and a significant feature of the health and social care sectors (**Figure 2**).

## 9. Growing need for care and support

A number of factors can be identified in looking to the health and social care needs of older people in this shifting Australian context. One is that the workforce needs to grow and diversify in terms of skills, qualifications, and experiences. Many nurses, for example, resigned during and after COVID-19 struck and it remains unclear if they will return to the workforce. The wider health workforce itself is ageing and so skilled workers were already a concern. This means that many of the older current health and social care workforce may yet become clients of the system in which they currently work. There is therefore a multi-level demographic patterning to the issue of how aged care will be resourced and by whom.

The past immigration pattern in Australia means that many older European cohorts may revert to their first language without a corresponding language skills base in the care providing workforce. So, for example, while a very large Italian (and Italian dialect) speaking cohort is ageing rapidly in Australia, recent arrivals from Italy are very low by comparison (see above). Countries of origin for the current and emerging aged care workforce do not correspond to the existing aged care patterning of the population and thus other cross-cultural skills may be needed to provide effective care. Even in large communities such as those from Mainland China, who are more recent arrivals, the risk exists that some individuals may be socially isolated by the lack of resources available in their first or primary language or dialect, with corresponding implications for communication and support in key areas of health, nutrition, self-care and end-of-life care where factors like consent are or should be central to service provision.

> *"At 30 June 2021 (or during the 2020–21 financial year for home support), across all mainstream aged care services, 33% of people were born overseas, of whom 66% were born in non-English-speaking countries. Significant proportions of people using aged care services had preferred languages other than English—9% in permanent residential aged care, 17% in home care and 10% in home support."* AIHW [27].

The AIHW [27] data indicates that one-third of all current aged care service recipients are overseas born and two-thirds of those are from non-English speaking countries. What also needs to be considered is the extent to which this group utilises formal aged care services in the first instance, given that language and cultural issues may be barriers to services that are not ethno-specific or able to meet care needs outside of an English-language mainstream model and its associated assumptions including food, religion and cultural practises. An associated concern is where and how Indigenous Australians are able to access safe and culturally appropriate care (especially if not living on country) and the role of the aged care workforce in facilitating that care [28]. Aboriginal people in aged care tend to be younger than non-Aboriginal residents and while the knowledge base on Aboriginal ageing is growing, it lags behind mainstream research.

One area that has received focused research over the past decade or so is how the dementias affect older Indigenous Australians including how to assess dementia and associated cognitive impairments and neurodegenerative problems [29]. As noted earlier, population diversity and epidemiological diversity are connected and the skills and knowledge required to address them effectively require support and development in training and educational programs for aged care staff, whether domestic or via immigration program(s).

## 10. The Australian aged care workforce

Pivotal to any and all of these issues is the nature, skill and capacity of the aged care workforce. In this context, we suggest, that workforce is not restricted to the residential care and community aged care sectors. Rather, it needs to be seen as a more integrated whole that includes any preventive work (e.g. social prescribing and community engagement) through primary care provided by GP's, nurses, pharmacies and allied health professionals on through ambulance and acute care services and then onwards to the aged care and disability care sectors. For the most part residential aged care is often, although not always (e.g. respite care) the tail end of a long health and illness trajectory. In our assessment, current fragment approaches are residual aspects of the system as it was rather than a system that needs to emerge.

While the majority of the aged care workforce remains locally born, the trend for immigrants to work as personal care workers, nursing and associated staff in the aged care sector has been growing for some time [30, 31]. Even with the temporary interruptions that COVID-19 produced in the existing immigration program(s), and its impact on the aged care sector itself, this dynamic is continuing. We can expect the analysis of the 2021 Census data to support the growing diversity of the aged care workforce to continue into the foreseeable future, and especially so as population ageing progresses and the demand for various forms of care and support grow. Underfunding remains a central feature of this problem [32, 33].

This situation will almost certainly be extended by imminent changes in government legislation, funding, policy and regulatory arrangements, such as requiring aged care facilities to have comprehensive registered nursing staff coverage. A factor driving some of this is the time it takes to produce skilled and experienced workers and develop them for emerging scenarios. In this context, immigration will remain central to the capability of the aged care system to meet current and emerging need.

## 11. Conclusion

In this chapter we have attempted to draw together some of the key demographic features of the Australian aged care environment through the lens of the aged care 'system,' its associated workforce concerns and the role of immigration in responding to current and future needs. We have done this in a 'post-COVID-19' setting although that is far from the reality of aged care and the larger issue of infectious disease re-emerging in high income countries cannot be ignored. The approach we suggest to resolving some of these issues is that national-level policies are likely to remain inadequate for managing local and regional level patterns of ageing and migration. More nuance is required if, for example, areas with well above average numbers of people aged in their 80s and above are to successfully respond to current and future health and social care needs. COVID-19 and especially long-COVID effects are likely to compound this situation for some time to come because the pandemic has had an acute phase, but we can expect a complicated post-acute phase to persist for some years to come.

To build and maintain a skilled workforce, immigration and internal migration factors will need to be managed more effectively and with a closer focus on the complexities experienced at and below the state/territory level. Current moves by the Australian Federal government to improve integration across the health, aged and social care sectors confirms the validity of this analysis and may see further initiatives in this space in coming months. This chapter comes at a time of considerable change and complexity in the Australian aged care environment and, seen through the lens of immigration and migration more broadly, we can expect these challenges to persist for the foreseeable future.

## Conflict of interest

The authors declare no conflict of interest.

## Author details

Hamish Robertson* and Nick Nicholas
University of Technology Sydney, Ultimo, NSW, Australia

*Address all correspondence to: hamish.robertson@uts.edu.au

## References

[1] Royal Commission into Aged Care. Final Report 2021, Canberra. 2021. Available from: https://agedcare.royalcommission.gov.au/

[2] Chan DK, Mclaws ML, Forsyth DR. COVID-19 in aged care homes: A comparison of effects initial government policies had in the UK (primarily focussing on England) and Australia during the first wave. International Journal for Quality in Health Care. 2021;**33**(1):mzab033

[3] Mansell V, Dykgraaf SH, Kidd M, Goodyear-Smith F. Long COVID and older people. The Lancet Healthy Longevity. 2022;**3**(12):e849-e854

[4] Powell T, Bellin E, Ehrlich AR. Older adults and Covid-19: The most vulnerable, the hardest hit. Hastings Center Report. 2020;**50**(3):61-63

[5] Ayton D, Soh SE, Berkovic D, Parker C, Yu K, Honeyman D, et al. Experiences of personal protective equipment by Australian healthcare workers during the COVID-19 pandemic, 2020: A cross-sectional study. PLoS One. 2022;**17**(6):e0269484

[6] PwC Australia. Recruiting, retaining and empowering the aged care workforce [online PwC article]. 2022. Available from: https://www.pwc.com.au/health/aged-care-royal-commission/workforce.html

[7] Aged Care Act 1997 [Internet]. Austlii.edu.au. 2015. Available from: http://www8.austlii.edu.au/cgi-bin/viewdb/au/legis/cth/consol_act/aca199757/

[8] Palmer E, Eveline J. Sustaining low pay in aged care work. Gender, Work and Organization. 2012;**19**(3):254-275

[9] Montague A, Burgess J, Connell J. Attracting and retaining Australia's aged care workers: Developing policy and organisational responses. Labour & Industry: A Journal of the Social and Economic Relations of Work. 2015;**25**(4):293-305

[10] Lanoix M. Labor as embodied practice: The lessons of care work. Hypatia. 2013;**28**(1):85-100

[11] Müller B. The careless society—dependency and care work in capitalist societies. Frontiers in Sociology. 2019;**3**:44

[12] Whitney S. Byproductive labor: A feminist theory of affective labor beyond the productive–reproductive distinction. Philosophy & Social Criticism. 2018;**44**(6):637-660

[13] Howe AL. International comparisons of long-term care: Australia. Canadian Journal on Aging/La Revue Canadienne du Vieillissement. 1996;**15**(S1):13-30

[14] Faulkner D, Feist HB, Lewis J. Ageing research in Australia: Reflecting on Graeme Hugo's four decades of contribution. Australian Geographer. 2016;**47**(4):399-415

[15] Fine MD, Mitchell A. Immigration and the aged care workforce in Australia: Meeting the deficit. Australasian Journal on Ageing. 2007;**26**(4):157-161

[16] Chand M, Tung RL. Skilled immigration to fill talent gaps: A comparison of the immigration policies of the United States, Canada, and Australia. Journal of International Business Policy. 2019;**2**:333-355

[17] CEDA. Duty of Care: Meeting the Aged Care Workforce Challenge.

Committee for the Economic Development of Australia; 2021. Available from: https://www.ceda.com.au/ResearchAndPolicies/Research/Health-Ageing/Duty-of-care-Meeting-the-aged-care-workforce-chal

[18] Hanna EG, McIver LJ. Climate change: A brief overview of the science and health impacts for Australia. Medical Journal of Australia. 2018;**208**(7):311-315

[19] Cosgrave C, Malatzky C, Gillespie J. Social determinants of rural health workforce retention: A scoping review. International Journal of Environmental Research and Public Health. 2019;**16**(3):314

[20] ABS. Census, 2023. Canberra: Australian Bureau of Statistics; 2021

[21] Ofori-Asenso R, Zomer E, Curtis AJ, Zoungas S, Gambhir M. Measures of population ageing in Australia from 1950 to 2050. Journal of Population Ageing. 2018;**11**:367-385

[22] Chatterjee SC, Chatterjee D. COVID-19, Older Adults and the Ageing Society. New York: Routledge; 2022

[23] Miller EA. Protecting and improving the lives of older adults in the COVID-19 era. Journal of Aging & Social Policy. 2020;**32**(4-5):297-309

[24] Wilson T, Temple J. New Population Projections for Australia and the States and Territories, with a Particular Focus on Population Ageing. CEPAR Working Paper. Sydney: UNSW; 2022. Available from: https://www.cepar.edu.au/publications/working-papers/new-population-projections-australia-and-states-and-territories-particular-focus-population-ageing

[25] Davies LE, Mercer SW, Brittain K, Jagger C, Robinson L, Kingston A. The association between multimorbidity and mobility disability-free life expectancy in adults aged 85 years and over: A modelling study in the Newcastle 85+ cohort. PLoS Medicine. 2022;**19**(11):e1004130

[26] Department of Home Affairs. Migration Program Report 2021-2022. Canberra: Australian Government; 2023. Available from: https://www.homeaffairs.gov.au/research-and-stats/files/report-migration-program-2021-22.pdf

[27] AIHW. GEN Fact Sheet People Using Aged Care 2021-2022. Canberra: Australian Institute of Health and Welfare; 2022. Available from: https://www.gen-agedcaredata.gov.au/Topics/Peopleusing-aged-care

[28] Sivertsen N, Harrington A, Hamiduzzaman M. Exploring Aboriginal aged care residents' cultural and spiritual needs in South Australia. BMC Health Services Research. 2019;**19**:1-3

[29] Bryant J, Noble N, Freund M, Rumbel J, Eades S, Sanson-Fisher R, et al. How can dementia diagnosis and care for Aboriginal and Torres Strait Islander people be improved? Perspectives of healthcare providers providing care in Aboriginal community controlled health services. BMC Health Services Research. 2021;**21**(1):1-1

[30] Negin J, Rozea A, Cloyd B, Martiniuk AL. Foreign-born health workers in Australia: An analysis of census data. Human Resources for Health. 2013;**11**(1):1-9

[31] Negin J, Coffman J, Connell J, Short S. Foreign-born aged care workers in Australia: A growing trend. Australasian Journal on Ageing. 2016;**35**(4):E13-E17

[32] Eagar K, McNamee J, Gordon R, Snoek M, Duncan C, Samsa P, et al. The Australian National Aged Care

Classification (AN-ACC). The Resource Utilisation and Classification Study: Report 1, 2019. Australian Health Services Research Institute, University of Wollongong; 2019

[33] Eagar K, Westera A, Kobel C. Australian residential aged care is understaffed. The Medical Journal of Australia. 2020;**212**(11):507-508

Chapter 5

# A Gendered Context of Reception: Understanding Immigrant Women's Workforce Incorporation in the United States

*Sandra Florian, Chenoa Flippen and Emilio Parrado*

## Abstract

The context of reception is an important theoretical and empirical tool for understanding immigrant assimilation. Yet, this concept has been narrowly defined as a gender-neutral socioeconomic and political context that immigrants encounter at arrival. We argue that this concept can be useful for understanding immigrant women's workforce assimilation, but that it needs to be expanded to incorporate the gender-specific characteristics of immigrant flows at arrival. Gendered cohort dimensions such as the sex ratio, share of women migrating unmarried, and share of men and women who are highly educated shape immigrant women's employment trajectories and contribute to national origin differences in labor force participation. We leverage a synthetic double-cohort approach using U.S. Census data from 1990 to 2019 to track immigrants' work trajectories over years since migration. We propose a five-group typology to simplify the analysis of national origin variation in patterns of workforce incorporation. We assess the impact of individual socioeconomic and gendered cohort characteristics at different points in the adaptation process (arrival, medium, and long term) to demonstrate the utility of a gendered context of reception for understanding national origin variation in immigrant's modes of incorporation.

**Keywords:** gendered context of reception, immigrant assimilation, immigrant women's labor force incorporation, modes of incorporation, trajectory typology, synthetic double-cohorts

## 1. Introduction

Immigrants represent more than 160 million workers worldwide, 42 percent of whom are women [1]. In the United States, where 13.7 percent of the population is foreign born, immigrant women constitute 16.3 percent of all employed women [2]. Scholars and politicians increasingly recognize the importance of immigrant women's economic contributions to their families and to the global economy [3, 4]. However, immigrant women in the U.S. hail from diverse countries and gender role contexts, and their labor force participation (LFP) rates vary greatly [5–7]. Understanding immigrant women's workforce incorporation requires considering how migration contributes to changing gender roles and female independence, dimensions of assimilation that do not readily apply to men [8, 9].

Research on immigrant women's employment has proliferated in recent decades. Most studies find that immigrant women exhibit lower LFP rates, higher unemployment, and lower wages than immigrant men and native-born women, revealing immigrant women's double gender- and nativity-based disadvantage in the labor market [4, 8]. However, patterns of female labor force assimilation vary dramatically across national origin groups. While traditional indicators of human capital, such as education and language proficiency, as well as individual's family structure account for part of this variation, large disparities remain even net of compositional differences across groups [6, 8, 10].

To account for these differences, scholars have turned their attention to how gender norms shape employment patterns. Studies have shown that factors such as sending country female LFP [11, 12], gender LFP ratio and fertility rates [5], gender equality indices [13], gender role attitudes, religion, and other measures of cultural traditionalism [14–16] correlate with immigrant women's LFP at destination. Findings indicate considerable continuity in labor market attachment with women from more gender traditional countries exhibiting lower LFP after migration than their counterparts from more gender egalitarian origins. Although analyzing indicators of gender norms in source countries has enhanced our understanding of immigrant women's LFP, these measures capture average population characteristics for entire sending countries, and fail to account for selectivity of migration flows [17]. Because immigrants differ in their levels of traditionalism from the overall population in their countries of origin, national-level indicators of cultural gender norms do not necessarily characterize immigrant women [18].

Moving forward the literature on immigrant women's labor market incorporation, we argue for the utility of three key methodological approaches. The first is assessing the impact of gendered characteristics of immigrant flows at the time of migration on immigrant women's labor supply. This approach takes into account the selectivity of migration flows produced by gendered aspects of both sending *and* receiving areas. We consider three gendered immigrant cohort aspects at arrival: characteristics relating to immigrant women themselves (the share of women arriving single and the share arriving with a college education); characteristics relating to immigrant men's economic potential (the share of men arriving with a college education); and relational dynamics (the cohort's gender ratio). We argue that higher shares of women migrating single and greater representation of women in immigrant cohorts signal demand for female immigrant labor in receiving areas, and thus will favor their LFP [9, 18]. A higher proportion of immigrant men arriving with a college education, in contrast, is indicative of male privilege and male immigrant labor demand, that until 2015 imposed restrictions on immigrants' wives' employment [19]. The impact of the share of immigrant women who are college educated could be more complex. Better-educated cohorts would be expected to average higher LFP, as human capital increases the returns to employment [20]. However, immigrant women's education is also highly correlated with that of immigrant men. To the extent that highly educated immigrant women are disproportionately accompanying men with restrictive employment visas, the educational composition of migration flows could have counterintuitive effects on female LFP.

Second, we argue for the importance of analyzing immigrant women's workforce trajectories, as opposed to average employment levels at a single point in time. We draw on data from the 1990 and 2000 U.S. Censuses and the American Community Survey corresponding to the periods between 2005 and 2009, 2010–2014, and

2015–2019 [21] to construct synthetic immigrant cohorts for different ages and periods of arrival. We include the 14 largest national groups in the United States, where sample sizes are too small for country-level analyses, we consider regional groups. Using synthetic cohorts, we are able to track immigrant women's LFP trajectories, analyzing cohort variation in LFP entry levels and growth rates over time.

Finally, to simplify the analysis and facilitate the drawing of broader conclusions, we use group-based trajectory modeling (GBTM) to identify groups that follow similar LFP patterns. We then use linear probability models with splines to analyze differences in LFP at arrival (starting points), and trajectories over time (growth rates) in the medium and long term. This strategy provides important insights into the evolution of national origin disparities in immigrant women's LFP over time that are not evident in group averages.

Results show that gendered migration cohort characteristics help explain immigrant women's LFP, accounting for between one-fourth to more than half of the remaining disparities after adjusting for individual characteristics across national origin for certain groups. Overall, findings document the importance of human capital characteristics and cultural gender norms, as well as historically produced structural aspects of the context of reception that shape immigrant women's LFP.

## 2. Theoretical background

Women's LFP has grown rapidly over the second half of the twentieth century, significantly reducing the gender gap in employment. For the 2010–2019 period, LFP rates in the United States were 74% for Black, White, and Hispanic native-born women, and 83% for Asian native-born women [21]. In contrast, the LFP rate for immigrant women was only 65% for the same period. However, LFP varies tremendously by country of origin. Immigrant women from Mexico, India, Korea, and of Arab descent exhibit LFP rates at or below 60%, while rates for women from the Philippines and the Caribbean exceed 80% [6, 7, 9]. Several theories have been proposed to explain this variation.

### 2.1 Modes of incorporation and immigrant women's LFP

Early theories of immigrant incorporation posited a relatively universal process of gradual assimilation driven largely by the characteristics of immigrants themselves [20, 22]. However, more recent and critical perspectives revealed a variety of modes of incorporation across groups [23, 24]. The concept of modes of incorporation draws attention to the importance of two sets of factors shaping adaptation: the context of origin and the context of reception.

The context of origin shapes immigrants' socioeconomic characteristics at the time of migration, including educational attainment, labor market experience, financial capital, and family structure, all factors that have a powerful impact on immigrant women's labor supply. Educational attainment increases LFP by raising the returns to employment and the opportunity cost of not working [20, 25]. LFP also increases with time of U.S. residence and fluency in English. In contrast, traditional gender expectations that come with marriage and childrearing increase women's domestic labor, constraining women's time for paid employment [4, 13, 15, 26].

These socioeconomic characteristics explain a significant proportion of national origin variation in immigrant women's LFP [6, 10]. Groups with higher human capital endowment, such as those from Europe, Canada, the Philippines, China, and the Caribbean, exhibit high employment rates, while those with lower levels of education and English language proficiency, such as Mexicans, have lower LFP [9, 10]. Yet, there are also notable exceptions who do not conform to these expectations. For example, women from India and South Korea average high levels of educational attainment, but exhibit relatively low levels of LFP [6, 9]. While a disproportionate share of these women are married and have young children at home, these characteristics do not completely explain the relatively low levels of LFP among these groups [9].

Indeed, after adjusting for individuals' levels of human capital, family characteristics, and length of residence, significant disparities in immigrant women's LFP remain [4, 6, 10, 11], prompting scholars to examine how other aspects of the context of origin, such as gender attitudes and roles, also influence immigrant women's LFP in receiving societies. Scholars have argued that source country gender norms infuse a repertoire of preferences, beliefs, and values that exerts a persistent influence on women's post-migration labor supply [13, 14]. Several measures have been used to assess the impact of gender cultural norms in countries of origin, including home country female LFP [11], fertility rates, gross domestic product [5], gender equality indices [13], gender role attitudes, religion, and other measures of cultural traditionalism [14, 16, 27, 28], which are all correlated to women's LFP after migration.

However, cultural norms are not homogenous within sending societies, but rather tend to vary across rural and urban areas and by level of education. In addition, women are not randomly drawn into migration, but are instead often selected on many dimensions that shape individuals' gender roles and attitudes [17]. As such, national level gender cultural measures do not necessarily apply well to immigrant women, particularly to female-driven migration and flows with more single women. Given these limitations, He and Gerber [18] proposed a sequence of marriage and migration framework, distinguishing between women who migrated single from those who migrated together with or after their husbands, as a way of capturing cultural norms net of immigrant selectivity.

Far less attention has been devoted to how the context of reception shapes national origin variation in immigrant women's economic assimilation. The context of reception refers to opportunity structures in communities of settlement. This includes factors such as immigration policies, economic opportunities, ethno-racial stratification, level of nativism and acceptance of newcomers, and social capital in co-ethnic communities. The context of reception can be positive (providing legal entry, access to jobs, and resettlement assistance); indifferent (providing legal entry, but without resettlement assistance), or negative (with hostility and active opposition to immigrants) [24, 29]. Social and economic opportunities in local communities, particularly related to the labor and housing market, are also important for immigrant's incorporation. Immigrants in welcoming communities that offer jobs and housing opportunities assimilate faster and more successfully, whereas those in hostile communities with barriers to employment and housing have a harder time incorporating into the host society [29].

While crucial for understanding immigrant incorporation, the context of reception has been described as a gender-neutral environment, overlooking the gendered nature of opportunity structures shaping economic assimilation. However, the demand for immigrant labor is highly gendered, with men and women often working in starkly different industries [7, 30, 31]. This gendered labor demand also intersects with immigration policies, which often favor certain classes of workers. When employment-based immigration pathways include sex-segregated occupational niches, they can have a profound effect on the LFP of immigrant spouses, who are often precluded from working in the formal economy for extended periods after migration. We argue that it is important to incorporate these gendered aspects of receiving contexts when attempting to explain immigrant women's incorporation [32].

### 2.2 Gendered migration cohort characteristics

One way to capture dimensions of both the context of origin and context of reception is to focus on gendered characteristics of migration flows at arrival, which reflect sending country norms, differential selection into migration, and gendered aspect of labor demand in receiving countries [9]. In this chapter we consider three dimensions of gendered migration dynamics: those pertaining to immigrant women themselves, those pertaining to their male peers, and relational dynamics.

For the characteristics of women themselves, we consider the share arriving single and their educational composition. Given that single immigrant women tend to marry soon after arrival, marital status years after migration does not adequately capture the greater economic independence implied by higher rates of single women at arrival [32]. We argue that the share of immigrant women arriving single captures gender roles in sending countries and receiving areas, including the forces shaping selection into migration [26, 33]. Countries with stronger patriarchal norms tend to discourage the migration of single women, such as Latin American, South Asian, and Arab countries [18, 28, 34]. Most women from these regions tend to arrive married. Marriage and young children have historically constrained women's employment; however, the effect of marriage and children significantly vary by national origin [4, 6]. Low proportions of single women at arrival may also indicate poor demand for immigrant women's labor in the receiving context, while the opposite is true in flows with high representations of single women. In the latter case, immigrant women are also more likely to find other employed co-ethnic women at arrival who can facilitate the search for employment.

Likewise, the educational composition of co-ethnic women at arrival could shape immigrant women's LFP even net of their own educational characteristics. All else equal, more well-educated women within a migration cohort should encourage the cohort's LFP, as they are more likely to find employment and, thus, constitute a form of social capital connecting co-ethnics to employment information and networks. However, the potentially employment-promoting effect of highly educated co-ethnic women could be hampered by other factors, such as immigration policies that restrict employment.

The second dimension we consider relates to migrant male peers. We considered the proportion of co-national men with college education at arrival as an indicator of their economic potential. Migrant flows comprised of highly educated men tend to signal male privilege in sending and receiving contexts. Having a highly educated partner could also reduce women's pressure to augment and diversify family income [6, 26]. Moreover, in disproportionately male, highly educated migration streams, women often enter the United States as spouses of H1-B visa holders. Prior to 2015 H1-B visa spouses were ineligible for employment, unless they were able to secure their own visa sponsor [19]. While a path to employment was subsequently created for those with dependent spousal visas, there remain numerous requirements that can delay or even preclude employment among this class of migrants. Because H1-B intensive industries employ a disproportionate share of men, the impact of these policies is highly gendered. Moreover, H1-B work visas are highly unevenly distributed across countries, with India and China alone accounting for 84% of such visas [35]. The gendered impact of these policies could therefore also contribute to national origin differences in immigrant women's LFP.

Finally, we also consider relational dynamics, namely the sex ratio of the migration flow. The gender composition often reflects cultural norms about women's roles [16, 18] and migration-related governmental strategies in sending countries [7], both of which could influence immigrant women's LFP in receiving communities. The gender ratio also signals the extent to which labor demand in receiving contexts is gendered [5, 7]. When migration is driven by labor demand in male-dominated sectors or more patriarchal sending environments, men tend to be overrepresented in the flow, such as the case of agriculture- and construction-driven Mexico-U.S. migration [32]. The converse is true when immigrant labor demand is female-dominated, such as nursing and other health-care driven migration from the Philippines, where the government also actively encourages women's migration [7, 36]. Thus, analyzing differences in the gender ratio of the immigrant flow at arrival provides insights into how cohort gender norms and gendered labor demand structure employment over and above individual level predictors.

## 3. Data and methods

### 3.1 Data

Data for the analysis come from the 5% samples of the 1990 and 2000 decennial U.S. Census, and the 5-year American Community Surveys 2009 (covering 2005–2009), 2014 (covering 2010–2014), and 2019 (covering 2015–2019). The sample includes immigrant women ages 16 to 54 living in U.S. households between 1990 and 2019 and who arrived between 1980 and 2014 at ages 15 to 44. Individuals living in group quarters and those enrolled in school are excluded from the sample.

### 3.2 Measurements

*Labor force participation (LFP)* is defined as being employed or unemployed but actively looking for employment, according to the U.S. Census definition. LFP is measured with a dichotomous variable, where 1 designates in the labor force, and 0 not in the labor force.

*National origin*. We used place of birth to identify immigrants' country of origin. We classified immigrants into 14 mutually exclusive dummy variables corresponding to their country or region of origin (the latter for groups with smaller sample sizes). The groups include Europe (referent), Canada, Mexico, Central America, South America, Cuba, China, Vietnam, Korea, India, other Asian countries, Africa, the Philippines, and Caribbean countries. We exclude immigrants of unknown origin and those from Australia/New Zeeland (0.33% and 0.31% of the original sample, respectively) due to small samples sizes.

*Years since migration* is a continuous variable used to trace LFP trajectories over time. It is measured in 3 splines, the first comprising 0–2 years (reference), which captures LFP rates at arrival; the second 3–10 years, assessing growth rates in the medium term; and the third 11 years or more, measuring growth rates in the long term.

*Age at migration* is measured in 5-year interval dummy variables including 15–19, 20–24 (referent), 25–29, 30–34, 35–39, and 40–44.

*Period of arrival* is measured in 4 categories 1980–1989 (referent), 1990–1999, 2000–2009, and 2010–2019.

*Human capital* is captured by indicators of education and English proficiency. *Education* is measured in four categories including less than high school, high school (referent), some college, or college degree or higher. *English proficiency* is measured with a dummy variable that takes the value of 1 for those who did not speak English well or at all, and 0 otherwise.

*Family structure* is assessed by marital status and the presence of young children. *Marital status* is measured with a dummy variable that takes the value of 1 for married women with a spouse present in the household, and 0 otherwise. *Young children* are assessed by a dummy variable that takes the value of 1 for individuals with pre-school age, less than 5 years old, children in the household at the time of the survey.

The *gendered context of reception* is assessed using four immigrant gender characteristics at the cohort level. The *proportion of single women at arrival* is calculated as the average proportion single in each cohort during the first 4 years in the U.S. Similarly, the *proportion of college educated women* and the *proportion of college educated men* is the average proportion with college education in each cohort by sex during the first 4 years in the U.S. The *sex ratio* is the number of men to women in each cohort at arrival, estimated as the average during the first 4 years after migration. A sex ratio equal to 1 represents a balanced sex composition, with equal numbers of men and women. A sex ratio greater than 1 reflects a male-predominant immigrant flow, whereas a sex ratio less than 1 indicates a female-predominant immigrant flow.

### 3.3 Analytic strategy: synthetic cohort LFP trajectories

Our primary analytic strategy is to assess immigrant women's LFP trajectories over time, and to examine differences across national origin groups at different points in the adaptation process. The study of immigrant assimilation has been limited by the lack of longitudinal data. Most studies rely on cross-sectional data, yet cross sectional approaches do not allow us to distinguish changes in labor market outcomes that accrue with assimilation, often measured as years since migration, from shifts in the composition of immigrant cohorts over time – for example, due to increases in education in sending countries [25, 26, 37].

Using synthetic cohorts, which combine multiple waves of cross-sectional data to track migration cohorts over time, represents a more adequate strategy to assess immigrant labor market assimilation. A limitation of this method is that it does not track the same individuals over time, but rather reconstructs cohorts' trajectories using demographic principles. Nevertheless, this method is able to take into account change across both birth and immigration cohorts. As **Figure 1** illustrates, birth cohorts (in black), address the issue of age-period-cohort identification, that is the impossibility of adding these three variables in a regression model because the third one, for example age, can be calculated using the other two (survey year minus year of birth). Immigration cohorts (in blue), address the duration-period-immigration age identification problem, considering years since migration (duration), year of migration (period), and age (at migration). A double cohort approach, which recreates trajectories for both birth and period of arrival cohorts, has been shown to be particularly advantageous [9, 38].

While this approach has become common in analyses of immigrant men's employment, it remains underutilized in studies of immigrant women's LFP. We propose a variation of the *double cohort approach* to analyze immigrant women's LFP

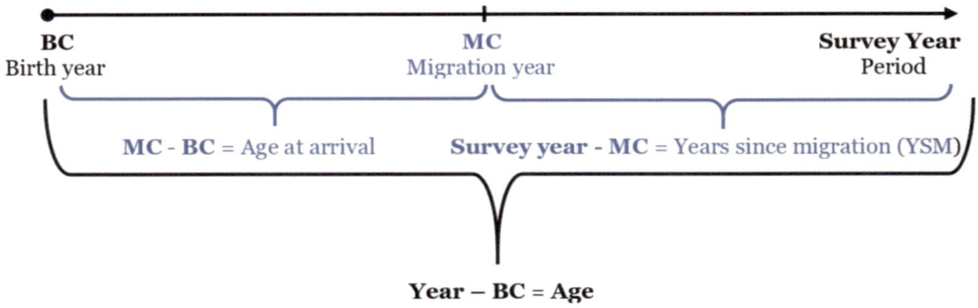


**Figure 1.**
*Double-cohort method: Birth cohort (BC) and migration cohort (MC).*

trajectories. Instead of tracking immigrant cohorts according to their year of birth and period of arrival, as in most prior studies, we follow cohorts as a function of their age at arrival, period of migration, and country/region of origin. For example, a cohort arriving to the United States in 1995 between ages 20–24 would have about 5 years of U.S. residence and be between ages 25–29 in 2000. By 2010, this cohort would have been in the U.S. for 15 years and would be between 35 and 39 years of age. While we do not track the same people over time, this variation of the double cohort approach allows us to better approximate LFP trajectories over years since migration, as cohorts age in the host country. The 14 national origin groups, 6 age-at-migration cohorts, and 4 periods of arrival results in 336 immigrant cohorts.

We further distinguish between the rates of LFP at arrival from growth rates over time to better understand whether the disparities in LFP across national origin groups are created at arrival or by differential rates of change with time in the host country. This approach also allows us to separately analyze the forces shaping immigrant women's LFP at different points of time after migration. Employment patterns, and differentials, shortly after arrival are likely to differ from those in the medium- and longer-term. Groups with high levels of LFP at arrival could be responding to labor demand in specific occupational niches [18, 36, 39]. For these flows, we should expect little increase in LFP over time and the most salient question is the extent to which participation remains high. Alternatively, flows with relatively low LFP at arrival could signal situations where women are likely not the primary economic providers. Nevertheless, there is likely important variation in the timing and extent of increasing LFP over time, even among groups that begin with relatively low levels of workforce engagement. The impact of socio-demographic factors on immigrant women's LFP could also vary depending on whether we consider participation soon after arrival or trajectories over time [5, 39]. For example, educational credentials are often not readily transferable across contexts [40, 41]. Thus, the impact of education on LFP at arrival may be muted. However, if highly educated women are able to gain employment opportunities more quickly than less educated women, human capital disparities in LFP could grow with longer durations of U.S. residence [25].

To facilitate the analysis and interpretation of LFP trajectories, we apply *Group-Based Trajectory Modeling (GBTM)* to the synthetic cohort trajectories to identify patterns of labor force assimilation. Similar to Latent Class Analysis (LCA), which aims at identifying groups or clusters with a similar categorical outcome, GBTM is designed to detect clusters that follow similar developmental trajectories [42]. The model assumes that the population distribution of trajectories emerges from a finite mixture of unknown order (or number of groups). The optimal number of groups is ultimately determined by the researcher. GBTM uses a multinomial modeling strategy to assign each immigrant cohort a probability of being in a cluster conditional on the number of groups and the shape of the group-specific trajectory. A limitation of GBTM is that the resulting clusters can be hard to interpret, demanding a thorough analysis from the researcher. We tested models with different group sizes from three to seven. We followed best accepted practices to determine the optimal number of groups using a combination of criteria, including the smallest Bayesian information criteria (BIC), parsimony in the number of groups that best fit the data, the size of the resulting groups, and the interpretability of the clusters [43]. We propose a five-group typology that we present in the results section.

We then use linear probability models for the multivariate analyses, specified in Eq. (1):

$$\begin{aligned} \Pr(Y_i = 1|X_i = x_i) = \beta_0 + \beta_1 p_i + \beta_2 n_i + \beta_3 a_i + \beta_4 t_i + \beta_5 e_i + \beta_6 g_c \\ + \beta_7 n_i^* t_i + \beta_8 a_i^* t_i + \beta_9 e_i^* t_i + \beta_{10} g_c^* t_i + \sigma_i \end{aligned} \tag{1}$$

where the probability of LFP for individual $i$ $Pr(Y_i = 1)$ is a function of the four mutually exclusive dummy variables $p$ indexing period of arrival; the mutually exclusive dummy variables $n_i$ indexing country/regions of origin; the six mutually exclusive dummy variables $a_i$ indexing age at arrival; the three variables from the years since migration spline specification $t_i$; the vector of individual's socioeconomic covariates, $e_i$, that is, human capital and family structure; and the vector of *gendered cohort-level characteristics*, $g_c$, including the ratio of men to women, the share of women single, and the share of women and men who are college educated upon arrival for each cohort $c$. National/regional origin, age-at-migration, socioeconomic, and gendered cohort characteristics are interacted with the spline indicators ($n_i^* t_i$; $ai^* t_i$; $e_i^* t_i$; $g_c^* t_i$; respectively), and $\sigma_i$ is the error term.

We compute predicted values to assess the extent to which individual- and cohort-level characteristics help explain variation in LFP trajectories. To account for the clustering of observations within period-of-arrival, age-at-arrival, and national/regional origin, we compute robust standard errors clustered at the cohort level. This specification assumes that observations are independent across cohorts, but allows observations to be correlated within cohorts.

## 4. Results

### 4.1 Immigrant women's labor force incorporation typology

**Figure 2** graphs the synthetic cohort LFP trajectories for immigrant women in the U.S. for the 14 national/regional origin groups. The different lines represent each cohort's LFP trajectory by years since migration. The curves show each cohort's initial LFP rate at arrival and the growth at roughly five-year intervals, reflecting changes in LFP as women age over time in the United States. Despite considerable variation in cohorts' LFP at arrival and growth rates over time, the spaghetti plots reveal some common patterns by national origin. We describe the different patterns using two extreme cases, Mexico and the Philippines. The trajectories of Mexican women show relatively low levels of LFP at arrival, around 40%. Over time, their LFP increases

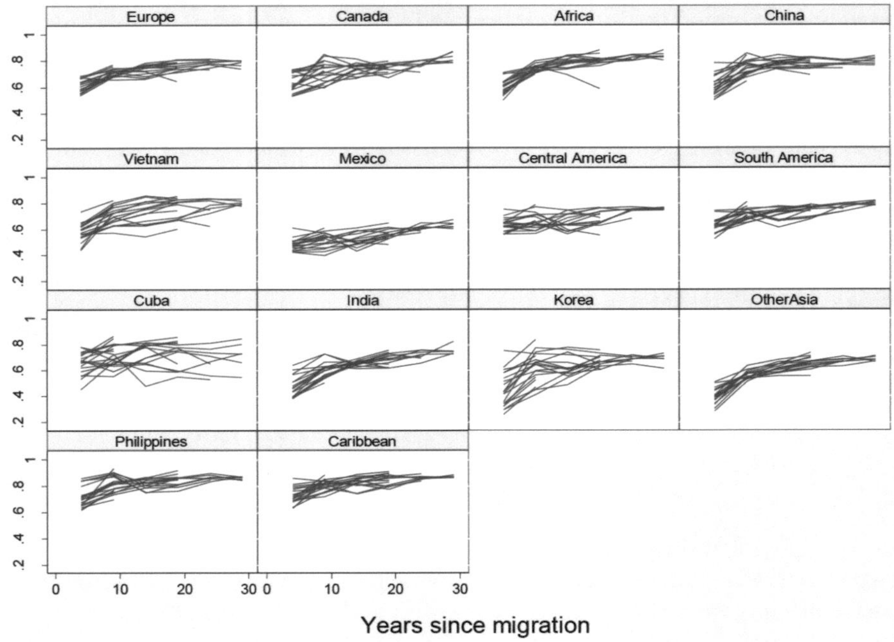


**Figure 2.**
*Immigrant women cohorts' LFP by national origin and years since migration to the United States (Spaghetti plots). Source: U.S. Census 1990, 2000; American Community Survey 2005–2009, 2010–2014, and 2015–2019.*

very slowly. The overall rate of LFP among Mexican immigrant women does not exceed 70% for any of the cohorts. In contrast, women from the Philippines exhibit much higher levels of LFP at arrival, close to 70%. Unlike the Mexican case, LFP increases almost immediately after arrival, quickly reaching nearly 80%. Filipinas maintain very high rates of LFP throughout the years of observation.

To better grasp this variation, we used Group-Based Trajectory Modeling (GBTM) to identify similar patterns of LFP trajectories across national groups. We propose a five-group typology, which synthesizes the patterns labor force incorporation by maximizing the between-group variation and minimizing within-group variation, as presented in **Figure 3**. While there is substantial heterogeneity among certain national origin cohorts, which are sometimes split among two or more clusters of the proposed typology, we assign national origin groups to the incorporation typology for which they have the highest probability of membership.

The first group illustrated in **Figure 3** shows a pattern of *gradual incorporation with moderate entry rates*, and comprises 39% of the cohorts. These cohorts averaged nearly 60% LFP rate at entry, gradually increasing to over 75% over time. Most of this gain occurs during the first 10 years in the U.S., then the growth rate slows down. This pattern corresponds to cohorts from Europe, Canada, Africa, and China, and some cohorts from Vietnam and South America as observed in the Spaghetti plots in **Figure 2**. The second group depicts a pattern of *delayed incorporation with low entry rates*, a pattern representing 8.5% of the cohorts, the vast majority coming from Mexico. These cohorts exhibit low starting rates of LFP, at around 45%, which are followed by sluggish growth rates over time. After 10 years in the U.S. their LFP rates increase to barely 50%, taking more than 15 years to reach levels of

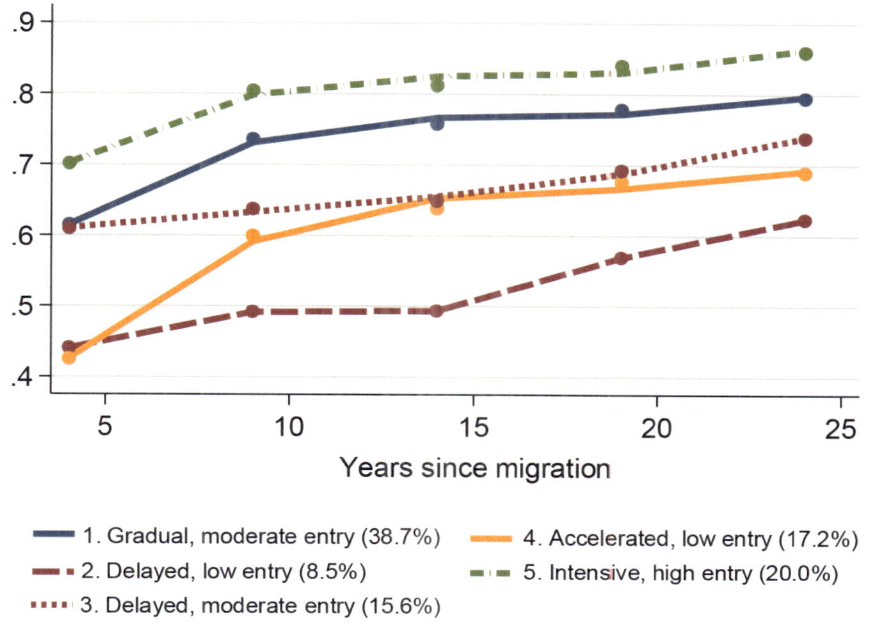


**Figure 3.**
*Group-based LFP trajectory model, 5-group solution.*

60%. The third group exhibits a pattern of *delayed incorporation with moderate entry rates*, and includes 16% of the cohorts. Similar to the former group, this group also exhibits slow growth rates, but start at rates slightly over 60%. This group illustrates the patterns found among cohorts from Central America and Cuba. A few cohorts from South America and India also fall into this group. It takes more than 15 years in the country for their LFP rates to increase to over 65%. The fourth group exhibits a pattern of *accelerated incorporation with low entry rates*, comprising 17% of the cohorts. These cohorts show rates of roughly 40% at arrival, but achieve rapid gains during the first years, surpassing the 60% level after 10 years in the country. This group describes the incorporation patterns of most cohorts from India, Korea, and other Asian countries. The last cluster shows a trajectory of *intensive LFP, with high entry levels*, and includes 20% of the cohorts, the vast majority coming from the Philippines and the Caribbean. These cohorts exhibit LFP rates over 70% at entry and after 10 years they surpass the 80% benchmark.

### 4.2 Explaining national origin differences in LFP trajectories

Explaining national/regional-origin differences in LFP requires first evaluating compositional differences in the predictors of employment across groups. **Table 1** reports socio-demographic individual and cohort-level characteristics of the sample by country/region of origin following the five-group typology. The lowest rates of LFP are observed for the groups with *delayed, low entry* and *accelerated, low entry* LFP rates, i.e., cohorts from Mexico, India, Korea and other Asia, who exhibit average LFP rates below 60%. In contrast, cohorts in the *intensive* employment group, such as immigrant women from the Philippines and the Caribbean, exhibit the highest

| | | | Demographic | | Human Capital | | Family | | Gender Cohort Characteristics at Arrival | | | |
|---|---|---|---|---|---|---|---|---|---|---|---|---|
| | *N* | LFP | Age at survey (mean) | Years in the U.S. (mean) | Years education (mean) | % English not well | Married (%) | Preschool children (%) | Sex Ratio (M/W) | % Women single | % Women w/ college | % Men w/ college |
| **Gradual, moderate entry** | | | | | | | | | | | | |
| Europe | 152,012 | 71.9 | 39.1 | 11.8 | 14.3 | 11.1 | 71.7 | 20.6 | 0.98 | 31.3 | 37.9 | 45.2 |
| Canada | 25,689 | 71.8 | 39.0 | 11.4 | 14.6 | 2.9 | 71.0 | 23.0 | 0.96 | 35.0 | 45.4 | 52.8 |
| Africa | 49,610 | 74.4 | 38.0 | 11.1 | 13.2 | 12.4 | 59.2 | 30.5 | 1.20 | 36.5 | 26.8 | 32.7 |
| China | 89,747 | 73.5 | 40.0 | 12.5 | 14.1 | 31.1 | 74.7 | 19.9 | 0.85 | 35.0 | 47.3 | 59.4 |
| Vietnam | 46,380 | 73.7 | 40.1 | 13.9 | 10.9 | 49.0 | 68.9 | 21.2 | 0.85 | 41.3 | 8.3 | 12.5 |
| **Delayed, low entry** | | | | | | | | | | | | |
| Mexico | 409,643 | 53.2 | 36.7 | 13.0 | 9.3 | 66.6 | 64.5 | 31.3 | 1.60 | 35.9 | 5.2 | 4.2 |
| **Delayed, moderate entry** | | | | | | | | | | | | |
| Central America | 143,569 | 67.9 | 37.7 | 13.1 | 10.0 | 56.0 | 50.2 | 25.0 | 1.30 | 46.8 | 7.9 | 5.7 |
| South America | 102,461 | 71.6 | 39.1 | 12.1 | 13.1 | 27.9 | 62.1 | 21.2 | 0.95 | 35.9 | 26.8 | 26.8 |
| Cuba | 22,674 | 72.3 | 39.9 | 11.2 | 12.5 | 54.1 | 54.9 | 15.7 | 1.08 | 27.7 | 18.7 | 16.6 |
| **Accelerated, low entry** | | | | | | | | | | | | |
| India | 103,582 | 59.5 | 36.9 | 10.5 | 15.1 | 12.1 | 87.3 | 30.8 | 1.18 | 17.4 | 66.4 | 73.7 |
| Korea | 37,345 | 58.7 | 40.4 | 12.6 | 14.2 | 36.3 | 77.0 | 19.2 | 0.75 | 27.8 | 44.0 | 51.9 |
| Other Asia | 88,479 | 57.1 | 38.6 | 11.9 | 12.8 | 24.5 | 75.0 | 26.0 | 1.03 | 33.1 | 35.3 | 43.4 |

| | | | Demographic | | Human Capital | | Family | | Gender Cohort Characteristics at Arrival | | | |
|---|---|---|---|---|---|---|---|---|---|---|---|---|
| | *N* | LFP | Age at survey (mean) | Years in the U.S. (mean) | Years education (mean) | % English not well | Married (%) | Preschool children (%) | Sex Ratio (M/W) | % Women single | % Women w/ college | % Men w/ college |
| **Intensive, high entry** | | | | | | | | | | | | |
| Caribbean | 53,093 | 82.1 | 40.1 | 14.0 | 12.5 | 10.0 | 44.0 | 18.8 | 0.92 | 52.7 | 9.7 | 9.9 |
| Philippines | 81,430 | 81.4 | 40.1 | 12.8 | 14.5 | 3.3 | 69.1 | 19.3 | 0.62 | 32.6 | 49.6 | 45.2 |

*Note: Immigrant women ages 16–54, who migrated from ages 15–44, not living in group quarters, not attending school.*
*Source: U.S. Census 1990, 2000; American Community Survey 2005–2009, 2010–2014, and 2015–2019.*

**Table 1.**
*Descriptive statistics for immigrant women's demographic, human capital, family, and group-level gendered migration characteristics by national origin.*

average LFP rates, above 80%. Most other groups exhibit rates slightly above 70%. The group typology does not clearly correlate with the length of residency; some of the longest settled groups exhibit relatively high LFP rates, such as women from the Caribbean who have been in the U.S. 14 years on average, whereas other exhibit the lowest average rates of LFP, such as cohorts from Mexico that have been in the U.S. for 13 years on average.

The lowest levels of human capital, measured by education and English ability, are observed for cohorts with *delayed incorporation* (*low* and *moderate entry* level), especially Mexican and Central American women. Low human capital is also observed for Vietnamese women, whose pattern of incorporation falls in between *gradual* and *delayed*. The opposite holds for cohorts in the *accelerated, low entry* incorporation group, such as women from India and Korea who have high levels of human capital, but still exhibit low rates of LFP. Other factors should also be considered, such as family characteristics, which roughly correlate with our LFP typology. High marriage rates, 75–87% are observed in the *accelerated, low entry* group, e.g. Indian and Asian women, whereas low marriage rates generally accompany high rates of LFP, such as for Caribbean and African women, who exhibit marriage rates of 44% and 59%, respectively. The presence of preschool-age children in the household also corresponds to low rates of LFP, such as the case of Mexican and Indian women, 31% of whom have preschool age children in the home, whereas cohorts in the *intensive* group exhibit a lower presence of young children in the home, such as Filipina and Caribbean women, among whom fewer than 20% have preschool age children in the home. The case of African women in the *gradual* group is more particular, combining a relatively high presence of young children in the home, 30%, with relatively high rates of LFP, 74%.

The gender cohort characteristics at arrival are estimated as cohort averages for the first 4 years after migration. A sex ratio higher than 1 indicates a male predominant flow, which is generally associated with lower female LFP, such as for cohorts from Mexico (1.60), Central America (1.30), and India (1.18). Conversely, sex ratios lower than 1, which indicate an overrepresentation of women, such as in cohorts from the Philippines (0.62) and the Caribbean (0.92) in the *intensive* group and China (0.85) in the *gradual* group, tend pair with high rates of immigrant women's LFP. The pattern is less clear for cohorts from Korea that combine a female predominant flow (sex ratio = 0.75) with low rates of LFP (59%).

We explored the correlations between different gendered cohort characteristics, as shown in **Table 2**. Results indicate that the share of immigrant men and women entering with a college degree is highly and positively correlated (0.88). In contrast, the percent of women arriving single is moderately and negatively correlated (−0.61) with the percent of men with college education at arrival. Cohorts from Mexico and Central America exhibit the lowest percentage of college educated women at arrival, 5% and 8%, respectively, and college educated men at arrival, 4% and 6%, respectively. By contrast, 66% of women as well as 74% of men from India are college educated at arrival, followed by cohorts from Korea, China, the Philippines, and Canada, among whom between 44–50% of women have a college degree at arrival, as well as between 45–59% of men. Women predominate at arrival in most of these flows, with the exception of cohorts from India. The case of India reflects migration driven by male labor demand; 87% of women in these flows arrive married, most of whom are spouses of H1-B visa holders that until 2015 restricted their right to work [19].

As expected, cohorts with higher percentages of single women at arrival tend to exhibit higher rates of LFP, such as the case of Caribbean cohorts in which the

| | Sex ratio (M/W) | % Women single | % Women w/ college | % Men w/ college |
|---|---|---|---|---|
| Sex ratio | 1 | | | |
| % Women single | 0.037 | 1 | | |
| % Women w/ college | −0.267* | −0.460* | 1 | |
| % Men w/ college | −0.160* | −0.610* | 0.884* | 1 |

*$p < 0.05$.
*Note: Cohort charatecteristics estimates for the first 4 years since migration.*

**Table 2.**
*Correlations among gender cohort charateristics at arrival.*

majority of women, 53%, arrive single. Whereas immigrant flows with fewer single women at arrival, such as cohorts from India (17%) and Korea (28%), tend to exhibit lower rates of LFP.

### 4.3 Multivariate results: Modeling LFP trajectories

We next investigate the extent to which national origin differences in LFP trajectories are explained by individual human capital and family characteristics. **Table 3** reports coefficients from linear probability models predicting LFP trajectories by national origin. The results are organized around the five-cluster typology, with European women with 0–2 years of U.S. residence as the referent. Model 1 includes national/regional origin, age at arrival, their interactions with the splines of years since migration, and period of arrival. Model 2 adds individual-level predictors, human capital and family characteristics, and their interactions with the splines.

Comparing the constants of the two models at the bottom of **Table 3**, we find an average LFP rate of 58% at arrival in Model 1, which increases to 77% after adjusting for human capital and family characteristics in Model 2. For European cohorts (the referent), the rate increases slightly every year during the medium term according to Model 2 (0.009 Column 4) and remains flat 10 years after migration (Column 6), reaching 85% after 10 years of U.S. residence. Differences in starting rates between European women and others in the *gradual* incorporation group are negligible, supporting the validity of the GBTM. There is also only moderate variation in medium-term growth across groups, and few differences in the long-term period. Overall, differences in socioeconomic characteristics, i.e. human capital and family composition, within the *gradual* group did little to alter the similarities in their LPF trajectories.

In contrast, controlling for socioeconomic characteristics reduced the disparities between European and Mexican women considerably, by 57% at arrival (reducing the coefficient from −0.144 to −0.061 in Columns 1 and 2, respectively) and by 51% in the medium-term growth rate (from −0.014 to −0.007 in Columns 3 and 4, respectively). The gap after 10 years between comparable European and Mexican women is reduced from 26 percentage points in Model 1 to only 12 percentage points in Model 2. Thus, compositional differences explain a relatively large share of differences between the *gradual* and *delayed* incorporation groups.

Accounting for individual characteristics also explained roughly 25% of the lower initial rates of LFP among the *accelerated* incorporation group relative to Europeans (26% for India (Columns 1 vs. 2); 22% for Korea, and 24% for other Asia). It also

| | Arrival (1–2 years) | | Medium term (3–10 years) | | Longer-term (11+ years) | |
|---|---|---|---|---|---|---|
| | Model 1 | Model 2 | Model 1 | Model 2 | Model 1 | Model 2 |
| | 1 | 2 | 3 | 4 | 5 | 6 |
| **Gradual, moderate entry** | | | | | | |
| Europe (ref.) | — | — | 0.017** | 0.009** | 0.004** | −0.001 |
| Canada | 0.033 | 0.018 | −0.007** | −0.006** | 0.002 | 0.001 |
| Africa | −0.009 | 0.016 | 0.006** | 0.004** | 0.000 | −0.002** |
| China | −0.033 | −0.016 | 0.009** | 0.009** | −0.002** | −0.002** |
| Vietnam | −0.016 | 0.045** | 0.002 | 0.005* | 0.001 | 0.000 |
| **Delayed, low entry** | | | | | | |
| Mexico | −0.144** | −0.061** | −0.014** | −0.007** | 0.006** | 0.005** |
| **Delayed, moderate entry** | | | | | | |
| Central America | 0.023 | 0.049** | −0.015** | −0.007** | 0.004** | 0.003** |
| South America | 0.003 | 0.012 | −0.004 | −0.002 | 0.001* | 0.001 |
| Cuba | 0.079** | 0.092** | −0.01** | −0.005 | −0.005** | −0.005** |
| **Accelerated, low entry** | | | | | | |
| India | −0.192** | −0.143** | 0.015** | 0.011** | 0.003* | 0.001 |
| Korea | −0.202** | −0.157** | 0.009** | 0.006 | 0.002 | 0.002 |
| Other Asia | −0.210** | −0.159** | 0.011** | 0.009** | 0.002* | 0.002** |
| **Intensive, high entry** | | | | | | |
| Philippines | 0.106** | 0.083** | −0.003 | −0.003 | 0.000 | 0.000 |
| Caribbean | 0.118** | 0.076** | −0.005* | 0.001 | 0.000 | −0.001 |
| **Education (ref. high school)** | | | | | | |
| Less than HS | | −0.027** | | −0.004** | | −0.001* |
| Some college | | 0.001 | | 0.005** | | 0.000 |
| College | | 0.019** | | 0.013** | | −0.001** |
| **English ability** | | | | | | |
| Does not speak English well | | −0.077** | | 0.001 | | −0.001* |
| **Family Characteristics** | | | | | | |
| Married | | −0.183** | | 0.005** | | 0.002* |
| Has children <5 in household | | −0.202** | | 0.008** | | 0.003** |
| **Controls** | | | | | | |
| **Age at arrival (ref. 20–24)** | | | | | | |
| 15–19 | −0.020 | −0.064** | 0.004* | 0.008** | −0.001 | 0.000 |
| 25–29 | −0.023* | 0.010 | 0.005** | −0.001 | 0.000 | 0.000 |
| 30–34 | −0.033** | 0.007 | 0.009** | 0.000 | −0.004** | −0.002** |
| 35–39 | −0.013 | 0.001 | 0.010** | 0.002 | −0.009** | −0.006** |
| 40+ | 0.016 | 0.000 | 0.003 | −0.001 | −0.012** | −0.009* |

| | Arrival (1–2 years) | | Medium term (3–10 years) | | Longer-term (11+ years) | |
|---|---|---|---|---|---|---|
| | Model 1 | Model 2 | Model 1 | Model 2 | Model 1 | Model 2 |
| | 1 | 2 | 3 | 4 | 5 | 6 |
| **Period of arrival (ref. 1980s)** | | | | | | |
| 1990s | 0.014** | −0.002 | | | | |
| 2000s | 0.032** | 0.008 | | | | |
| 2010s | 0.041** | 0.009 | | | | |
| Constant | 0.577** | 0.773** | | | | |
| *N* | 1,405,714 | 1,405,714 | | | | |
| R-squared | 0.067 | 0.129 | | | | |

**p* < 0.10.
***p* < 0.05.
*Note: Immigrant women ages 16–54, who migrated from ages 15–44, not living in group quarters, not Attending school.*
*Source: U.S. Census 1990, 2000; American Community Survey 2005–2009, 2010–2014, and 2015–2019.*

**Table 3.**
*Coefficients from linear probability models predicting immigrant women's LFP at arrival, medium- and longer-terms years after migration.*

effectively reduced the difference in growth rates over the medium-term relative to European women (Columns 3 vs. 4). Similar explanatory power was evident among the *intensive* LFP group; the higher rate of LFP at arrival for Caribbean relative to European women is reduced from 0.118 (Column 1) to 0.076 (Column 2) and for Filipinas from 0.106 to 0.083, respectively.

The bottom part of **Table 3** reports coefficients for the socioeconomic predictors of LFP for the three splines of years since migration. Consistent with our expectations, in several cases the effects vary over time. For example, compared to women with a high school education, those with a college degree were more likely — and those lacking a high school diploma were less likely — to be in the labor force in the years immediately after arrival. These educational disparities in LFP grew more pronounced over time, as the advantage of college educated women, and the disadvantage of the least educated women, expanded with increased U.S. experience. Likewise, women with some college increased LFP more rapidly than those who did not advance beyond high school. Thus, while European women with less than high school education could expect a LFP rate of 79% after 10 years in the United States, the rate would be 89% for those with some college. Moreover, accounting for human capital explained a sizeable share of the slow growth in LFP for less educated, *delayed* incorporation cohorts. Lacking English proficiency exerted a steadier influence on LFP over time, having a large negative effect on LFP (−0.077 in Column 4) that does not seem to diminish with time in the United States.

Likewise, the impact of family structure on immigrant women's LFP varied over time. Both being married and having children under five are associated with lower LFP at arrival (−18% and − 20% in Column 2, respectively). However, these dampening effects attenuated somewhat with time in the United States, both during the medium and long term. In the medium term, for every year of U.S. residence (after the initial two) the LFP of married women and women with young children grew by 0.5% and 0.8%, and in later years by 0.2% and 0.3%, respectively.

The final step in the analysis is to examine the link between gendered characteristics and national/regional origin variation in immigrant women's LFP. **Table 4** reports summary results for models incorporating the four cohort-level gender characteristics. The models also control for national origin, age at arrival, period of arrival, and individual socioeconomic characteristics (full models not reported but available upon request). The top panel of **Table 4** reports results from models estimated including one cohort-level variable at a time and then an integrated model, estimated with all four group-level variables. The integrated model should be interpreted with caution given the strong correlation between the share of men arriving with a college education, on the one hand, and the share of women with college education and the share of single at arrival, on the other. **Table 4** reports overall effects, i.e., without interactions with the splines (Column 1), and the interaction effects (Columns 2, 3, and 4).

The results in Column 1 of **Table 4** document two salient group-level processes affecting LFP trajectories, namely the gender ratio and share of women single at arrival. They work in opposite directions. The gender ratio at arrival is negatively associated with immigrant women's LFP (−0.017), while the opposite is the case for the share of women arriving single (0.042). These effects reflect gendered demand for immigrant labor. The interactions with the splines show that most of the effect of the gender ratio acts by reducing the medium-term growth rate (−0.012 Column 2), though the positive coefficient in the long term (Column 4) indicates that the impact of the gender ratio attenuates over time. The opposite holds for the impact of the share of women single at arrival, which may signal the extent to which migration is driven by women's economic versus family considerations [18]. Results show that a higher representation of unmarried women at arrival is associated with an overall higher likelihood of women's LFP (Column 1), net of individual-level characteristics, supporting the interpretation that women migrate in search of jobs within those flows. Although the association is negative at arrival (−0.121 Column 2), it is positive for the medium-term growth rate (0.027 in Column 3).

| | | Interaction with time in the U.S. (Splines) | | |
|---|---|---|---|---|
| | **Overall effect** | **Arrival** | **Medium-term** | **Longer-term** |
| | 1 | 2 | 3 | 4 |
| Individual models | | | | |
| Sex ratio at arrival | −0.017$^{*}$ | 0.035 | −0.012$^{**}$ | 0.004$^{**}$ |
| % Women single at arrival | 0.042$^{*}$ | −0.121$^{*}$ | 0.027$^{**}$ | −0.001 |
| % Women w/college at arrival | −0.030$^{*}$ | −0.164$^{**}$ | 0.023$^{**}$ | −0.002 |
| % Men w/college at arrival | −0.043$^{**}$ | −0.134$^{**}$ | 0.013$^{*}$ | 0.001 |
| Integrated models | | | | |
| Sex ratio at arrival | −0.010 | 0.048$^{*}$ | −0.013$^{**}$ | 0.005$^{**}$ |
| % Women single at arrival | 0.013 | −0.223$^{**}$ | 0.039$^{**}$ | 0.000 |
| % Women w/college at arrival | 0.010 | −0.072 | 0.018$^{**}$ | −0.003 |
| % Men w/college at arrival | −0.039 | −0.184$^{**}$ | 0.021$^{*}$ | 0.001 |
| *N* | 1,405,714 | | | |

$^{*}p < 0.10$.
$^{**}p < 0.05$.
*Source: U.S. Census 1990, 2000; American Community Survey 2005–2009, 2010–2014, and 2015–2019.*

**Table 4.**
*Coefficients for gendered cohort characteristics from linear probability models predicting immigrant women's LFP.*

The effect of the share of co-ethnic women and men arriving with a college degree also varies by years since migration. The overall effect is negative for both of these variables at arrival (−0.164 and − 0.134 in Column 2, respectively), but the associations reverse during the medium-term years (0.023 and 0.013 in Column 3, respectively) and even off in later years. The integrated models (bottom panel of **Table 4**) show a similar pattern of effects, though the high correlation among these variables, as previously discussed, obscures their independent effects. Yet, the integrated models indicate a stronger effect for men's than for women's education at arrival. Cohorts with high representation of college educated men, like India, reflect the gendered nature of immigrant labor demand with a strong male preference. In these flows, women tend to follow their husbands and arrive with H1B dependent visas, which until 2015 prevented them from working, undermining women's LFP at arrival [19]. However, since women in these flows also tend to be highly educated, the initial penalty dissipates rapidly during the medium term, and levels off over the longer term.

To help illustrate the different roles of socioeconomic background and gendered migration cohort characteristics, **Table 5** reports the predicted probability of LFP for women arriving to the United States between 1990 and 1999 at the ages of 20 to 24. Model 1 presents the predicted probability of LFP with basic demographic controls

| | At arrival | | | 10 Years | | | 20 Years | | |
|---|---|---|---|---|---|---|---|---|---|
| | M1 | M2 | M3 | M1 | M2 | M3 | M1 | M2 | M3 |
| **Gradual, moderate entry** | | | | | | | | | |
| Europe | 59.1 | 56.4 | 63.1 | 70.8 | 68.6 | 66.8 | 76.8 | 70.6 | 69.7 |
| Canada | 62.4 | 58.2 | 67.6 | 68.9 | 66.1 | 64.0 | 75.7 | 68.7 | 66.8 |
| Africa | 58.2 | 58.0 | 60.8 | 74.0 | 73.2 | 72.6 | 80.8 | 74.1 | 73.0 |
| China | 55.8 | 54.8 | 64.9 | 73.6 | 73.3 | 71.0 | 78.2 | 73.9 | 71.7 |
| Vietnam | 57.5 | 60.9 | 60.3 | 70.3 | 76.6 | 74.4 | 77.5 | 79.0 | 77.2 |
| **Delayed, low entry** | | | | | | | | | |
| Mexico | 44.7 | 50.3 | 43.9 | 46.7 | 57.8 | 59.0 | 57.7 | 64.4 | 64.9 |
| **Delayed, moderate entry** | | | | | | | | | |
| Central America | 61.4 | 61.3 | 59.3 | 62.7 | 68.5 | 67.6 | 71.1 | 72.6 | 72.0 |
| South America | 59.4 | 57.6 | 61.2 | 68.6 | 68.7 | 66.5 | 75.8 | 71.5 | 70.3 |
| Cuba | 67.0 | 65.6 | 64.5 | 72.0 | 73.9 | 72.7 | 72.5 | 70.5 | 70.7 |
| **Accelerated, low entry** | | | | | | | | | |
| India | 39.9 | 42.1 | 50.9 | 61.9 | 61.7 | 61.5 | 71.9 | 66.3 | 65.7 |
| Korea | 38.9 | 40.7 | 50.4 | 57.2 | 57.0 | 54.3 | 66.1 | 62.2 | 61.1 |
| Other Asia | 38.1 | 40.5 | 46.7 | 57.8 | 58.6 | 57.2 | 66.7 | 63.7 | 62.1 |
| **Intensive, high entry** | | | | | | | | | |
| Philippines | 69.7 | 64.7 | 73.8 | 79.4 | 74.8 | 70.8 | 84.8 | 77.0 | 74.6 |
| Caribbean | 70.9 | 64.0 | 66.3 | 79.2 | 76.8 | 73.8 | 85.0 | 78.3 | 76.1 |

*Note: Predicted probabilities for women arriving between 1990 and 1999 at age 20–24 at means based on the models presented on **Tables** 3 and **4**.*

**Table 5.**
*Predicted probabilities of being in the labor force with demographic controls (M1), human capital and family characteristics (M2), and gendered cohort characteristics (M3).*

(based on **Table 3**, Model 1). Model 2 shows the probabilities controlling for average socioeconomic characteristics, that is, individual human capital and family characteristics (based on **Table 3**, Model 2), and controlling for cohort gender characteristics (based on **Table 4**, integrated model with spline interactions). We present the probabilities at arrival, after 10 years, and 20 years since migration, respectively. As discussed in the multivariate results, socioeconomic composition explains a large portion of the differences in employment probabilities across national origin groups. If European women had the average socioeconomic composition of the whole immigrant sample their probability of employment after 20 years in the United States would decline from 76.8% (M1) to 70.6% (M2). The opposite applies to Mexican women, although the effect is larger at 10 years in the United States, consistent with the pattern of delayed incorporation. Mexican women would see their predicted probability of LFP after 10 years increase from 47% (M1) to 58% (M2) if they had the average socioeconomic characteristics of immigrant women, and to 59% (M3) if they had average gender cohort characteristics.

In comparing the disparity between Europeans and Mexicans at 10 years after migration, European women exhibit 24 percentage points higher probability of LFP than Mexican women (M1), a difference that is decreased to 11 percentage points adjusting for individual socioeconomic characteristics (M2), and to 8 percentage points after controlling for gendered cohort characteristics (M3). That is, socioeconomic composition explains more than 55% of the disparity after 10 years, whereas 28% of the disparity between the two groups is attributable to gendered migration cohort characteristics.

An interesting pattern is evidenced for countries in the accelerated incorporation with low initial participation group, for whom adjusting for cohort gender characteristics increase their LFP at arrival. The effect is dominated by the high representation of educated men in Indian cohorts at arrival and women's tendency to arrive married. For example, Indian women LFP rate at arrival would increase from 42% (M2) to 51% (M3) if they had average gender cohort characteristics. This finding suggests that a different gender context would increase Asian women's LFP at arrival. Finally, the group with intensive employment, Filipinas and Caribbeans, would see their LFP rates decline over the medium and long term, if they were to have the average socioeconomic and gender cohort characteristics of all immigrant women.

## 5. Conclusions

The literature on immigrant assimilation has emphasized the heterogeneity in modes of incorporation, yet the limitations of traditional analyses of cross-sectional data have undermined our understanding of how these processes play out among immigrant women. In this chapter, we analyze the factors that shape the variation in labor force participation (LFP) trajectories for the 14 largest national/regional origin groups. We construct synthetic immigrant cohorts using U.S. Census and American Community Survey (ACS) data from 1990 to 2019, to track immigrant women's LFP trajectories investigating national origin variation in LFP rates at entry, and growth rates in the medium, and long terms. We propose a five-group typology that synthesizes immigrant women's national origin variation in patterns of labor market incorporation. We elaborate on the usefulness of the notion of the gendered context of reception for understanding different modes of assimilation.

Our analysis revealed that national origin variation in LFP trajectories clusters into five distinct patterns of workforce incorporation: (1) *Gradual incorporation from moderate entry rates*, typified by cohorts from Europe, Canada, Africa, China, and Vietnam; (2) *Delayed incorporation with low initial participation*, exemplified by Mexico, with low starting rates and slow growth rates; (3) *Delayed incorporation with moderate entry rates*, which characterizes cohorts from Central America, South America, and Cuba; (4) *Accelerated incorporation with low entry rates*, including India, Korea, and other Asian countries, with fast growth in the medium-term years; and (5) *Continuous intensive LFP with high entry rates*, which includes the Philippines and Caribbean countries. Despite this variation, the results show that most groups show evidence assimilation, increasing their rates of LFP in the years after migration.

Consistent with prior studies, controlling for individual socioeconomic characteristics, including educational attainment, English proficiency, and family characteristics, explains a large portion of LFP disparities across groups [6, 9, 10]. We contribute to the prior literature by showing that the effects of these individual-level characteristics vary by group and depend on whether we focus on the rates at arrival or change with time in the United States. We show that socioeconomic characteristics explain nearly half of the lower LFP at arrival among the groups with delayed incorporation, which includes Latin American countries, especially Mexico, relative to the gradual incorporation group, exemplified by Europe. They also explain a similar proportion of the slower rate of growth in LFP among the delayed incorporation group. Conversely, for the group with accelerated incorporation, including India, Korea, other Asian countries, around 25% of the lower entry level LFP at arrival relative to Europeans is explained by individual characteristics. For the accelerated group, the initial constraint stems not from lack of human capital, but the much higher propensity for women to arrive married. Moreover, accounting for individual-level characteristics, particularly education, explains a large part of their more rapid growth in LFP over time. A different pattern is found for the group with continuous intensive LFP. For this group, which includes cohorts from the Philippines and the Caribbean, socioeconomic controls reduced 22% and 36% of the higher LFP at arrival relative to Europeans, respectively, and for Caribbeans, explained their slower medium-term growth rate.

We found that educational attainment shapes LFP differently across periods of incorporation. While better educated women average higher LFP than their less educated counterparts, the differences are significantly smaller at arrival, and widen with longer durations of U.S. residence. Those with more than a high school education increase faster their rates of LFP over time, while the opposite is true of their less educated counterparts. These patterns highlight the difficulties faced by less educated immigrant flows, such as Mexicans, Central Americans, and some Asian groups, in finding work in the increasingly skill-oriented U.S. labor market. In contrast, the constraints on immigrant women's LFP associated with family responsibilities, that is, being married and having children younger than age five in the household, significantly reduce LFP mainly at arrival. Married women and those with young children seem better able to combine work and family over time, as their LFP increases at a faster rate than other women with longer periods of U.S. residence.

Finally, we show that gendered migration cohort characteristics, namely the gender ratio at arrival, share of women arriving single, and share of women and men arriving with a college education, help explain an additional proportion of LFP gaps across groups. For example, the overrepresentation of men in migrant flows, such as the cases of Mexican and India, undermines immigrant women's LFP rates, while the opposite holds for flows dominated by women, such as the Philippines. The link between these group-level characteristics and LFP changes over time. It is only after many years in the United States, i.e., more than 11, that women's LFP in male-dominated migration streams begins to converge with those from more gender-balanced flows.

The share of immigrant women arriving single, in contrast, reflects the degree of female independence and labor demand driving women's migration decisions. Results show that higher representations of single women in migration cohorts were associated with higher LFP, even net of individual-level characteristics. The share of women and men arriving with college education were associated with lower women's LFP, with a stronger effect for the proportion of men with college education at arrival, an indicator of male privilege and male labor demand. While the aggregated effect on LFP was not significant, separating by length of U.S. residence showed that highly educated male flows, such as from India, were negatively associated with immigrant women's LFP at arrival. Despite their initial disadvantage, these flows show more rapid increases in LFP over time. Taken together, national origin differences in these four gendered dimensions of migration flows help explain the gap in LFP that remains after controlling for individual-level characteristics.

Overall, this chapter shows the advantage of using a synthetic double-cohort approach and group-based trajectory modeling to summarize and understand the variation in the patterns of immigrants' modes of incorporation. It also shows the importance of distinguishing LFP rates at arrival from growth rates in the medium and long term, and highlights the need to integrate the gender dimension in the concept of context of reception. This methodology also shows a more impressive and nuanced process of assimilation among immigrant women than that evinced in prior studies [4, 5, 10]. We argue that immigrant cohort gender characteristics at arrival can help us understand the variation in immigrant labor supply, providing important insights into the evolution of national-origin disparities in immigrant women's LFP. Immigrant incorporation is shaped by not only by individual and family characteristics, but also by larger contextual forces, including cultural norms, government policies, and gendered labor demand.

Results also suggest the need for continued exploration of creative methodologies to capture the complexity of modes of immigrant assimilation. Future research should examine whether immigrant cohort effects largely follow national origin lines, as we suggest here, whether and how they are shaped by racial and ethnic lines, as well as by internal geographical patterns of settlement.

## Author details

Sandra Florian[1]*, Chenoa Flippen[2] and Emilio Parrado[2]

1 French Institute for Demographic Studies (INED), Aubervilliers, France

2 University of Pennsylvania, Philadelphia, USA

*Address all correspondence to: sandra.florian@ined.fr

## References

[1] Rakotonarivo A. Who are the women on the move? A portrait of female migrant workers – ILOSTAT. *International Labour Organisation ILO, ILOSTAT.* 2020. Available from: https://ilostat.ilo.org/who-are-the-women-on-the-move-a-portrait-of-female-migrant-workers/ [Accessed 17 November 2022]

[2] Carratala S, Svajlenka NP, Glynn SJ. A Profile of Immigrant Women in the Workforce – Center for American Progress. *Center for American Progress (CAP)*. 2021. Available from: https://www.americanprogress.org/article/profile-immigrant-women-workforce/ [Accessed 17 November 2022]

[3] Adserà A, Ferrer AM. The myth of immigrant women as secondary workers: Evidence from Canada. American Economic Review. 2014;**104**:360-364

[4] Donato KM, Piya B, Jacobs A. The double disadvantage reconsidered: Gender, immigration, marital status, and global labor force participation in the 21st century. International Migration Review. 2014;**48**:S335-S376

[5] Blau FD, Kahn LM, Papps KL. Gender, source country characteristics, and labor market assimilation among immigrants. Review of Economics and Statistics. 2011;**93**:43-58

[6] Read JG, Cohen PN. One size fits all? Explaining U.S.-born and immigrant Women's employment across 12 ethnic groups. Social Forces. 2007;**85**:1713-1731

[7] Donato KM, Gabaccia D. Gender and International Migration. New York: Russell Sage Foundation; 2015

[8] Lee T, Peri G, Viarengo M. The gender aspect of migrants' assimilation in Europe. Labour Economics. 2022;**78**:102180

[9] Florian S, Flippen C, Parrado E. The labor force trajectories of immigrant women in the United States: intersecting individual and gendered cohort characteristics. International Migration Review. 2023;**57**(1):95-127. DOI: 10.1177/01979183221076781

[10] Schoeni RF. Labor market assimilation of immigrant women. Industrial and Labor Relations Review. 1998;**51**:483-504

[11] Antecol H. An examination of cross-country differences in the gender gap in labor force participation rates. Labour Economics. 2000;7:409-426

[12] Blau FD, Kahn LM. Substitution between individual and source country characteristics. Journal of Human Capital. 2015;**9**:439-482

[13] Blau FD, Kahn LM, Comey M, et al. Culture and gender allocation of tasks: Source country characteristics and the division of non-market work among US immigrants. Review of Economics of the Household. 2020;**18**:907-958

[14] Polavieja JG. Capturing culture: A new method to estimate exogenous cultural effects using migrant populations. American Sociological Review. 2015;**80**:166-191

[15] Apgar L, McManus PA. Cultural persistence and labor force participation among partnered second-generation women in the United States. Social Forces. 2019;**98**:211-244

[16] Wang S. The role of gender role attitudes and immigrant generation in

ethnic minority Women's labor force participation in Britain. Sex Roles. 2019:234-245

[17] Feliciano C. Immigrant selectivity effects on health, labor market, and educational outcomes. Annual Review of Sociology. 2020;**46**:315-334

[18] He Q, Gerber TP. Origin-country culture, migration sequencing, and female employment: Variations among immigrant women in the United States. International Migration Review. 2020;**54**:233-261

[19] Banerjee P. Subversive self-employment: Intersectionality and self-employment among dependent visas holders in the United States. American Behavioral Scientist. 2019;**63**:186-207

[20] Borjas GJ. Assimilation, changes in cohort quality, and the earnings of immigrants. Journal of Labor Economics. 1985;**3**:463-489

[21] Flood S, King M, Rodgers R, et al. Integrated Public Use Microdata Series, Current Population Survey: Version 10.0 [Dataset]. Minneapolis, MN; 2022. DOI: 10.18128/D030.V10.0

[22] Gordon MM. Assimilation in America: Theory and reality. Daedalus. 1961;**90**(2):263-285

[23] Alba R, Nee V. Rethinking assimilation theory for a new era of immigration. International Migration Review. 1997;**31**:826-874

[24] Portes A, Zhou M. The new 2nd-generation - segmented assimilation and its variants. Annals of the American Academy of Political and Social Science. 1993;**530**:74-96

[25] Borjas GJ. The slowdown in the economic assimilation of immigrants: Aging and cohort effects revisited again. Journal of Human Capital. 2015;**9**:483-517

[26] Baker M, Benjamin D. The role of the family in immigrants' labor-market activity: An evaluation of alternative explanations. The American Economic Review. 1997;**87**:705-727

[27] McManus PA, Apgar L. Parental origins, mixed unions, and the labor supply of second-generation women in the United States. Demography. 2019;**56**:49-73

[28] Read JG. Cultural influences on immigrant Women's labor force participation: The Arab-American case. International Migration Review. 2004;**38**:52-77

[29] Portes A, Rumbaut R. Immigrant America: A Portrait. 4th ed. Irvine, CA: University of California Press; 2014

[30] Flippen CA. Intersectionality at work: Determinants of labor supply among immigrant Latinas. Gender & Society. 2013;**28**:404-434

[31] Flippen CA. Laboring underground: The employment patterns of Hispanic immigrant men in Durham, NC. Social Problems. 2012;**59**:21-42

[32] Flippen CA, Parrado EA. A tale of two contexts: U.S. migration and the labor force trajectories of Mexican women. International Migration Review. 2015;**49**:232-259

[33] Parrado EA, Flippen CA. Migration and gender among Mexican women. American Sociological Review. 2005;**70**:606-632

[34] Hondagneu-Sotelo P. Gendered Transitions: Mexican Experiences of Immigration. Berkeley: University of California Press; 1994

[35] USCI. H-1B Petitions by Gender and Country of Birth Fiscal Year 2018.

Washington, D.C.; U.S. Citizenship and Immigration Service; 2018

[36] Kofman E. Gendered global migrations. International Feminist Journal of Politics. 2004;**6**:643-665

[37] Chiswick BR. The effect of Americanization on the earnings of foreign-born men. Journal of Political Economy. 1978;**86**:897-921

[38] Myers D, Lee SW. Immigration cohorts and residential overcrowding in Southern California. Demography. 1996;**33**:51

[39] Fuller S. Do pathways matter? Linking early immigrant employment sequences and later economic outcomes: Evidence from Canada. International Migration Review. 2015;**49**:355-405

[40] Chiswick BR, Miller PW. The international transferability of immigrants' human capital. Economics of Education Review. 2009;**28**:162-169

[41] Fuller S, Martin TF. Predicting immigrant employment sequences in the first years of settlement. International Migration Review. 2012;**46**:138-190

[42] Jones BL, Nagin DS. A note on a Stata plugin for estimating group-based trajectory models. Sociological Methods and Research. 2013;**42**:608-613

[43] Jung T, Wickrama KAS. An introduction to latent class growth analysis and growth mixture Modeling. Social and Personality Psychology Compass. 2008;**2**:302-317

Chapter 6

# Youth and Migration: Perspective of African Countries

*Lesego Selotlegeng-Mbe*


## Abstract

Most of the estimated 3,6 million Africans residing abroad are highly educated professionals. This migration has resulted in the loss of expertise in vital economic sectors. This chapter addresses the relationship between migration and youth in African nations. Many youth move in response to inadequate living conditions, unemployment, famines, the effects of climate change, and armed conflicts. Since 2012, more than 260,000 people migrated from African continent to other continents, most of them young. They respond to both push and pull factors, whether these are economic, political, cultural, or environmental. In 2017, there were approximately 420,000 more sub-Saharan African migrants living in Europe than in 2010. An estimated 1.55 million sub-Saharan African migrants resided in the United States in 2017, an increase of approximately 325,000 from 2010, when an estimated 1.22 million sub-Saharan African migrants resided in the country. As of 2017, 72% of Europe's sub-Saharan African immigrant population was concentrated in four countries: the United Kingdom (1.27 million), France (980,000), Italy (370,000), and Portugal (370,000). Most migrants hail from Nigeria (17487), Syrian Arab Republic (16568), Guinea (12158) and Côte d'Ivoire (11966). In 2015, Greece overtook Italy as the primary point of arrival.


**Keywords:** migrants, youth, Africa, Mediterranean route, drivers of youth migration

## 1. Introduction

There is little consistency in the definition of youth across countries and organizations (see **Table 1**). The United Nations set the year range 15–24 years to define youth. However, several United Nations agencies (United Nations Fund for Population Activities (UNFPA), the United Nations Children's Fund (UNICEF), and the World Health Organization (WHO)), define youth as people aged 10 to 24 [1]. The World Bank keeps the top age limit of 24 years but lowers the starting age to 12 years. These parameters differ from the African Youth Charter's broader age span of 15–35 years [2].

In 2013, there were 28.2 million international migrants between the ages of 15 and 24, representing one-eighth of the 232 million international migrants worldwide [3]. The proportion of young migrants is greater in developing nations than in developed



IntechOpen

| Organization | Definition of youth (year) | Sources |
|---|---|---|
| Africa Union | 15–35 | African Youth Charter |
| The Commonwealth | 15–29 | Commonwealth Youth Programme |
| United Nations | 15–24 | UNFPA framework for action on Adolescents and Youth |
| World Bank | 15–24 | Africa Development Indicators 2008/2009;Youth and Employment in Africa |
| World Health Organisation | 15–24 | World Report on Violence and Health; Youth Violence |

**Table 1.**
*Age-based definition of youth.*

nations, whereas the proportion of young females and women who migrate is greater in developed nations than in developing nations [4]. There are many reasons why young people migrate. The decision to migrate is frequently associated with key life transitions, such as attaining a higher education, locating and beginning a new job, or getting married. With approximately 71 million youth unemployed worldwide in 2016, job search remains a major factor in youth migration in both developed and developing countries. In addition, many young people migrate to escape poverty, violence, or conflict, or because they are displaced by war or climate change. Consequently, youth are highly represented in humanitarian migration, including as refugees, asylees, and unaccompanied minors.

## 2. International youth migrants: Numbers and trends

International migration is a global issue of importance. Whether alone or with family, more and more adolescents and youth migrate in search of survival, security, improved living standards, education, or protection from maltreatment [5]. The United Nations report focuses on migrants between 15 and 24 years of age, who in 2013 represented about one-eighth (28.2 million) of the 232 million international migrants worldwide. The United Nations Children's Fund (UNICEF) divides adolescence into three periods for analytical purposes: early (10-to-13 years), middle (14-to-16 years), and late (17-to-19 years). There is no legal definition of 'youth,' although the United Nations (UN) defines it as those aged 15 to 24 "without prejudice to other definitions by Member States" [6]. An international migrant is any individual who has changed their country of usual habitation, with "short-term migrants" (those who have changed their country of usual residence for at least 3 months but less than 1 year) and "long-term migrants" (those who have done so for at least 1 year) distinguishing between them [7]. Overall, the estimated number of international youth migrants has increased over the past year. The total estimated of over 10 million youth living in a country other than their country of birth in 2020 is almost over 4 million more than in 2000 when it was over 3 million (see **Figure 1**).

Between 2000 and 2019, the stock of young international migrants increased slightly (**Figure 2**). It grew from 1990 to 2015 across all African Countries but it

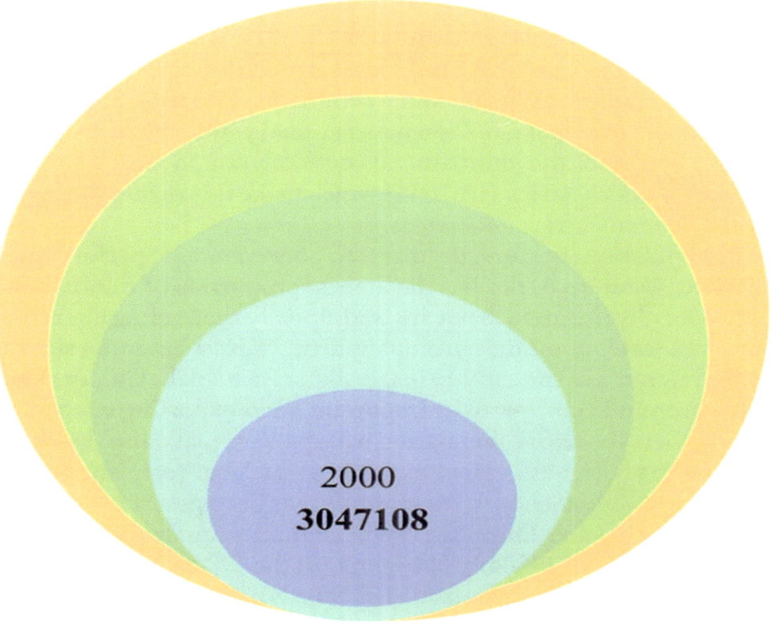


**Figure 1.**
*International Youth migration, Africa 2000-2020. Source: United Nations Department of Economic and Social Affairs, Population Division (2020). International Migrant Stock 2020. https://www.un.org/development/desa/pd/content/international-migrant-stock NB: This figure use the United Nations (UN) defines persons aged 15-to-24 as youth.*

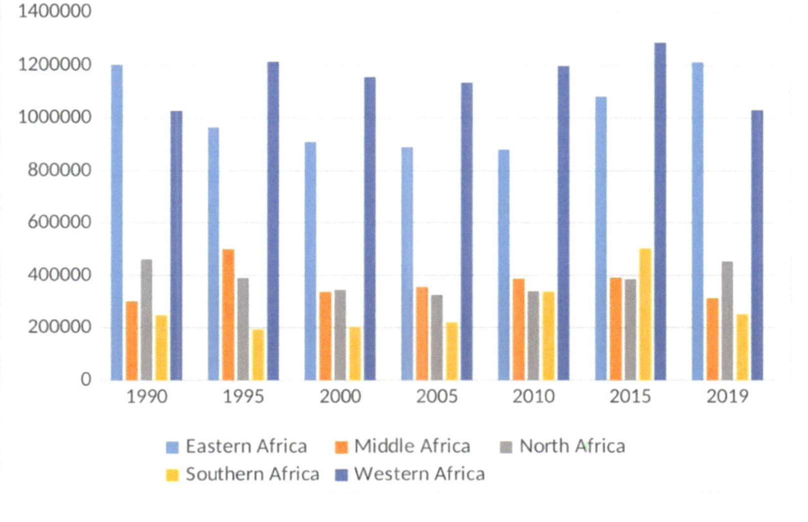


**Figure 2.**
*Trends in International Young migrants from 1990-2019. Source: United National, Department of Economic and Social Affairs 2019. https://www.un.org/development/desa/pd/content/international-migrant-stock NB: This figure use the United Nations (UN) defines persons aged 15-to-24 as youth.*

subsequently decreases slightly around 2019. Western African countries had the highest number of international youth migrants in 2015, with 1,2 million, followed by Eastern African countries with 1,1 million. It is much lower in Middle African with less than half a million (390347) and North Africa (385384). Southern African countries host almost over half a million international youth migrants (503189). In 2019 there was a decline of the international youth migrant in most Africa Region but an increase in Eastern Africa (1212645) which make this region the highest and followed by the Western Africa (1030112).

Because of population pressure, destitution, poor economic performance, and endemic conflicts, Western Africa has the highest proportion of international youth migrants [8]. Côte d'Ivoire and Ghana are traditionally the leading countries of immigration. As a result of oil-driven employment, Nigeria became a significant destination for migrants in the early 1970s. Burkina Faso, Mali, Guinea, Cape Verde, and Togo have been and continue to be important labor exporting countries. The diaspora outnumbers the native population in Cape Verde, making the situation unusual. Senegal has been both a labor exporter and a labor recipient. All of this has shifted in recent years. Senegal, for example, has become a transit country for migrants attempting to enter European Union countries clandestinely via Las Palmas to Spain. Ghana (in the late 1960s) and Nigeria (in the 1980s) became exporters of labor when economic conditions worsened. Ghana is presently experiencing return migration as a result of the government's progressive economic policies and the country's political stability.

### 2.1 Determinants of migration

People migrate for a variety of reasons. According to the International Organization for Migration (IOM), these reasons are economic, social, political, and environmental. According to the IOM, economic migration is to pursue a specific vocation. Social migration is moving closer to family or friends for a better quality of life, whereas political migration is moving to another location to escape war or political persuasion. The employment crisis drives millions of people, particularly young women and men, to migrate in order to improve their job prospects. Many of them migrate to urban areas and large cities in their home nations, or they pursue new opportunities abroad. According to IOM figures (2017), around 244 million people leave their home countries to seek jobs abroad [9]. International migration can provide new opportunities for employment and training, but youth workers, particularly young men and women and undocumented migrants, confront unique challenges and vulnerabilities. Labor migration experiences can be either an opportunity or a risk for young people, depending on the policies and measures that support them, such as increased and improved social protection, education and training for employment, entrepreneurship development, social inclusion, and an effective institutional framework [10].

Historically, international youth migration Africa has been modest compared with that from other continents. The rate of migration from South Africa has increased dramatically in recent years. **Figure 3** indicated South Africa as the region with the largest population of international youth migrants. The other countries on that list, in order, include Côte d'Ivoire, Kenya, Burkina Faso,

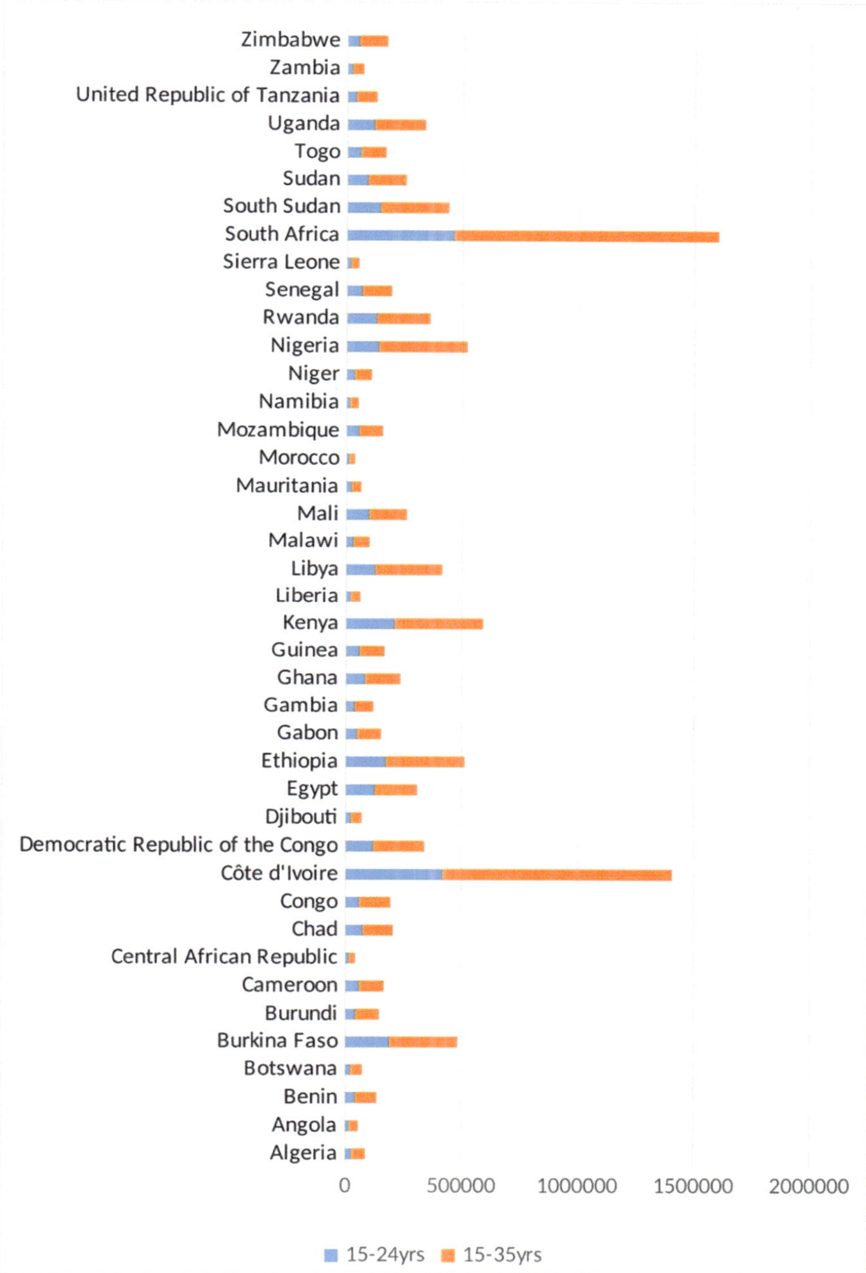


**Figure 3.**
*Trends in International Young migrants for African countries 2015. Source: United National, Department of Economic and Social Affairs 2015. https://www.un.org/development/desa/pd/content/international-migrant-stock NB: This figure uses the United Nations (UN) defines persons aged 15-to-24 as youth and African Youth Charter's wider age range of 15–35 years.*

Ethiopia, South Sudan, Nigeria, Rwanda and Libya. In Africa, the majority of the population is youthful and increasingly well-informed due to access to mobile phones and the internet, which continues to fuel migration aspirations. Numerous African youths are exposed to compelling examples (in their cities, on television, and online) of successful migrants and growing remittances [11]. Youth Migration within Africa is partially a disaster-driven. Many migrate to urban areas and large cities in their home countries, or they seek out new opportunities abroad. It is anticipated that climate change-induced land degradation, violence, freshwater scarcity, and more extreme weather conditions such as droughts and floods will propel international youth migration from Africa. As a result, concerns have been expressed regarding the loss of skilled labor from already impoverished countries and the potential for migration to lead to violent conflict.

## 3. Drivers of youth migration

Migration refers to a permanent or semi-permanent change of residence. People migrate due to push and pull factors, whether these are economic, political, cultural, or environmental in nature. Conditions that can push people from their communities include insufficient livelihood opportunities, poverty, rapid population growth, or poor living conditions, desertification, famines/droughts, fear of political persecution, inadequate healthcare, loss of wealth, and natural disasters are considered push factors. Pull factors, on the other hand, attract individuals to a particular location. Typical examples include employment opportunities and better living conditions, easy access to land for settlement and agriculture, political and/or religious freedom, superior education and welfare systems, improved transportation and communication facilities, a superior healthcare system and a stress-free environment, and safety.

Young people migrate for many reasons. Migration is frequently associated with key life transitions, such as continuing education, locating and beginning a job, or getting married. With an estimated 71 million youth unemployed worldwide in 2016 [12], the pursuit for employment remains a significant driver of youth migration in both developed and developing nations. Many young people migrate to escape poverty, violence, or conflict, or because they have been displaced by war or climate change. Consequently, youth are highly represented in humanitarian migration, including as refugees, asylees, and unaccompanied minors. Some move to avoid poverty, violence, unemployment, or the effects of climate change, while others relocate to study abroad, reunite with family, or marry. Young Africans' migration decisions are primarily influenced by significant life transitions, such as obtaining a higher education, beginning work, or getting married. Since the 1970s, more than 2.5 million young migrants have traversed the Mediterranean without authorization. In response to the introduction of visa requirements for people who had previously been exempted – the majority of whom were temporary labor migrants from North Africa and Turkey – irregular sea travel increased during these years, as Western states grappled with rising unemployment during the 1973 oil crisis. At mid-September 2017, it was evident that the Mediterranean migration crisis was diminishing. Since the beginning of the year, "only" 130,000 migrants have arrived by sea in Italy, Greece, Spain, Malta, and Cyprus without a visa. Even though 2017 is not yet over, it is unlikely that the total number of juvenile migrants crossing the Mediterranean will reach the peaks of previous years. 368,080 in 2016, 908,558 in 2015, and 209,664 in 2014; totaling 368,080 [13].

### 3.1 Unemployment

Africa's current population is estimated to more than double by 2050, when it will account for one-fourth of the global population. This young generation could lead the economic transformation of Africa. However, the majority of young people lack economic stability and employment security. The majority of Africa's 420 million adolescents aged 15 to 35 are unemployed, insecurely employed, or have temporary jobs [14]. The average unemployment rate for young persons is roughly twice that of older individuals. However, there are substantial differences between African nations. According to the World Bank, youths account for 60% of Africa's unemployed. The adolescent unemployment rate in North Africa is 25%, particularly in Botswana, the Republic of the Congo, Senegal, and South Africa, among others. Africa has the world's largest youth population, with 200 million individuals between the ages of 15 and 24. As shown in **Figure 4**, young women experience the effects of unemployment even more acutely than young men. In the majority of sub-Saharan African countries and all North African countries, it is easier for males to obtain employment than it is for women, even with similar skills and experience.

According to the International Labour Organization (ILO) [15], youths account for 70% of all of Africa's jobless. According to **Figure 4** unemployment rate among youth is high in females compared to male. From 1991 until to 2023 more women are losing jobs, as it was indicated by national statistics institute (ISTAT), in 2020, 326,000 women had lost their employment, compared to 141,000 men. The most recent global female labor force participation rate is roughly 47%, compared to 72% for men (ILO, 2022), this indicates that globally are unemployed. In Africa, youth unemployment is high in southern African region by over 35% and less in the Eastern part by less than 10% (**Figure 5**).

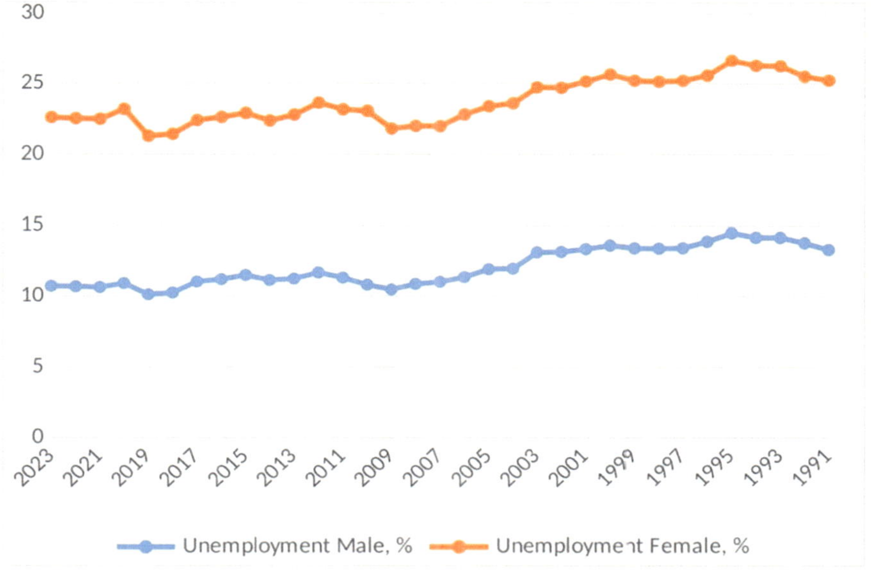


**Figure 4.**
*The unemployment youth (% of male, female labor force age 15–24) in Africa. Source: International Labour Organisation, https://ilostat.ilo.org/data/#.*

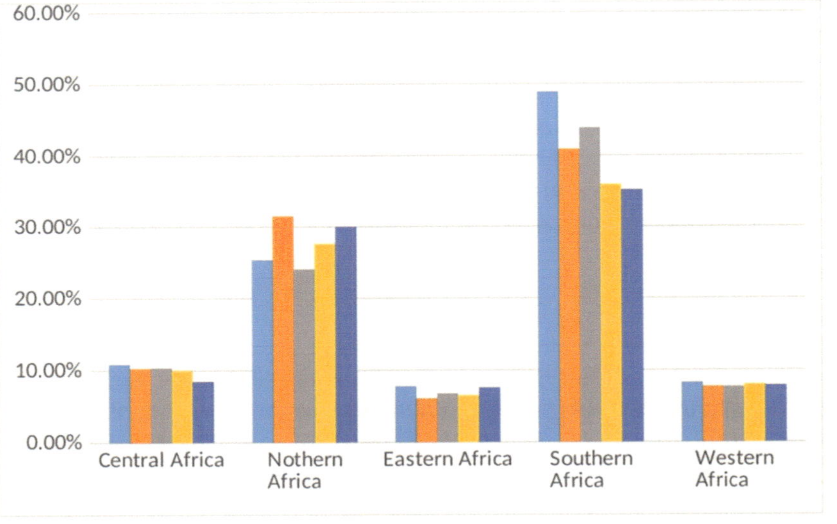


**Figure 5.**
*The unemployment youth (% of labor force age 15–24) in Africa. Source: International Labour Organisation, https://ilostat.ilo.org/data/#.*

According to **Figure 6**, unemployment is a major challenge among youth. Countries with the highest rate of youth unemployment (over 35%) include Somalia, Gabon, Rwanda, Tunisia, Botswana, Namibia, Eswatini. In the majority of African nations, adolescent unemployment is higher than that of adults (African Development Bank (date)). Africa's unemployment statistics exclude those in precarious employment and underemployed individuals in informal sectors. In Africa, young people can find employment, but not in positions that offer decent wages, skill development, or job security. At least 70% of adolescents in the Republic of the Congo, the Democratic Republic of the Congo, Ethiopia, Ghana, Malawi, Mali, Rwanda, Senegal, and Uganda are either self-employed or participate in family work. In Ghana, only "52% of people aged 15-24 were employed, compared to 77% of the entire population," indicating that 48% of these youths were unemployed. Although some of this high unemployment is driven by low levels of schooling, this figure highlighted the challenge confronting the nation [16]. Even though they have jobs, a disproportionate number of young people in emerging and developing nations live in extreme or moderate poverty. In actuality, 156 million or 37.7% of working adolescents live in extreme or moderate poverty, compared to 26% of working adults [17]. According to a publication of the United Nations Economic Commission for Africa, young migrants frequently face obstacles, such as discrimination, due to their inexperience. Even those fortunate enough to obtain employment are the first to be let go during hard economic times. Industrial development is most closely associated with employment-intensive expansion, so the majority of countries must focus on manufacturing. Additionally, increased investment in agriculture, tourism, and construction, as well as youth-employment initiatives. Young employees have access to opportunities through public works programs. The African Union also supports the demand for increased agricultural investment. The Africa Union (AU) requests that its member states allocate 15% of their national budgets to agriculture.

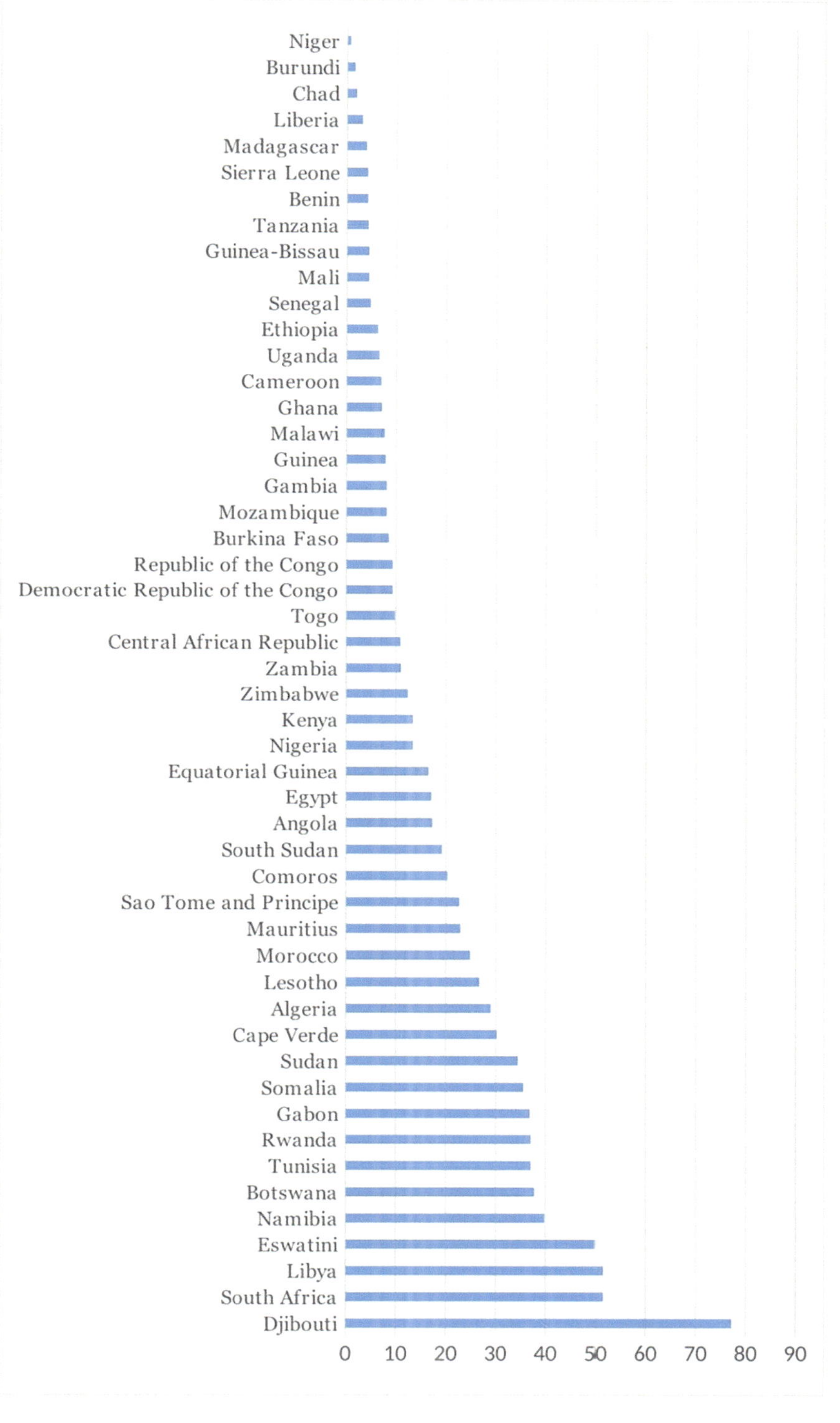


**Figure 6.**
*Unemployment rate for African Countries, 2016. Source: International Labour Organization (ILO), 2016, https://ilostat.ilo.org/data/#.*

### 3.2 Education

With the global expansion of global education, skill transmission through migration has also intensified. The percentage of migrants with a higher level of education increased from 29.8 to 34.6% between 1990 and 2013, while the percentage of migrants with a low level of education decreased from 44.9 to 36.4%. A significant portion of the education-migration literature focuses on the influence of education on the decision to migrate and choice of destination country. In past few years, youth who are most likely to migrate are with a middle level of education (i.e., upper secondary and post-secondary non-tertiary education).

Education plays a crucial role in youth migration. The returns to skills in both the country of origin and the country of destination are particularly important. The youth immigrant's economic success in the destination country is largely determined by their educational background and the transferability of their abilities to the local labor market. **Figure 7** indicated that majority of youth migrated to France, United States of America in order to development themselves. The desire to acquire skills in the destination country that have a high return in the country of origin may also be a key reason for migration and, in some cases, the sole reason.

Between 1963 and 2006, the number of pupils studying in a foreign country increased ninefold. In 2006, 2,7 million pupils studied abroad, and it is anticipated that by 2025, the demand for cross-border education will increase to 7,2 million.[6] There is great preponderance of international students in six OECD countries. In 2007, the United States accounted for 21,4% of international enrollments, followed by

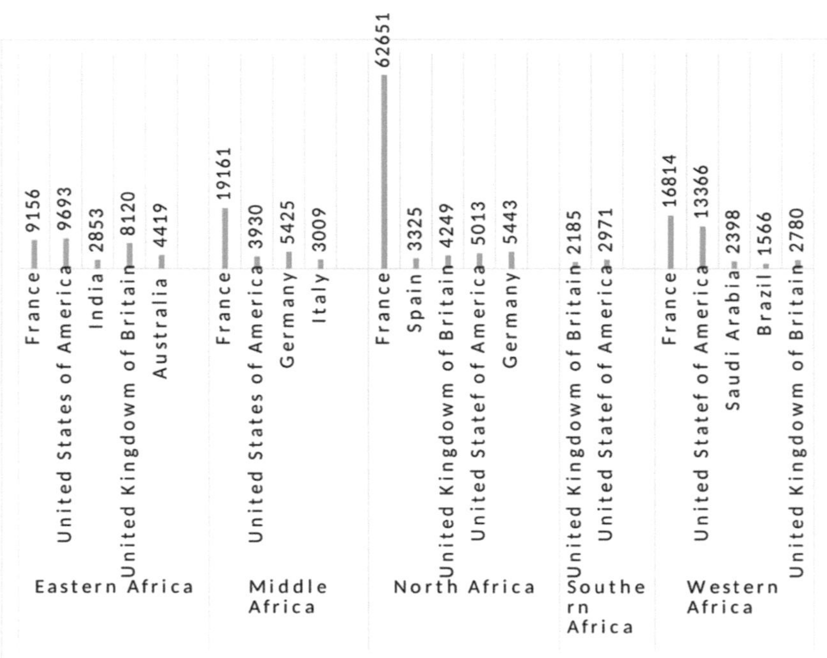


**Figure 7.**
*Youth Migrants by Destination, 2017. Source: United Nations, Department of Economic and Social Affairs, Population Division (2017). World Population Prospects: The 2017 Revision. https://www.un.org/development/desa/pd/content/international-migrant-stock.*

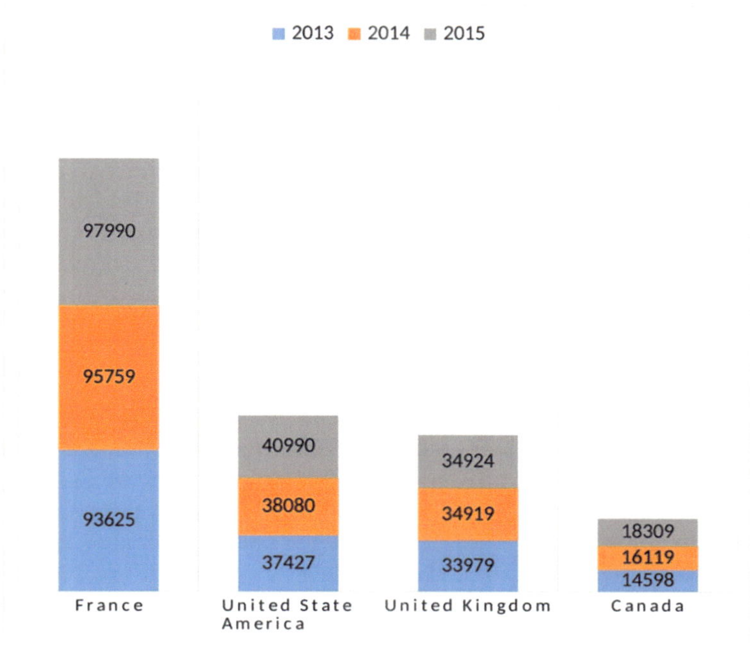


**Figure 8.**
*International Youth migrants from Africa: Tertiary enrolment, 2015.*

the United Kingdom, France, Australia, Germany, and Japan. Europe is the leading region for international students, with approximately 840,000 international students [18]. **Figure 6** indicated that majority of youth migrate to France for further studies. In addition, **Figure 8** indicated that France since 2013 enrolled more than 90,000 African youth in tertiary education.

Educational mobility policies can benefit both individuals and communities in destination nations. Educational mobility affords individuals the chance to develop personally, realize their potential, and alter their worldviews without placing their lives in danger. These avenues enable youth to learn new ideas and encounter people from around the globe. Even more tangible benefits, including brain gain, skill transfer, and remittances, accrue in the countries where their voyages began. It is imperative that, as the United Nations discusses ways to expand legal migration routes from Africa to the rest of the world, sufficient attention is paid to education routes. Even when there are universities available in their home countries, many young migrants often consider these to provide a poor standard of education that will not propel them into good careers. The expectation of studying in a developed country has become a key part of some societies, and it signals a transition to adulthood along with qualifications.

### 3.3 Environmental change

According to the United Nations Economic Commission for Africa (UNECA), while irregular migration from Africa to Europe has garnered considerable attention, intra-African migration dominates the movement of African migrants. About 80% of Africans who migrate do so within the continent, with only 15–20% taking the route to Europe, which indicates that there are 18,6 million African migrants. Women now make up nearly half (49%) of the international migrant population, which is estimated to be 3% of the world's population. This is because more women now have access to education and employment opportunities outside of the continent. Numerous women who work as nurses, housekeepers, or caregivers pursue employment in the West, particularly in Europe, where, in addition to better employment conditions, there is a demand for their services. More than half of all highly educated African migrants currently reside in the United States, Germany, the United Kingdom, France, Canada, Australia, and Spain, according to the report. This has a negative effect on the continent's economic growth [19]. As depicted in **Figure 9**, the majority of migrant youth from Africa hold non-graduate jobs in their host countries. These jobs include crosswalk attendant, factory laborers, and hospital porters.

According to OECD statistics, France provides employment for young African migrants, with an estimated 50,559 young African migrant laborers employed in elementary occupations and 29,923 youth migrants employed in sales and services elementary occupations. Hence, a small number of youth migrants are in management, architecture and engineering and legal occupation. Being in a foreign land is not easy to get a job that matches one's qualification. Most of young graduate African migrants work undeclared employment particularly in the areas of agriculture, construction, catering, tourism, household services and cleaning in the host countries. In Belgium, public authority inspections have uncovered a substantial number of youthful illegal immigrants working in the hospitality and construction industries. In Lombardy, the northern region with the highest concentration of immigrants, an estimated 55.3% of males in the active migrant population have declared employment, while 14.4% have unreported employment. Significant numbers of young migrants are employed illegally as menial construction workers, cleaners, dishwashers, and packers; sawmill workers, woodcutters, or warehouse workers in the Czech Republic. In France, there

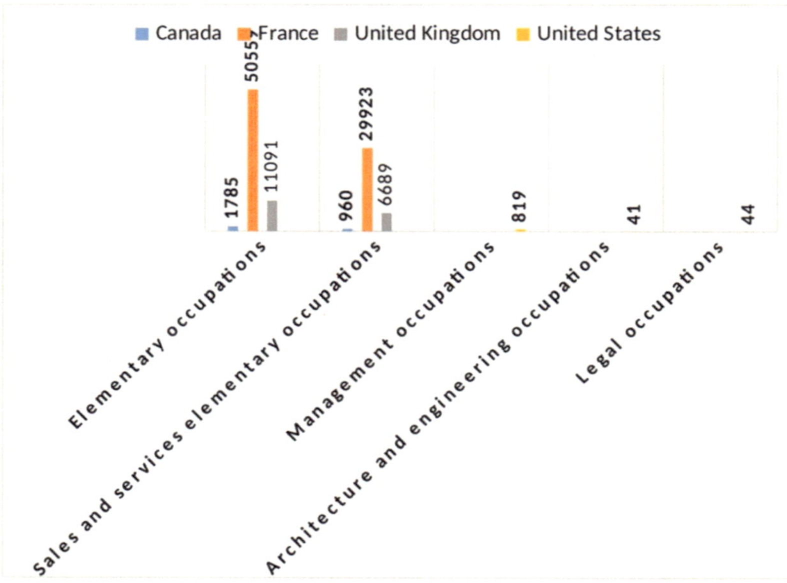


**Figure 9.**
*Occupation of African youth migrants in host countries. Sources: OECD.Stat Dec 2017 NB: African youth migrants age 15–35.*

is a correlation between recruitment challenges in certain industries, such as construction, hotels and restaurants, retail, and agriculture, and the illicit employment of foreigners. Overall, it can be concluded that in a number of nations, expatriates are exposed to undeclared employment, which has detrimental effects on their working conditions.

Both labor migrants and international students must be able to support themselves until they find employment. As shown in **Table 2**, tuition and fees for international students can be quite expensive, preventing many young people from studying abroad without a scholarship or grant.

### 3.4 Marriage and personal relationships

Marriage and family formation have been linked to adolescent mobility, especially among women in the global South. In Malawi, for instance, 'the transition to adulthood centers on marriage, labor, and school, all of which are linked to local mobility' [20]. This study discovered that marriage was a significant motivator for relocation, particularly for women. Among men between the ages of 15 and 24 who had never been married, 80% had lived in the same community for at least 5 years, compared to only 66% of those who were married. For women, the respective ratios were 82% and 57%. In addition, marriage-related migration was typically shorter in distance, whereas migration for employment opportunities was typically longer.

### 3.5 Culture and coming of age

Migration, whether from rural to urban environments or internationally, is frequently cited as a means by which young people pursue greater independence during their transition to adulthood. This may be associated with a shift from potentially more conservative rural environments to contemporary urban lifestyles. In Estonia, for instance, even though rural youth workers were concerned about youth emigration, they characterized it as a form of self-empowerment and self-expression that

| Country | Annual students fees (US Dollar) |
|---|---|
| Australia | 25375 |
| United States | 25226 |
| United Arab Emirates | 21371 |
| United Kingdom | 19921 |
| Canada | 18474 |
| Singapore | 14885 |
| Japan | 6522 |
| China | 3983 |
| Russian Federation | 3131 |
| Spain | 1002 |
| Germany | 635 |

*Source: HSBC (2013).*

**Table 2.**
*International student fees.*

was "forward" rather than "away" [21]. Similarly, in Mali, migration from rural to urban areas is described as a step toward modernity and "a way of life free from the constraints of the countryside" [22]. Kandel and Massey contend that migration from Mexico is a rite of passage for adolescent boys who share a 'culture of migration': those who move away experience elevated social status upon their return, while those who do not emigrate are negatively viewed by peers [23].

## 4. Migration across the mediterranean

### 4.1 A dangerous route

Migrants who enter Europe through the Mediterranean choose a more dangerous route due to border restrictions in Europe, which increases the risk of death, according to International Organization for Migration. An estimated 22,500 migrants have died on the way to Europe since 2014 [24]. International Organization for Migration reported that when it comes to Central Mediterranean route ending at the Sicily, only about a quarter of almost 1.5 million people who have arrived. According to the United Nations High Commissioner for Refugees (UNHCR), nearly 80% of migrants in Libya were young men, on average 22 years old, and these young migrants travel alone [25], as illustrated in **Figure 10** where 84% of African young migrants aged 15–35 travel alone in search of greener pastures. Most of the migrants who travel through Mediterranean route are youth.

### 4.2 Mediterranean Sea arrivals

In 2016, more than 362,376 migrants risked their lives by crossing the Mediterranean Sea to reach Europe. In early 2015, more than one million refugees and migrants traveled across the Mediterranean Sea in unseaworthy vessels. The number of new arrivals decreased marginally in 2016. 53% of those who have reached European shores so far in 2017 originated from the ten nations that presently produce the most refugees worldwide.

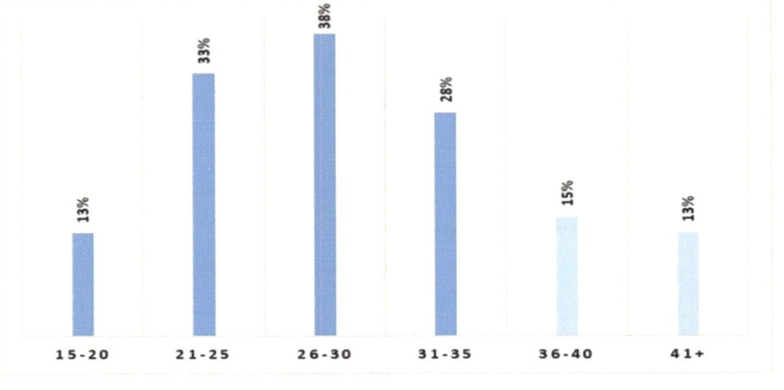


**Figure 10.**
*Aged of migrant who travelled via Mediterranean route. Source: UNHCR, Note: This graph is based on the In-depth interviews with refugees and migrants in Niger, Algeria, Italy and Chad (140 interviews) https://popstats.unhcr.org/refugee-statistics/download/.*

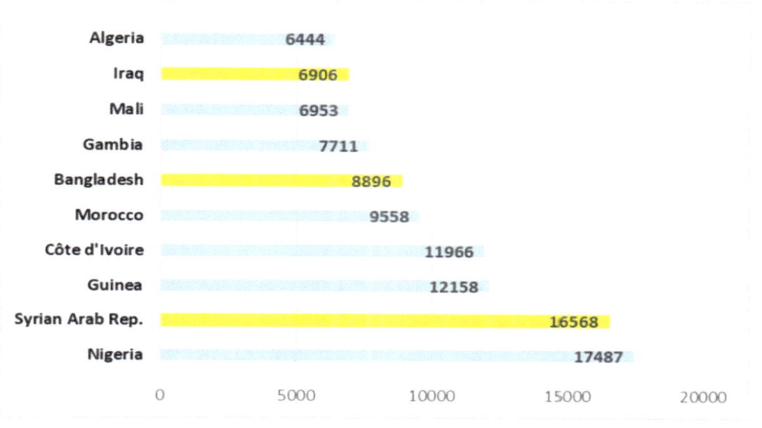


**Figure 11.**
*Most common nationalities of Mediterranean Sea arrivals (2017). Source: UNHCR, https://popstats.unhcr.org/refugee-statistics/download/ Note: the blue color represented African countries.*

**Figure 11** indicated that arrivals most commonly originated Nigeria, Guinea and Côte d'Ivoire. The majority of arrivals are from the Nigeria (17487), Syrian Arab Republic (16568), Guinea (12158) and Côte d'Ivoire (11966). In 2015, Greece overtaking Italy as the primary point of arrival and surpassing in the early 2015 the numbers for the whole of 2014. More than 67,500 people arrived in Italy, mainly coming from Eritrea (25%), Nigeria (10%) and Somalia (10%) [26]. IOM reported that Nigeria is among the top ten nationalities arriving in Italy through the Central Mediterranean route. Nigeria remains the single largest sender, with just over 17,000 registered arrivals through the end of September in 2017 [27]. In 2017 almost 83,000 migrants who have arrived by sea in Europe, the vast majority have crossed the central Mediterranean between Libya and Italy now the deadliest sea passage in the world. Five in addition Nigerians were by far the most numerous to arrive with 37,551 arrivals in 2016 [28].

According to the Missing Migrants Project (MMP) of the International Organization for Migration, 4757 migrants died in 2017. In the past five days around 21 July 2016–2025 July 2016, nine corpses have been recovered off the coast of Libya in the Central Mediterranean; one body was discovered in Al Maya on October 19, 2017 and eight bodies were recovered near Al Khums on October 21 and 22. Additionally, one individual drowned off the coast of Melilla, Spain, on October 22, 2017. The total number of fatalities in the Mediterranean in 2017 is now 2793. **Table 3** indicated that since 2014 there is a decline in number of sea arrivals

| Previous years | Sea arrivals | Dead and missing |
|---|---|---|
| 2017 | 171332 | 3082 |
| 2016 | 362753 | 5096 |
| 2015 | 1015078 | 3771 |
| 2014 | 216054 | 3538 |

*Source: UNHCR, https://popstats.unhcr.org/refugee-statistics/download*

**Table 3.**
*Mediterranean Sea arrivals from 2014 to 2017.*

from 216,054 (2014) to 171,332 (2017). The table continued reporting that number of deaths increased from 2014(3538) to 5096 in 2015, then we notice a decline in 2017 by 3082. The United Nations' Refugee Agency (UNHCR) indicated that 129 asylum seekers were missing and presumed dead after a dinghy launched by smugglers in Libya started taking on water and sank, leaving only four survivors from Sub-Saharan Africa [29].

### 4.3 Characteristics of mediterranean sea migrants

According to International Organization for Migration, more than 442,000 refugees and migrants so far this year have made it to Europe by sea [30]. Young migrants set out to secure better futures and face great risks in the process. For young migrants crossing the Mediterranean Sea to reach Europe, the voyage is marked by high levels of abuse, exploitation, and trafficking. Those traveling alone, those with low levels of education, and those undertaking extended journeys are more susceptible than others. **Figure 12** depicts the principal maritime migration routes. As for the Eastern Mediterranean route, the passage long used by migrants crossing Turkey into the European Union has become increasingly congested since the outbreak of the Syrian civil conflict in 2011. People fleeing conflict in Somalia, the Democratic Republic of the Congo, and South Sudan have long used a migration route in East Africa that has recently merged with Syrian routes along the easternmost points of the Mediterranean Sea [31]. The Central Mediterranean Route is considered the most deadly migration route in the world, with over 14,500 fatalities since 2014. IOM recorded 2224 migrant fatalities in the Central Mediterranean during the middle of 2017. In 2017, one out of every thirty-six migrants attempting to traverse the Central Mediterranean route succumbed [32].

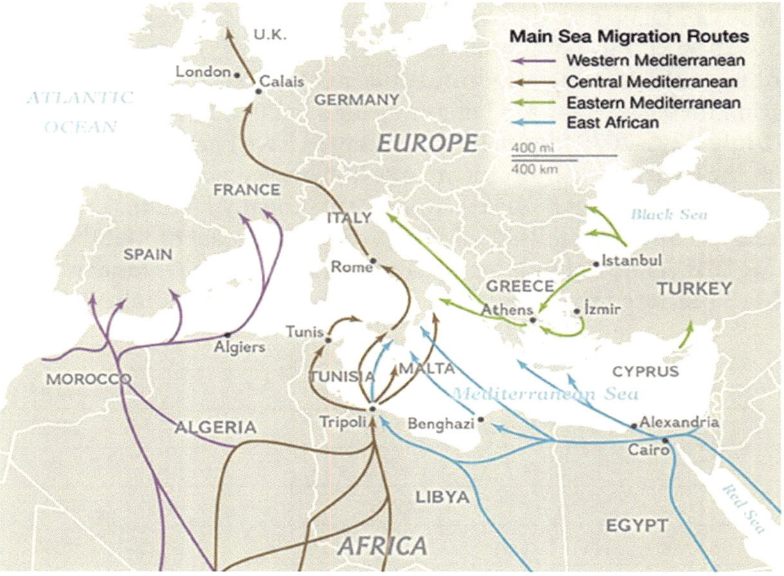


**Figure 12.**
*Main Sea Migration Routes. Source: Missing migrants project, international organization for migration; UNHCR; i-map; regional mixed migration secretariat, https://popstats.unhcr.org/refugee-statistics/download/.*

### *4.3.1 Age of migrants*

**Figure 13** shows that in the Central Mediterranean route most of the migrants are between the ages 14–24 years. According to the UNHCR, nearly 80% of the refugees and migrants in Libya were young men (80%), on average 22 years old, and traveling alone (72%). This is evidence that the majority of migrants along the Mediterranean route are young males aged 15 to 25 who are typically unattached. In contrast to Eastern routes, families almost never travel together on Western routes. Usually, extended families collect the funds necessary to support a member's attempt to reach Europe in the hopes that he or she will find employment and send money home [33, 34].

According to **Figure 14**, most of youth travel alone in central Mediterranean route while those that use the Eastern travel in groups. Previous research has raised concern

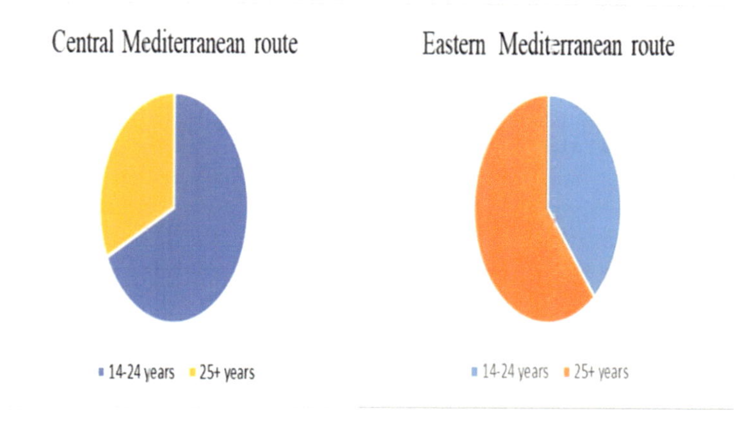


**Figure 13.**
*Adolescents and youth made up a greater proportion of migrants and refugees interviewed on the Central Mediterranean route. Source: International Organization for Migration, Displacement Tracking Matrix Flow Monitoring Surveys, January 2016–May 2017. https://migration.iom.int/datasets.*

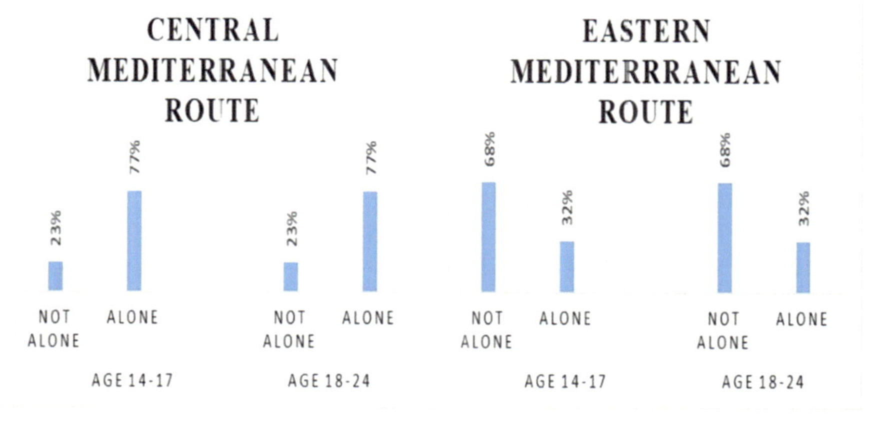


**Figure 14.**
*On the Central Mediterranean route, most travelled alone, while on the Eastern route, most travelled in groups. Source: International Organization for Migration, Displacement Tracking Matrix Flow Monitoring Surveys, January 2016–May 2017. https://migration.iom.int/datasets.*

over the rise in the number of unaccompanied and separated children traveling alone, which now accounts for approximately 14% of all arrivals in Europe via the Central Mediterranean route, as well as women, especially those from West and Central Africa, who may be victims of human trafficking. In 2016, 181,436 migrants arrived in Italy via the Central Mediterranean Route (CMR), which in 90% of instances involves transiting Libya. This represented an increase of 18% compared to 2015 [35], in contrast to a decline in the number of persons traveling along the two other major migration routes to Europe (Western Mediterranean Route (WMR) and Eastern Mediterranean Route (EMR)) [36].

### *4.3.2 Gender of migrants*

A previous study reported that almost 80 per cent of the migrants in Libya were young men (80 per cent) (reference?). The above **Figure 15** indicated that male travel more than females. Most migrants in Libya are young single men [37]. Women are usually from East Africa and transit to Europe over a short period, with the addition of some from West and Central Africa who are more likely victims of trafficking. Families traveling as a unit are rare, except among Syrians and Palestinians [38]. People who travel along Western routes are predominantly in search of economic opportunities, although some originate from nations that produce refugees. Gambians, Malians, Nigerians, and Central Africans, for example, may have fled due to conflict, instability, or human rights violations, or for political reasons [39]. Very few women were reported on the Western routes to and through Libya, and those who were, were usually victims of trafficking. Because they are fleeing some mixture of war, oppression, civil disorder, and poverty. Most of the migrants are young men. They make their journeys in sections, stopping and working at various places along the route.

### *4.3.3 Education of migrants*

The study found that migrants in Libya tended to have a low level of schooling, with 49% having little or no formal education and 16% having received vocational training or higher education [40]. The above **Figure 16** reported that most of the migrants the highest education is secondary education. The majority of migrants on Western routes

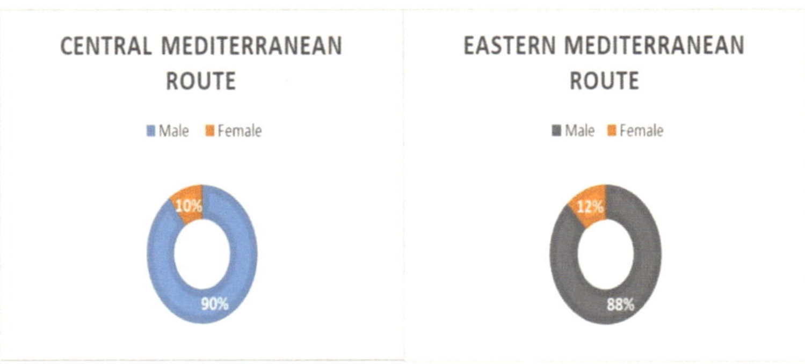


**Figure 15.**
*Aged 14-24 on the Central Mediterranean route by sex. Source: International Organization for Migration, Displacement Tracking Matrix Flow Monitoring Surveys, January 2016–May 2017. Note: Central Mediterranean route sample size is 6248 while Eastern Mediterranean route is 4811. https://migration.iom.int/datasets.*

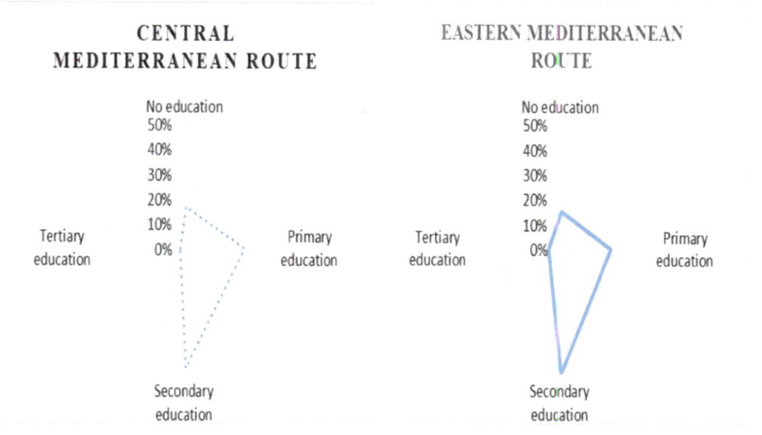


**Figure 16.**
*Aged 14–24 on the Central and Eastern Mediterranean routes by education. Source: International Organization for Migration, Displacement Tracking Matrix Flow Monitoring Surveys, January 2016–May 2017. Note: Central Mediterranean route sample size is 6248 while Eastern Mediterranean route is 4811. https://migration.iom.int/datasets.*

are illiterate, having bowed out of school at an early age, frequently because their parents could not afford to pay for their education or because they intended to travel to Europe. However, some are college graduates who were unable to obtain employment in their home countries despite having degrees. The majority have limited to no prior employment experience. Only about 5% of respondents waiting in smuggler-owned "ghettos" for a transport to Libya were female in 2016, according to data collected in Agadez, which remains the principal hub on the route from West Africa to Libya.19 Most were under 25 years old, and many had not completed their education.

### *4.3.4 Duration of journey*

In the majority of cases, migrants learn about the journey from friends, acquaintances, or members of their communities prior to embarking on it, indicating that the vast majority were aware of the hazards the journey entailed. When young migrants travel through unauthorized channels, they run the risk of being detained and deprived of their freedom of movement. The above **Figure 17** indicated that most of the migrant's journey is more than 6 months before reaching their destination or preferable countries. This is because the migration occurs is multiple steps. The journey starts from the country of origin, then internal migration before thinking of international migration.

### *4.3.5 Intended country of destination*

The massive majority of migrants who leave Libya end up in Italy often the small island of Lampedusa. Greece and Malta are also common destinations. The above **Figure 18** indicated that Italy, Germany and France are the destination countries that migrants prefer to migrate. According to the Dublin regulation of the European Union, the first EU country a migrant arrives in is responsible for them; southern countries say this places a significant burden on their border management [41]. Because southerners encourage migrants to migrate north, Germany, France, and the

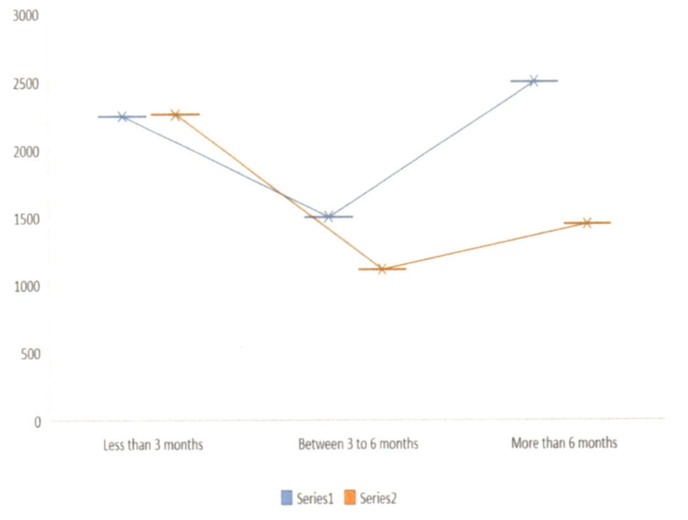


**Figure 17.**
*Aged 14–24 on the Central and Eastern Mediterranean routes by duration of journey. Source: International Organization for Migration, Displacement Tracking Matrix Flow Monitoring Surveys, January 2016–May 2017. Note: Central Mediterranean route sample size is 6248 while Eastern Mediterranean route is 4811; Series 1 refers to Central Mediterranean route, series 2 refers to Eastern Mediterranean route.*

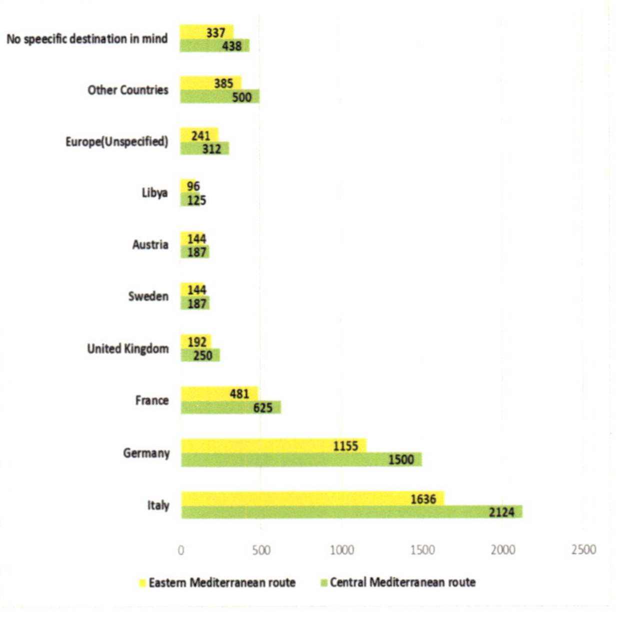


**Figure 18.**
*Intended country of destination at the time of departure as reported by youth (14–24 years), by migration route, 2016–2017. Source: International Organization for Migration, Displacement Tracking Matrix Flow Monitoring Surveys, January 2016–May 2017. https://migration.iom.int/europe/arrivals#content-tab-anchor. Note: Series 1 refers to Central Mediterranean route and Series 2 refers to Eastern Mediterranean route. https://migration.iom.int/datasets https://migration.iom.int/europe/arrivals.*

| | Central Mediterranean route | Eastern Mediterranean route |
|---|---|---|
| Held against will, forced to work and worked without expected payment | 1749 | 1347 |
| Held against will, only | 1625 | 1299 |
| Worked without expected payment and forced to work | 759 | 577 |
| Held against will and forced to work | 688 | 529 |
| Worked without expected payment, only | 562 | 433 |
| Held against will and worked without expected payment | 562 | 433 |
| Forced to work, only | 187 | 144 |
| Other | 125 | 96 |

*Source: International Organization for Migration, Displacement Tracking Matrix Flow Monitoring Surveys, January 2016–May 2017.*
*Note: Other refers to "received offers of arranged marriage"*

**Table 4.**
*On the Central and Eastern Mediterranean route, many youths experienced multiple types of exploitation.*

United Kingdom end up accepting more migrants. The inability to reach an agreement on the equitable distribution of the burden is primarily due to the political sensitivity of northern nations to immigration. Per capita, Sweden has taken in the highest number of Syrian refugees in Europe [42].

#### *4.3.6 Types of exploitation of migrant*

Nearly two thirds of youth on the Central Mediterranean route reported being held against their will and worked without expected payment, the same with Eastern Mediterranean route migrants, compared with about half of people 25 and older [43]. This experience is nearly as common as indicated in above **Table 4** that most of migrants are held against will. Older people, upon whom children depend to assist them during their journeys, may take advantage of their vulnerability. Children are susceptible to abuse and violence, as well as human trafficking for sexual exploitation or coerced labor [44]. There are numerous reports of youthful Eastern Route migrants falling victim to exploitative labor.

## 5. Conclusion

International migration can potentially yield favorable outcomes for young migrants, as it presents them with new opportunities, avenues for engaging in higher education, improved employment opportunities, opportunities for professional growth, and avenues for personal development. Nevertheless, some problems arise and vulnerabilities are conferred onto young migrants, particularly young women, during the migration process. The vulnerabilities encompass various forms of discrimination, such as those rooted in gender, migration status, ethnicity, or religion. Additionally, young migrant workers often face substandard working conditions, which are further aggravated by their relatively limited bargaining power and lower trade union participation compared to adult workers. Hence, the migratory phenomenon has the potential to serve as either a favorable prospect or a potential hazard for young individuals, thereby influencing their personal growth or conversely, impeding it. This outcome is contingent upon the implementation of policies and procedures that provide enough assistance to these individuals. The resolution of the Mediterranean migrant issue requires the concerted endeavors and cooperation of states, organizations, and communities. In order to efficiently solve this dilemma, it is imperative to also confront its underlying factors, which encompass conflict, poverty, and limited possibilities. Through the implementation of sustainable development initiatives, provision of support to countries of origin, and establishment of secure and authorized channels for migration, it is possible to mitigate the dire circumstances that drive persons to undertake hazardous adventures. It is imperative for African and European leaders to collaborate in order to establish a novel partnership with the objective of reducing migration from northern Africa into Europe. This collaboration should involve providing aid, particularly in Nigeria, as it is the primary source of migrants along the Mediterranean route. It is imperative for the heads of state of France, Germany, and Italy to collaborate in providing assistance to Niger in order to effectively address the issue of border control, thereby mitigating the influx of migrants transiting through Libya and crossing the Mediterranean Sea. The migration crisis continues to provide a significant challenge for both European and African nations, necessitating a compassionate and effective strategy.

## Author details

Lesego Selotlegeng-Mbe
Institute of Development Management (IDM), Botswana

*Address all correspondence to: dr.lselotlegeng@gmail.com

## References

[1] United Nation Fund for Population Activities. Framework for action on adolescents & youth. 2007. Available from https://www.unfpa.org/sites/default/files/pub-pdf/framework_youth.pdf

[2] World Bank. World Development Report. Washington, D.C; 2007

[3] Global Migration Group. Migration and youth. 2014. Available from: http://www.globalmigrationgroup.org/sites/default/files/0._Cover_and_Acknowledgements_%281%29.pdf

[4] ILO. World employment and social outlook trends for youth. International Labour Organization. 2016. Available from: http://www.ilo.org/global/research/globalreports/youth/2016/lang--en/index.htm

[5] GMG. International Migration and Human Rights: Challenges and Opportunities on the Threshold of the 60th Anniversary of the Universal Declaration of Human Rights. 2008; p. 53

[6] Migration and Youth: Challenges and Opportunities, Edited by Jeronimo Cortina, Patrick Taran and Alison Raphael on behalf of the Global Migration Group © 2014 UNICEF

[7] International Organization for Migration. Results of the survey engaging Diasporas as agent for development. 2005

[8] AU. Common African Position (CAP) on the Post 2015 Development Agenda. 2014. Available from: http://www.uneca.org/sites/default/files/uploaded-documents/Macroeconomy/post2015/cap-post2015_en.pdf

[9] International Organization for Migration. International Organization for Migration, Displacement Tracking Matrix Flow Monitoring Surveys. Geneva: IOM; January 2016–May 2017

[10] ILO (International Labour Organization). World Employment Social Outlook Trends for Youth 2016. Geneva Switzerland; 2016

[11] International Monetary Fund, World Economic Outlook, Subdued Demand: Symptoms and Remedies. IMF. 2016. Available from: http://www.imf.org/external/pubs/ft/weo/2016/02/pdf/c4.pdf

[12] International Labour Organization. World employment and social outlook trends for youth. International Labour Organization. 2016. Available from: http://www.ilo.org/global/research/globalreports/youth/2016/lang--en/index.htm

[13] International Organization for Migration (IOM). Unless stated otherwise, numbers of arrivals at sea are those provided. Available from: http://iom.maps.arcgis.com/apps/MapAndAppGallery/index.html?appid=3af3e9630ab849e99e6970a29aa25ff5

[14] The African Development Bank. Jobs for Youth in Africa, 2017

[15] ILO. Database of labour statistics. Key indicators of the labour market. 2017. Available from: http://www.ilo.org/ilostat/faces/wcnav_defaultSelection?_afrLoop=428483334979709&_afrWindowMode=0&_afrWindowId=null#!%40%40%3F_afrWindowId%3Dnull%26_afrLoop%3D428483334979709%26_afrWindow Mode%3D0%26_adf.ctrl-state%3Dnkidt7v7t_14

[16] ILO. Upgrading informal apprenticeship. 2017. Available from: http://ilo.org/skills/projects/WCMS_158771/lang--en/index.htm

[17] United Nations Development Programme. What is inclusive growth? 2017. Available from: http://www.ipc-undp.org/what-inclusive-growth

[18] Varghese NV. Globalization of Higher Education and Cross-Border Student Mobility. International Institute for Educational Planning, UNESCO; 2008

[19] ILO. A Global Alliance Against Forced Labour. 2005. Available from: www.ilo.org/wcmsp5/groups/public/@ed_norm/@declaration/documents/publication/ wcms_081882.pdf

[20] Beegle K, De Weerdt J, Dercon S. Migration and economic mobility in Tanzania: Evidence from a tracking survey. Review of Economics and Statistics. 2011;**93**(3):1010-1033

[21] Jentsch B. "I think that they should go. Let them see something". The context of rural youth's out-migration in post-socialist Estonia. Journal of Rural Studies. 2014;**34**:51-64

[22] Kovacheva S, Kabaivanov S, Roberts K. Interrogating waithood: Family and housing life stage transitions among young adults in North-West Africa countries. International Journal of Adolescence and Youth. 2018;**23**:4

[23] Kandel W, Massey D. The culture of Mexican migration: A theoretical and empirical analysis. Social Forces. 2002;**80**(3):981-1004

[24] IOM. Mediterranean update report. Migration Flows Europe: Arrivals and Fatalities. 2016. Available from: https://www.iom.int/news/mediterranean-migrant-arrivals-reach345440-deaths-sea-4655 [Accessed: 7 December 2016]

[25] The UN Refugee Agency. Mixed migration trends in Libya. Changing dynamics and protection challenges. The UN Refugee Agency. 2017

[26] UNHCR. The sea route to Europe: The Mediterranean passage in the age of refugees. UNHCR. 2016

[27] IOM. Migration flow to Europe. Quarterly Overview. September 2017

[28] IOM. Migration flow to Europe. Quarterly overview. June 2017

[29] IOM. Migration flow to Europe. Quarterly overview. March 2017

[30] United Nations High Commissioner Refugee (UNHCR). Refugee and migrant flows from Libya to Europe on the rise. 2017

[31] IOM. Humanitarian Emergencies, missing migrants, refugee and Asylum issues

[32] United Nations High Commissioner Refugee (UNHCR). Missing migrant project international organization for migrants. 2015

[33] IOM. The Central Mediterranean route. Migrant fatalities. January 2014–July 2017

[34] ILO. Youth and Covid-19: Impacts on Jobs, Education, Rights and Mental WellBeing. Geneva: International Labour Organization; 2020 Available from: https://www.ilo.org/global/topics/youthemployment/publications/WCMS_753026/lang--en/index.htm

[35] UNHCR. Mixed migration trends in Libya: Changing dynamics and protection challenges. 2017

[36] ECOWAS. A Survey on Migration Policies in West Africa. Second ed2016

[37] UNHCR. Desperate Journeys. 2017. Available from: https://data2.unhcr.org/fr/documents/download/58838

[38] UNHCR. Europe Monthly Update. November 2010. Available from: https://data2.unhcr.org/en/documents/download/61424

[39] UNHCR. Italy Update #10. December 2016. Available from: https://reliefweb.int/sites/reliefweb.int/files/resources/2016_12_UNHCRCountryUpdateItaly-December_2016_V8.pdf

[40] Mandic D. Trafficking and Syrian Refugee Smuggling. Evidence from the Balkan route. Social inclusion. 2017

[41] UNHCR. Mixed migration trends in Libya: Changing dynamics and protection challenges. 2017

[42] UNSMIL. Detained and Dehumanized, Report on Human Rights Abuses against Migrants in Libya. 2016; 17. Available from: https://unsmil.unmissions.org/Portals/unsmil/Documents/Migrants report-EN.pdf

[43] International Organization for Migration. Migration Trends across the Mediterranean: Connecting the Dots. Cairo: ION Middle East and North Africa Regional Office; 2015

[44] International Labour Organization. ILO Global Estimate of Forced Labour: Results and Methodology. Geneva: International Labour Office, Special Action Programme to Combat Forced Labour, SAP-FL; 2012

Chapter 7

# Socioeconomic Conditions and Infant Mortality: The Recent Experience of Francophone Africa

*Gervais Beninguisse and Claude Mbarga*


## Abstract

This chapter highlights the impact of socioeconomic conditions on infant mortality trends, based on the experience of 18 French-speaking African countries over the past 30 years. We use a mix of classification, decomposition, and regression methods to highlight convergences and divergences between countries. The analyses show steep declines in five countries (Congo, DRC, Burundi, Central African Republic, Niger, and Mali). For most (14 out of 18) countries, the analyses also show a narrowing of the rural-urban gap that is unfortunately due to slow declines or a rise in the risk of mortality in urban areas. Elsewhere, this gap remains steady. Decomposition analyses underscore the role of general improvements in health services and infrastructure, which appear as the main driver of change.


**Keywords:** infant mortality, rural-urban differences, socioeconomic conditions, countries convergences and divergences, French-speaking African countries

## 1. Introduction

Since 1990, child mortality has been nearly halved worldwide, but it is now concentrated in sub-Saharan Africa and South Asia, where the burden is greatest [1, 2]. Nearly, 56% of all child deaths occur in sub-Saharan Africa and 26% in South Asia [1–3]. At the same time, there are profound rural-urban differences in the chances of survival. Although sub-Saharan Africa still holds the record for the highest level of child mortality in the world, it also showed the fastest decline. Between 1997 and 2017, child mortality fell from 166 to 78 deaths per 1000 live births, a 53% decline concomitant with an 11-year gain in life expectancy [4].

Sub-Saharan Africa itself is not homogeneous, and its contextual diversity is likely to induce variability in child mortality. French-speaking sub-Saharan Africa exemplifies this diversity. This group of 23 countries[1] have French as their official language

[1] Bénin, Burkina Faso, Burundi, Cameroun, Comores, Congo, Ivory Coast, Djibouti, Gabon, Guinée, Guinée Equatoriale, Madagascar, Mali, Maurice, Mauritanie, Niger, République Centrafricaine, République Démocratique du Congo, Rwanda, Sénégal, Seychelles, Tchad, Togo.

and share the French or Belgian colonial heritage that still affects their economic performance and governance[2].

Yet there are questions as to whether this group of countries is itself homogenous. To what extent do they show the same trends in infant mortality? What similarities and differences can be found? This is the central question in this chapter.

Its objective is to describe trends in levels and rural-urban differences in infant mortality over the past 30 years across a sample of 18 French-speaking African countries for which data are available, and to highlight the impact of socioeconomic status.

## 2. Socioeconomic status and infant mortality: the expected links

Models of child mortality point to several levels of influence involving policy, community, family resources, parental characteristics, and individual factors [10, 11]. Socioeconomic policies influence child mortality indirectly through literacy, health behaviors and standard of living, residence environment, etc. At the community level, the availability of basic social services and infrastructure (markets, drinking water, electricity, health and family planning services, etc.) has a direct or indirect influence on child mortality.

Thus, socioeconomic theories differ according to whether they emphasize selection or causal effects [12]. Selection means a systematic filtering during the process of social mobility: people with better health have a greater opportunity to move up the socioeconomic ladder. Selection can be direct, with healthy people moving upward and unhealthy people moving downward. It can also be indirect if the standard of living exposes or does not expose people to risk factors (the higher the standard of living, the less people are exposed to risk factors, and the lower the standard of living, the more people are exposed to risk factors). On the other hand, causal arguments assume that the socioeconomic status of individuals affects health through influences that may be structural (living conditions, neighborhoods, urban or rural residence, etc.) or cultural/behavioral (knowledge, attitudes, values, lifestyle, etc.) but also depending on the political and ecological context [10, 13–15].

---

[2] In a study based on 63 ex-colonies [5, 6], it was found that the economic performance of the former British colonies was much better than that of their French or Spanish counterparts over the period 1961–1990, due in part to a more developed educational capital over a longer period of colonization. Even today, French-speaking countries in Africa differ from their English-speaking counterparts in having lower levels of development. Of the 33 African countries classified as "least developed," nearly half (16 countries) are francophone. See UN list of least developed countries in 2022: https://unctad.org/topic/least-developed-countries/list. French-speaking sub-Saharan Africa is also characterized by political instability, with recurrent internal and cross-border conflicts and little political alternation. Since the 1990s, some French-speaking African countries have been plagued by conflict. This is the case in northern Mali, in the east of the Democratic Republic of Congo and in some regions of Niger, Chad, and Cameroon, where the Boko Haram group is active. This is also the case in the northwest and southwest regions of Cameroon, as well as in the Central African Republic and Burundi. Most of these countries in conflict have insecure borders, where forced migration is developing with strong social marginalization, displaced populations, and sociocultural destructuring [7, 8].

Based on United Nations estimates [9], French-speaking sub-Saharan Africa, representing 23 countries, will have 377,653,521 inhabitants in 2022, accounting for 32.4% of the population of sub-Saharan Africa and 26.4% of the African population.

This study explores the influence of economic conditions on aggregate levels of child mortality by distinguishing the effect related to the change in the distribution of the population between different socioeconomic categories (composition effect) from that related to the influence of the change in the risk of death within different groups (rate or behavior effect). Because these two types of effects call for different policies — redistribution of economic wealth versus general improvement of health services and infrastructure, or public sector investments and diffusion versus selective modernization and individual progress — their relative importance deserves attention. The methods used in this study make it possible to dissociate these complementary influences. Most French-speaking African countries have experienced remarkable economic growth over the last 30 years, but efforts to redistribute wealth have not led to a significant reduction in poverty. Therefore, we assume that progress in reducing child mortality is mainly driven by overall improvement in health services and infrastructure that has led to a significant reduction in the vulnerability of the poor.

## 3. Materials and methods

The study covers a sample of 18 French-speaking sub-Saharan African countries and draws on a database from two main sources:

- The demographic and health surveys (DHS) whose infant mortality quotient indicators are produced by standard of living and area of residence to produce rural-urban differences) are produced from the DHS program's Statcompiler tool [16].

- World Population Prospect (WPP)[3] child mortality indicators [17]. To provide estimates of mortality over a long period from 1990 to 2022.

The analysis was based on decomposition methods. Decomposition methods allow us to determine the source of change of levels in infant mortality. First, a simple decomposition separates out the share of change due to variation in the distribution of the population across socioeconomic categories (demographic or compositional effect) from that due to behavioral change (performance or behavioral effect). When the behavioral effect is predominant, an advanced decomposition is used to dissociate the part due to an overall, baseline gain that reflects public policies from the part due to a change in the health returns to socioeconomic status (differential effect).

Note that decomposition methods best reveal the "sources" rather than the root "causes" of change. While it does not support specific causal claims, it can provide a detailed "an accounting of the proximate sources" of a change. In short, it does not reveal "why," "from what," or "from whom" the change occurred [18]. In our analysis, we aim to understand the sources of changes in infant mortality based on the type of residence (urban-rural) and wealth quintile.

The actual calculation follows the formula below, where $Y_t$ is a weighted average (by $w_{jt}$) of the values of individual subpopulations ($y_{jt}$) (socioeconomic categories). From this formula, the national change in infant mortality is decomposed as follows:

[3] https://www.wpp.com/fr

$$Y_t = \sum_{j=1}^{n} w_{jt} * y_{jt} \quad (1)$$

$$\Delta Y_t = \underbrace{\sum \bar{y}_j * \Delta w_j}_{\uparrow\ \text{Composition effect}} + \underbrace{\sum \overline{w}_j * \Delta y_j}_{\uparrow\ \text{Behavior effect}} \quad (2)$$

The dependent variable here is the infant mortality rate, and the classificatory variables are wealth index.

The extension of the behavioral effect is based on the socioeconomic category function $y_j$, which represents the performance on infant mortality of socioeconomic groups:

$$y_j = \alpha + \beta x_j + \varepsilon_j,$$

where

$\alpha$ represents the baseline performance, when $x = 0$;

$\beta$ is the increase in mortality related to a unit increase in the variable, and

$\varepsilon_j$, the error, (relative outperformance/underperformance of the group, or as the residual effect of factors other than, or as the residual effect of factors other than, not considered in the analysis $x_.$

The change in the value of between two groups is obtained as follows: $y_j$.

$$\Delta y_j = \Delta\alpha + \overline{\beta}\Delta x_j + \Delta\varepsilon_j + \overline{x}\Delta\beta + \Delta\varepsilon_j, \quad (3)$$

Inserting (3) into (2), we have:

$$\Delta Y_t = \underbrace{\sum_{n=1}^{n} \bar{y}_j \Delta w_{jt}}_{\substack{A \\ \uparrow \\ \text{Composition effect}}} + \underbrace{\underbrace{\sum_{n=1}^{n} \overline{w}_j \Delta\alpha}_{B_1} + \underbrace{\sum_{n=1}^{n} \overline{w}_j \overline{\beta} \Delta x_j +_j \sum_{n=1}^{n} \overline{w}_j \overline{x} \Delta\beta}_{B_2} + \underbrace{\sum_{n=1}^{n} \overline{w}_j \Delta\varepsilon_j}_{B_3}}_{\text{Behavior effect}} \quad (4)$$

$A$ : The composition effect.

$B_1$ : The baseline performance effect, which reflects the decline in infant mortality due to improvements in the basic health conditions of populations, is attributable to public policies.

$B_2$: The differentiation effect, which measures the decrease in infant mortality associated with the overall improvement in the standard of living of populations (improvement in the standard of living of different categories and change due to the socioeconomic effect).

$B_3$: The residual effect.

### 3.1 Distribution of the countries covered by the study according to the period of change

The study covers 18 countries in French-speaking sub-Saharan Africa, namely: Benin, Burkina Faso, Burundi, Cameroon, Central African Republic, Chad, Comoros, Congo, DRC, Ivory Coast, Gabon, Guinea, Madagascar, Mali, Mauritania, Niger, Senegal, and Togo. The DHS data from these countries have varying periodicity for studying changes in rural-urban levels and differences in child mortality. **Table 1** below summarizes the periodicity of DHS data for each country (time between the first and last survey). It shows that the duration of available DHS surveys ranges from

| Countries | Period | Duration |
|---|---|---|
| Benin | 1996–2017 | 21 |
| Burkina Faso | 1993–2017 | 24 |
| Burundi | 2010–2017 | 7 |
| Cameroon | 1991–2018 | 27 |
| Central Africa | 1994–2019[1] | 25 |
| Chad | 1997–2014 | 17 |
| Comoros | 1996–2012 | 16 |
| Congo | 2005–2012 | 7 |
| DRC | 2007–2014 | 7 |
| Ivory Coast | 1994–2012 | 18 |
| Gabon | 2000–2012 | 12 |
| Guinea | 1999–2021 | 22 |
| Madagascar | 1992–2021 | 29 |
| Mali | 1996–2021 | 25 |
| Mauritania | 2000–2020 | 20 |
| Niger | 1992–2012 | 20 |
| Senegal | 1993–2020 | 27 |
| Togo | 1998–2017 | 19 |

[1]*MICS 2019.*

**Table 1.**
*Presentation of the countries covered by the study according to the period of coverage of the DHS surveys.*

7 years in Burundi, Congo, and DRC to 29 years in Madagascar, over a period from 1991 to 2021.

## 3.2 The infant mortality transition in francophone sub-Saharan Africa

Overall, child mortality in the 18 French-speaking sub-Saharan African countries studied has declined over the last three decades despite some reversals in some countries (Burkina Faso, Cameroon, Ivory Coast, and Rwanda) between 1990 and 2010 [10]. French-speaking sub-Saharan African countries have each gone through a significant transition phase in child mortality. According to United Nations estimates [17], child mortality has declined from a peak of 139 deaths to less than 68 deaths per 1000 live births. The transition of child mortality can be assessed by grouping these countries into four categories between the following groups of levels, from highest to lowest.

- The highest-level group with infant mortality between 115.1 and 139.6 deaths per 1000 live births.

- The second group whose infant mortality is between 96.6 and 115.1 deaths per 1000 live births.

- The third level group with infant mortality between 73.0 and 96.6 deaths per 1000 live births.

- The fourth group with the lowest infant mortality, ranging from 0.1 to 72.9 deaths per 1000 live births.

**Figure 1** and **Table 2** describe the mobility of countries between the four levels of child mortality over the four time periods: 1990, 2000, 2015, and 2020. Overall, there

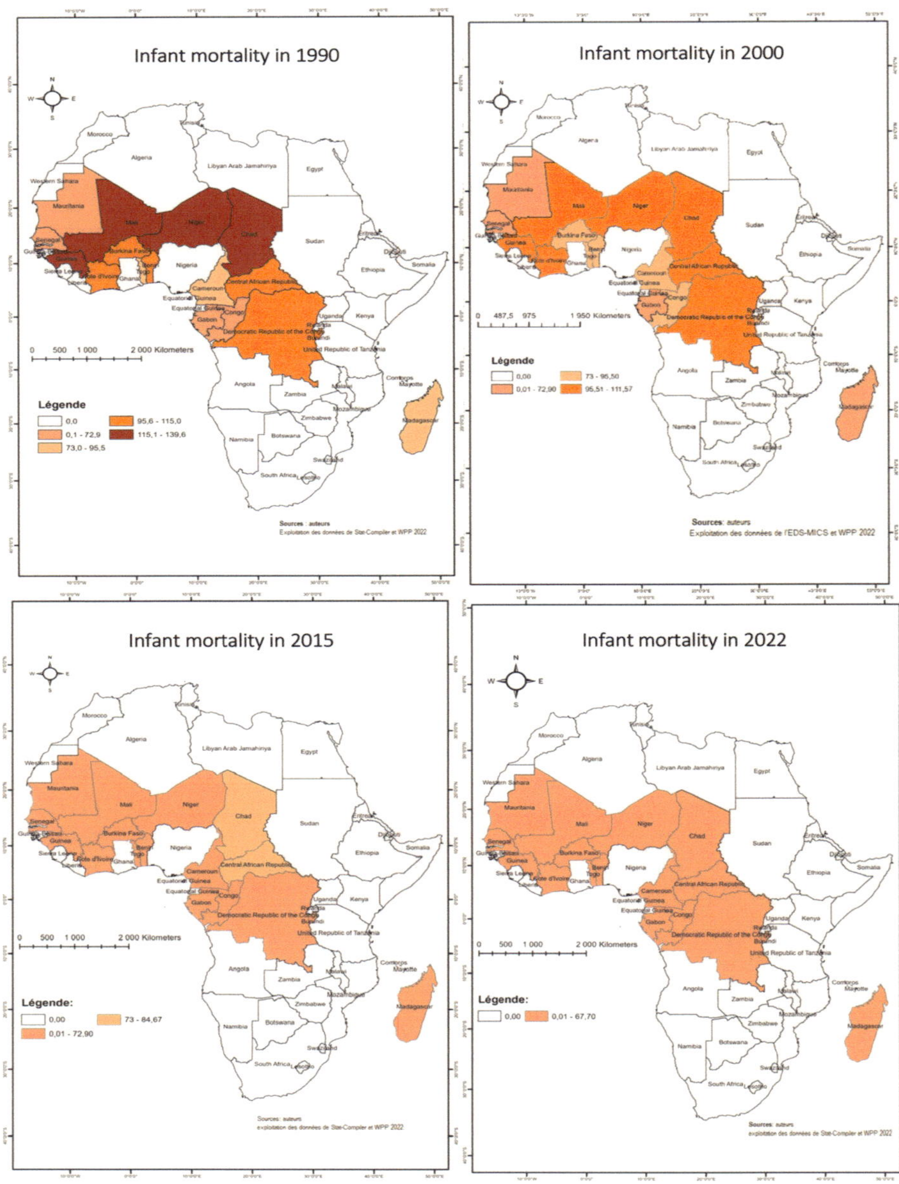


**Figure 1.**
*Health transition in francophone sub-Saharan Africa from 1990 to 2022.*

| Infant mortality level group | 1990 | 2000 | 2015 | 2022 |
|---|---|---|---|---|
| Groupe 1 (115,1‰ - 139,6‰) | Chad, Niger, Mali, Guinea. | N/A | N/A | N/A |
| Groupe 2 (96,6‰ - 115,0‰) | Ivory Coast, Benin, Burkina Faso, Central African Republic, DRC. | CAR, Chad, Guinea, Mali, Niger, Ivory Coast, DRC | N/A | N/A |
| Groupe 3 (73,0‰ - 96,5‰) | Cameroon, Madagascar, Togo, Comoros. | Cameroon, Burundi, Burkina Faso, Comoros, Congo, Togo, Benin | Chad, CAR | N/A |
| Groupe 4 (0,1‰ - 72,9‰) | Mauritania, Senegal, Gabon, Congo. | Mauritania, Gabon, Senegal, Madagascar | Mauritania, Gabon, Senegal, Cameroon, Burundi, Burkina Faso, Comoros, Congo, Togo, Chad, Guinea, Mali, Niger, Ivory Coast, DRC | Chad, CAR, Mauritania, Gabon, Senegal, Cameroon, Burundi, Burkina Faso, Comoros, Congo, Togo, Chad, Guinea, Mali, Niger, Ivory Coast, DRC |

**Table 2.**
*Distribution of French-speaking African countries covered by the study according to the downward trend in infant mortality between 1990 and 2022.*

has been a shift from the highest-level group in the 1990s, represented by four countries (Chad, Niger, Mali, and Guinea) to the lowest-level group in 2022 with 17 countries (Chad, CAR, Mauritania, Gabon, Senegal, Cameroon, Burundi, Burkina Faso, Comoros, Congo, Togo, Chad, Guinea, Mali, Niger, Ivory Coast, and DRC).

In 1990, Group 3 included four countries whose mortality levels were already at an average level, but which stagnated in 2000, with the exception of Madagascar which migrated to Group 4.

Between these two periods, there were not only certainly rapid changes but also stagnation. But overall, the transition in infant mortality has been significant but at different rates and levels in different countries.

### 3.3 Uneven progress in reducing infant mortality

#### *3.3.1 Overall rate of change by country*

Over the last 30 years (1990–2022), infant mortality rates have declined overall in French-speaking sub-Saharan Africa. However, the pace of the decline has varied across countries and between rural and urban areas.

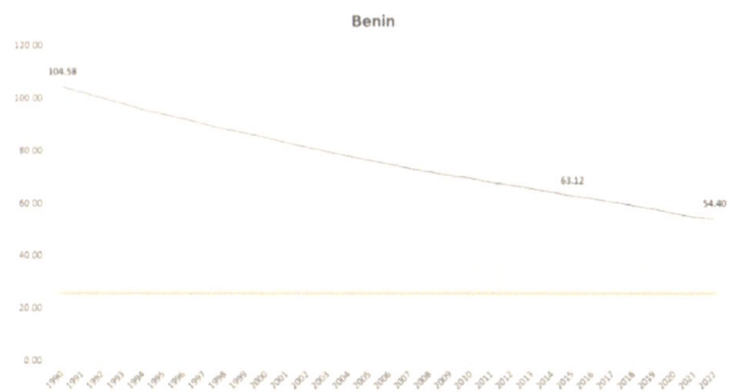


**Benin**

The evolution of infant mortality has continuously decreased from 104.58 to 54.40 deaths per 1,000 live births between 1990 and 2022. In 2015, the level was far above the 1/3 required by MDG 4, that is, 34.86 deaths per 1,000 live births. The value in 2022 is still far from the 25 deaths per 1,000 births required to achieve the SDG3[1]. The country must make a large effort to improve investments in health to achieve the SDG3 by 2030.

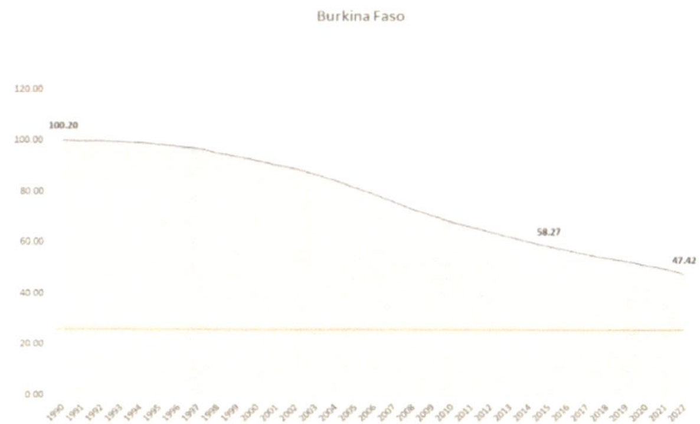


**Burkina Faso**

In Burkina Faso, infant mortality declined between 1990 and 2022, from 100.20 to 47.42 deaths per 1,000 live births. But at a different rate than the decline in Benin. Also, in 2015, the value of child mortality was 58.27 deaths per 1,000 live births, above the 1/3 (33.4 deaths per 1,000 births) required by MDG 4. Reaching the 25 deaths per 1,000 marks will be a difficult to achieve within 8 years. The country needs to provide increase its health investment.

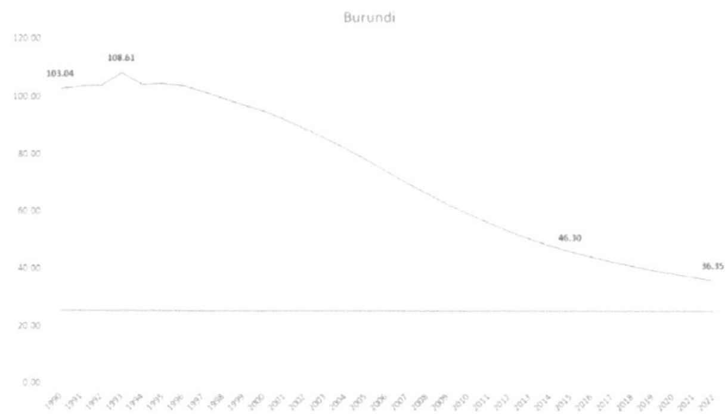


**Burundi**
The evolution of infant mortality in Burundi first increased slightly by 5.6 points between 1990 and 1993, and then declined slowly until 1999, and then a sharp decline until 2022, when the country shows a level of 36.4 deaths per 1,000 live births.
In 2015, the value of infant mortality was 46.30 deaths per 1,000 live births, higher than the 1/3 required in MDG 4, or 34.4 deaths per 1,000 live births. To reach the 25 deaths per 1,000 live births mark, the country must close the gap of 11.4 deaths per 1,000 within the next 8 years.

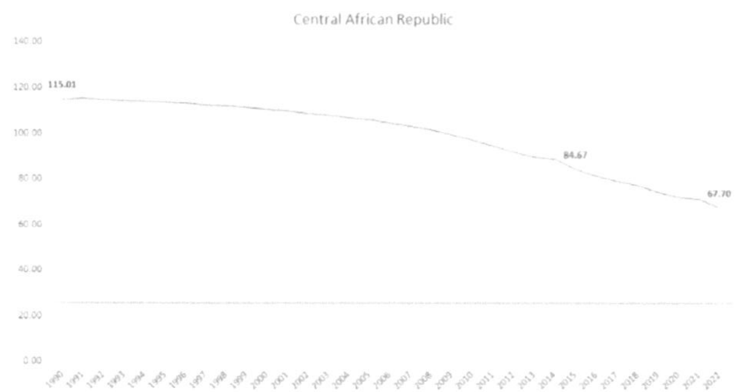


**Central African Republic**
The evolution of infant mortality in the Central African Republic shows a slow but significant decline from 115.01 to 67.70 deaths per 1,000 live births. In 2015, the country had not reached the maximum of 1/3 required by MDG 4 (i.e., 38.33 deaths per 1,000 live births). In 2022, the country has an infant mortality rate of 67.70%, which is still far from the maximum of 25 deaths per 1,000 births by 2030, especially given the overall downward trend in child mortality.
The country still needs to make efforts to invest in health.

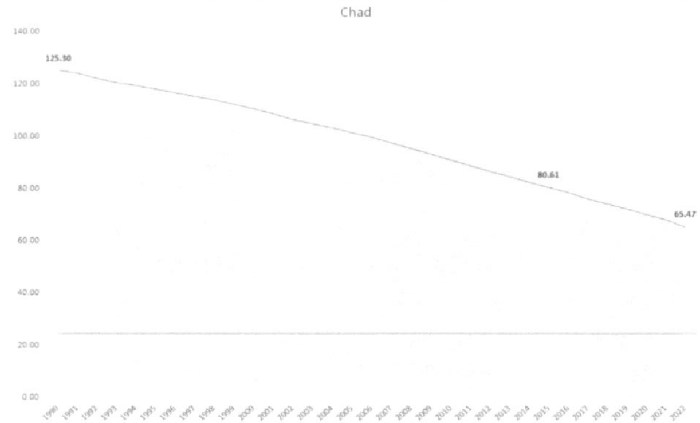


**Chad**

Infant mortality in Chad has changed considerably, from 125.30 deaths per 1,000 live births in 1990 to 65.47 deaths per 1,000 live births in 2022. This represents a decrease of 59.83 points. The country has not reached the bar of 1/3 required by the MDG 4, which should be located at most 41, 46 deaths per 1,000 live births. In 2022, the country has an infant mortality rate of 65.47%, which is still above the 25 deaths per 1,000 births threshold by 2030. The country still has considerable efforts to make in terms of investment in health.

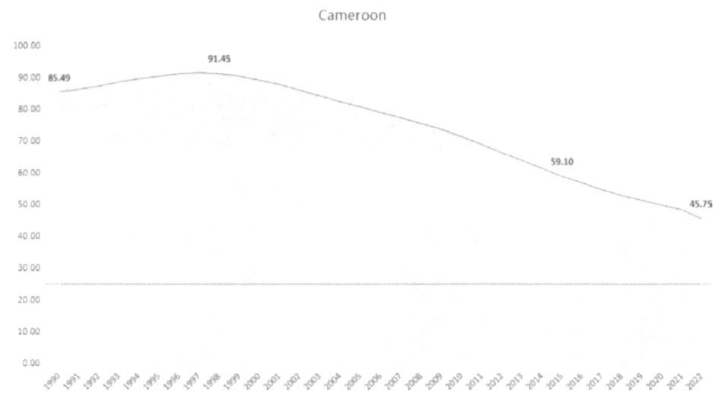


**Cameroon**

Cameroon has experienced two trends in infant mortality between 1990 and 2022. An increase from 84.49 to 91.45 deaths per 1,000 inhabitants between 1990 and 1998 and a decrease from 91.45% to 45.75 deaths per 1,000 between 1998 and 2022. In 2015, the country failed to reach the required 1/3 of MDG 4 (28.49 deaths per 1,000 live births). The value of mortality in 2022 shows that the country has not yet reached the minimum 25% for MDG 3. The country still needs to make efforts in terms of investment in health.

*DOI: http://dx.doi.org/10.5772/intechopen.1002675*

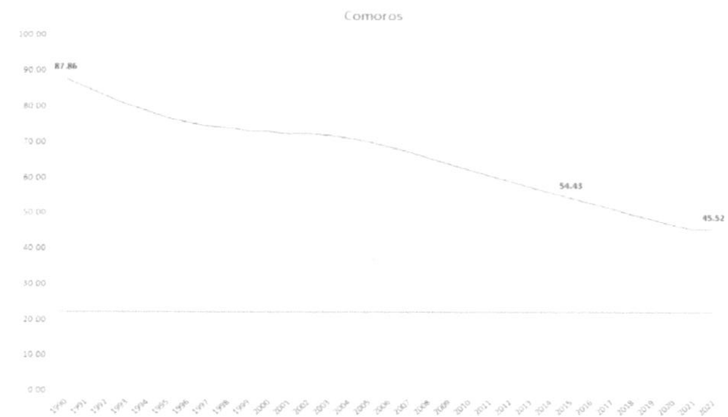


**Comoros**

Comoros has experienced a downward trend in infant mortality from 87.36 deaths per 1,000 live births to 45.52 deaths per 1,000 between 1990 and 2022. In 2015, the country failed to reach the MDG 4 threshold of 1/3 or 29.28 deaths per 1,000 births. In 2022, the country is still far from the 25 deaths per 1,000 births needed to achieve MDG 3 on child health. It is important that Comoros continues to make investments in health.

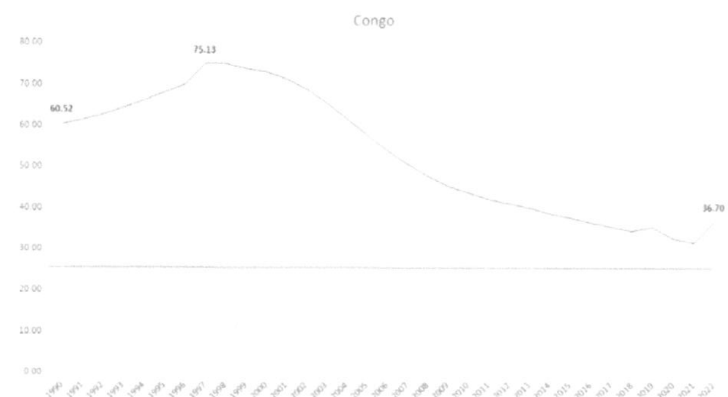


**Congo**

The Congo is experiencing several trends in infant mortality. It increased from 60.52 to 75.13 deaths per 1,000 live births between 1990 and 1998 and decreased between 1998 and 2021 when it increased again and reached 36.70 deaths per 1,000 live births in 2022. In 2015, the country failed to reach the MDG 4 threshold of 20.17 deaths per 1,000 live births. The country is at least 11.7 points away from reaching the 25 deaths per 1,000 live births mark by 2030.

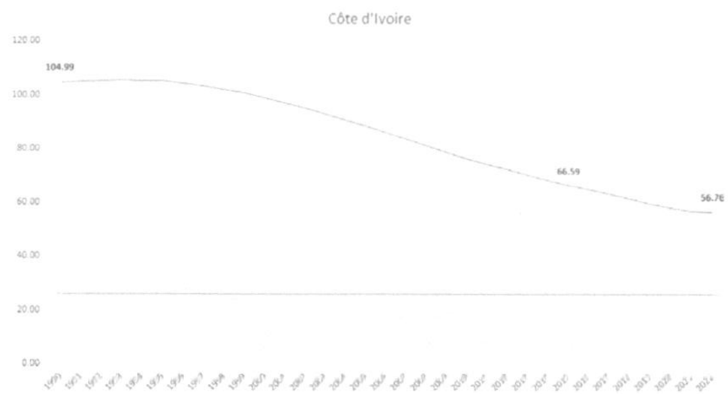


**Ivory Coast**

Ivory Coast shows a slow but single trend of decline in child mortality between 1990 and 2022. In fact, the country has a differential of 48.23 points between the two dates, and in 2015, it was insufficient to reach MDG 4, which should have been at most 34.99 deaths per 1,000 live births. In addition, the country still has a 31.76-point gap to reach the 25 deaths per 1,000 live births mark of MDG 3. Closing this gap will require further investments in health.

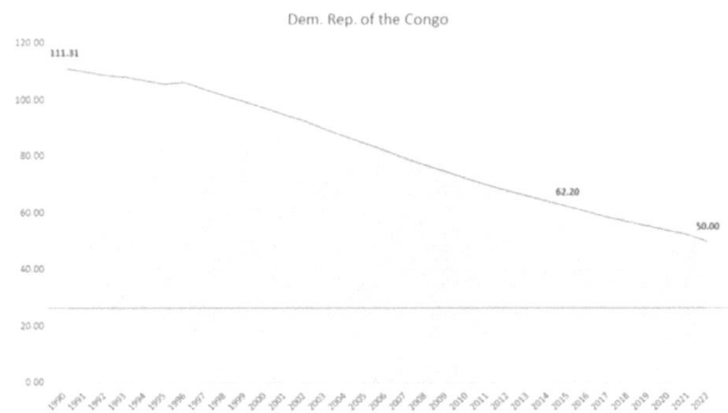


**Democratic Republic of Congo**
The Democratic Republic of the Congo shows a relatively slow change in infant mortality between 1990 and 2022. Mortality declined from 111.3 to 50.0 deaths per 1,000 live births between 1990 and 2022. In 2015, the country did not reach the maximum 1/3 for the achievement of MDG 4. In 2022, the overall level of mortality is still high (50.0 deaths per 1,000 live births) to reach the minimum 25 deaths required to achieve MDG 3 by 2030. This country must meet the huge challenge to invest in children's health.

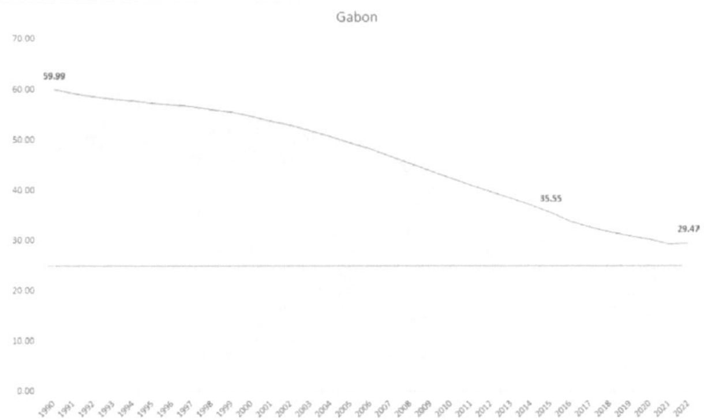


**Gabon**
Gabon's results on infant mortality are quite encouraging. In 1990, the infant mortality rate was 59.9 deaths per 1,000 live births despite the failure to achieve MDG 4 in 2015 (the rate should have been below 19.9 deaths per 1,000 live births). In 2022, this country is 4.5 points away from reaching the 25 deaths per 1,000 live births MDG 3 by 2030. This is feasible despite the slow pace of overall decline in child mortality over the past 30 years.

DOI: http://dx.doi.org/10.5772/intechopen.1002675

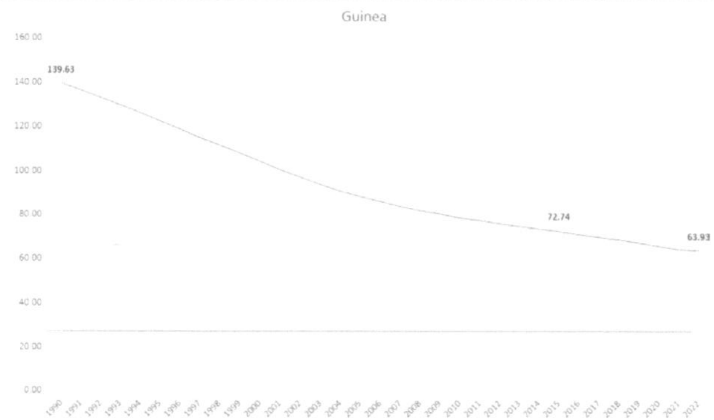


**Guinea**

Between 1990 and 2022, the country recorded a decline in infant mortality from 139.63 to 63.93 deaths per 1,000 live births. This rate of decline was not sufficient to achieve MDG 4 in 2015 (at a rate of 46.54 deaths per 1,000 live births). By 2030, the country must exceed 25 deaths per 1,000 live births. That is a gap of 38.93 points. It is important to make efforts to invest in health.

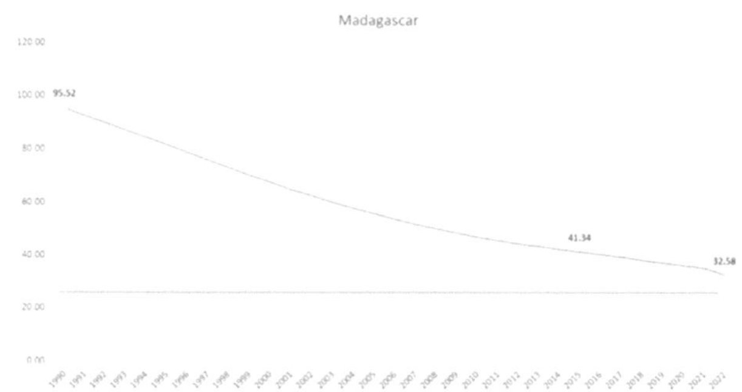


**Madagascar**

Between 1990 and 2022, the country experienced a significant decline in infant mortality from 95.52 to 32.58 deaths per 1,000 live births. In 2015, the country was unable to reach the 1/3 mark required in MDG 4, with a rate of 41.34 above the 31.52 deaths per 1,000 live births required. To achieve MDG 3, the country must reduce by at least 7.58 points to be below the 25 deaths per 1,000 live births mark by 2030.

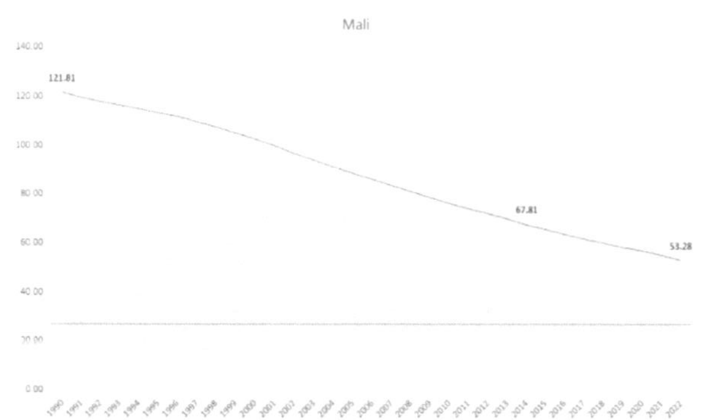


**Mali**

Mali shows a decline in child mortality from 121.81 to 53.28 deaths per 1,000 live births between 1990 and 2022. In 2015, the country had a child mortality rate of 67.1 deaths per 1,000 live births above the minimum 40.60 deaths per 1,000 live births required to achieve MDG 4. In 2022, the country is still far from the threshold of 25 deaths per 1,000 live births to achieve MDG 3 by 2030. This is a significant challenge and requires additional health investments.

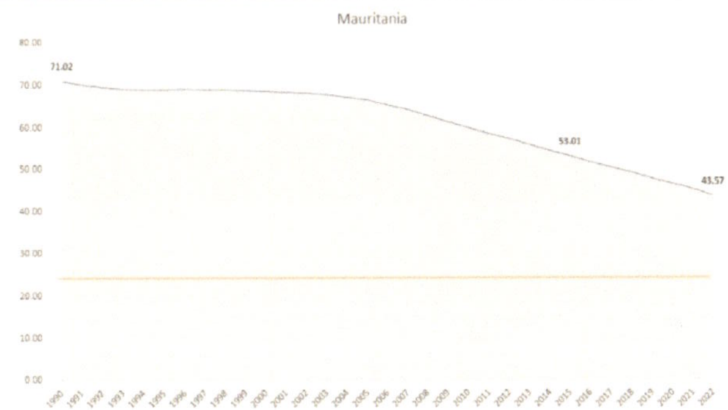


**Mauritania**

Mauritania has a slow rate of change in the infant mortality rate, from 71.02 to 43.57 deaths per 1,000 live births between 1990 and 2022. In 2015, the country failed to achieve MDG 4 (23.67). The country needs to make considerable efforts to reach MDG 3, which is 25 deaths per 1,000 live births, through health investments.

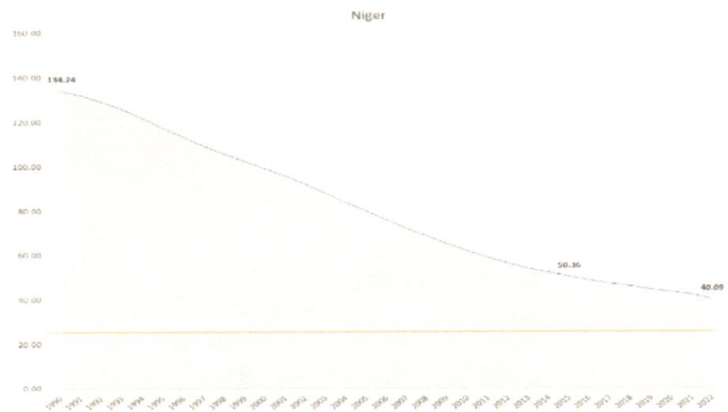


**Niger**

Niger's infant mortality rate has been relatively high, falling from 134.24 to 40.09 deaths per 1,000 live births between 1990 and 2022. Despite this sharp decline in child mortality, the country was not able to reach the MDG 4 target of 44.74 deaths per 1,000 live births in 2015. Moreover, the country should continue and provide additional efforts in investment on health to reach at least the 25 deaths per 1,000 required by MDG 3.

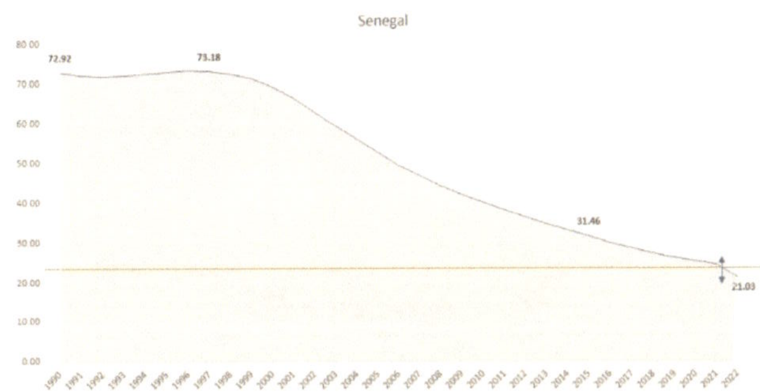


**Senegal**

Senegal also experienced a two-stage evolution of infant mortality, from 72.92 to 73.18 deaths per 1,000 live births between 1990 and 1997. Then a sharp decline until 2022, when the country has a value of 21.03 deaths per 1,000 live births, below the 25 deaths per 1,000, the minimum threshold for achieving MDG 4. Senegal has demonstrated a good performance in the health transition, reflected in the sharp decline in infant mortality, even though it has not reached the threshold of 1/3 set by MDG 4, that is, less than 24.30 deaths per 1,000 live births.

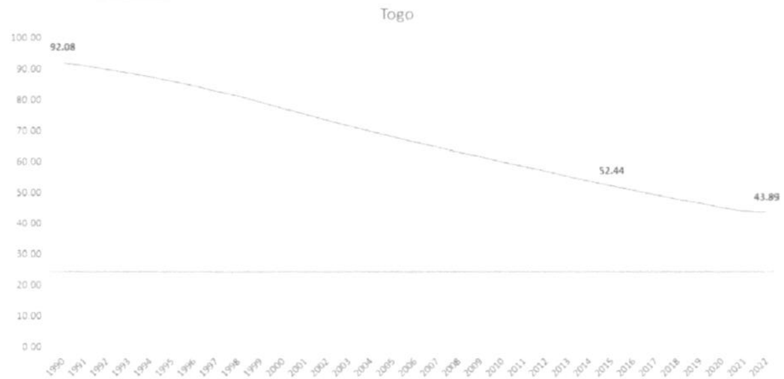


**Togo**

Togo experienced a decline in mortality from 92.08 to 43.89 deaths per 1,000 live births, a 48.19-point drop, between 1990 and 2022. In 2015, the country was unable to surpass the one-third mark in infant mortality (30.69 deaths per 1,000 live births). Moreover, the country must make considerable efforts to reach the mark of 25 deaths per 1000 births in 2030.

[1] *SDG 3 target for under-five mortality is no more than 25 deaths per 1000 live births. In this study, this target was assumed to be identical for infant mortality.*

### *3.3.2 Cross-country comparison*

The ranking of countries according to the level of average annual decline in infant mortality shows that Congo, DRC, Burundi, Central African Republic, Niger, and Mali are the top five countries with the highest decline over the last 30 years with respectively −4.86, −4.29, −4.14, −3.60, and −3.55. At the bottom of the scale are Togo, Burkina, Senegal, Cameroon, and Ivory Coast with respectively −1.42, −1.25, −1.22, −1.00, and −0.83.

At the global level, analysis of the estimated infant mortality rates of the WPP 2022 shows that Niger, Guinea, Mali, Burundi, Madagascar, and the DRC are the countries with the fastest decline in mortality since 1990, with respective variations of 94.15, 75.70, 68.53, 66.69, 62.94, and 61.31. On the other hand, the countries with the slowest decline are Comoros, Cameroon, Gabon, Mauritania, and Congo, with variations of 39.7, 30.5, 27.5, and 23.82, respectively. These results show that the countries with the fastest decline in infant mortality are those that initially had the highest mortality rates (Niger, Guinea, Mali, Burundi, and DRC) or average rate (Chad, Burkina Faso, Benin, and Ivory Coast) in 1990. These countries are all from West Africa, with the exception of Burundi and the DRC, and had infant mortality rates in excess of 100 deaths per 1000 live births in 1990. The geographic location of these countries suggests a climate that is not conducive to child survival (cold and dry tropical climate where certain germs and insects thrive), nutritional problems prevalent at that time, cholera and Ebola epidemics, and the incidence of other water-related diseases. The decline in infant mortality has been impacted by urbanization and efforts to provide access to health care, clean water/sanitation, and national programs to combat malaria, Ebola, and cholera. There are also numerous free vaccination and vitamin A programs for children.

### *3.3.3 Ranking of French-speaking sub-Saharan African countries by average annual rural-urban difference in infant mortality over the past 30 years*

Analysis of changes in rural-urban differences in infant mortality over the past 30 years reveals two major trends (**Table 3**):

- The increase or stagnation of rural-urban inequalities in infant mortality (four countries).

Within this trend, there are countries where rural-urban differences are significantly increasing (Mauritania, Comoros, and Cameroon), mainly due to an increase in the risk of mortality in the countryside. In these countries, the vulnerability of urban areas is reinforced, probably because of the persistent inadequacy and precariousness of health care provision. There is also one country (Benin) where rural-urban differences in child mortality have not changed over time, with a prevalent rural excess mortality.

- Reducing rural-urban inequalities in infant mortality (14 countries).

In these countries (Gabon, Ivory Coast, Togo, Central African Republic, Chad, Senegal, Burkina Faso, Mali, Madagascar, Guinea, Niger, DR Congo, Congo, and Burundi). In these countries, the significant reduction in rural-urban differences in child mortality is due to a significant increase in the risk of mortality in urban areas probably inherent to the growing phenomenon of rural exodus associated with the development

| | Infant mortality rate (IMR) | | |
|---|---|---|---|
| **Countries** | **1990** | **2022** | **Overall decrease** |
| Niger | 134.24 | 40.09 | 94.15 |
| Guinea | 139.63 | 63.93 | 75.70 |
| Mali | 121.81 | 53.28 | 68.53 |
| Burundi | 103.04 | 36.35 | 66.69 |
| Madagascar | 95.52 | 32.58 | 62.94 |
| Dem. Rep. of Congo | 111.31 | 50.00 | 61.31 |
| Chad | 125.30 | 65.47 | 59.83 |
| Burkina Faso | 100.20 | 47.42 | 52.78 |
| Senegal | 72.92 | 21.03 | 51.89 |
| Benin | 104.58 | 54.40 | 50.19 |
| Ivory Coast | 104.99 | 56.76 | 48.23 |
| Toga | 92.08 | 43.89 | 48.19 |
| Central African Republic | 115.01 | 67.70 | 47.31 |
| Comoros | 87.86 | 45.52 | 42.34 |
| Cameroon | 85.49 | 45.75 | 39.74 |
| Gabon | 59.99 | 29.47 | 30.52 |
| Mauritania | 71.02 | 43.57 | 27.46 |
| Congo | 60.52 | 36.70 | 23.82 |

**Table 3.**
*Distribution of French-speaking sub-Saharan African countries covered by the study according to the overall level of decline in infant mortality between 1990 and 2022.*

of slums. The five countries with the greatest reduction in rural-urban disparities in child mortality are Guinea, Niger, DR Congo, Congo, and Burundi (**Table 4**).

### *3.3.4 Sources of change*

Analysis of the sources of changes in infant mortality levels by socioeconomic status using decomposition methods in the 18 French-speaking sub-Saharan. African countries studied show the overall preponderance of behavioral rather than composition influences. In other words, the downward trends in mortality in the 18 countries are largely attributable to improvements in health care provision and behavior. The composition effect, that is, changes in the distribution of births across socioeconomic categories, had a more marginal influence on the decline in infant mortality in the countries studied over the past 30 years.

### *3.3.5 Ranking of French-speaking sub-Saharan African countries by type of behavioral effect*

An advanced behavioral effect decomposition analysis was performed to assess whether it was due mostly to an overall improvement in the baseline mortality or instead to an improvement in the returns to socioeconomic status. The results (**Table 5**) show the dominance of the baseline effect, suggesting an improvement in public health

| Countries | Rural-Urban differences in IMR | | Total rural-urban differences in IMR | Average annual change in Rural-Urban differences in IMR | Period | Duration | Rank |
|---|---|---|---|---|---|---|---|
| | Base | Final | | | | | |
| Mauritania | −9 | 11 | 20 | 1.00 | 2020–2000 | 20 | 1 |
| Comoros | 7 | 18 | 11 | 0.69 | 2012–1996 | 16 | 2 |
| Cameroon | 4 | 14 | 10 | 0.37 | 2018–1991 | 27 | 3 |
| Benin | 17 | 17 | 0 | 0.00 | 2017–1996 | 21 | 4 |
| Gabon | 4 | 3 | −1 | −0.08 | 2012–2000 | 12 | 5 |
| Ivory Coast | 16 | 11 | −5 | −0.28 | 2012–1994 | 18 | 6 |
| Togo | 18 | 12 | −6 | −0.32 | 2017–1998 | 19 | 7 |
| Central Africa | 28 | 14 | −14 | −0.56 | 2019–1994 | 25 | 8 |
| Chad | 7 | −3 | −10 | −0.59 | 2014–1997 | 17 | 9 |
| Senegal | 30 | 10.8 | −19.2 | −0.71 | 2020–1993 | 27 | 10 |
| Burkina | 32 | 9.7 | −22.3 | −0.93 | 2017–1993 | 24 | 11 |
| Mali | 48 | 23 | −25 | −1.00 | 2021–1996 | 25 | 12 |
| Madagascar | 32 | 0 | −32 | −1.10 | 2021–1992 | 29 | 13 |
| Guinea | 38 | 4.4 | −33.6 | −1.53 | 2021–1999 | 22 | 14 |
| Niger | 51 | 20 | −31 | −1.55 | 2012–1992 | 20 | 15 |
| DR Congo | 32 | 8 | −24 | −3.43 | 2014–2007 | 7 | 16 |
| Congo | 38 | −2 | −40 | −5.71 | 2012–2005 | 7 | 17 |
| Burundi | 32 | −10 | −42 | −6.00 | 2017–2010 | 7 | 18 |

**Table 4.**
*Distribution of 18 French-speaking sub-Saharan African countries covered by the study according to changes in rural-urban differences in infant mortality over the past 30 years.*

| Countries | Total change | Composition effect | Behavioral effect |
|---|---|---|---|
| Benin | −41.85 | −1.2% | 101.2% |
| Burkina | −30.15 | −2.4% | 102.4% |
| Burundi | −29.12 | −0.4% | 100.4% |
| Cameroon | −26.96 | −6.5% | 106.6% |
| Central Africa R | −77.96 | −4.9% | 104.9% |
| Chad | −25.96 | −2.5% | 102.5% |
| Comores | −44.01 | −1.0% | 101.0% |
| Congo | −32.94 | 0.1% | 99.9% |
| DR Congo | −28.50 | −0.3% | 100.3% |
| Ivory Coast | −14.44 | −4.8% | 104.8% |
| Gabon | −17.08 | −1.2% | 101.2% |
| Guinea | −50.62 | −0.3% | 100.3% |
| Madagascar | −52.05 | −1.2% | 101.2% |

| Countries | Total change | Composition effect | Behavioral effect |
|---|---|---|---|
| Mali | −72.48 | −1.1% | 101.1% |
| Mauritania | −33.53 | −0.2% | 100.2% |
| Niger | −68.96 | −0.8% | 100.8% |
| Senegal | −32.80 | −2.8% | 102.8% |
| Togo | −26.92 | −1.2% | 101.2% |

**Table 5.**
*Decomposition of the total change in infant mortality according to the contributions of the composition effect and the behavior effect in the 18 French-speaking sub-Saharan African countries studied.*

that lifted everyone in all the study countries. It is therefore mainly thanks to the action of maternal and child health policies and programs (vaccinations, nutrition, vitamin supplementation, measures to prevent malaria and diarrhea, medical care for newborns, etc.) that infant mortality has fallen significantly in the countries studied. The differentiation effect inherent in the variation of the individual risk of mortality was less important but noticeable. In most cases, this premium to socioeconomic status was negative, meaning it worked to narrow the gaps in child mortality between the rich and poor, a finding that reinforces the importance of public health investments. Only in Burkina Faso, Mauritania, and Togo did the gap widen (**Table 6**).

| | BASE % | Differentiation % | Error % |
|---|---|---|---|
| Benin | 145.87 | −46.02 | 0.15 |
| Burkina | 87.12 | 12.37 | 0.50 |
| Burundi | 129.93 | −30.51 | 0.58 |
| Cameroon | 179.55 | −79.61 | 0.07 |
| Central Africa | 168.20 | −68.27 | 0.07 |
| Chad | 80.79 | −21.08 | 40.29 |
| Ivory Coast | 214.74 | −114.65 | −0.08 |
| Comoros | 150.42 | −48.59 | −0.28 |
| Congo | 142.94 | −44.14 | 1.20 |
| Gabon | 36.03 | −45.32 | 109.29 |
| Guinea | 169.34 | −69.39 | 0.05 |
| Madagascar | 172.70 | −72.62 | −0.08 |
| Mali | 110.63 | −10.57 | −0.06 |
| Mauritania | 42.24 | 32.15 | 25.61 |
| Niger | 131.91 | −31.72 | −0.19 |
| DR Congo | 202.50 | −102.54 | 0.04 |
| Senegal | 135.24 | −35.60 | 0.36 |
| Togo | 85.13 | 14.75 | 0.12 |

**Table 6.**
*Decomposition of the predominant behavior effect into base and differentiation effects in the 18 sub-Saharan African countries studied.*

## 4. Discussion, conclusion, and policy implications

The purpose of this chapter was to describe trends of levels and rural-urban differences in infant mortality over the past 30 years (1990 to 2022) in 18 French-speaking African countries and to highlight the impact of socioeconomic status.

The decline in infant mortality levels was substantial overall, but its rate varied by country and period. The ranking of countries according to the level of average annual decline in child mortality shows that Congo, DRC, Burundi, Central African Republic, Niger, and Mali are the top five countries with the highest. At the bottom of the scale are Togo, Burkina, Senegal, Cameroon, and Ivory Coast.

Analysis of the evolution of rural-urban differences in child mortality over the past 30 years has revealed two major trends. In some countries, rural-urban inequalities have grown or stagnated (Mauritania, Comoros, Cameroon, and Benin) due to an increase in the risk of mortality in the rural areas. On the other hand, these rural-urban inequalities have decreased (Gabon, Ivory Coast, Togo, Central African Republic, Chad, Senegal, Burkina Faso, Mali, Madagascar, Guinea, Niger, DR Congo, Congo, and Burundi) due to a significant increase in the risk of mortality in urban areas probably inherent to the growing phenomenon of urban slums. Analysis of the sources of changes in infant mortality levels by socioeconomic status using decomposition methods confirms the preponderant influence of general improvement in health services and infrastructure on the reduction of infant mortality, which has led to a significant reduction in the vulnerability of the poor. One of the challenges for future studies is to identify the programs or areas of intervention that have had the greatest impact on this decline in infant mortality. But infant mortality remains high in francophone Africa and is associated with very high levels of out-of-pocket health expenses with a proportion of 50% in Congo, Guinea, and Togo, 51% in Mauritania, 52% in Senegal, 59% in Niger, 61% in Chad, and 70% in Cameroon against 8% in English-speaking countries such as South Africa. Namibia and Mozambique [19].

Ultimately, the main policy implications of the findings of this study are to continuously improve the supply of maternal and child health services, achieve universal health coverage (UHC), and to educate the target populations on their optimal use and the adoption of healthy behaviors.

## Author details

Gervais Beninguisse* and Claude Mbarga
Institut de Formation et de Recherche Démographiques (IFORD), Yaounde, Cameroon

*Address all correspondence to: gbeninguisse@gmail.com

## References

[1] UNICEF 2023. Mortalité infantile: 1,9 million de bébés sont morts tragiquement en. 2021. Available from: https://www.unicef.fr/article/rapport-de-lonu-toutes-les-44-secondes-un-enfant-ou-un-jeune-est-decede-en-2021

[2] Banque mondiale, ONU: le nombre de décès d'enfants dans le monde a diminué de près de moitié depuis. 1990. Available from: https://www.banquemondiale.org/fr/news/press-release/2013/09/13/un-global-child-deaths-down

[3] IGME 2021. Levels and trends in child mortality: report 2021: Estimates developed by the UN Inter-agency Group for Child Mortality Estimation. Report 2021, United Nations Children's Fund, World Health Organization, World Bank Group Emi Suzuki United Nations, Department of Economic and Social Affairs, Population Division 2021. Available from: https://childmortality.org/wp-content/uploads/2023/01/UN-IGME-Child-Mortality-Report-2022.pdf

[4] Tabutin D, Schoumaker B. La démographie de l'afrique subsaharienne au xxie siècle, Bilan des changements de 2000 à 2020, perspectives et défis d'ici 2050. Ined Éditions ed. Vol. 75. Population 2020/2; 2020. pp. 169-295. DOI: 10.3917/popu.2002.0169. ISSN 0032-4663, ISBN 9782733220450. Available from: https://childmortality.org/wp-content/uploads/2023/01/UN-IGME-Child-Mortality-Report-2022.pdf

[5] Grier RM. Colonial legacies and economic growth. Public Choice. 1999; **98**:317-335. DOI: 10.1023/A:1018322908007Grier (1999 & 1997)

[6] Grier R. The effect of religion on economic development: A cross national study of 63 former colonies. Kyklos. 1997;**50**(1):47-62

[7] Calvin M. S'engager quand on est réfugié centrafricain à Garoua-Boulaï (Cameroun). Analyse des formes de mobilisation et des luttes dans un champ associatif-humanitaire local. Carnets de géographes 12, 2019. Géographie(s) des mobilisations; 2019. Available from: https://journals.openedition.org/cdg/4493

[8] Zozime TA. Le Cameroun face aux réfugiés centrafricains: Comprendre la crise migratoire et les résiliences subséquentes, Note d'analyses Sociopolitiques. Vol. 1. Montréal: CARPADD; 2018

[9] Nations Unies 2022. UN Population Division Data Portal Interactive Access to Global Demographic Indicators (2022 Revision). 2022. Available from: https://population.un.org/dataportal/home

[10] Beninguisse G, Eloundou Enyegue P, Nsoa Mbondo, Tanang Tchouala P. Les tendances de la mortalité des enfants selon le statut socio-économique en Afrique subsaharienne: effet de composition ou de performance? In Tabutin, D, Masquelier B. (Sous la Direction de), Ralentissements, résistances et ruptures dans les transitions démographiques, Centre de recherche en démographie et sociétés, Presses Universitaires de Louvain, Université catholique de Louvain, Belgique. 2014. pp. 213-256

[11] Masuy-Stroobant G. The determinants of infant mortality: How far are conceptual frameworks really modelled? In: Franck R, editor. The Explanatory Power of Models. Methodos Series. Vol. 1. Dordrecht: Springer; 2002. DOI: 10.1007/978-1-4020-4676-6_2

[12] De Maeseneer J, Willems S, De Sutter A, Ilse Van de Geuchte MD, Billings M. Primary health care as a

strategy for achieving equitable care: A literature review commissioned by the health systems knowledge network. WHO Mars; 2007. Available from: https://pure.itg.be/files/2202299/2017phca0032.pdf

[13] Mosley WH, Chen LC. An analytical framework for the study of child survival in developing countries. In: Mosley WH, Chen LC, editors. Child Survival: Strategies for Research, Population and Development Review. Vol. 10. New York: Population Council; 1984. pp. 25-48

[14] Garenne M, and Vimard P. A framework for the analysis of the determinants of childhood mortality. Cahiers O.R.S.T.O.M. Seŕie Sciences Humaines. 1984;**20**(2):305-310. Available from: https://horizon.documentation.ird.fr/exl-php/accueil

[15] Meegama SA. Socio-Economic Determinants of Infant and Child Mortality in Sri Lanka: An Analysis of Post-War Experience. 1980. Available from: https://wfs.dhsprogram.com/WFS-SR/ISI-WFS_SR-08_Meegama_1980_Socio-Economic%20Determinants%20of%20Infant%20and%20Child%20Mortality%20in%20Sri%20Lanka%20-%20An%20Analysis%20of%20Post-War%20Experience.pdf

[16] StatCompiler. 2022. Available from: https://www.statcompiler.com/fr

[17] WPP. 2022. Available from: https://www.wpp.com/fr

[18] Eloundou-Enyegue P, Giroux S, Tenikue M. Demographic analysis and the decomposition of social change. In: Demographic, Analysis-Selected Concepts, Tools, and Applications. London, UK: IntechOpen; 2021. Available from: https://www.intechopen.com/chapters/75618

[19] WHO. Global Health Expenditure Database. 2023. Available from: https://apps.who.int/nha/database/Select/Indicators/en

Chapter 8

# Trends in Maternal Health Care Utilization in West Africa: Diffusion or Modernization?

*Siaka Cissé and Imad Rherrad*


## Abstract

Maternal health care remains a major concern in developing countries, but many sub-Saharan countries have achieved substantial reduction in maternal and neonatal mortality rates. This chapter seeks to account for the sources of these reductions, focusing on the role of socioeconomic changes and the health system and using Mali, Burkina Faso, Niger, and Senegal as case studies. The results of our decomposition analysis suggest that, overall, changes in the use of maternal health care reflect behavioral changes associated with improvements in the performance of health systems in these countries. Exceptions were observed for pregnancy and delivery assistance in Mali between 2001 and 2006, and in Burkina Faso between 1999 and 2003. Despite this overall progress, inequalities between socioeconomic groups persist, particularly in Mali and Senegal.


**Keywords:** maternal health, socioeconomic changes, health care system, inequality, decomposition analysis

## 1. Introduction

Maternal and neonatal mortality remain a major concern in developing countries. Sub-Saharan Africa is the region in the world with the highest level of maternal mortality and the lowest rate in the use of maternal health services. Despite numerous policies and programs to improve access to maternal care and reduce maternal deaths, many populations are excluded from modern care, especially the most socioeconomically vulnerable groups [1–3]. Costs (both direct and indirect) are disincentives for women and their households to use health services during pregnancy and childbirth [4, 5].

Women who belong to a disadvantaged social group [6], living in poor households [7], or have difficulties paying for pregnancy [8] may be less likely to attend antenatal clinics or seek assistance from skilled health personnel in child delivery. As the costs of antenatal care and child delivery-related services are not affordable for all households, women living in poor households are more likely to receive less care during pregnancy and more likely to give birth at home. Thus, exorbitant costs (both direct and indirect) of care services for some poor households partly condition their decisions to use maternal health services. These costs represent factors that may discourage women from going to health facilities for pregnancy monitoring or for assistance at the time of child delivery [4, 5, 9]. In this way, Titaley and his colleagues [10] note that "Cost was one of the main reasons reported by participants in all villages for using traditional birth attendants' services." Referring to additional financial barriers induced by the increase in the cost of service provision in rural Zaire, a longitudinal study showed a decrease in the use of health services by almost 40% between 1987 and 1991 [11]. According to these authors, 18 to 32% of this decrease can be explained by the cost of using these services. Therefore, a reduction in these costs could lead to an increase in the use of health services. Ridde and colleagues [3] point to an increase in the use of facility-based delivery following cost suppression in some African countries.

However, the impact of cost reduction on the increase in the use of health services does not seem to be verified in all studies. This is the case, for example, in Kenya and Tanzania, where the quality of services seems to be more important than cost issues, supporting the complexity of the relationship among cost reduction, provider motivation, quality of services, and use of health service during pregnancy and childbirth [4, 12].

Furthermore, women's education is widely reported in almost all studies on maternal health because of its undeniable effect on health care-seeking behavioral changes. Education facilitates, among other things, more egalitarian relationships within the couple, better communication with the spouse, and consequently greater decision-making power; better adaptability and negotiation skills; greater familiarity with health services; and better ability to communicate with health care providers and thus to demand adequate services [7, 13–16]. Thus, the vast majority of educated women are able to turn away from traditional practices that are harmful to their health. Education also increases knowledge of motherhood-associated risks. An educated woman is more likely to be better informed about the need for antenatal visits or skilled attendance at birth and the benefits of care for her and her children. All studies indicate that relatively better educated women make better use of maternal health services than those with lower levels of education, who are more likely to seek care late in pregnancy and give birth at home [6, 7, 15].

The same is true for the education of spouses. The education level of husband is equally important in the decision to use maternal health care, although it appears to have less influence than that of the wife [7, 17]. When educated, husbands can understand the benefits of antenatal care and assisted delivery for their wives, allowing them to be more open to modern medicine [18]. Furthermore, financial access of pregnant and parturient women to care is facilitated by the fact that husband's education is also associated with occupation and wealth of the household [19]. It is true that in some cases, the education of the partner has no significant effect on the use of antenatal care and assisted delivery compared to that of the woman [20]. But in most cases, this is because there is a high probability that an educated woman is in a relationship with an educated man [21].

The effect of education can go beyond individuals and affect the role of the community on health issues. For example, communities with more educated people may get organized to demand better public services and a higher profile for health on political agenda [7].

Clear disparities in access to obstetric care between rich and poor people and by level of education are combined with uneven distribution and inadequacy of human resources (health workers) and infrastructure, and poor quality of care provided by public health system [3, 22, 23].

In this context of inequalities in access to health care, several African countries have adopted subsidy and/or free health care policies in recent years. Among these, we can mention Burkina Faso, Mali, Niger, and Senegal, which have implemented measures of total or partial exemption from payment in 2006 (Burkina Faso) and 2005, respectively. Indeed, Cesarean sections are officially free in Mali, Niger, and Senegal, and deliveries are subsidized in Burkina Faso [3, 22, 23]. Even though these policies vary from one country to another, the objective is the same everywhere, namely, to make health care more accessible, particularly to the most vulnerable. These actions to improve health also include free treatment of malaria, one of the major causes of mortality in these countries, among pregnant women and children under five, particularly through the free provision of antimalarial drugs and impregnated mosquito nets.

Since the implementation of these different free and/or subsidized interventions, several studies have looked at their effects on the use of health services. This is the case for Ridde and his colleagues [3] who show an increase in the use of delivery in a health center induced by the removal of costs in some African countries (Ghana, Kenya, Madagascar, Senegal, South Africa, Tanzania, and Uganda). In the context of Burkina Faso, the subsidy and free care at the time of delivery has allowed for some empowerment of women in a context where the decision to seek care was subject exclusively to the husband's discretion [24, 25]. Subsidies and free health care seemed to contribute to an increase in the use of health services. According to Samb [25], the majority of women report that they no longer need their husbands to pay for childbirth-related costs, although most still seek their husband's "approval" before visiting health centers, out of respect for them.

As mentioned above, the role of health service provision and health system, more generally, in improving the level of service use during pregnancy and childbirth is more or less documented. However, the effect of changes on the population socioeconomic structure on the use of healthcare services at national level remains largely unexplored. It is true that in contexts such as those of poor countries, the costs of antenatal care and assisted childbirth remain out of reach for most individuals and their households. From this point of view, subsidy and/or exemption policies seem important for greater access to care, especially for the poorest, even if difficulties are observed in their implementation[1]. But certainly, the improvement in the supply of services alone cannot explain the increase in the national level of use of maternal care.

There are still very few studies that seek to identify the contribution of changes in average living standards and educational attainment on national maternal health service utilization patterns. Canning et al. [27] find that the reduction in total female fertility induced by the increase of an additional year of schooling is smaller than that due to the average improvement in schooling in many developing countries. This implies that the change, observed at an aggregate level, produces a larger effect than that at the individual level. This is a valid argument for exploring the contribution of

[1] Despite the efforts made under these policies and programs, difficulties of implementation persist. Even where the official policy is to provide free health care, there are difficulties associated with the implementation of payment systems, the official work exemption given to some health workers [3, 22] and the non-compliance with subsidized prices [26]. Therefore, changes in the demand for health care cannot be attributed exclusively to subsidy and/or free health care policies [25].

changes in the socioeconomic structure of the female population to recent trends in the national level of the use of health care. Examining the contribution of changes in the structure of the female population, and thus of improvements in their level of socioeconomic and human development, is all the more relevant as the living conditions of populations change and those of women with them.

Therefore, in the overall effort to improve health, socioeconomic development also matters. Beyond the improvement of supply through health policies and programs, highlighted by some authors [28], it is important to identify the effect of socioeconomic changes (change in the socioeconomic structure of the female population). Understanding the precise dimensions of this development would help guide actions to improve maternal health. This raises questions about the sources of progress in improving maternal health. Does the increase in the use of maternal health care stem from effective health programs and policies (more generally from the health system) or from global changes in the level of socio-economic and human development?

The objective of this chapter is to identify the respective roles of changes in the socioeconomic composition and the health system in general in the upward trend in the use of maternal care at the national level. The aim is to examine whether positive changes in the use of maternal health care are the result of the performance of health policies and programs (contextual health resources) or of an overall improvement in the ability of women of childbearing age to make better use of available services in favor of effective use of maternal health care. In addition, we examine whether inequalities in health care utilization between socioeconomic groups have increased or decreased by examining their respective contributions to the total change observed at the national level by comparing the situation in Mali with that in three neighboring countries (Burkina Faso, Niger, and Senegal).

The rest of the chapter is structured as follows: Section 2 present the data, the methodology, and the variables, while Section 3 reports and discusses the results. Section 4 concludes.

## 2. Data, methodology, and variables

### 2.1 Data sources

The dataset used for this chapter comes from the Demographic and Health Survey (DHS). The DHS are nationally representative surveys, conducted in different countries including Sub-Saharan Africa. We focus on three rounds for each country, namely, Mali (2001, 2006, 2012), Burkina Faso (1999, 2003, 2010), Niger (1998, 2006, 2012), and Senegal (1997, 2005, 2011).

With respect to Mali, it is important to note that the last survey (2012) occurred in the context of high political instability coupled with terrorism conflict in the northern and the central regions. So, it did not fully cover the national territory, missing the northern area (Timbuktu, Gao, and Kidal regions) and three circles of the Mopti region located in the center of the country (Douentza, Ténenkou, and Youwarou). Therefore, the 2012 data may not be comparable to the previous data, which were carried out on all regions of the country and according to a sampling procedure stratified by the region and place of residence. To circumvent this problem, we chose to work only on the southern zone, consisting of the first five regions (Kayes, Koulikoro, Sikasso, Ségou, and Mopti located in the south and center of the country, respectively) and the district of Bamako (the capital) for the examination of trends and comparison with other countries.

## 2.2 Methodology

In terms of methodology, the questions and hypotheses formulated in this work are addressed by means of the decomposition method developed by Eloundou-Enyegue and Giroux (2010). The decomposition method is based on the principle that the prevalence of maternal health service utilization at the national level ($Y_t$) is an average of the prevalence in the different socioeconomic categories ($y_{it}$) weighted by the proportion of women in each category at the same time t ($_{\text{wit}}$). The basic decomposition formula is obtained by expressing the national performance as a weighted average of group performance.

$$Y_t = \sum w_{it} * y_{it} \tag{1}$$

$Y$ is the national average for the substantive variable (health service utilization during pregnancy or delivery at the national level). $y_{it}$ is the prevalence of maternal health service utilization for group I in year $t$. $w_{it}$ is the proportion of women belonging to group i at time t.

Based on this formula, the change in the prevalence of maternal health service utilization at the national level can be broken down as follows:

$$\Delta Y = \sum \bar{y_l} * \Delta w_i + \sum \bar{w_l} * \Delta y_i \tag{2}$$

The decomposition thus expresses the total variation due to the change in "composition" (first term in the above equation) and due to "performance/behavior" within different socioeconomic classes.

For the advanced decomposition, the performance effect is further decomposed, noting that the performance of a given group (i) can be expressed as a function of another variable(s). In the case of a linear relationship, for example,

$$y_{it} = \alpha_t + \beta_t x_{it} + \mu_{it} \tag{3}$$

where the constant $\alpha$ represents baseline performance when $x = 0$, β is the increase in prevalence of service use associated with a unit increase in variable $X$ (in our case, household socioeconomic status or female education level), and $\mu$ is the error that is interpreted as the residual effect of factors other than $X$ not considered in the analysis.

In this case, the change in the value of $y_i$ between two periods is obtained as follows:

$$\Delta y_i = \Delta\alpha + \bar{\beta}\Delta x_i + \bar{x_l}\Delta\beta + \Delta\mu_i \tag{4}$$

Since the definitions of the categories of $x$ do not change between dates $t_1$ and $t_2$, the second term in this equation is equal to zero, and $x_i = x_i$.

Thus, the equation is reduced to:

$$\Delta y_i = \Delta\alpha + x_i\Delta\beta + \Delta\mu_i \tag{5}$$

Replacing this Eq. (5) in the basic decomposition Eq. (2) gives the general equation for the advanced decomposition below:

$$\Delta Y = \sum_j \bar{Y}_J * \Delta w_j + \sum_j \bar{w}_J * \Delta\alpha + \sum_j \bar{w}_J * x_j \Delta\beta + \sum_j \bar{w}_J * \Delta\mu_j \qquad (6)$$

The first term in this advanced decomposition equation represents the compositional effect, and the last three components refer respectively to the change attributable to improvement in basic health conditions, the effect of differentiating the prevalence of health service use by the classification variable used, and the residual effect of other variables not considered.

## 2.3 Variables

### *2.3.1 Prevalence of prenatal consultations and assisted deliveries*

The main interest variable is the maternal health care service utilization. The variable is constructed using the women's questionnaire. Women aged 15 to 49 who had their last birth in the 5 years preceding the surveys were asked whether they had received antenatal care from a health worker at least once and whether they were assisted by a trained provider (doctors, nurses, midwives, and matrons) at the time of childbirth. The maternal health service utilization is defined as a dummy variable if a woman who had a child in the last 5 years responded "yes" and 0 otherwise. These individuals' responses are used to calculate the national prevalence of antenatal visits and assisted deliveries for all countries and years.

### *2.3.2 Socioeconomic resources of the context: Decomposition of the socioeconomic and human structure of the female population of reproductive age*

National variables of living standard indicators and education are calculated. More concretely, the national proportions of women of childbearing age in each standard of living (low, intermediate, and high) and education category (none, primary, and secondary or higher) are calculated to see how these proportions change over time. Any temporal increase in the national proportions of women living in the most affluent households with high levels of education is broadly interpreted as an improvement in national socioeconomic and human development.

### *2.3.3 Change in socioeconomic situation at the national level: Standardized living by country*

Given that the surveys were conducted at different dates, the living standard indicators available in the databases cannot be used for comparison purposes. Indeed, the households in the different surveys are not classified according to the same standard of living score scale, which varies from 1 year to another. We combined the data from three DHS round to estimate how the distribution of women by living standard categories changes over time within each country and the implication that this structural change may have on the national level of health care utilization.

We then use the characteristics of the housing and the facilities owned by households in a Principal Component Analysis (PCA) procedure to construct our country-specific standard of living indicators. These indicators are calculated, taking into

| Country | DHS round | Indicator of living conditions | | | Total |
|---|---|---|---|---|---|
| | | Low | Middle | High | |
| Burkina Faso | 1999 | 53.7 | 23.4 | 22.8 | 100.0 |
| | 2003 | 43.3 | 25.0 | 31.8 | 100.0 |
| | 2010 | 33.4 | 31.2 | 35.3 | 100.0 |
| | Total | 40.5 | 27.7 | 31.9 | 100.0 |
| Mali | 2001 | 18.0 | 59.0 | 23.0 | 100.0 |
| | 2006 | 14.7 | 56.8 | 28.5 | 100.0 |
| | 2012 | 7.1 | 58.7 | 34.2 | 100.0 |
| | Total | 13.7 | 58.1 | 28.2 | 100.0 |
| Niger | 1998 | 73.7 | 12.9 | 13.4 | 100.0 |
| | 2006 | 72.7 | 14.0 | 13.3 | 100.0 |
| | 2012 | 60.3 | 20.6 | 19.1 | 100.0 |
| | Total | 68.0 | 16.3 | 15.6 | 100.0 |
| Senegal | 1997 | 19.8 | 21.1 | 59.2 | 100.0 |
| | 2005 | 11.2 | 19.8 | 69.1 | 100.0 |
| | 2011 | 8.4 | 19.5 | 72.1 | 100.0 |
| | Total | 11.9 | 20.0 | 68.1 | 100.0 |

**Table 1.**
*Distribution of women aged 15–49 by standardized standard of living, by country and year.*

account the specificities between urban and rural areas, in order to assess the living environment of a household compared to households living in a similar environment. The choice of an indicator calculated separately by environment is justified by the vast socioeconomic and infrastructure disparities that are found between urban and rural areas in most sub-Saharan countries [29–31]. The main factors derived from the PCA are used to construct categories of households, prioritized on a standard of living scale. For each of the four countries, these factors are divided into three quantiles: The first third of households are considered as having a low standard of living, the second as the intermediate group, and the last third represents households with a high standard of living.

The distribution of women of childbearing age by standard of living categories, shown in **Table 1**, shows an increase in the proportion of women living in households with better living conditions, except for the period 1998–2006 for Niger.

### *2.3.4 Trends in educational attainment at the national level*

Another indicator used in the decomposition procedure is the change in the distribution of women by educational attainment at the national level. The level of education, which we use to perform the aggregate calculation, refers to the highest level of education attained by women at the time of the surveys. This variable, available in the databases, has been categorized in three modalities: "No level," "Primary," and "Secondary or higher."

| Country | DHS round | Education level | | | Total |
|---|---|---|---|---|---|
| | | No education | Primary | Secondary and more | |
| Burkina Faso | 1999 | 85.8 | 8.4 | 5.8 | 100.0 |
| | 2003 | 80.3 | 11.0 | 8.7 | 100.0 |
| | 2010 | 74.0 | 13.6 | 12.4 | 100.0 |
| | Total | 78.3 | 11.8 | 9.9 | 100.0 |
| Mali | 2001 | 80.0 | 11.3 | 8.7 | 100.0 |
| | 2006 | 78.2 | 11.4 | 10.3 | 100.0 |
| | 2012 | 75.8 | 9.3 | 14.9 | 100.0 |
| | Total | 78.2 | 10.8 | 11.0 | 100.0 |
| Niger | 1998 | 84.8 | 9.9 | 5.3 | 100.0 |
| | 2006 | 83.5 | 10.4 | 6.1 | 100.0 |
| | 2012 | 80.1 | 11.4 | 8.5 | 100.0 |
| | Total | 82.5 | 10.7 | 6.8 | 100.0 |
| Senegal | 1997 | 66.6 | 20.9 | 12.5 | 100.0 |
| | 2005 | 59.6 | 25.2 | 15.2 | 100.0 |
| | 2011 | 57.9 | 21.8 | 20.4 | 100.0 |
| | Total | 60.4 | 22.9 | 16.7 | 100.0 |

**Table 2.**
*Distribution of women by standardized standard of living, education level by country, and year.*

The data (**Table 2**) show progress in the average education levels of women of reproductive age. Progress is slow overall, although Senegal is ahead of the others. Progress is slowest in Niger, followed by Burkina Faso, and Mali.

## 3. Results

### 3.1 Trends in maternal health services utilization

The results indicate that antenatal visits are more frequent in Burkina Faso and Senegal ahead of Mali and Niger. Mali has the lowest current rate of antenatal care utilization. Over the past twenty years, the prevalence of prenatal consultations has increased in all four countries but at different rates. Maternal care has greatly increased in Burkina Faso and Niger, particularly during the periods 2003–2010 in Burkina and 2006–2012 in Niger, when it almost doubled. Senegal and Mali also registered an increase in maternal care use, but it was slower compared to Burkina Faso and Niger. In terms of absolute levels, Senegal has been ahead of these other countries for a long time and already had a higher prenatal consultation rate in 1997 than Niger and Mali in 2012 and Burkina Faso in 2003. In the case of Mali, it was during the period 2001–2006 that a sharp increase[2] was observed.

[2] It should be noted, however, that the analyses cover only the five southern and central regions and the district of Bamako because of security problems that prevented coverage of the entire country by the 2012 survey.

*DOI: http://dx.doi.org/10.5772/intechopen.1002664*

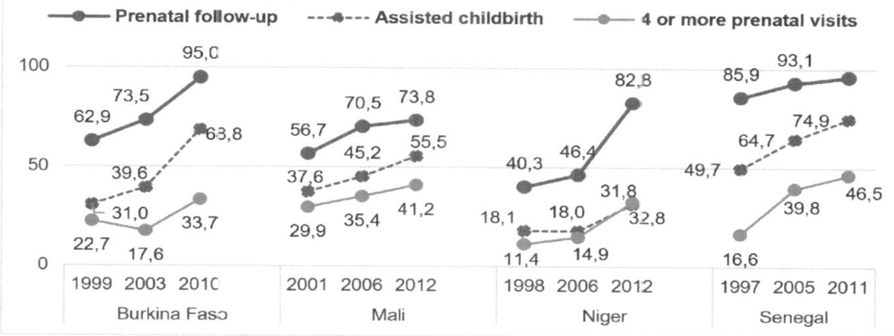


**Figure 1.**
*Trends in maternal health service utilization by study countries.*

In all four countries, less than half of pregnant women consult a health care professional more than three times. In Niger and Burkina Faso, only one-third of pregnant women visit a health care professional at least four times during their pregnancy. We observe that the prevalence of maternal care utilization doubled in Burkina Faso during the period 2003–2010 (after a deceleration between 1999 and 2003), in Niger during 2006–2012, and in Senegal already during the period 1997–2005. In Mali, however, the increase was less marked.

Overall, assisted delivery is less common than antenatal care, and Niger stands out for having a much lower level than the others. Its prevalence in 2012 is still below that of Mali in 2001 and Senegal in 1997 and is equivalent to that of Burkina Faso in 1999. In terms of trends, Burkina Faso stands out for a more significant increase, especially during the 2003–2010 period. The 1998–2006 period was marked by stagnation in Niger (**Figure 1**).

### 3.2 Basic decomposition

#### *3.2.1 Compositional effect of improving women's socioeconomic status at the national level on increasing trends in care utilization*

Using a basic decomposition, we account for the observed changes in national-level utilization of care in terms of changes in the educational composition of women versus changes in group-specific rates of care utilization (behavior or performance effect).

The results of the prenatal consultation highlight the preponderance of the effect of behaviors in all countries and for all periods except Mali between 2006 and 2012. In Mali, during this period, the improvement in the socioeconomic situation of households where women of childbearing age live had a very significant effect on the increase in the national level of care utilization. In other words, the increase in antenatal care at the national level during this period is mainly the result of the improvement in women's collective capacity to use antenatal care services. Except in this case, progress in antenatal care attendance is mainly attributable to behavioral change across socioeconomic groups.

The results indicate that the behavioral effect predominates, apart from the case of Mali reported above, but even if it is in a relatively smaller proportion, a composition effect of the female population is also observed. Thus, in Senegal for the period

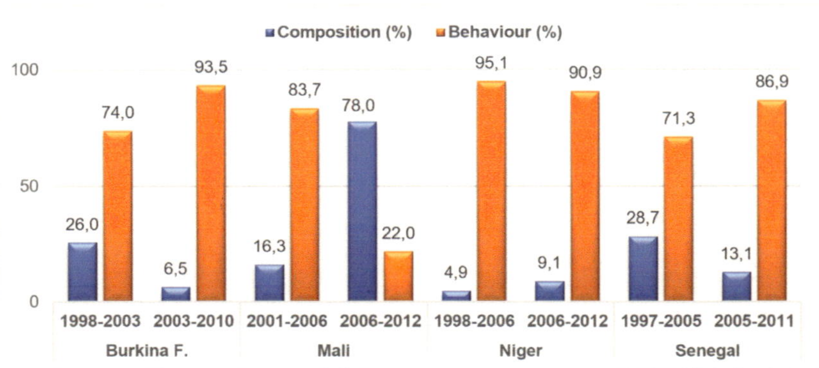


**Figure 2.**
*Simple decomposition of the effect of standardized living in prenatal care utilization patterns.*

1997–2005, nearly one-third of the increase in the prenatal follow-up rate was due to this compositional effect and a little more than one-quarter in Burkina Faso for the period 1999–2003. This effect is therefore not negligible (**Figure 2**).

For assisted delivery, the behavioral effect always dominates in all countries (**Figure 3**). However, this effect is smaller than for antenatal care, as the compositional effect, which is related to improvements in women's socioeconomic conditions, is larger for assisted childbirth. In Burkina Faso, nearly half of the increase in the assisted childbirth rate between 1999 and 2003 was due to the compositional effect. Similarly, the share of the increase related to women's collective capacity to use services exceeded one-third in Niger between 2006 and 2012 and in Mali in all periods and exceeded one-fifth in Senegal during the period 1997–2005. This result highlights a distinct role of improvement in socioeconomic status according to the maternal health component: It has a greater effect in increasing the overall level of use of assisted childbirth than of prenatal care.

As with the prenatal consultation, in Burkina Faso, the compositional effect was much smaller during the 1999–2003 period, during which the socioeconomic situation improved only slightly. In Niger, since the socioeconomic situation of women did not improve at all between 1998 and 2006, the compositional effect was negative, thus constituting an obstacle to increasing the national use of assisted childbirth. Moreover, this could explain, in part, the stagnation of the assisted childbirth rate during this period in Niger (**Figure 3**).

### *3.2.2 Compositional effect of overall improvement in women's human capital on changes in care use*

The results of the decomposition associated with women's education level are similar in all the countries studied regardless of the period except in Niger between 1998 and 2006 for assisted childbirth. This case aside, the trends in both antenatal care and assisted childbirth, mostly result from changes in the behavior of mothers regardless of education level. This preponderance of the behavioral or performance effect is slightly stronger for the prenatal consultation component than for assisted delivery. Still, the educational component is also important. In Mali, the improvement in women's education made a substantial contribution to the increase in the national prevalence of antenatal visits during the 2006–2012 period. During this period, slightly more than a quarter of the increase in the national level of use of assisted

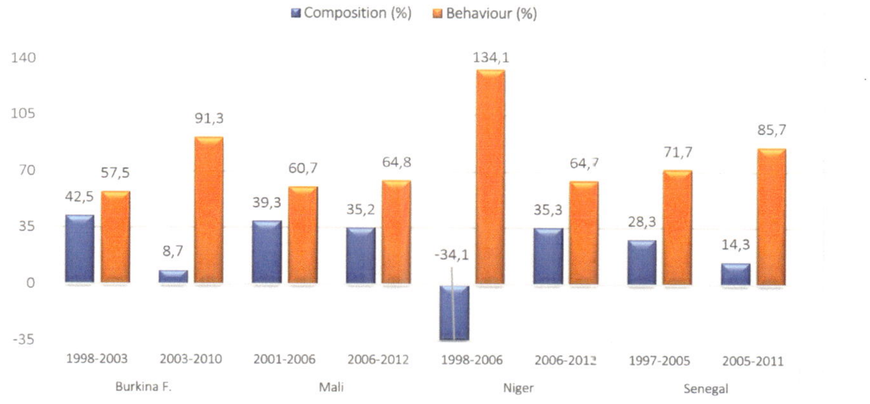


**Figure 3.**
*Simple decomposition of the sources of change in health care utilization: Effect of changes in standard of living (composition effect) versus changes in group-specific behavior (behavior effect).*

childbirth was due to the overall increase in women's human capital. The same is true in Burkina Faso and to a lesser extent in Senegal with respect to assisted childbirth.

The situation in Niger highlights how gains in women's education between 1998 and 2006 helped maintain the level of assisted childbirth constant during this period. This very large share, despite the stagnation of the national assisted childbirth rate, suggests that the overall proportion of assisted childbirth in Niger between 1998 and 2006 would have declined if there had not been this slight increase in women's human capital.

In conclusion, progress in school enrolment did not raise the national rate at which women used delivery health services. Their effect remains below that relating to behavioral changes linked to the relative performance of the health system (**Figures 4** and **5**).

### 3.3 Advanced decomposition

The advanced decomposition shows that the behavioral effect mostly reflects a baseline change for all women (baseline performance) rather than differential progress between groups (**Table 3**). The upward trend in health care utilization is the result of overall changes in behavior resulting mainly from improvements in the health system (service provision, awareness, policies and programs, etc.), with the exception of assisted childbirth during the periods 1998–2003 and 2001–2006 in Burkina Faso and Mali, respectively. Indeed, in these cases, differential changes in the propensity to use health care between socioeconomic categories are observed.

In Burkina Faso, the increase in the prevalence of childbirth, which occurred between 1998 and 2003 and during the 2001–2006 period in Mali, is due to a higher propensity to use health care among women belonging to less disadvantaged socioeconomic groups: intermediary or wealthy (**Table 3**).

### 3.4 Analyses of trends in inequalities between social groups in the use of maternal care

We examine trends in inequality across socioeconomic categories through changes in their relative contributions (**Table 4**). Results vary across countries. In Mali,

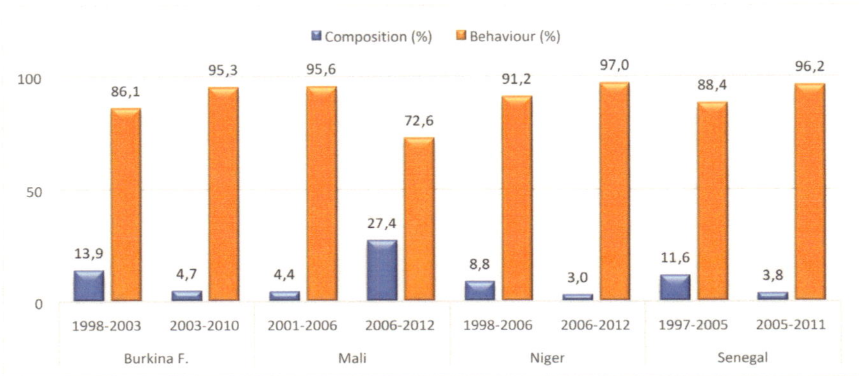


**Figure 4.**
*Simple decomposition of the effect of education in prenatal care utilization patterns.*

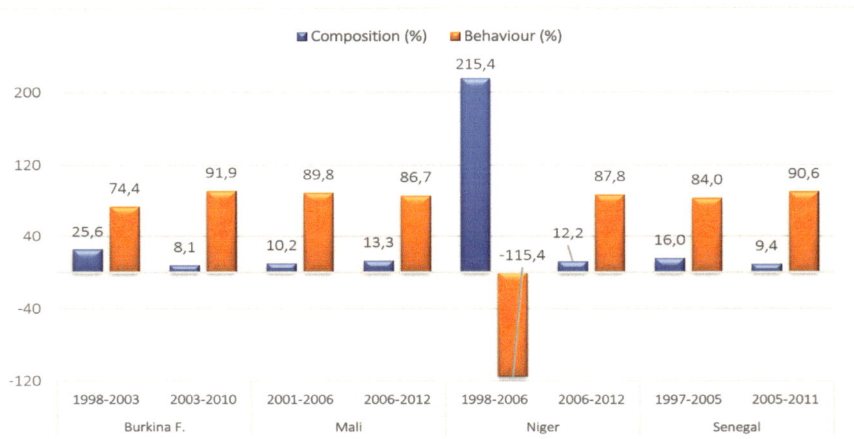


**Figure 5.**
*Simple decomposition of the effect of education on health care utilization patterns at delivery.*

| Pays | Variables | DHS round | Antenatal follow-up | | | | |
|---|---|---|---|---|---|---|---|
| | | | Total change (b-a) | Composition (%) | Performance effect | | |
| | | | | | Base (%) | Difference (%) | Residual (%) |
| Burkina F. | Living standard | 1999–2003 | 10.6 | 26.0 | 79.0 | 17.1 | −22.1 |
| | | 2003–2010 | 21.5 | 6.5 | 135.7 | −51.1 | −3.62 |
| | Education | 1999–2003 | 10.6 | 13.9 | 131.5 | −45.4 | −0.1 |
| | | 2003–2010 | 21.5 | 4.7 | 179.8 | −175.1 | −0.13 |
| Mali | Living standard | 2001–2006 | 13.9 | 16.3 | 91.0 | 12.7 | −20.1 |
| | | 2006–2012 | 3.2 | 78.0 | 195.1 | −122.7 | −43.4 |
| | Education | 2001–2006 | 13.9 | 4.4 | 162.8 | −68.8 | 1.6 |
| | | 2006–2012 | 3.2 | 27.4 | 186.5 | −207.1 | −1.7 |

| Pays | Variables | DHS round | Antenatal follow-up | | | | |
|---|---|---|---|---|---|---|---|
| | | | Total change (b-a) | Composition (%) | Performance effect | | |
| | | | | | Base (%) | Difference (%) | Residual (%) |
| Niger | Living standard | 1998–2006 | 6.1 | 4.9 | 130.6 | −26.5 | −9.0 |
| | | 2006–2012 | 36.4 | 9.1 | 121.1 | −33.5 | −8.1 |
| | Education | 1998–2006 | 6.1 | 8.8 | 90.5 | 0.8 | −0.2 |
| | | 2006–2012 | 36.4 | 3.0 | 159.3 | −118.7 | 0.1 |
| Sénégal | Living standard | 1997–2005 | 7.3 | 28.7 | 159.5 | −62.8 | −25.4 |
| | | 2005–2011 | 3.0 | 13.1 | 246.5 | −171.4 | 2.9 |
| | Education | 1997–2005 | 7.3 | 11.6 | 194.8 | −103.7 | −2.7 |
| | | 2005–2011 | 3.0 | 3.8 | 257.6 | −323.8 | 16.4 |
| Assisted childbirth | | | | | | | |
| Burkina F. | Living standard | 1999–2003 | 8.5 | 42.5 | 26.7 | 69.7 | −39.0 |
| | | 2003–2010 | 29.2 | 8.7 | 130.1 | −29.7 | −5.01 |
| | Education | 1999–2003 | 8.5 | 25.6 | 51.5 | 23.2 | −0.4 |
| | | 2003–2010 | 29.2 | 8.1 | 172.1 | −130.2 | −0.15 |
| Mali | Living standard | 2001–2006 | 7.6 | 39.3 | 10.6 | 100.8 | −50.6 |
| | | 2006–2012 | 10.3 | 35.2 | 146.4 | −40.9 | −17.9 |
| | Education | 2001–2006 | 7.6 | 10.2 | 127.9 | −41.4 | 3.3 |
| | | 2006–2012 | 10.3 | 13.3 | 142.8 | −81.8 | −1.2 |
| Niger | Living standard | 1998–2006 | −0.2 | −34.1 | 110.1 | −23.3 | 47.3 |
| | | 2006–2012 | 13.8 | 35.3 | 115.7 | −18.9 | −27.6 |
| | Education | 1998–2006 | −0.2 | 215.4 | −1398.7 | 1790.2 | −6.9 |
| | | 2006–2012 | 13.8 | 12.2 | 134.1 | −52.6 | −0.9 |
| Sénégal | Living standard | 1997–2005 | 15.0 | 28.3 | 97.3 | −2.2 | −23.3 |
| | | 2005–2011 | 10.2 | 14.3 | 178.3 | −60.8 | 0.1 |
| | Education | 1997–2005 | 15.0 | 16.0 | 121.0 | −34.3 | −2.8 |
| | | 2005–2011 | 10.2 | 9.4 | 207.3 | −184.1 | 4.2 |

**Table 3.**
*Results of the advanced decomposition for the contributions of baseline gains versus differential progress in maternal health care utilization.*

inequalities between the different socioeconomic categories increased during the 2006–2012 period. This is undoubtedly why composition is the dominant source of the increase in the use of prenatal care during this period (see **Figure 2**). This probably explains the timid increase in the use of care (from 70% in 2006 to 74% in 2012), compared, for example, to Niger during the same period. The prevalence of health care utilization in Niger in 2006 was lower than that observed in Mali in 2001 (46% in Niger and 57% in Mali), but by 2012, it had become much higher in Niger (84%) than in Mali (74%) (see **Figure 1**). This slower increase in Mali, where the current

| Variables | Burkina Faso | | Mali | | Niger | | Senegal | |
|---|---|---|---|---|---|---|---|---|
| | 1998–2003 | 2003–2010 | 2001–2006 | 2006–2012 | 1998–2006 | 2006–2012 | 1997–2005 | 2005–2011 |
| Living standard | | | | | | | | |
| Low | −20.7 | 19.5 | 8.3 | −100.7 | 96.4 | 58.0 | −73.4 | −67.5 |
| Middle | 32.4 | 52.8 | 45.9 | 63.0 | 11.1 | 24.5 | 6.6 | 22.4 |
| High | 88.3 | 27.7 | 45.8 | 137.6 | −7.5 | 17.5 | 166.8 | 145.1 |
| Education level | | | | | | | | |
| No education | 44.5 | 64.7 | 79.2 | 28.8 | 69.7 | 83.8 | −9.4 | 40.4 |
| Primary | 27.2 | 17.4 | 9.1 | −66.4 | 12.5 | 8.8 | 68.0 | −123.1 |
| Secondary and more | 28.3 | 17.9 | 11.7 | 137.6 | 17.9 | 7.4 | 41.3 | 182.7 |
| Total | 100.0 | 100.0 | 100.0 | 100.0 | 100.0 | 100.0 | 100.0 | 100.0 |

**Table 4.**
*Relative contributions of women in different socioeconomic and educational categories to total change in use of antenatal care by country.*

level of prenatal monitoring is the lowest of the four countries considered, is also the result of this significant increase in inequalities in contributions between socioeconomic groups. Niger is the country where the poorest group of women has contributed the most to the change in the level of prenatal care since 1998. The more rapid increase in the prenatal care rate observed in Niger, particularly between 2006 and 2012, also stems from this strong contribution of the poorest socioeconomic groups, even though a downward trend is observed between 2006 and 2012. It is especially in Burkina Faso that inequalities between socioeconomic categories, in terms of their contribution to changes in the use of prenatal care, have decreased. This is also the case in Senegal, but to a lesser extent, because even though the gaps between socioeconomic categories are gradually narrowing, the contributions of the poorest women's group are still low.

With regard to the education effect, there is an increase in the contributions of the least educated group of women to the increase in the prenatal follow-up rate in Burkina Faso and Niger, respectively, during the periods 2003–2010 and 2006–2012. These periods were also marked by a much greater increase in prenatal follow-up in these two countries, no doubt due to the observed decrease in inequalities between the least educated and educated women. On the other hand, in Mali and Senegal, there has been an increase in inequalities between the most educated and less educated women, but their contribution to the overall increase in the prenatal follow-up rate remains significant.

### *3.4.1 Trends in the unequal contributions of different socioeconomic groups to increased use of assisted childbirth*

The results show a decrease in inequalities between socioeconomic groups in Burkina Faso and Niger in terms of their contribution to the overall change in the use of assisted childbirth. In both countries, there was an increase in the contribution to changes in the use of assisted childbirth of the most disadvantaged group of women (those in the lowest

| Variables | Burkina Faso | | Mali | | Niger | | Sénégal | |
|---|---|---|---|---|---|---|---|---|
| | 1998–2003 | 2003–2010 | 2001–2006 | 2006–2012 | 1998–2006 | 2006–2012 | 1997–2005 | 2005–2011 |
| Living standard | | | | | | | | |
| Low | −9.3 | 29.0 | 5.6 | −12.8 | −19.6 | 48.7 | −6.0 | −7.3 |
| Middle | 26.0 | 47.8 | 35.4 | 56.3 | 20.8 | 19.0 | 4.3 | 28.8 |
| High | 83.2 | 23.2 | 59.0 | 56.5 | 98.8 | 32.3 | 101.7 | 78.5 |
| Education level | | | | | | | | |
| No education | 37.7 | 74.6 | 63.3 | 70.1 | −380.3 | 73.2 | 37.4 | 68.8 |
| Primary | 30.9 | 14.3 | 21.5 | −14.8 | 67.4 | 15.1 | 39.2 | −20.7 |
| Secondary and more | 31.4 | 11.1 | 15.2 | 44.7 | 412.9 | 11.7 | 23.4 | 52.0 |
| Total | 100.0 | 100.0 | 100.0 | 100.0 | 100.0 | 100.0 | 100.0 | 100.0 |

**Table 5.**
*Relative contributions of women in different socioeconomic and educational categories to total change in the use of assisted childbirth by country.*

socioeconomic category or with no education at all). This therefore implies a reduction in inequalities in this respect between socioeconomic groups. This increase in the contribution of the most disadvantaged women, from a socioeconomic or educational point of view, is the most apparent in Niger, a country where the national level of use of assisted childbirth did not increase between 1998 and 2006. This stagnation, therefore, would be due to the significant disadvantage of the group of uneducated women (who are the most numerous). It can also be assumed that, during this period, health services were not easily accessible to the poorest. During the following period, between 2006 and 2012, the reduction in the disadvantages of the least advantaged women resulted in a significant increase in the use of assisted childbirth. It was also during the period 2003–2010 that the increase in the rate of assisted childbirth was the greatest in Burkina Faso.

In Senegal, we also observe a decrease in inequality, but contrary to what is observed in Burkina Faso and Niger, it is the middle class that benefits. It is the gap between the most affluent women and those in the middle class that is narrowing the most, while the contribution of the poorest women remains low. It could therefore be said that the disadvantage of the poorest women in Senegal continues. In terms of education, the opposite situation is observed in this country, that is, an increase in inequalities to the detriment of women at the primary level.

Mali, unlike in the other three countries, shows an increase in inequalities in the use of assisted childbirth, which is expressed by the widening gap between the poorest women and others. However, despite this decrease in the contribution of uneducated women, it is mainly due to them that the slight overall increase in the national level of use of assisted childbirth in Mali between 2006 and 2012 was observed (**Table 5**).

## 4. Discussion and conclusion

This chapter shed light on the roles of socioeconomic changes on living conditions of the female in maternal care service utilization in Mali, Burkina Faso, Niger, and

Senegal. We also examine the trends in inequalities between socioeconomic groups in maternal health care use at the national level.

The results highlight both a behavioral and a compositional effect, but the former clearly predominates regardless of the country, except in Mali and Niger, respectively, for the periods 2006–2012 for prenatal follow-up and 1998–2006 for assisted childbirth. In Mali, during the 2006–2012 period, the increase in the use of antenatal care was marked by a predominant effect of improving women's socioeconomic conditions. On the other hand, in Niger between 1998 and 2006, a negative effect of socioeconomic composition was observed: the stagnation in the level of use of assisted childbirth stems from the fact that the socioeconomic situation did not improve during this period. During this same period in this country, however, a slight improvement in the human capital of women of childbearing age helped keep the level of assisted childbirth constant. Except in these cases, the socioeconomic composition of the female population is not the main factor. Rather, we observe an overall trend toward behavioral change.

This predominant change in behavior is mainly due to basic performance (except for assisted childbirth in Mali between 2001 and 2006 and in Burkina Faso between 1999 and 2003). This increase in the use of maternal health services may be partly a reflection of different policy actions to improve the health status of mothers. The establishment of community health centers in the countries has brought health services closer to users. In addition, there are policies to waive the cost of Cesarean sections, to treat cases of severe malaria among pregnant women, and to make insecticide-treated nets available despite multiple dysfunctions and problems observed in their development and implementation [22, 23].

The gains permitted by service provision or policies and programs are often accompanied by inequalities across socioeconomic categories. While the contributions of the poorest people to changes in levels of health care utilization are rising in Burkina Faso and Niger, the same cannot be said for Mali and, to a lesser extent, Senegal. Contrary to our hypothesis 2, the relative disadvantage of the poorest women (especially the group of women living in poor households, slightly less so for the group of uneducated women), compared to those from the most advantaged socioeconomic strata, has increased in Mali and remained constant in Senegal despite the overall performance in health care utilization. This could explain the importance of compositional effects of Mali's change on the national rate of antenatal monitoring between 2006 and 2012. Health services are still relatively inaccessible to the poorest socioeconomic strata, and new interventions often produce new inequalities [31].

With respect to inequalities, they tend to grow along economic, rather than educational, lines, both for prenatal monitoring and assisted childbirth. Such a result highlights the greater role of poverty as an obstacle to seeking maternal care. This suggests that the need for care to reduce the risks associated with pregnancy and childbirth is increasingly understood among the population. Maternal care tends to be widely perceived as a need, even among the least educated women, but it is financial inaccessibility combined with insufficient supply believed to be the real barriers to seeking care, rather than cultural barriers.

Finally, progress remains slow in Mali and in the other countries included in this analysis. These results warrant attention to inequalities that go beyond the health system alone. The local context (including availability of services) matters even when laudable policies and programs are adopted nationally. Another issue is women's overall empowerment, that is, their real opportunity to use services if they so desire.

This also translates into a lower contribution of the socioeconomic resources of the context (compositional effect) to the progress made in the use of care in these countries.

## Author details

Siaka Cissé[1*] and Imad Rherrad[2]

1 National Institute of Statistics of Mali (INSTAT), Bamako, Mali

2 Ministère des Finances du Québec (MFQ), Canada

*Address all correspondence to: siakacisse79@gmail.com

## References

[1] Balique H, Ouattara O, Iknane AA. Ten years of experience in community health Centers in Mali. Santé Publique. 2001;**13**:35-48

[2] Gilson L, Kalyalya D, Kuchler F, Lake S, Oranga H, Ouendo M. Strategies for promoting equity: Experience with community financing in three African countries. Health Policy. 2001;**58**:37-67

[3] Ridde V, Robert E, Meessen B. A literature review of the disruptive effects of user fee exemption policies on health systems. BMC Public Health. 2012;**12**:1-7

[4] Peters DH, Garg A, Bloom G, Walker DG, Brieger WR, Hafizur RM. Poverty and access to health care in developing countries. Annals of the New York Academy of Sciences. 2008;**1136**: 161-171

[5] Perkins M, Brazier E, Themmen E, Bassane B, Diallo D, Mutunga A, et al. Out-of-pocket costs for facility-based maternity care in three African countries. Health Policy and Planning. 2009;**24**:289-300

[6] Van Eijk AM, Bles HM, Odhiambo F, Ayisi JG, Blokland IE, Rosen DH, et al. Use of antenatal services and delivery care among women in rural western Kenya: A community based survey. Reproductive Health. 2006;**3**:1-9

[7] Gabrysch S, Cousens S, Cox J, Campbell OM. The influence of distance and level of care on delivery place in rural Zambia: A study of linked national data in a geographic information system. PLoS Medicine. 2011;**8**:e1000394

[8] Gross K, Alba S, Glass TR, Schellenberg JA, Obrist B. Timing of antenatal care for adolescent and adult pregnant women in South-Eastern Tanzania. BMC Pregnancy and Childbirth. 2012;**12**:1-12

[9] Koblinsky M, Moyer CA, Calvert C, Campbell J, Campbell OM, Feigl AB, et al. Quality maternity care for every woman, everywhere: A call to action. The Lancet. 2016;**388**:2307-2320

[10] Titaley CR, Dibley MJ, Agho K, Roberts CL, Hall J. Determinants of neonatal mortality in Indonesia. BMC Public Health. 2008;**8**:1-15

[11] Haddad S, Fournier P. Quality, cost and utilization of health services in developing countries. A longitudinal study in Zaire. Social Science & Medicine. 1995;**40**:743-753

[12] Kruk ME, Paczkowski M, Mbaruku G, De Pinho H, Galea S. Women's preferences for place of delivery in rural Tanzania: A population-based discrete choice experiment. American Journal of Public Health. 2009;**99**:1666-1672

[13] Thaddeus S, Maine D. Too far to walk: Maternal mortality in context. Social Science & Medicine. 1994;**38**: 1091-1110

[14] Burgard S. Race and pregnancy-related care in Brazil and South Africa. Social Science & Medicine. 2004;**59**: 1127-1146

[15] Furuta M, Salway S. Women's position within the household as a determinant of maternal health care use in Nepal. International Family Planning Perspectives. 2006:17-27

[16] Navaneetham K, Dharmalingam A. Utilization of maternal health care

services in southern India. Social Science & Medicine. 2002;**55**:1849-1869

[17] Paul BK, Rumsey DJ. Utilization of health facilities and trained birth attendants for childbirth in rural Bangladesh: An empirical study. Social Science & Medicine. 2002;**54**: 1755-1765

[18] Glei DA, Goldman N, Rodríguez G. Utilization of care during pregnancy in rural Guatemala: Does obstetrical need matter? Social Science & Medicine. 2003;**57**:2447-2463

[19] Short SE, Zhang F. Use of maternal health services in rural China. Population Studies. 2004;**58**:3-19

[20] Kamiya Y. Women's autonomy and reproductive health care utilisation: Empirical evidence from Tajikistan. Health Policy. 2011;**102**:304-313

[21] Adjiwanou V. Contexte de genre, autonomie des femmes et utilisation des services de santé maternelle en milieu rural africain: analyse par modèles d'équations structurelles [Thèse]. Université de Montréal; 2014

[22] de Sardan J-PO, Ridde V. L'exemption de paiement des soins au Burkina Faso, Mali et Niger. Afrique Contemporaine. 2012;**243**:11-32

[23] Witter S, Dieng T, Mbengue D, Moreira I, De Brouwere V. The national free delivery and caesarean policy in Senegal: Evaluating process and outcomes. Health Policy and Planning. 2010;**25**:384-392

[24] Nikièma B, Haddad S, Potvin L. Women bargaining to seek healthcare: Norms, domestic practices, and implications in rural Burkina Faso. World Development. 2008;**36**:608-624

[25] Samb OM, Belaid L, Ridde V. Burkina Faso: la gratuité des soins aux dépens de la relation entre les femmes et les soignants? Humanit Enjeux Prat Débats. 2013;**35**:34-43

[26] Agyepong IA, Nagai RA. "We charge them; Otherwise we cannot run the hospital" front line workers, clients and health financing policy implementation gaps in Ghana. Health Policy. 2011;**99**: 226-233

[27] Canning D, Raja S, Yazbeck A. Africa's Demographic Transition: Dividend or Disaster? World Bank Publ; 2015

[28] Fournier P, Dumont A, Tourigny C, Dunkley G, Dramé S. Improved access to comprehensive emergency obstetric care and its effect on institutional maternal mortality in rural Mali. Bulletin of the World Health Organization. 2009;**87**: 30-38

[29] Rutstein SO. DHS working papers. DHS Wealth Index Approaches Rural Urban Areas USAID 2008

[30] Rutstein SO. Steps to Constructing the New DHS Wealth Index. Rockville, MD: ICF International; 2015

[31] White M, Adams J, Heywood P. How and why do interventions that increase health overall widen inequalities within populations? In: Social Inequality and Public Health. Policy Press; 2009. pp. 65-82

Section 2

# An Anthropocentric Perspective: How the World Will Change Demography

Chapter 9

# Improving the Measurement of Women's Work: The Contribution of Demographic Surveys in Francophone West Africa

*Anne E. Calvès and Agnès Adjamagbo*

## Abstract

Since the 1970s, the measurement and recognition of women's work and their contributions to family well-being and economic development have been a matter of academic interest, as well as feminist advocacy. The interrelationships between women's work and demographic processes, especially decisions regarding fertility, have also attracted the attention of demographers for some time. However, despite long-standing efforts to capture all aspects of women's work, large-scale demographic and economic surveys conducted in the Global South still fail to approach work as a gendered concept and continue to make much of women's labor invisible. The measurement of unpaid care and household responsibilities is particularly scarce. In such a context, the purpose of this chapter is twofold. First, it retraces the long history of the global efforts of feminist scholars and activists to enhance the measurement of women's work. Second, it illustrates how recent data collection initiatives in francophone West Africa, building on the experience of collaborative research conducted by demographers in the region since the 1970s, have attempted to fill some of the persisting gaps in data on women's activity, especially on household domestic and care, voluntary collective/community work, as well as on women's contribution to household expenses and family support.

**Keywords:** women's work, unpaid care, labor force participation, gender division of labor, family dynamics, measurement, surveys, indicators, demography, francophone West Africa

## 1. Introduction

The COVID-19 pandemic and the associated lockdowns declared by governments around the world have shed some light on the gender inequalities in paid and unpaid work. Not only have women been hit harder in the labor market, suffering from greater employment loss than men [1], but there is mounting evidence that the pandemic has exacerbated gender gaps in domestic work and childcare responsibilities within the household [2]. Globally, the COVID-19 crisis has highlighted several aspects of women's work, such as their frontline role in health and social care, their involvement in precarious and survival activities in the informal sector, and their double burden of paid and unpaid care and domestic labor. While these are issues that have gained attention with the pandemic, they have been the focus of feminist scholars and activists for decades.

In fact, since the 1970s, the measurement and recognition of the extent of women's work and their contributions to family well-being and economic development have been a matter of academic interest, as well as feminist advocacy. The interrelationships between women's work and demographic processes, especially decisions related to fertility, also started to attract the attention of demographers at that time. From the 1990s onwards, with women's empowerment increasingly becoming a stated priority of governments and global development institutions, efforts have intensified to better capture all aspects of women's work, including unpaid care and domestic activities. Today, employment variables, along with other proxies or measures of women's empowerment included in international surveys, such as the Demographic and Health Survey (DHS), are widely used in the demographic analysis [3]. Despite these efforts, however, large-scale demographic and economic surveys conducted in the Global South, critics argue, still fail to approach work as a gendered concept and continue to make much of women's work invisible [4, 5].

In such a context, the purpose of this chapter is two-folded: first, to retrace the long history of the global efforts of feminist scholars and activists to enhance the measurement of women's work, underlining the persisting gaps in data on women's activity, and second, to illustrate how recent data collection initiatives in francophone West Africa, building on the experience of collaborative research conducted by demographers in the region since the 1970s, have attempted to fill some of these gaps.

## 2. Making women's work visible: five decades of global feminist efforts

Advocacy to better capture women's work and their contribution to family well-being and economic development is not new. It can be traced to the 1970s when feminist scholars and activists started to point out the mismeasurement and underestimation of women's activities in official statistics and national surveys. The publication in 1970 of Ester Boserup's book, *Woman's Role in Economic Development*, undoubtedly represents a milestone in the recognition of the need to tackle the invisibility of women's work. Based on empirical studies in Asia, Africa, and Latin America, the economist illustrates how development policies have ignored Third World women or confined them to their reproductive and domestic roles. In Africa, for instance, although traditional agricultural systems are what she describes as "women's farming systems" par excellence, since the colonial period agricultural modernization policies have largely favored men over women [6]. Subsistence activities, such as unpaid agricultural work and domestic labor, as well as employment in the informal sector of the economy, where women are over-represented, are not only ignored by developers, Boserup and others argue, but they are also hidden by census and national labor data that tend to focus on formal employment [7].

After its publication, Boserup's book became an essential reference both for the work of academics and for the development programs that would mark the entire United Nations (UN) Decade for women (1976–1985) under what is referred to as the women in development (WID) approach. In line with Boserup's work, this perspective, articulated mostly by liberal feminists in the United States, views the lack of integration of women into economic development programs as a central issue. In 1973, following feminist lobbying, the US congress adopted a bill (the *Percy amendment*), which required that programs financed by Agency for International Development (USAID) include some measures to improve women's access to resources and participation in economic development. In 1974, a WID Office was created within the agency, to monitor the progress made in achieving this goal [8]. During the first UN conference on Women in Mexico City in 1975, all member states also committed to better integration of women in development assistance. From the mid-1970s, with the support of bilateral and multilateral international aid agencies as well as private foundations, and thanks to transnational feminist advocacy and lobbying activities, WID programs to such as income-generating and microcredit projects designed to enhance the productive role of women flourished in Africa, as in other parts of the Global South [9]. The recognition of the need to make women's work more visible in labor force statistics and gross domestic product (GDP) also started to strengthen among international agencies, non-governmental organizations (NGOs), and governments. In 1980, the Program of Action adopted at the 2nd World Conference on Women in Copenhagen made the collection of disaggregated statistics and the development of databases about women one of its objectives. The WID Office started to sponsor time-use data collections that recorded detailed information on all activities carried out by individuals in a specific period, to document the extent of women's unpaid household work [10]. The International Research and Training Institute for the Advancement of Women (INSTRAW), created in 1976 after the Mexico conference, and the Statistical Office of the UN Secretariat also played a key role in promoting national statistics on women's work [11]. As pointed out by Goetz [7], generating and analyzing data on women, including women's economic activities, was "one of the main objectives, and an enduring success, of the UN Decade for Women." In the context of rising concerns about rapid population growth in the Third World, demographers were also interested in exploring the relationships between women's labor force participation and fertility at that time [12]. The World Fertility Surveys (WFSs) conducted from 1974 to 1982 in 62 countries, mostly developing ones, to measure fertility and its determinants, including a series of 17 questions on women's employment explicitly designed to test the widespread idea that economic modernization factors such as increased economic opportunities for women outside the home would reduce fertility [13].

Interest in women's economic activities gained further momentum after the world conference on women held in Nairobi in 1985 and throughout the 1990s. The writings of feminist scholars on the repercussions of the economic crisis and structural adjustment programs (SAPs) implemented across the Global South in the 1980s and 1990s on the living and working conditions of women have multiplied, inaugurating a new field of research [14]. Analyses illustrate how, in cities, the increased cost of living and rising unemployment among men forced women to multiply "survival" activities in the informal sector of the economy, particularly in Latin America and Africa [15–17]. Across the Global South, studies show an intensification of the individual as well as collective involvement of women in the survival of impoverished households and communities [9, 16]. Evaluations also point out the exploitation of women's work induced by a globalized economy and the accelerated relocation of transnational companies in the Global South [18]. In the 1990s, the new boom in female employment in areas such as data entry and computer programming, female subcontracting, and informal work at home further attracted the attention of researchers. Overall, feminists argue, with women increasingly bearing the burden of household survival, one has witnessed over the years a "feminization of responsibilities and obligations" [19]. This "feminization of survival" extends beyond households and national borders. To cope with poverty and unemployment and meet the increased needs of the care industry in industrialized countries, women from East Asia, Africa, and Latin America are migrating in increasing numbers to Western Europe, the Middle East, and North America, to be employed in precarious and socially devalued jobs such as domestic work, childcare, or nursing [20, 21].

This sustained academic interest in women's work took place in a context of progressive institutionalization of the "gender and development" (GAD) agenda, resulting, in large part, from the extensive advocacy work of feminist activists during the UN conferences that marked the 1990s. Rooted in the writing of socialist, post-colonial and anti-globalization feminists, especially scholars from the Global South, the GAD perspective criticizes the dominant WID paradigm for its narrow focus on the provision of resources to women, its Western hegemonic view of women, and its failure to address the fundamental and structural causes of women's subordination [8, 10]. Development initiatives, tenants of the GAD approach argue, should not consider women in isolation from men but rather focus on transforming unequal gender relationships. Development planners should also favor participatory approaches with women in diverse settings defining their own needs and adopt "gender mainstreaming" that integrates gender in all development projects [10].

After the 4th World conference on women in Beijing in 1995, the development industry operated a gradual shift from "women" to "gender" and promoting gender equality became a stated priority for governments and international donors and development agencies. The population field was no exception, and the 1994 International Conference on Population and Development in Cairo undoubtedly marked a turn toward "a feminization of population and development issues" [22]. The new approach adopted at the end of the conference placed sexual and reproductive rights and the empowerment of women at the heart of population issues and put an unprecedented emphasis on gender relations as determinants of demographic processes [23, 24]. From the 1990s onwards, UN agencies and international donors further encouraged the collection, production, and analysis of gender statistics and gender-disaggregated socioeconomic indicators to monitor progress toward gender equality. Influenced by the work of feminist scholars, especially economists, data collection initiatives to quantitatively capture women's nonmarket and market work also increased greatly. In 1993, the System of National Accounts (SNA) of the United Nations was revised to include subsistence or "primary" activities, primarily undertaken by women, such as water fetching or firewood collection in the calculation of the GDP [25]. Initiatives to theorize and collect data on the gendered dimensions of the informal economy initiated by research groups, UN agencies such as the International Labor Organization (ILO) or the UN Economic Commission for Africa, or advocacy networks such as Women in Informal Employment: Globalizing and Organizing (WIEGO) also multiplied [26, 27].

Following a formal recommendation from the Beijing Platform for Action, time-use surveys flourished in the Global South after the conference, often with the involvement of feminist scholars [28]. At the end of the 1990s, time-use surveys at the national level were conducted for the first time in Africa [25]. Despite a lack of harmonization across countries and other methodological issues, these new data have been very useful in documenting the magnitude of unpaid care work performed by women across the world [29]. The increased availability of time-use data in the 2000s also allowed economists and family demographers in industrialized countries to study trends in the division of labor within two-parent households and the relationships between women's unpaid care work and labor force participation in both Western and non-Western countries [30–32]. Changes adopted in 1999 by the DHS, an essential source of demographic data, are also emblematic of the effort to make gender a central variable in demographic analyses [3]. In the wake of the Cairo conference, in addition to the indirect measures of women's status such as education and employment, the program decided to introduce direct assessments of gender relations in the questionnaire, such as questions on women's participation in household decision-making, control over financial resources and attitude toward gender norms. Since their introduction into datasets, these empowerment indicators, along with the variables related to women's labor force participation and earnings, have been widely used by demographers. Empirical research on Africa, for instance, has utilized the DHS questions on women's work to explore the relationships between women's employment and fertility [33, 34], contraceptive use [35], child survival [36], or intimate partner violence [37], to cite a few examples.

The increasing availability of data on women's work and especially on time-use data has also been useful for feminist activists to further advocate for the global recognition of women's work, particularly the unpaid domestic and care types. Despite the global feminization of the labor force, they argue, there is still a universal "male breadwinner bias" that permeates social policies in both Western and non-Western countries and a lack of consideration of existing gender imbalances in the distribution of unpaid care within households. Studies have documented that regardless of their level of participation in the labor market, and despite the increase in men's involvement in household work in several countries, globally, women are still responsible for the majority of household chores (such as cleaning, cooking, and shopping for groceries) and for the care of family members, including children and the elderly. Across the world, time-use data illustrate the double burden many women bear and its potential detrimental consequences for themselves and their children in poorer countries [32, 38]. In recent years, women's rights advocates have been instrumental in putting the issue of care on the global development agenda. In 2013, in a landmark decision, the International Conference of Labor Statisticians (ICLS) adopted a new and broader definition of work that includes unpaid care work [29]. In 2015, "recognizing and valuing unpaid care and domestic work" was defined by United Nations as one of the Sustainable Development Goals for achieving gender equality [39].

Today, however, despite the high visibility of women's work on the international policy agenda and the improved availability of statistics on all dimensions of women's work, data gaps remain. First, nationally representative time-use data are still rare in the Global South. Second, the tendency to only view women's activity through the lens of labor force participation is still strong, especially in large-scale international surveys [5, 32, 40]. Not only is unpaid care work ignored by widely used surveys, such as the DHS or the World Bank's Living Standards Measurement Survey (LSMS), but they also often underestimate women's paid activities. In fact, based on examples in Africa, researchers demonstrate that the phrasing and administration of the work-related questions in these two surveys prime female respondents to declare that they do not work because they believe the economic activities they perform do not qualify as actual work [6, 41]. Thus, informal, episodic, and seasonal economic activities or work combined with unpaid household duties carried out by women in several countries remain hidden by the male bias prevailing in the framing of work questions in large demographic or economic surveys. Too often, critics argue, women's labor force participation is treated in isolation from their responsibilities within the family, while market and nonmarket activities should be viewed as a continuum rather than a dichotomy [6, 41]. In the same vein, data on women's activity and responsibilities within formal or informal associations and organizations at the community level also referred to as "community managing work" [9] or "collective provisioning work" [42], are rarely considered or measured.

## 3. Capturing women's work: the contribution of early demographic surveys in francophone West Africa

Women paid and unpaid work and the gender division of labor within urban households in francophone West Africa have received a fair amount of attention from family demographers in the last decade. Mirroring global trends, the origin of this interest can be traced to the 1970s. While women's work was not the focus of early empirical demographic research in West Africa, several population surveys conducted at that time helped document women's activities in the region and their interrelationships with demographic processes, such as migration or fertility. This was the case of Hoe and Wage, an ambitious research project initiated in 1973 by Gregory and Piché at the Department of Demography at the University of Montreal in collaboration with the Volta Center for Scientific Research. The purpose of the project was to trace the history of national and international circular labor migration in Burkina Faso from 1900 to 1973. To do so, the project used a unique national migration survey conducted in 1974–1975 that collected retrospective data on mobility among a nationally representative sample of men and women, along with information on migrants' economic activity at their destination [43]. Documenting for the first time the colonial and early postindependence migration history of Burkinabè women, the analyses show the role played by female migration within family networks and confirm the importance of women's domestic and agricultural labor in sustaining rural households' production. From a methodological point of view, the experience of the national migration survey also points out the difficulties in collecting data on women's activities and especially when attempting to "draw a line between household work and agricultural work" in rural Burkina Faso [43]. From a conceptual point of view, the empirical results provided strong support for the idea that demographic behaviors in rural Africa, such as circular migration or high fertility, need to be studied within the context of a familial/domestic mode of production, that is, in connection with household strategies, to draw resources from both the agricultural subsistence economy for women and the capitalist market economy for men to ensure household social reproduction [44]. Thus, according to this view, women's work in West Africa must also be analyzed as part of the "household's strategies of social reproduction," rather than as a factor of modernization and vector of ideational change [13].

Throughout the 1970s and 1980s, several other demographers stressed the crucial role played not only by domestic modes of production, including women's responsibilities in subsistence production, but also cultural and social factors, such as family and kinship structures, as well as conjugal relationships, in explaining persistent high fertility and the failure of family planning programs in rural West Africa [45–47]. As elsewhere, feminist scholars also increasingly pointed out the necessity of taking into account women's subordination and unequal access to production resources, as well as intra-household power relationships, when considering household reproductive strategies in rural Africa [48]. The adoption of these macrostructural or "institutional" approaches [49] to fertility in rural West Africa had some methodological implications. It meant moving away from large-scale standardized demographic data, such as the WFS or the DHS, to favor case studies, combining small-scale surveys and ethnographic data from in-depth field works to situate fertility behaviors within their relevant social, economic, and cultural contexts [50]. The work carried out by French demographers such as Thérèse Locoh, André Quesnels or Patrice Vimard in rural societies in Southeastern Togo and Southwestern Côte d'Ivoire provides examples of such focused fieldwork approaches [45, 51].

If these early demographic surveys on migration and fertility provided some valuable insights into women's subsistence work and the sexual division of labor within rural households in francophone West Africa, the development of retrospective longitudinal surveys starting in the 1990s was an important milestone in capturing women's work in the region. From 1989 onwards, as part of collaborative research projects between French-speaking research institutes and demography departments in Africa, France, and Québec, numerous biographical or event history surveys were performed in West Africa, both in capital cities and at the national level [52]. The first series of collections of life history was carried out in francophone African cities, including Bamako in 1992, Abidjan in 1996, Yaoundé in 1996, Antananarivo in 1998, Lomé in 2000, and again in Dakar in 2001 [53]. In Dakar and Lomé, individual interviews and focus group discussions were also conducted in addition to the life course surveys [54]. To this list of the first series of urban surveys should be added two surveys with national coverage administered in 2000, one in Burkina Faso [55] and one in Mali [56], as well as a survey targeting youth and young adults in Ouagadougou in 2010 [57].

In a context of growing rural out-migration and rising poverty due to the economic recession, the adoption of structural adjustment programs, and the 1994 devaluation of the Financial Community of Africa (CFA) franc, the overall purpose of the first wave of surveys was to evaluate the impact of the worsening living conditions on the urban integration of rural migrants, as well as on the demographic behaviors and coping strategies of individual city-dwellers and urban families. Even if the focus of the survey differed from one study to the next, the biographical questionnaires used retraced key events in at least three spheres of their respondents' lives: residence/housing, education/employment, and family (union/birth). Prior to completing these survey questions, interviewers generally utilized an "Ageven form" [58], a life history calendar organized in three columns to chronologically report the main events in the three spheres of respondents' lives and the dates on which these events occurred, in Ref. to each other. In all these retrospective longitudinal surveys, the section of the questionnaire devoted to the occupational history of men and women collected detailed information on each period of paid and unpaid labor market participation from age 12 or six (depending on the survey) to the date of the survey. Information on respondents' market work included questions related to the sector of activity, the occupational status (e.g., self-employed, employee, or unpaid family helper), whether the work was occasional or not, the form of payment, the link with the employer, and the level of formality of the job (written contract/pay slip or not).

Thus, the analyses of these event history data have not only made a particularly significant contribution to the study of migration and urban integration in West Africa, but they have also contributed to making several aspects of women's labor force participation in West African cities visible. First, data collected among different generations of city-dwellers show that the deteriorating economic conditions, men's unemployment, and increased poverty, especially during the 1990s, have pushed women to intensify and multiply their economic activities in the informal sector economy [59, 60]. Qualitative data collected in Dakar and Lomé further suggest that the growing contribution of women to household income often extends well beyond the simple additional contribution to small daily expenses [54]. The work and educational survey histories of urban men and women also reveal striking gender inequalities in the labor market. In Dakar, Yaoundé, Antananarivo, and Ouagadougou, women of all generations are still significantly more likely than men to be self-employed or perform family work in the more unstable and less profitable subsector of the informal economy [59, 61–63]. The life histories of city-dwellers in francophone West Africa were also very useful in documenting differences over time in the timing and patterns of the transition to market work by old and young generations, as well as among subgroups of adolescent girls and women, especially according to their socioeconomic origins and their migration history [64].

One of the strengths of life history data is the ability to analyze interactions between different spheres of respondents' lives over time. Some interesting results on the interaction between women's employment and demographic events, such as marriage or childbearing, emerge from the analysis of the life course data. In Ouagadougou, for example, the results show that access to employment income seems to make the social and economic imperative of marriage less pressing for young urban women, at least in the short term, and young working women tend to delay their first union [65]. Marital life is also not incompatible with the pursuit of professional activity in Sahelian cities and many women in Ouagadougou [64] and Dakar [54] balance family and paid employment. In Lomé, where the economic activity of women has always been socially valued, this reconciliation is nothing new. Single women are heavily involved in the job market, particularly in informal petty trade, and marriage only interrupts this activity briefly [66]. As for the women working as employees in the formal sector of the economy in the Togolese capital, data suggested that they tend to space out their pregnancies to remain in employment [67].

By the mid-2000s, data from demographic event history surveys had helped document women's changing experience of labor force participation in francophone West Africa and explore the potential interactions between occupational history and marital and childbearing trajectories. Although the work module of these surveys was better suited to capturing informal, episodic, and seasonal economic activities, compared to large-scale surveys, such as the DHS, it still focused on women's labor force participation and treated employment in isolation from unpaid care and household work and responsibilities, rather than conceptualizing it as a continuum. Education surveys focusing on children and adolescents contributed to showing the disproportional share of domestic chores performed by schoolgirls compared to schoolboys in urban West African households, and how this heavy domestic workload, including daily tasks such as water fetching, house cleaning, and cooking, negatively impacts their schooling trajectories [68]. As in other parts of the world, time use and ethnographic data also increasingly illustrate the heavy double burden carried by working women in francophone African cities, even among educated ones working in the formal sector of the urban economy [69]. The 1-2-3 employment surveys series conducted in 2001/2002 in seven economic capitals in francophone West Africa, for instance, included an additional time-use module where, based on an activity list, household members were asked to recall the weekly time spent on selected activities, including domestic work and caring for children, gathering wood, fetching water and shopping, working in main and second jobs, providing voluntary community services, and studying. The results demonstrate that, unlike in other regions of the world, women in West African cities do not "specialize" in domestic activities while their husbands work for pay, but instead participate in both market and domestic work. In fact, women in francophone

African cities account for a significant percentage of household hours spent working in the labor market (40% on average) while undertaking the very large majority of the household domestic work at the same time [69].

## 4. Women's unpaid household and care work and contributions: the focus of recent surveys in francophone West Africa

Building on the efforts of employment surveys to produce data on the intra-household division of labor in the region, from 2012 to 2022, three collaborative demographic research projects were developed in four francophone West African capitals, including Cotonou, Lomé, Ouagadougou, and Dakar. While the focus and the format of these projects slightly differed, all three of them were interested in capturing both women's market and nonmarket work and responsibilities within the context of households' gender relationships, family dynamics, and domestic organization. The objectives were also to assess women's strategies for combining market work and domestic and care responsibilities and produce quantitative measures of women's current contributions to family well-being. The first of these projects was a comparative multidisciplinary research program initiated in 2012 by the French Laboratoire population, environnement et développement (LPED) in collaboration with four West African demographic institutions[1]. The data collected combined qualitative interviews and quantitative data from a survey entitled "*Activité économique, partage des ressources et prise en charge des dépenses au sein des Ménages urbains*" (AEMU), conducted in three West African cities (Cotonou, Lomé and Ouagadougou). The survey included a household questionnaire as well as an individual one administered to both men and women in each city. The second survey, "Enquête Femmes et Organisation Travail – Famille à Dakar" (FORTE) was performed in Dakar in 2018, as part of a larger collaborative research program.[2] FORTE's objectives and structure were very similar to those of AEMU, with a focus on highly educated women. Initiated by the University of Montreal and two African research institutes[3], the last of the three surveys was a longitudinal retrospective survey, entitled "*Travail au Féminin*" (TAF), which was carried out in Ouagadougou in 2019/2020 and in Lomé in 2021/2022. The purpose of the AEMU, FORTE, and TAF surveys was not only to examine the intra-household division of labor but also to explore the interrelationships between women's work (both market and domestic) and family structure and dynamics. Thus, in addition to the modules on work and the household division of labor, each survey questionnaire includes questions on union and marriage, in addition to childbearing behaviors, as well as the sociodemographic characteristics of households and individuals (the

[1] The research was funded by the French National Research Agency (ANR-10-SUDS-005-01). The scientific partners included the Laboratoire population, environnement et développement (LPED), a research laboratory from the French Institut de Recherche pour le Développement (IRD), the Center of Formation and Research in Population (CEFORP), Abomey-Calavi University in Cotonou (Bénin), the Demographic Research Unit (URD), University of Lomé (Togo), and the Higher Institute of Population Sciences (ISSP), Joseph Ki Zerbo University, Ouagadougou (Burkina Faso).

[2] The project, funded by French National Research Agency (ANR - young researcher program), was developed by IRD in collaboration with the Senegalese National Statistics and Demography Agency (INSD).

[3] TAF is a collaborative project between the Department of Sociology at the University of Montreal, ISSP in Ouagadougou (Burkina Faso) and URD in Lomé (Togo), funded by the Canadian Social Sciences and Humanities Research Council (SSHRC).

| Sphere of work/responsibilities | Selected dimensions measured |
|---|---|
| Market work | Type and sector of activity |
| | Occupational status and category, relationship to employer, employer type |
| | Level of formalization and protection of job (registered, account keeping, pay slip, formal contract) |
| | Job quality: level, type, and regularity of income, public/private insurance, retirement funds, social security, promotion |
| | Work location, commuting time and means of transport to work, job-related monthly travels |
| | Level of job satisfaction |
| Household domestic and care work | Household chores (meal preparation, household repairs, cleaning, washing dishes, doing laundry, fetching water, gardening) |
| | Childcare (taking children to school and picking them up, showering and bathing them, supervision of homework, care when sick) |
| | Help with domestic chores and/or childcare services and use of domestic and or childcare services<br>Recruitment, management, and working conditions of domestic staff |
| | Provision of advice/mediation in case of family or community conflicts |
| | Perceived difficulties in combining market economic activities and domestic responsibilities (most draining domestic chores, feeling of stress or exhaustion associated with workload) |
| Voluntary collective/community work | Participation in formal and informal associations/groups/organizations (professional, neighborhood, community, religious, rotating saving and credits associations): average weekly time spent, responsibilities within the association |
| Contribution to household expenses and family support | Recurrent household expenses: water, electricity, gas, coal, rent, food, health costs, daily travel costs, school fees, children's clothing and health expenses, professional services (maid, waste collection service, others) |
| | Major household expenses: furniture, car, motorbike, piece of land, house construction, household appliances |
| | Contributions to expenses related to community/extended family events (marriages, baptisms, religious celebrations) |
| | Financial support to elderly parents, in-laws, siblings, cousins, adult children, and other relatives |

**Table 1.**
*Selected dimensions of women's work measured by the AEMU, FORTE, and TAF questionnaires.*

woman and her husband/partner). **Table 1** presents selected dimensions considered and measured by AEMU, FORTE, and TAF to capture women's work and responsibilities outside and within their households, as well as their contributions to family well-being.

In all three questionnaires, the section on individual market work (both paid and unpaid) is more detailed than the typical occupational section used in previous demographic surveys in francophone West African cities. Besides questions regarding activity type, occupational status, and category, several questions were asked to assess the level of informality of job and sector of employment, as well as job quality (level and regularity of earnings, health insurance, social security, and promotion for formal employees). Information regarding job location, commuting time, and means of transport to work as well as job-related monthly travel was also collected. The TAF questionnaire also included a subjective question on job satisfaction. To assess the division of labor within the household and the extent of women's unpaid domestic and care work, the three questionnaires used activity list questions that have been proven superior to keyword questions in measuring women's work [41]. The first activity list refers to household chores, such as cleaning, preparing meals, washing dishes, doing laundry, grocery shopping, water fetching, gardening, and household repairs. The AEMU household questionnaire recorded who in the household was usually responsible for each activity. In the TAF individual questionnaire, for each chore listed, the female respondent was asked whether she had done the chore the previous week, and if yes, how many hours she spent doing it, and if not, who was mainly responsible for it. The second list discussed childcare for children under 12 residing in the household and included activities such as taking children to school and collecting them, supervising their homework, and showering and bathing them, as well as taking care of them when sick. The surveys also tried to capture whether women were helped in their domestic and care work. In the FORTE survey, specific questions were asked about the recruitment and payment of domestic workers as well as about their working conditions. In the TAF survey, for each activity women were involved in, they were asked whether someone else was also responsible for the activity, and if yes, who that person was. All questionnaires inquired about the use of paid domestic and childcare services.

Additionally, women interviewed in the TAF survey in Ouagadougou and Lomé were asked how often they were consulted for advice within the family or community and for mediation in case of family conflicts. They were also questioned on the potential difficulties they faced in combining economic activities and domestic responsibilities and whether they ever felt any stress or exhaustion associated with the workload outside or at home. Besides market and household work, the TAF survey also tried to capture women's community work and responsibilities. The questionnaire included a module on the respondent's history of involvement in voluntary associations or groups since age 15, with questions to estimate the level of women's involvement in each association (time spent, type of responsibilities). Each survey, through its individual or household questionnaire, also measured women's contribution to household expenses, distinguishing between recurrent ones (food, water, and rent, as well as energy bills, health costs, daily travel costs, school fees, children's clothing and health expenses and professional services for cleaning, waste management or other chores) and major household expenses (furniture, car, motorbike, piece of land, house construction and household appliances). Women's financial contribution outside the household was also estimated with questions regarding their yearly participation in expenses related to community/extended family events (marriages, baptisms, and religious celebrations), as well as the level of financial support they provided to immediate and extended family members.

Although these survey data, especially the most recent ones, have not yet been fully explored, the first analyses provide valuable insight into women's work. First, data confirm the high female labor force participation in francophone West African cities, with working women generally self-employed in the informal sector of the economy (in petty trade, for most of them), declaring rather low incomes [70]. Data further show that however modest it may be, women's income allows them to participate in a substantial way in the payment of household expenses and in meeting basic household consumption needs [71, 72]. In Cotonou, Ouagadougou and Lomé, food, water, coal (or gas), medical care for children and school fees were expenditure items that women declared that they paid on a regular basis, fully or partially. Data also confirm that men in the four cities are still performing very few domestic chores. In Dakar and Lomé, the core of domestic work, including time-consuming, repetitive, and tedious chores (preparing meals, washing dishes, doing laundry, and cleaning), remains almost exclusively female work, and men's involvement is often limited to children's educational support (the supervision of homework or driving children to school) [73]. Despite some timid transformations among the younger generation of highly educated men, the division of labor between women and men within households overall remains highly unbalanced [71, 74]. Furthermore, AEMU data demonstrate that in Cotonou and Lomé, when controlling for the generation the men belong to, the husband's involvement in household work tends to further decrease over the couple's life cycle, as the pressure to care for young children diminishes [75]. In these two cities, men's participation in domestic work, particularly in the preparation of meals, depends on their professional activity. In Ouagadougou, qualitative data suggest domestic help has become scarce and the day of active women, who generally "resigned themselves" to the lack of involvement of their husbands in household domestic and care work, is a real "obstacle course" [71]. In fact, more than a third of economically active women interviewed by the TAF survey in Ouagadougou (36%) and more than a quarter (26%) of their counterparts in Lomé declared feeling "often" or "very often" depleted by their daily workload. In Cotonou, qualitative data further posits that women's ability to withstand the stress of combining market work and household responsibilities depends on their educational and financial capital as well as their ability to mobilize a social network. Some of the more privileged women may even choose to divorce to pursue their professional ambitions [76].

Despite the contribution of recent data collection in West African cities in improving the measurement of women's work and responsibilities, some important work dimensions are still missing from family demography surveys in the region. First, the measurement of women's care of family members should be expanded beyond childcare to include indicators of women's involvement in the care of elderly parents, as well as relatives who are ill or living with disabilities. Indicators should measure the provision of regular care to any vulnerable person, with or without family ties. Second, capturing the extent of women's emotional workload associated with the daily management of family responsibilities, as well as the physical and psychological consequences of the heavy burden of paid and unpaid work both for women and their families require further attention. Third, as revealed by the recent COVID-19 crisis, women's work and care can be crucial to the survival of the family in times of emergency. Survey data on women's individual and collective activities to cope with a health crisis or environmental disasters such as drought episodes, inflow of environmental refugees, sudden depletion of natural resources, disease outbreaks, or more generally, to deal with family traumatic events (death, illness, accident, and employment loss) could also be useful in documenting women's contribution to family and community survival in time of hardships. Finally, the potential impact of the exponential growth in the use of information and communication technologies (ICTs) over the last decades in Africa on women's work, needs further investigation. Survey data on ICT use, especially through mobile phones, along with indicators of paid and unpaid work could help assess the impact of ICTs not only on women's labor force participation but also on domestic and care responsibilities, including "kin work" at home and abroad [77], as well as community and social activities.

## 5. Conclusions

Since the 1970s, feminist scholars and activists have constantly pointed out the need to recognize and tackle the mismeasurement of women's activities and the underestimation of their contribution to family well-being and economic development. From their early research on women's agricultural subsistence activities, domestic labor, and informal sector work around the world, as well as the damaging effects of colonial and post-colonial agricultural policies, to the examinations of local, national, and global survival strategies developed by women in the context of the 1980s and 1990s economic crisis and neoliberal reforms, and the recent analysis of persisting gender inequality in household and unpaid care work, feminist scholars, especially economists, have tried to make all aspects of women's work visible. Their longstanding efforts have been instrumental in promoting the collection and analysis of time-use data, in enhancing female work indicators in employment surveys, and in revising international guidelines to progressively include women's nonmarket work in national accounts and official statistics. Over the last five decades, demographers have also been interested in capturing women's work and exploring the interactions between work and demographic processes. In francophone West Africa, for instance, throughout the 1970s and 1980s, several demographers, based on focused case studies, stressed the crucial role played by domestic modes of production, including women's responsibility in subsistence production, in explaining gendered patterns of migration or persistent high fertility. From the 1990s onwards, the adoption of the life course approach by numerous collaborative research teams, and the production of event history survey data in francophone West Africa, was another milestone in the analysis of women's work in the region. The retrospective occupational, residential, and familial history data collected by these surveys uniquely documented the changing employment experience of generations of women, the persisting gender inequalities on the urban labor market, and the heterogeneity of work experiences among sub-groups of female city-dwellers. They have also allowed for exploring the interactions between women's employment and demographic events, such as marriage or childbearing, over time. Despite these contributions, however, these survey data, like most data on the topic in and outside Africa, still focus on women's market work and treat the labor force participation of women in isolation from their responsibilities within the family. Recent demographic surveys conducted in francophone West Africa have attempted to fill these data gaps and have collected, in addition to classic demographic data on family dynamics, statistics on women's market work, nonmarket domestic and care responsibilities, and community activities as well as their current contributions to household expenses and family support.

These new data provide promising analysis opportunities that could help inform the design and implementation of policies and programs promoting women's work in the region. In fact, today, the promotion of "decent work" is at the top of the agenda for African governments, as well as regional and international development institutions. Female entrepreneurship, in particular, occupies a prominent place in the narrative of Africa's future. In a "smart economics" approach to women's work, which sees investing in women essentially as a way to spur economic growth, initiatives encouraging women's entrepreneurship that has flourished on the continent in the last decade have focused on the provision of technical training or finance to help women develop their businesses. They tend to ignore crucial structural issues, such as the unequal division of labor and power relationships within households, that contribute to the reproduction of gender inequalities, including inequalities in the labor market.

In such a context, the production, analysis, and diffusion by feminist scholars, including demographers, of both qualitative and quantitative data on all aspects of women's work, including unpaid care and household responsibilities, remain as critical today as they were 50 years ago.

## Author details

Anne E. Calvès[1]* and Agnès Adjamagbo[2]

1 Sociology Department, University of Montreal, Montreal, Canada

2 Population Environment and Development Laboratory, Research Institute for Development, Aix-Marseille University, France

*Address all correspondence to: anne.calves@umontreal.ca

## References

[1] International Labour Organisation. An Uneven and Gender-Unequal COVID-19 Recovery: Update on Gender and Employment Trends 2021. Geneva: ILO; 2021. p. 16. Available from: https://www.ilo.org/employment/Whatwedo/Publications/policy-briefs/WCMS_824865/lang--en/index.htm

[2] Kabeer N, Razavi S, Van der Meulen RY. Feminist economic perspectives on the COVID-19 pandemic. Feminist Economics. 2021;**27**(1-2):1-29. DOI: 10.1080/13545701.2021.1876906

[3] Riley NE. Demography of gender. In: Handbook of Population. Cham: Springer; 2019. pp. 107-142. DOI: 10.1007/978-3-030-10910-3

[4] Elson D. Recognize, reduce, and redistribute unpaid care work: How to close the gender gap. New Labor Forum. 2017;**26**(2):52-61. DOI: 10.1177/1095796017700135

[5] Finlay JE, Efevbera Y, Ndikubagenzi J, Karra M, Canning D. Reframing the measurement of women's work in the Sub-Saharan African context. Work, Employment and Society. 2019;**33**(3):518-528. DOI: 10.1177/095001701877424

[6] Boserup E. Woman's Role in Economic Development. London: George Allen and Unwin; 1970. p. 283. DOI: 10.2307/1238241

[7] Goetz AM. From feminist knowledge to data for development: The bureaucratic management of information on women and development. IDS Bulletin. 1994;**25**(2):27-36. DOI: 10.1111/j.1759-5436.1994.mp25002003.x

[8] Rathgeber EM. WID, WAD, GAD: Trends in research and practice. The Journal of Developing Areas. 1990;**24**(4):489-502. Available from: http://www.jstor.org/stable/4191904

[9] Moser CO. Gender planning in the third world: Meeting practical and strategic gender needs. World Development. 1989;**17**(11):1799-1825. DOI: 10.1016/0305-750X(89)90201-5

[10] Jaquette JS. Women/gender and development: The growing gap between theory and practice. Studies in Comparative International Development. 2017;**52**(2):242-260. DOI: 10.1007/s12116-017-9248-8

[11] Benerìa L. Accounting for women's work: The progress of two decades. World Development. 1992;**20**(11):1547-1560. DOI: 10.1016/0305-750X(92)90013-L

[12] Lloyd CB. The contribution of the World Fertility Surveys to an understanding of the relationship between women's work and fertility. Studies in Family Planning. 1991;**22**(3):144-161. DOI: 10.2307/1966642

[13] Poirier J, Piché V, Neill G. Travail des femmes et fécondité dans les pays en développement: que nous a appris l'Enquête mondiale de la fécondité? Cahiers québécois de démographie. 1989;**18**(1):159-184. DOI: 10.7202/010006ar

[14] Antrobus P. The Global women's Movement: Origins, Issues and Strategies. New York: Bloomsbury Publishing; 2008. p. 197

[15] Elson D. The Impact of Structural Adjustment on Women. In: Onimode B, editor. The IMF, the World Bank, and

African Debt. London, New York: Zedbooks; 1989. pp. 56-74

[16] Benerìa L, Feldman S. Unequal Burden: Economic Crisis, Persistent Poverty and Women's Work. Boulder: Westview Press; 1992. p. 278. DOI: 10.5860/choice.30-5128

[17] Afshar H, Dennis C, editors. Women and Adjustment Policies in the Third World. 2e éd. ed. London: MacMillan; 2016. p. 271. DOI: 10.1007/978-1-349-11961-1

[18] Elson D, Pearson R. Nimble fingers make cheap workers: An analysis of Women's employment in third world export manufacturing. Feminist Review. 1987;7:87-107. DOI: 10.1057/fr.1981.6

[19] Chant S. The 'feminisation of poverty' and the 'feminisation' of anti-poverty programmes: Room for revision? The Journal of Development Studies. 2008;**44**(2):165-197. DOI: 10.1080/00220380701789810

[20] Pareñas RS. Servants of Globalization: Women, Migration, and Domestic. Palo Alto: Stanford University Press; 2001. p. 309. DOI: 10.1515/9780804796187

[21] Ehrenreich B, Hochschild AR, editors. Global Woman. Nannies, Maids and Sex Workers in the new Economy. New York: Metropolitan Books; 2002. p. 336

[22] Cleland J. ICPD and the feminization of population and development issues. Health Transition Review. 1996;**6**(1):107-110. Available from: https://www.jstor.org/stable/40608710

[23] Halfon SE. The Cairo Consensus: Demographic Surveys, women's Empowerment, and Regime Change in Population Policy. Plymouth: Lexington Books; 2007. p. 261

[24] Calvès AE. Empowerment: The history of a key concept in contemporary development discourse. Revue Tiers Monde. 2009;**4**(200):735-749. DOI: 10.3917/rtm.200.0735

[25] Charmes J. A review of empirical evidence on time use in Africa from UN-sponsored surveys. In: Blackden CM, Wodon Q, editors. Gender, Time Use, and Poverty in Sub-Saharan Africa. Washington DC: The World Bank; 2006. pp. 39-72. DOI: 10.1596/978-0-8213-6561-8

[26] Charmes J, Wieringa S. Measuring Women's empowerment: An assessment of the gender-related development index and the gender empowerment measure. Journal of Human Development. 2003;**4**(3):419-435. DOI: 10.1080/1464988032000125773

[27] Chant S, Pedwell C. Women, Gender and the Informal Economy: An Assessment of ILO Research and Suggested Ways Forward. Geneva: International Labour Organization Publishing; 2008. p. 64

[28] Esquivel V, Budlender D, Folbre N, Hirway I. Explorations: Time-use surveys in the south. Feminist Economics. 2008;**14**(3):107-152. DOI: 10.1080/13545700802075135

[29] Charmes J. The Unpaid Care Work and the Labour Market. An Analysis of Time Use Data Based on the Latest World Compilation of Time-Use Surveys. Geneva: International Labour Office; 2019. p. 161

[30] Bianchi SM, Milkie MA. Work and family research in the first decade of the 21st century. Journal of Marriage and Family. 2010;**72**(3):705-725. DOI: 10.1111/j.17413737.2010.00726.x

[31] Casper LM. Family demography, chapter 3. In: Poston DL, editor.

Handbook of Population. Cham: Springer; 2019. pp. 79-105. DOI: 10.1007/978-3-030-10910-3

[32] Chopra D, Zambelli E. No Time to Rest: Women's Lived Experiences of Balancing Paid Work and Unpaid Care Work. Global Synthesis Report. Brighton: Institute of Development Studies; 2017. p. 60. Available from: https://www.ids.ac.uk/publications/no-time-to-rest-womens-lived-experiences-of-balancing-paid-work-and-unpaid-care-work/

[33] Derose L. Continuity of women's work, breastfeeding, and fertility in Ghana in the 1980s. Population Studies. 2002;**56**(2):167-179. DOI: 10.1080/00324720215924

[34] Bongaarts J, Blanc AK, McCarthy JK. The links between women's employment and children at home: Variations in low- and middle-income countries by world region. Population Studies. 2019;**73**(2):149-163. DOI: 10.1080/00324728.2019.1581896

[35] Yaya S, Uthman OA, Ekholuenetale M, Bishwajit G. Women empowerment as an enabling factor of contraceptive use in sub-Saharan Africa: A multilevel analysis of cross-sectional surveys of 32 countries. Reproductive Health. 2018;**15**(1):1-12. DOI: 10.1186/s12978-018-0658-5

[36] Akinyemi JO, Solanke BL, Odimegwu CO. Maternal employment and child survival during the era of sustainable development goals: Insights from proportional hazards modelling of Nigeria birth history data. Annals of Global Health. 2018;**84**(1):15-30. DOI: 10.29024/aogh.11

[37] Tandrayen-Ragoobur V. Intimate partner violence and women's labour force participation in Sub Saharan Africa. Community, Work & Family. 2020;**23**(1):19-43. DOI: 10.1080/13668803.2018.1540400

[38] International Labour Office. Women at Work: Trends. Geneva: International Labour Organization; 2016 Available from: http://www.ilo.org/gender/Informationresources/Publications/WCMS_457317/lang--en/index.htm

[39] United Nations General Assembly. Transforming our world: The 2030 agenda for sustainable development. A/RES/70/1. 2015

[40] Razavi S. Rethinking care in a development context: An introduction. Development and Change. 2011;**42**(4):873-903. DOI: 10.1111/j.1467-7660.2011.01722.x

[41] Langsten RS. Two approaches to measuring women's work in developing countries: A comparison of survey data from Egypt. Population and Development Review. 2008;**34**(2):283-305. DOI: 10.1111/j.1728-4457.2008.00220.x

[42] Neysmith S, Baker-Collins S, Reitsma-Street M. Beyond Caring Labour to Provisioning Work. Toronto: University of Toronto Press; 2012. p. 208. DOI: 10.3138/9781442695726

[43] Cordell D, Gregory JW, Piche V, editors. Hoe and Wage: A Social History of a Circular Migration System in West Africa. New York: Routledge; 1996. p. 400. DOI: 10.4324/9780429037092

[44] Gregory JW, Piché V. Mode de production et régime démographique. Canadian Journal of African Studies. Revue canadienne des études africaines. 1985;**19**(1):73-79. DOI: 10.1080/00083968.1985.10804099

[45] Locoh T. Fécondité et famille en Afrique de l'Ouest. Paris: INED; 1984. p. 182

[46] Frank O, McNicoll G. An interpretation of fertility and population policy in Kenya. Population and Development Review. 1987;**1987**:209-243. Available from: https://www.jstor.org/stable/1973192

[47] Lesthaeghe RJ. Reproduction and Social Organization in sub-Saharan Africa. Berkeley: University of California Press; 1989. p. 556

[48] Vock J. Demographic theories and Women's reproductive labour. In: Stichter S, Parpart J, editors. Patriarchy and Class: African Women in the Home and Workforce. London: Westview Press; 2019. pp. 81-96

[49] McNicoll G. Institutional determinants of fertility change. Population and Development Review. 1980;**6**(3):441-462. DOI: 10.2307/1972410

[50] Oppong C. Relationships between women's Work and Demographic Behaviour: Some Research Evidence in West Africa. Geneva: International Labour Organisation; 1991. p. 63. DOI: 10.13140/RG.2.2.25617.35683

[51] Quesnel A, Vimard P. Dynamique de population en économie de plantation. Le plateau de Dayes au Sud-ouest du Togo. Paris: ORSTOM; 1988. p. 505

[52] Calvès AE, Marcoux R. Réponses des populations à la crise en Afrique francophone: l'éclairage des enquêtes biographiques récentes. Cahiers québécois de démographie. 2004;**33**(2):161-165. DOI: 10.7202/011106ar

[53] Antoine P, Bocquier P, Marcoux R, Piché V. L'expérience des enquêtes biographiques en Afrique. In: Schoumaker B, Tabutin B, editors. Les systèmes d'information en démographie et en sciences sociales: nouvelles questions. Louvain-La-Neuve: Presses universitaires de Louvain; 2010. pp. 103-130

[54] Adjamagbo A, Antoine P, Beguy D, Dial FB. Comment les femmes concilient-elles mariage et travail à Dakar et à Lomé? Working Papers DT/2006/04. Paris: DIAL; 2006. p. 18

[55] Poirier J, Piché V, Le Jeune G, Dabiré B, Wane HR. Projet d'étude des stratégies de reproduction des populations sahéliennes à partir de l'enquête «Dynamique migratoire, insertion urbaine et environnement au Burkina Faso». Cahiers québécois de démographie. 2001;**30**(2):289-309. DOI: 10.7202/010312ar

[56] Marcoux R, Guèye M, Konaté MK. Environnement familial, itinéraires scolaires et travail des enfants au Mali. Dans: Actes du colloque de l'AIDELF sur Enfants d'aujourd'hui. Diversité des contextes, pluralité des parcours; 10-13 décembre 2002. Paris: AIDELF-PUF; 2006. pp. 961-973

[57] Calvès AE. First union formation in urban Burkina Faso: Competing relationship transitions to marriage or cohabitation. Demographic Research. 2016;**34**:421-450. DOI: 10.4054/DemRes.2016.34.15

[58] Antoine P, Bry X, Diouf PD. La fiche «Ageven»: un outil pour la collecte des données rétrospectives. Bulletin de liaison STATECO. 1987;**49**:33-52

[59] Antoine P, Razafindrakoto M, Roubaud F. Contraints de rester jeunes? Évolution de l'insertion dans trois capitales africaines: Dakar, Yaoundé, Antananarivo. Autrepart. 2001;**2**:17-36. DOI: 10.3917/autr.018.0017

[60] Adjamagbo A, Antoine P, Dial FB. Le dilemme des Dakaroises: entre travailler

et «bien travailler». In: Diop MC, editor. Gouverner le Sénégal: entre ajustement structurel et développement durable. Paris: karthala; 2004. pp. 247-272

[61] Calvès AE, Schoumaker B. Deteriorating economic context and changing patterns of youth employment in urban Burkina Faso: 1980-2000. World Development. 2004;**32**(8):1341-1354. DOI: 10.1016/j.worlddev.2004.03.002

[62] Diagne A, Lessault D. Émancipation résidentielle différée et recomposition des dépendances intergénérationnelles à Dakar. Paris: Les Collections du CEPED; 2007. p. 41

[63] Zourkaléini Y, Piché V. Economic integration in a West-African urban labour market: Does migration matter? The case of Ouagadougou, Burkina Faso. Demographic Research. 2007;**17**:497-540. DOI: 10.4054/DemRes.2007.17.17

[64] Calvès AE, Kobiané J. Genre et nouvelles dynamiques d'insertion professionnelle chez les jeunes à Ouagadougou. Autrepart. 2014;**3**:33-56. DOI: 10.3917/autr.071.0033

[65] Calvès AE, Kobiané JF, Martel E. Changing transition to adulthood in urban Burkina Faso. Journal of Comparative Family Studies. 2007;**38**(2):265-283. DOI: 10.3138/jcfs.38.2.265

[66] Adjamagbo A, Antoine P. Être femme autonome dans une capitale Africaine: les cas de Dakar et Lomé. In Vallin J, éditeur. Du genre et de l'Afrique, ouvrage en hommage à Thérèse Locoh. Paris: Éditions de l'INED; 2009, 2009. pp. 305-318

[67] Beguy D. The impact of female employment on fertility in Dakar (Senegal) and Lome (Togo). Demographic Research. 2009;**20**:97-128. DOI: 10.4054/DemRes.2009.20.7

[68] Marcoux R. Le travail des enfants au Mali. Tentative de mesure et inégalités de genre. Revue de droit comparé du travail et de la sécurité sociale. 2016;**2015**(2):84-90

[69] Herrera J, Torelli C. Domestic work and employment in Africa: What is the tradeoff for women? In: De Vreyer P, Roubaud F, éditeurs. Urban Labor Markets in Sub-Saharan Africa. Washington DC: World Bank Publications et Agence française de développement; 2013. pp. 221-249. 10.1596/9780821397817_ch07

[70] Kpadonou N. Travail-famille: conciliation des rôles économiques et domestiques dans trois capitales d'Afrique de l'Ouest. Louvain-La-Neuve: Presses universitaires de Louvain; 2019. p. 299

[71] Gnoumou Thiombiano B. Le travail et la famille en milieu urbain. Un défi pour les femmes à Ouagadougou. In: Calvès AE, Dial FB, Marcoux M, éditeurs. Nouvelles dynamiques familiales en Afrique. Québec: Presses de l'Université du Québec, Coll. Les sociétés africaines en mutation; 2018. pp. 155-181

[72] Adjamagbo A, Gastineau B, Kpadonou N. Travail-famille: un défi pour les femmes à Cotonou. Recherches féministes. 2016, 2016;**29**(2):17-41. DOI: 10.7202/1038719ar

[73] Moguérou L, Wayack-Pambè M, Awissi M. Les femmes chefs de ménage célibataires à Dakar et à Ouagadougou. Matérialité et vécu d'une situation atypique. In: Calvès AE, Dial FB, Marcoux M, editors. Nouvelles dynamiques familiales en Afrique. Québec: Presses de l'Université du

Québec, Coll. Les sociétés africaines en mutation; 2018. pp. 93-118

[74] Moguérou L, Vampo C, Kpadonou N, Adjamagbo A. Les hommes au travail domestique en Afrique de l'Ouest. Cahiers du GEN. 2019;**67**:97-119. DOI: 10.3917/cdge.067.0097

[75] Kpadonou N, Adjamagbo A, Gastineau B, Toudeka MR. Cycle de vie des couples et partage des tâches domestiques au sein des couples à Cotonou et Lomé. In: Pennec S, Girard C, Sanderson JP, editors. Trajectoires et âges de la vie. Paris: AIDELF; 2016. p. 14

[76] Adjamagbo A. Femmes africaines et vulnérabilité; la situation est-elle en train de changer? In: Adjamagbo A, Gastineau B, Golaz V, Ouattara F, editors. La vulnérabilité à l'encontre des idées reçues. Marseille: Les impromptus du LPED; 2020. pp. 35-51

[77] Bakuri AZ, Amoabeng D. Doing kin work among Ghanaians home and abroad: A paradigm shift to ICT. Family Relations. 2023:1-16. DOI: 10.1111/fare.12838

Chapter 10

# Perspective Chapter: Foreign Residents Providing Eldercare in Japan – Government Data and Their Limitations

*Deborah J. Milly*

## Abstract

How many foreign residents in Japan are caring for Japanese senior citizens? What trends will likely characterize reliance on foreign residents for caregiving? Japan leads the world in its proportion of seniors, but many other countries are following a similar path. The visa system and the care industry in Japan are highly institutionalized and diverse, posing challenges for assessing the extent of foreign residents' contribution to care. Scholars, policy professionals, and those advising potential migrants from other countries should recognize the pros and cons of the major government data sources and not rely on just one source. This chapter provides guidance on these sources and suggestions for using them effectively. It further highlights that, given recent access to new visa options, employers are opting for workers with more skills and the possibility of remaining in Japan for a longer period of time.

**Keywords:** Japan, aging society, eldercare, care workers, migration, administrative data

## 1. Introduction

How many foreign residents in Japan are caring for Japanese senior citizens? Answering this question is not straightforward, even though Japanese policy discussion has focused on the need for foreign migrants to take up some of this role. Among the many challenges population-aging brings across countries, the demand for eldercare, especially for the old-old population over 80 years old, is a major one. Japan is not alone: many countries in both the industrialized and industrializing world can expect the portion of their population over 65 years old to increase. As of 2021, persons 65 and older made up 30% of Japan's population, compared to 24% in Italy and between 22% and 23% in several other countries, including Finland, Portugal, Bulgaria, and Greece. By 2050, China, the Republic of Korea (South Korea), Japan, Italy, and Spain are all projected to have aged populations of over 35%, with China surpassing 40% [1].

The demand for care for older citizens collides with realities of a shrinking labor force in which tightened competition for labor across sectors contributes further to the difficulty of securing care providers. Despite technological innovations to improve working conditions and somewhat reduce the need for care industry staff, and even if wages can be raised for underpaid care workers, labor market conditions work against such efforts. More attractive forms of employment are increasingly available for persons who otherwise might choose to be care workers. Some countries have already made a practice of relying on foreign-born care workers to take up needed caregiving, but patterns of migration and the institutional contexts of care provision vary across countries, affecting opportunities for migrating and the methods for estimating how many foreign migrants are providing care labor.

The Japanese case highlights the significance of the institutional contexts of care provision and visa systems for the data available. In some countries, lack of documentation status and a largely informal labor sector for domestic work can obstruct data-gathering efforts. But even when administrative data are available, administrative purposes do not necessarily align with the goals of researchers who might want to use those data. This article addresses recent patterns of foreign residents in Japan providing "care work," including migrants whose migration status recognizes their care work employment and those persons whose residence status makes no distinction as to their employment. The article explains the hazards of using Japanese data sources, as they often are partial and tend to underrepresent care workers among certain categories of foreign migrants. The main intent here is to provide some guidance to researchers and policy experts from outside Japan concerning the *types* of administrative data available and what they contribute for understanding the extent to which foreign migrants in Japan are coming to occupy a position in providing care, mainly for those sixty-five and older. Disparate groups of foreign residents in the country under different visa conditions are working in a largely formal care industry. Different agencies gather data to suit their purposes, producing inconsistencies despite some overlap. By referring to multiple data sources, it becomes clear that employers prefer workers with more training and who can work fulltime and with visas that in future may allow them to remain longer-term in Japan.

This chapter proceeds as follows. It first provides critical context as to how the term "care work" is linked to formal institutions and explains the variety of visa statuses through which foreign migrants may end up performing care. It then introduces the method and justification for examining administrative data. It proceeds to compare the major types of relevant government data in Japan, focusing on their usefulness, the hazards of relying on one data source alone, and putting the numbers into the bigger context of the care labor market. The concluding discussion addresses which data, when used together, may be useful for answering which questions.

## 2. Context

### 2.1 Long-term care as an industry

When speaking about "care work" and "care work migration" with respect to Japan, it is critical to understand three points. First, the Long-term Care Insurance (LTCI) program, passed into legislation in 1997 and implemented in 2000, frames and defines the general use of the term "care" (*kaigo*). Second, "care work" and categories of care worker are defined through both the same public insurance system and through legislation that specifies the credential of Certified Welfare Worker (CWW) and Certified Care Worker (CCW) and requirements for other types of care workers. Third, childcare is separate from this system and informal live-in domestic care is not the norm in Japan. This means that the country differs from countries that either provide a formal possibility of live-in domestic care work to foreign migrants or that rely on the informal sector and possibly on undocumented foreign migrants to provide care to individual households. Instead, speaking of "care work" involves a formal care labor market and a sprawling set of institutions in the care industry that have grown up to meet demands for a variety of forms of care and differing degrees of need for care.

Although the care industry has burgeoned and includes many different types of enterprises, many of which are owned and run by the same management, typically in surveys of employers about care workers some of the main categories addressed are: home-visit care worker, general "care worker," certified care worker, nurse, care manager, nutritionist, physical therapist, and occupational therapist. Among these groups, however, the general term care worker (*kaigo shokuin*) may variously apply to home-visit care workers, certified care workers, and entry-level care workers; these workers are often the focus of discussion about difficulties in hiring and retaining staff and problems of low wages. Certified Care Worker (CCW) is a credential obtained through several routes, including by graduating from some type of higher education program (such as a two-year vocational program in care work or a college-level program for social welfare training). In the past, graduates of two-year care training programs were exempt from passing the national certification exam, but the requirements are currently in transition such that from 2027 all graduates will be required to pass the national exam [2]. This matters currently for international student graduates who have been able to delay passing the exam and continue working for an additional five years.

Entry-level care workers, however, can work after a basic set of training, often provided by the employer or a local government. They can be found in residential facilities and working for providers of in-home visits for specified services. Such services do not require workers to contract with individual families or live with them. A key problem among entry-level care workers is that not only is the pay very low, but workers in these positions have themselves been aging. In 2021, 45% of employers in a large-scale survey reported employing workers 65 or older as "care workers" and 34% as home-visit caregivers [3].

### 2.2 The care labor supply and foreign migrants

The number of care workers has steadily grown to meet the needs of the aging population since the implementation of long-term care insurance, and officials expect that number continue to grow (see **Figures 1** and **2**). As of 2017, the Ministry of Health, Labor, and Welfare (MHLW) estimated that Japan would need 380,000 additional care workers by 2025 [4]. In 2021, the MHLW estimated that by 2040 an additional 690,000 care workers would be needed over the current levels [5]. In the meantime, government efforts to encourage technological improvements have expanded, measures to promote employment of Japanese workers have continued, and the immigration control system has been modified to enable foreign migrants to work as care workers through a variety of routes.

Even before Shinzō Abe became prime minister for a second time in 2012 and embarked on wide-ranging reforms, including labor migration reforms, portions of the long-term care industry were advocating changes. Under Abe's administration, several adjustments to the overall labor migration options, and some specific to care workers, created more options for care businesses to employ foreign care workers.

The visa options that allow for care work migration have increased, as has the number of care-providing migrants. Visa statuses not designed to allow "care work migration"

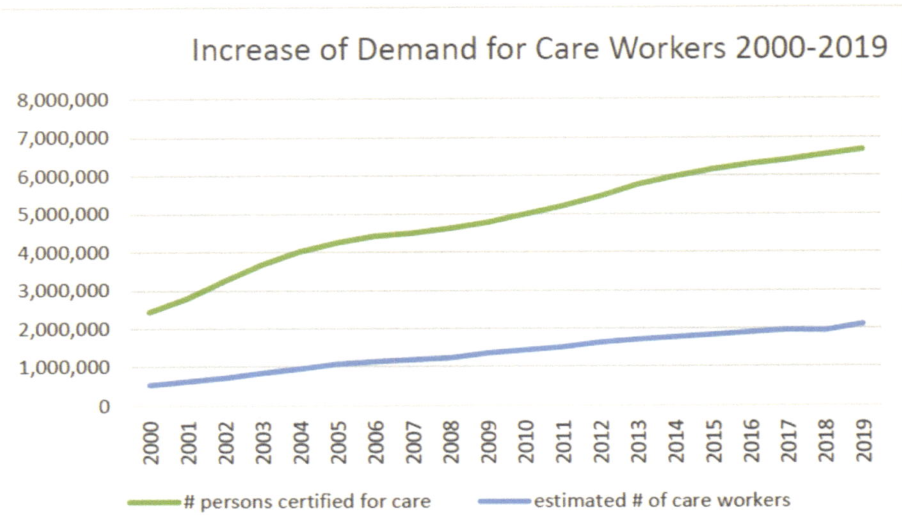


**Figure 1.**
*Increase of demand for Care Workers in Japan, 2000–2019. Source: [6]. Note: The LTCI provides for certifying the level of care needed for individuals as assessed by local care managers.*

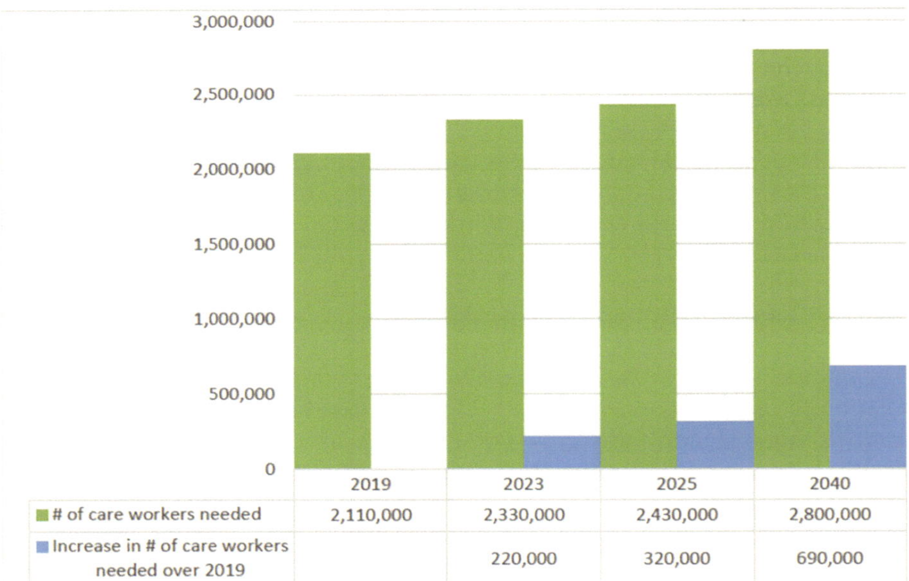


**Figure 2.**
*Estimate of future demand for care workers above the 2019 level. Source: [7].*

as such but that enable migrants to work as care workers include status visas and those of others who are eligible to work part-time with a visa for a different purpose. Persons holding status visas may be permanent residents, long-term residents (*teijūsha*) who are mainly those with documented family ties to Japanese citizens, and spouses and children of Japanese citizens or permanent residents. Because they hold status visas, their access to employment is not restricted by immigration regulations. International students and spouses of foreign residents on certain other visas are also eligible to work, usually up to 28 hours per week, provided they receive permission from the Immigration Services Agency (ISA). Through Economic Partnership Agreements (EPA) with the Philippines, Indonesia, and Vietnam, apprentices to work as CCWs (and nurses as well) have received a visa for Designated Activities (a catch-all visa applied to multiple circumstances) for study and on-the-job training to become CCWs and to remain in Japan to work as CCWs if they pass the certification exam. Very recently, in 2020, the Ministry of Justice issued a change in regulations to allow EPA care workers entering with nursing credentials in hand to obtain a separate Care Work visa (below), but the implementation is only beginning to take place [8].

Some visa categories specifically for employment incorporate care work as one occupational option. These include visas for workers in the Technical Intern Training Program (TITP), a work-intern system, which was amended in 2017 to incorporate basic care work; a visa specifically for Care Work (*kaigo*) intended for those who have a Japanese CCW credential; and the status of Specified Skilled Worker (SSW), an employment visa that was approved in 2018 and in the implementation stages in 2019 just before the Covid-19 pandemic began. The TITP is based on agreements between Japan and currently 13 countries in the Asia-Pacific region (3 other countries have yet to ratify the agreements). It has existed since 1993 but care work was only included in 2017 and requires that entrants meet a language test [9]. The SSW program was created to enable qualified workers who have worked in the TITP for at least three years to transfer to this employment visa, which is still temporary for up to five years. It also allows those who can pass required standards to be hired directly without passing through the TITP. The SSW was designed to apply to fourteen occupational categories in which there is a severe shortage of workers; each industry creates its own language and skill requirements. Tests for care work and language skills were begun in 2019, in Japan and in other countries, before the Covid-19 pandemic put a temporary stop to migration for work and study. As with the TITP, the SSW program is based on bilateral agreements between Japan and specific Asian countries, currently twelve, and another three countries with which negotiations are ongoing [10]. Although the visas for technical intern and for specified skilled worker do not indicate the occupational field, other data provide more specific data for those working in care work.

The Covid-19 pandemic understandably affected migration and mobility to Japan for a variety of purposes, but it also affected domestic labor conditions, including the conditions of migrants in Japan who lost jobs or whose visas may have expired yet could not leave the country. Several ad hoc measures were taken and then further extended as the pandemic continued. Some of the major changes included allowing TITP workers to change employers in the same occupational sector, allowing TITP workers to change to SSW status if employment was found and if they could qualify, and allowing others who found work to remain with a visa for Designated Activities [11]. Health and welfare sector employers continued to need workers, and both Japanese and foreign workers were encouraged to seek work in the care industry. For purposes here, data are presented for 2019 before the pandemic and, as available, for 2021 or 2022, after conditions had begun to improve.

## 3. Method and justification

Administrative data are a potentially important resource for researchers, but they pose obstacles that vary by the research purpose [12–15]. One fundamental challenge is that administrative agencies in the same country often differ in how they gather related data to suit their policy purposes. For researchers, access to data is not just about having the data but includes finding ways to interpret and possibly merge data gathered by different agencies to make them applicable to research questions [16].

A first step in using Japanese administrative data is to grasp the scope and data-gathering methods used by agencies to recognize the source of the data, how data overlap across agencies, and how they are inconsistent as to whom or what they include or exclude. This chapter considers data that reflect the care-provision roles of migrants formally in Japan as care workers as well as of other foreign residents. It focuses on two main forms of government data—those compiled by the Ministry of Justice's Immigration Services Agency and related agencies and those compiled by the Ministry of Health, Labor, and Welfare (MHLW) on the employment of foreign residents. In addition, it examines other data sources that give further context for interpreting immigration and employment data. Each type of data omits different categories of foreign care workers, and each depends on a different type of reporting. Immigration-related data arise from border control administrative processes whereas MHLW data use an employer-reporting system. A simple comparison of these data highlights why considering multiple data sources is important for grasping the extent of Japanese reliance on foreign care workers even if the portion of businesses employing them remains modest.

## 4. What the data tell us

### 4.1 Data on visas and approved plans for TITP workers

If one looks simply at visa data, it is quite difficult to grasp how many foreign residents are performing care work in Japan. **Table 1** presents data for 2019 and 2022 using Immigration Services Agency and related sources. The Ministry of Justice makes available the number of those staying in Japan according to visa categories, but not all categories are explicitly limited to care workers.

Persons with status visas accounted for about 51% of all foreign residents in Japan in 2019, but in 2021, given the reduced migration to Japan due to the pandemic, they made up 54.8% [20, 21]. This is a substantial number whose visas tell us nothing about their employment and the same is true of international students, the large majority of whom work. Those with visas for Care Work (also referred to as nursing care by ISA) are a small group, but their numbers are increasing. The visa data for Designated Activities are broken down by purpose, so EPA workers' visa data are clear, but care workers and nurses are lumped together. For the SSW program workers, the Immigration Services Agency *does* currently provide data on its website for the SSW program broken down by occupation, but these specific data are not included in the semi-annual data regularly posted in the government's statistical portal (see **Table 1** sources for details). For TITP interns, visa status data alone tell us nothing about the occupational sector in which they are working, but the organization responsible for managing the TITP (Organization for Technical Intern Training) publishes annual data on the number of approved plans for interns for the year, as indicated on **Table 1** [19]. In short, only a few visa categories clearly indicate care work is being done.

Especially given the newness of the visas for nursing care, SSW program, and incorporation of care work into the TITP, the data in **Table 1** give a snapshot of very recent trends in Japan. Despite the pandemic and possibly because some TITP workers

| Visa type | Care work[a] | TITP Intern[b] | SSW (for care work Only) | Designated activities (EPA only)[c] | Total | Unspecified potential sources of care workers | |
|---|---|---|---|---|---|---|---|
| | | | | | | Students (total)[d] | Status Visas (total) |
| 2019 | 499 (3.7) | 8967 (65.8) | 0 (0) | 4166 (30.6) | 13,632 (100.1) | 336,915 | 1,481,744 |
| 2022 | 5339 (19.2) | 8384 (30.1) | 10,411 (37.4) | 3721 (13.4) | 27,855 (100.1) | 260,884 | 1,673,696 |

*Sources: [17–19].*[a]*Official translation is "nursing care."*
[b]*As reported by OTIT as of March of the year.*
[c]*Per ISA data. Refers to both nurse and care worker candidates.*
[d]*Indicates total number of international students. Breakdown of those receiving permission to work in care industry not available.*

**Table 1.**
*Visa Statuses and Employment in Care Work, June 2019 and June 2022, according to Immigration Services Agency and Organization for Technical Intern Training (OTIT).*

were eligible to shift to SSW visas, the numbers of SSW care workers and Care Work visa-holders have soared in a brief amount of time. Given the ISA data that are available, however, this picture of dependence on foreign care workers is skewed toward those who have visas specifically for this purpose. As indicated in **Table 1**, holders of other types of visas may be an important source of care workers. Other data are needed to give us a fuller picture of both the numbers and the extent to which foreign workers are meeting the demand for care labor.

### 4.2 Reporting system on the employment status of foreigners

ISA data reveal a part of the migrant care work labor force, but other types of data do better at grasping the care workers hidden in the categories of international student and status visas and providing a more comprehensive view. The MHLW's annual survey, *Reporting system on the employment status of foreigners* (*gaikokujin koyō jōkyō chōsa tokode)* requires all employers to report the number of foreign residents they are employing as of October each year [22]. As seen in **Table 2**, although employers' failure to report may lead to underestimates, these data have two benefits: they include workers with international student visas and status visas and they provide data by occupational sector. The microlevel data are not available. Although the system does not include a narrowly-defined category of care work, it includes the general category of Medical and Welfare services and some tables break this category further down into medical and welfare categories. Care workers are more likely to be employed by welfare organizations.

There is, however, a disadvantage to the results as compiled. Workers who hold an SSW visa and those with a Care Work visa are difficult to identify, as they are lumped together with all other professional and technically-skilled workers. This means that those in the professional category in the medical/welfare category may be medical doctors, radiologists, or registered nurses, or they may be SSW care workers. However, comparing 2022 immigration data on those with Care Work or SSW visas with those identified in the MHLW data as having professional visas suggests that most of those identified as working in the Medical and Welfare fields by MHLW likely hold Care Work or SSW visas (See **Table 2**).

| | TITP Intern | Int. Studs. | Design Activs.[a] | Status Visa | Prof. Visas[b] | Total | Unspecified visa categories from Table 1 | |
|---|---|---|---|---|---|---|---|---|
| | | | | | | | Care Work | Care Work SSW |
| 2019 | 3304 (10.3) | 4046 (12.7) | 4329 (13.6) | 17,760 (55.6) | 2494 (7.8) | 31,933 (100.0) | 499 | 0 |
| 2022 | 14,063 (19.9) | 6033 (8.5) | 9277 (13.1) | 25,279 (35.7) | 16,147 (22.8) | 70,799 (100.0) | 5339 | 10,411 |

*Source: [22].[a]Designated Activities is not limited to EPA-based workers but includes other care workers with this visa; the 2022 numbers are partially influenced by special adjustments in regulations made during the Covid-19 pandemic. [b]Unlike the ISA data, the MHLW survey combines SSW workers with others with professional and highly-skilled visas. Professional data presented here exclude mechanical engineers, international business, language teachers, marketing specialists, etc.*

**Table 2.**
*MHLW Employer Survey on Foreign Employees in Medical and Welfare Sectors, October 2019 and October 2022.*

## 4.3 Annual employer survey on care labor conditions

Another source of data is from the Care Work Foundation of Japan (*kaigo rōdō antei sentā*), a public corporation linked to the MHLW. The Care Work Foundation conducts an annual large random-sample survey of businesses in the care industry, the Care Work Conditions Survey (*kaigo rōdō jittai chōsa*) [23]. Employers respond to one part of the survey and individual employers select a small number of workers to fill out the survey, making the care workers' survey portion less representative. The survey is sent to about 18,000 firms, with a response rate usually of about 50%. Because the survey has been administered annually since 2003, albeit with some changes in questions, it is possible to track employer perspectives on employment conditions in the care labor market across several years.

The questions on the survey range across many topics, but especially relevant here are questions on difficulties of securing workers, changes in the use of technology, changes that employers have made to hire and retain workers, and experience with employment of foreign workers. A consistent finding has been that employers who have experience hiring foreign residents tend to be more positive about them than those who have not done so. **Table 3** presents data from recent surveys. Although these surveys are useful, they still leave an area of missing data and likely underestimate the extent of foreign workers in the care industry.

The survey has both advantages and disadvantages for answering how many foreign residents are working in the care field in Japan. The advantage is that the results enable situating in percentage terms the likely *portion* of *employers* who are currently hiring or intend to hire foreign migrant care workers, at least as they are framed in the survey. Even with the recent increased numbers of foreign care work employees seen in immigration data and the MHLW's employer survey, the survey shows that only a small percentage of employers are hiring foreign residents, despite the increased opportunities to do so. The benefits of the survey are that it is comprehensive across all types of care industry employer and that it includes groups less easily identified from ISA visa data, such as international students and EPA workers. A major disadvantage, however, is that that the way the questions are asked fails to clearly

*DOI: http://dx.doi.org/10.5772/intechopen.1002389*

| | | EPA program worker | Care Worker (visa) | TITP Intern | SSW | Student (visa) | No details |
|---|---|---|---|---|---|---|---|
| 2019 (n = 9080) | Employing (n = 1197; 6.6%) | 22.7 | 19.9 | 25.1 | 2.3 | 30.0 | n.a. |
| | Plan to employ (n = 1425; 15.7% of total) | 23.0 | 37.2 | 56.3 | 21.1 | 16.7 | 4.3 |
| 2021 (n = 8201) | Employing (n = 541; 6.2%) | 10.7 | 32.2 | 41.6 | 25.1 | 20.5 | n.a. |
| | Plan to employ (n = 1019; 11.7% of total) | 15.5 | 41.0 | 50.2 | 39.5 | 14.6 | 3.5 |

*Sources: [3, 24].*
*Note: One question asked employers to indicate whether they were currently employing foreign care workers with any of the five statuses. A second asked whether they expected to hire workers in any of the five statuses. Formulation of questions was not fully consistent across the two questions or years of the survey.*

**Table 3.**
*Those hiring and planning to employ foreign care workers (%).*

include those with status visas. For instance, in the 2021 survey, when asking about the immigration status of those working in the establishment, the response options included only those with visas for Care Work, the TITP, the SSW, and international student, with another option of "not employing any of the above"; it omitted foreign residents with status visas as a category [3]. An additional potential disadvantage is that because the survey is so heavily focused on the business of providing care, questions do not address the presence of workers who do not provide care but provide other essential work such as cleaning, laundry, and cooking, jobs that foreign residents might be given if they do not have adequate skills for care work.

Given the timing of the reports for the annual surveys, currently we can only draw on the 2019 and 2021 surveys to parallel the immigration data used above. Because this is a survey using a random sample, the percentages of responses only are presented here. Stark patterns over the two-year span stand out, and they parallel findings in the other data sources. First, the portion currently employing or planning to employ EPA care workers has declined, but those employing or planning to employ workers with Care Work, TITP, or SSW visas has increased. This suggests that these systems offer better trade-offs in investment and long-term employment possibilities. In parallel, the portion employing or expecting to employ international students has declined, likewise indicating that better-trained workers are available and desirable. Overall, the data are useful for suggesting that although the portion of all care industry employers interested in employing foreign care workers remains limited (15.5% in 2021), the target workers are those who already have training and who have the possibility of renewing their visas indefinitely. (Although those with Care Work visas can renew indefinitely, SSW Category 1 workers in principle cannot renew beyond 5 years, but the possibility remains open that there may be an SSW Category 2 status with unlimited renewals for care work.) More importantly, TITP workers who transition to SSW and previously unsuccessful EPA workers who qualify as SSW workers will have received training to meet Japanese workplace expectations. The statuses of SSW and Care Work give workers regular employment status and, in principle, the ability to change employers to work where they choose.

### 4.4 Supplemental data

A couple of other sources may be useful supplements for providing a further grasp of those training to be CCWs. Data on international students enrolled in post-high school training programs for care work are assembled by the Japan Association of Training Institutions for Certified Care Workers (*nihon kaigo fukushishi yōsei shisetsu kyōkai*). These indicate the numbers of those migrants preparing to obtain employment after graduation, but also hint at the number of students who are likely working part-time in care businesses with ties to the training schools. In 2022, 1880 international students from 22 countries were studying in such schools and made up 27.6% of students enrolled [25].

For the EPA care workers, the Ministry of Health, Labor, and Welfare (MHLW) makes data available on the number of candidates who take and pass the national certification exam. The way these are often presented is through press releases or, occasionally, in materials provided to deliberative councils [26]. These results, however, do not indicate how many of those passing the exam subsequently end up working in Japan as care workers.

## 5. Conclusion

The above discussion should be helpful for those who wish to use Japanese administrative data on care work migration to grasp how many foreign residents are shouldering part of the care labor demand, yet it also highlights gaps and ambiguities in data that are gathered regularly. **Tables 1–3** illustrate what is possible to know, but highlight the need for caution. The *purpose* of examining the data is important for determining which data are going to be more useful.

For those wishing to estimate the total number of foreign care workers in Japan, using a combination of ISA data on visa statuses together with MHLW data on foreign residents' employment may be the best way to develop an approximate estimate. Immigration data specify the numbers of those with Care Work visas and SSWs performing care work; OTIT data give a rough estimate of the number of TITP workers doing care work; and the data for Designated Activities in the semi-annual data for foreign residents provide the number of EPA-based care workers and care-work candidates with that visa. But because the MHLW employer reporting system also includes workers in the medical and welfare fields who have status visas and student visas, those data should be given consideration. Even though the two sources of data are not consistent and the MHLW data on employed foreigners may involve underreporting, taken together they should be able to produce a whole picture with a very rough estimate of foreign care workers supporting the system.

For those wishing to understand employer preferences and the possible future direction of the care labor market, however, the Care Work Foundation's annual survey together with the ISA's immigration data can be helpful. The ISA's visa data highlight the increase of workers with Care Work visas and SSW visas for care work. OTIT, a government agency, provides data on the number of technical trainees in care work for a given year. The increase in those numbers is easy to track. Placing those data in relation to the Care Work Foundation's surveys clarifies *which foreign migrants with which visas* are performing care. Certain visas are new options and recently created (since 2017 and 2019 for the Care Work and SSW visas, respectively) and border closures associated with the pandemic have intervened, but the snapshots of data shown here give hints as to what employers want. These include a clear preference for those who have visas that include training, allow fulltime work, and may in future lead to long-term stays, even if the current visa system precludes this for many workers now. Although the MHLW employer survey places SSW and Care Work visa holders into a large, amorphous category of skilled professionals, the Care Work Foundation survey indicates a preference for TITP, SSW, and Care Work (i.e., CCW) visa holders as these relatively-new systems are taking hold.

Other options exist for those wishing to understand how local areas in Japan approach foreign care workers, but these are not uniformly available across areas. *Some subnational governments* (either prefectures or municipalities) collect data concerning the number of foreign residents working in the care industry in their jurisdictions and have developed other documents that illustrate employer demand for care work. Some local employers, NGOs, and/or local governments provide training for foreign residents already in the area or for EPA care work candidates working toward the certification exam. Obtaining these data requires assessing each prefecture or major city separately and exploring their systems for the data they gather and for coordinating with employers. These data can reveal local commitment to foreign care workers, but the negative side is that variation across localities prevents generalizing to the entire country.

*The interest of migrants and would-be migrants in performing care work* is reflected in data on migrants and would-be migrants taking the qualifying tests to become SSW care workers. The results include tests given in Japan and many more administered in other Asian countries since 2019 [27]. However, because the tests for skills and language are separate tests, results on skill and language performance often diverge, the data suggest more about those who are interested in coming to Japan than they do about those in a good position to do so.

All told, although the data for foreign migrant care workers to Japan may be disjointed, it is possible to use them if one starts with an awareness of what they obscure and what they have to say. Looking at data from different sources in combination provides the basis for grasping the whole picture, if not for arriving at a fully quantifiable one.

At the same time, the focus on data alone should not obscure the complex dynamics that influence patterns of migration from other parts of Asia to Japan for care work. Patterns of aging range across Asian origin countries, leading some governments to focus more on promoting their own health systems than to encourage health-worker migration. Transnational relationships that support care work migration also vary, in some cases setting the foundation for circular migration and providing investment in the health systems abroad [28]. As countries age and demand for care workers increases at home and abroad, competition among countries for these workers, the availability of workers, and development of new care provision options will no doubt contribute to further changing the dynamics.

## Conflict of interest

The author declares no conflict of interest.

## Author details

Deborah J. Milly
Virginia Polytechnic Institute and State University, Blacksburg, Virginia, United States

*Address all correspondence to: djmilly@vt.edu

## References

[1] United Nations Department of Economic and Social Affairs. Leaving No One Behind in an Ageing World: World Social Report 2023. New York: United Nations. Document No. ST/ESA/379. [Internet]. 2023. Available from: https://desapublications.un.org/publications/world-social-report-2023-leaving-no-one-behind-ageing-world [Accessed: February 25, 2023]

[2] Social Welfare Promotion and National Examination Center (*Shakai fukushi shinkō-shiken sentā*). Kaigo fukushishi kokka shiken [National exam for becoming a Certified Care Worker]. [Internet]. 2023. Available from: https://www.sssc.or.jp/kaigo/shikaku/k_05.html [Accessed: February 02, 2023]

[3] Care Work Foundation of Japan (*Kaigo rōdō antei sentā*). Reiwa-3-nendo kaigo rōdō jittai chōsa. Tokyo. [Internet]. 2022. Available from: http://www.kaigo-center.or.jp/report/2022r01_chousa_01.html [Accessed: February 02, 2023]

[4] Ministry of Health, Labor, and Welfare (MHLW). Fukushi-kaigo jinzai no kakuho ni muketa torikumi ni tsuite. Tokyo. [Internet]. 2017. Available from: https://www.mhlw.go.jp/file/05-Shingikai-12201000-Shakaiengokyokushougaihokenfukushibu-Kikakuka/0000167734.pdf [Accessed: January 29, 2020]

[5] Ministry of Health, Labor, and Welfare (MHLW). Dai-8-ki kaigo hoken jigyō keikaku ni motozuku kaigo shokuin no hitsuyōsū ni tsuite [press release]. [Internet]. 2021. Available from: https://www.mhlw.go.jp/stf/houdou/0000207323_00005.html [Accessed: February 28, 2023]

[6] Ministry of Health, Labor, and Welfare. Kaigo shokuin-sū no sui-i. [Internet]. 2021. Available from: https://www.mhlw.go.jp/content/12004000/000804139.pdf [Accessed: June 25, 2023]

[7] Ministry of Health, Labor and Welfare. Dai-8-ki kaigo hoken jigyō keikaku ni motozuku kaigo shokuin no hitsuyō-sū ni tsuite. [Internet]. 2021. Available from: https://www.mhlw.go.jp/content/12004000/000804129.pdf [Accessed: June 25, 2023]

[8] Kokusai kōsei jigyōdan (JICWELS). Change of Status of Residence from "Designated Activities (EPA Care Worker)" to "Nursing Care". [Internet]. 2022. Available from: https://jicwels.or.jp/?p=49275 [Accessed: February 25, 2023]

[9] Japan International Trainee and Skilled Worker Cooperation Organization. Gaikokujin ginō jisshū seido to wa. [Internet]. 2023. Available from: https://www.jitco.or.jp/ja/regulation/send/ [Accessed: February 28, 2023]

[10] Japan International Trainee and Skilled Worker Cooperation Organization. Zairyū shikaku tokutei ginō to wa. [Internet]. 2023. Available from: https://www.jitco.or.jp/ja/skill/send/ [Accessed: February 27, 2023]

[11] Milly DJ. Multilevel governance, community and emergency management during the pandemic: Migrants in Japan. International Journal of Sociology and Social Policy. 2023;**43**(3/4):384-401. DOI: 10.1108/IJSSP-06-2022-0172

[12] Cole S, Dhaliwal I, Sautmann A, Vilhuber L. Using administrative data for research and evidence-based

policy: An introduction. In: Cole S, Dhaliwal I, Sautmann A, Vilhuber L, editors. Handbook on Using Administrative Data for Research and Evidence-based Policy. Cambridge, MA: Abdul Latif Jameel Poverty Action Lab; 2020. Available from: https://admindatahandbook.mit.edu/book/v1.0/intro.html [Accessed June 25, 2023]

[13] Johnson DS, Massey C, O'Hara A. The opportunities and challenges of using administrative data linkages to evaluate mobility. Annals of the American Academy of Political and Social Science. 2015;**657**:247. DOI: 10.1177/0002716214552780

[14] Davern M, Thiede Call K, Ziegenfuss J, Davidson G, Beebe TJ, Blewett L. Validating health insurance coverage survey estimates: A comparison of self-reported coverage and administrative data records. Public Opinion Quarterly. 2008;**72**(2):241-259. DOI: 10.1093/poq/nfn013

[15] Allard SW, Wiegand ER, Schlecht C, Datta AR, Goerge RM, Weigensberg E. State agencies' use of administrative data for improved practice: Needs, challenges, and opportunities. Public Administration Review. 2018;**78**(2):240-250. DOI: 10.1111/puar.12883

[16] Maxwell K. Issues in Accessing and Using Administrative Data. Washington, DC: Office of Planning, Research and Evaluation. 2017. Contract No.: OPRE Report #2017-24. [Internet]. Available from: https://www.acf.hhs.gov/sites/default/files/documents/opre/issues_in_accessing_and_using_administrative_data_3617_508.pdf [Accessed June 25, 2023]

[17] Japan Immigration Services Agency (ISA). Tokutei ginō zairyū gaikokujin ninsū no kōhyō. [Internet]. 2023. Available from: https://www.moj.go.jp/isa/policies/ssw/nyuukokukanri07_00215.html [Accessed: February 26, 2023]

[18] Japan Immigration Services Agency. Zairyū gaikokujin tōkei. Multiple years. [Internet]. Available from database at www.e-stat.go.jp [Accessed: February 26, 2023]

[19] Organization for Technical Intern Training. Internet. 2023. Available from: https://www.otit.go.jp [Accessed: February 26, 2023]

[20] Japan Immigration Services Agency. White Paper: 2020 Immigration Control and Residency Management, Part 1. [Internet]. 2020. Available from: https://www.moj.go.jp/isa/policies/policies/03_00003.html [Accessed: February 26, 2023]

[21] Japan Immigration Services Agency. 2022 Immigration Control and Residency Management, Part 1. [Internet]. 2022. Available from: https://www.moj.go.jp/isa/policies/policies/03_00032.html?hl=en [Accessed: February 26, 2023]

[22] Japan Ministry of Health, Labor, and Welfare. Gaikokujin koyō jōkyō no tokede jōkyō ni tsuite. Multiple years. [Internet]. Available from: https://www.mhlw.go.jp/stf/seisakunitsuite/bunya/koyou_roudou/koyou/gaikokujin/gaikokujin-koyou/06.html [Accessed: February 26, 2023]

[23] Care Work Foundation of Japan (*kaigo rōdō antei sentā*). Kaigo rōdō antei sentā (Care Work Foundation of Japan). [Internet]. 2023. Available from: http://www.kaigo-center.or.jp/report/ [Accessed: February 26, 2023]

[24] Care Work Foundation of Japan (*kaigo rōdō antei sentā*). Reiwa-gan-nendo kaigo rōdō jittai chōsa jigyōsho ni okeru

kaigo rōdō jittai chōsa kekka hōkokusho. [Internet]. 2020. Available from: http://www.kaigo-center.or.jp/report/2020r02_chousa_01.html [Accessed: February 27, 2023]

[25] Japan Association of Training Institutions for Certified Care Workers (*Nihon kaigo fukushishi yōsei shisetsu kyōkai*). Kaigo fukushishi yōsei shisetsu ni okeru gaikokujin ryūgakusei ukeire-sū no suii-tō (heisei 30-nendo kara reiwa 4-nendo). [Internet]. 2022. Available from: https://kaiyokyo.net/news/r4_ryuugakusei.pdf [Accessed: February 28, 2023]

[26] Ministry of Health, Labor, and Welfare. Dai-34-kai kaigo fukushishi kokka shiken ni okeru EPA kaigo fukushishi kōhosha no shiken kekka. [Internet]. 2022. Available from: https://www.mhlw.go.jp/stf/newpage_24688.html [Accessed: February 28, 2023]

[27] Ministry of Health, Labor, and Welfare. Kaigo bun'ya ni okeru tokutei ginō gaikokujin no ukeire ni tsuite. [Internet]. 2023. Available from: https://www.mhlw.go.jp/stf/newpage_000117702.html [Accessed: February 28, 2023]

[28] Milly DJ. Eldercare in Japan, transnational care labor, and emerging welfare regimes. International Journal of Sociology and Social Policy. 2022;**42**(1/2):141-158. DOI: 10.1108/IJSSP-10-2020-0485

Chapter 11

# Formal and Social Demography: Current Links in Tanzania

*Christopher S. Awinia*

## Abstract

This chapter sheds light on recent population trends in Tanzania. It explores the contribution of fertility, mortality, and migration to population growth. It uses social demography as an analytical framework to identify social, cultural, economic, and behavioral drivers of population trends. It highlights the importance of location most notably in rural areas where fertility rates are high and literacy is low. Rural-urban migration is also influential in driving recent urbanization. Because the majority of urban migrants are poor, low-skilled, and unemployed, this fuels high rates of poverty among urban youth. Their low human capital also restricts full participation in the productive economy, preventing the harnessing of a large dividend from recent demographic changes.

**Keywords:** social demography, population growth, poverty and human development, migration and urbanization, population trends

## 1. Introduction

This chapter explores the interrelationship between formal and social demography. Formal demography focuses on measuring formal demographic processes by relying on rigorous statistical and quantitative methods. It emphasizes quantification and statistical measures such as rates, ratios, and projections [1]. However, the field of demography has evolved over the past three decades to give increasing attention to social consequences [2] and drivers of the dynamics of fertility, mortality, and migration. These social forces include household structure, gender relations, culture, economic organization, and political economy [1–3]. Work in this vein includes Durkheim's study of suicide rates and their relation to social structural arrangements [4]. With increasing population data from Tanzania's Population and Housing Census, Demographic and Health Survey (DHS), and Household Budget Survey (HBS) Tanzanian demographers can increasingly study the social dimensions of recent demographic change, but also the implications of these demographic shifts.

## 2. Formal versus social demography

Formal demography as a subfield relies on statistical methods and analysis to describe population trends and dynamics [3]. It studies quantitative aspects of population data and statistics [5]. It typically relies on advanced mathematical methods and modeling drawn from population censuses and surveys in order to present and forecast key population indicators. In Tanzania, the Population and Housing Census (Census) analyzes sex ratios, cohorts, population growth rates, trends, density, geographic distribution, household size, dependency ratio, housing and land ownership, and key population characteristics such as marital status, disability, orphanhood, literacy, occupation and employment, mortality, fertility, migration, and urbanization [3, 6].

Social demography, on the other hand, seeks to understand the dynamics that underlie formal demographic trends [7–9]. While formal demography provides statistical description, social demography analyzes underlying causes, enabling factors, and drivers of change [5]. It examines how demographic change relates to social and economic inequality, literacy levels, gender roles, and other social factors. Social demography also looks at how demographic patterns vary across different groups within a population, such as by race, ethnicity, and income groups. In summary, formal demography focuses on the mathematical and statistical analysis of population data, while social demography is concerned with understanding the socio-cultural context in which demographic patterns occur [1, 10].

Recent intercensal studies with data to inform social demography analysis in Tanzania include the DHS and HBS [11]. The DHS offers a comprehensive analysis of sample-size population and housing characteristics, household composition, parental survival, school attendance rates, access to water and sanitation, health insurance coverage, tobacco use, wealth index, birth registration, food security, fertility, contraceptive use, family planning, birth intervals, age at first marriage, sexual activity, child and maternal mortality, nutrition, care, gender-based violence, female genital cutting, women's economic empowerment, malaria, and Human Immunodeficiency Syndrome (HIV) [10, 12]. In essence, they document the social context that underlies recent demographic change.

HBS on the other hand provides information on social implications of recent demographic change. In Tanzania, the HBS provides information on dwelling facilities and asset ownership, household size, composition and dependents, marital status, ownership of birth certificates, national identity cards, housing construction materials, number of persons sleeping in a room, housing tenure, housing connection to facilities and connection to the national electricity grid, sources of energy for lighting and cooking, drinking water, sanitation facilities, financial access, health and education, food security. Others are household expenditure, poverty, inequality, and time use [7, 13].

Current demographic changes in Tanzania can alter the core of its society [14]. These changes are themselves driven by social, cultural, economic, reproductive, biological, behavioral, and human development forces [10, 14]. In turn, they affect the rate of population growth, migration, fertility rate, and age structure [1, 5, 6, 15]. The Total Fertility Rate (TFR) at the time of writing this Chapter was 5.2 births per woman. The intercensal population growth rate (PGR) 2012–2022 was 3.7 percent translating to a population doubling time (PDT) of 22 years 2022–2044 [6].

### 2.1 Social demography methods

Tanzania's social demography data come from three main sources, including the Census, intercensal surveys, and administrative records [16]. Census is usually conducted every 10 years and intercensal surveys every 5 years in between the censuses. Administrative data was being collected routinely, continually, and administratively [16–18].

The Census is a classical source for formal demographic analysis [9, 16, 19]. A population census is a total process of collecting, compiling, evaluating, analyzing, publishing, and disseminating demographic data taken at a specified time to all persons in a country or specified location of a country [6, 19]. The population census attempts a comprehensive coverage of the national population, yielding a large sample size that allows it to produce estimates to the smallest geographical levels, and population subgroups. It produces core population statistics that can be used to calculate vital rates from civil registration data, and it also supplies the sampling frame for intercensal surveys.

There are several steps in preparing a census. The process begins with the demarcation of enumeration areas (EAs), producing questionnaires, preparation of instruction manuals, conducting a pilot census, and training of census personnel. Subsequently, the launching of publicity campaigns, preparing for data processing, tabulation, production, and dissemination of census results [18–20].

The Census methodology adopted was typical of formal demography. It has two types of questionnaires namely (a) a short-form questionnaire with 37 questions which are administered in about 70 percent of all enumeration areas and (b) a long-form questionnaire with 62 questions was administered to the remaining 30 percent of the enumeration areas. The questions in the short form include the respondents' name, relationship to the head of household, sex, age, disability, marital status, citizenship, place of residence, the place where the respondent spends most of his/her daytime, birth certificate, literacy, education attainment, levels of education, general and maternal deaths, agriculture and livestock, citizen in diaspora, social security fund, and lastly the total number of persons in the household by sex. The long form includes 25 extra questions under the following themes:

- Survival of parents
- Place of birth
- Place of residence
- Education levels attained
- Economic status
- Fertility
- Mortality
- Housing conditions and ownership of selected assets

Census results were presented in district estimates broken down into rural and urban parts. Sample households for the long questionnaires were determined through cluster sampling where a cluster of an EA was first selected. Each district was divided into rural and urban parts. Within the rural and urban parts of the EA, a sample was selected at random with an equal probability by systematic sampling. The use of systematic sampling ensured a good balance between urban and rural representation in the sample from the districts.

Census information involves drawing estimation on the number of persons in the different categories such as educational attainment, number of children, or occupation usually analyzed by basic sex-age breakdown.[1]

[1] The estimation was arrived by following formula [21].
Let $X_c^b$ be the number of persons in category c of a variable in sex-age group $b$ in the rural/urban part of a district. An estimate $\hat{X}_c^b$ of $X_c^b$ was computed by the following formula:

$$\hat{X}_c^b = \frac{M}{m}\sum_{i=1}^{m} x_{c_i}^b \tag{1}$$

Where;
$X_{ci}^b$: Number of persons in category c of a variable in sex-age group b in the $i^{th}$ sample EA in the rural/urban part of a district
M: Number of EAs in the rural/urban part of the district
m: Number of sample EAs in the rural/urban part of the district
Estimates at a regional level were derived by summing up district estimates over all districts within the region. National level estimates were the sum of regional estimates. The linear estimates thus obtained were adjusted by using ratio estimation in order to result in the same age and sex composition as the results on a complete basis.
Let denote the population in sex-age group $b$ derived on a complete basis by $X^b$, and the estimate of number of persons in sex-age group b obtained on the basis of data from long questionnaires by $\hat{X}^b$. The estimate $\hat{X}^b$ may not coincide with $X^b$. The final estimate for $X_c^b$ was derived by multiplying the ratio of $X^b$ to b $\hat{X}^b$ into the linear estimate $\hat{X}_c^b$
Census data based on the long questionnaire is subject to sampling errors. Sampling errors of estimates for selected variables were estimated. For the sake of simplification

$$V(\hat{X}) = M^2(1-f)\frac{1}{m(m-1)}\sum_{i=1}^{m}(x_i - \bar{x})^2 \tag{2}$$

Where;
$V(\hat{X})$: Variance of the estimate $(\hat{X})$
$x_i$: Value of the variable X in the $i$th sample EA, e.g., the number of literate persons in the $i$th sample EA
$\bar{x}$: Mean of $x_i$ within the district, i.e., an average of $x_i$ for m sample EAs in that district
f: Sampling fraction, i.e., m/M
M: Number of EAs in the rural/urban part of the district
Variance of the estimate at a regional level was calculated for rural and urban parts separately as the sum of district level variances within the region, and variance of the national estimate was the sum of regional level variances. Variance for the total of rural and urban areas was the sum of variances for rural and urban parts. The standard error is the standard deviation of the estimates, namely the square root of variance and the relative standard error is the coefficient of variation (C.V.) of the estimate, i.e., the ratio of standard error to the estimate as expressed in percentage. Standard errors and the coefficients of variation for selected items are at a national level.
The sampling error of the estimate was considered approximately twice the standard error. Estimates at regional level were derived by summing-up district estimates from all districts within the Region. National level estimates were the sum of regional estimates. Linear estimates that were obtained were adjusted by using ratio estimation in order to result in the same age and sex composition as the result on a complete basis [6, 21].

The census provides a snapshot of population rates, ratios and distribution, and intercensal trends. It, however, does not provide information on underlying dynamics that drive observed demographic change. The main drivers of demographic change were fertility, mortality, and migration. Tanzania conducted intercensal surveys focused on behavioral, social, cultural, gender, income, and non-income determinants of main drivers of demographic change [9, 10, 16, 17]. Intercensal surveys were useful for collecting detailed social, economic, cultural, and political data, which cannot be accommodated in the full-scale census. They were also instrumental in identifying emerging issues in between censuses. Several factors were taken into account in determining the nature of questions to be collected in intercensal surveys. These included the information needs of stakeholders, information availability, international comparability, willingness of respondents to provide information, and resource availability. Intercensal surveys can take many forms including multi-subject, specialized surveys, multi-phased, panel, and longitudinal surveys [12, 16, 18, 22].

Social demographers in Tanzania rely on the DHS to link formal and social demography. The main objective of DHS is to calculate demographic rates including fertility, infant and child mortality, adult and maternal mortality, and disability. It also collected the following set of information to provide an explanation of social demography and demographic change. These include:

The HBS also used a two-stage cluster sample design. The first stage involved the selection of EAs as primary sampling units (PSUs) which were also based on the sampling frame that was delineated for the census. A total of 796 PSUs (69 from Dar-es-Salaam, 167 from other urban areas, and 560 from rural areas) were selected.

Social demographers also rely on routine administrative data that are compiled from various administrative processes. They were mainly extracted from vital statistics recorded in civil registration systems such as birth, death, divorce, school, hospital, employment, food production, distribution, market price information records, and statistics [13].

Intercensal surveys and administrative data provided vital information for triangulating formal and social demography. They allowed social demographers to delve into underlying dynamics that can explain the demographic change.

## 3. Social dimensions of demographic change

Tanzania's population structure is changing, and these changes can have lasting effects on society, culture, economy, and political life. Already, the nation's growth rate has been steadily rising since the first census in 1967. The population sex distribution had not changed significantly over the decades. However, the proportion of youth has increased where youth under 35 now account for more than half of the total population [6, 23, 24]. This is a significant demographic change because for the first time youth dominate the population pyramid, increasing the dependency rate, and subsequently as a proportion of the population under poverty [6, 23–25].

Another remarkable demographic change is urbanization [10, 26]. As seen in **Figure 1**, the percentage of urban population has steadily grown since the first post-independence census of 1967.

The rate of urban growth has remained high above the national rate of population growth of 3.2 percent [6, 14, 23, 24]. The concentration of youth was higher in urban areas, largely driven by youth-dominated rural-urban migration [26]. Dar-es-Salaam,

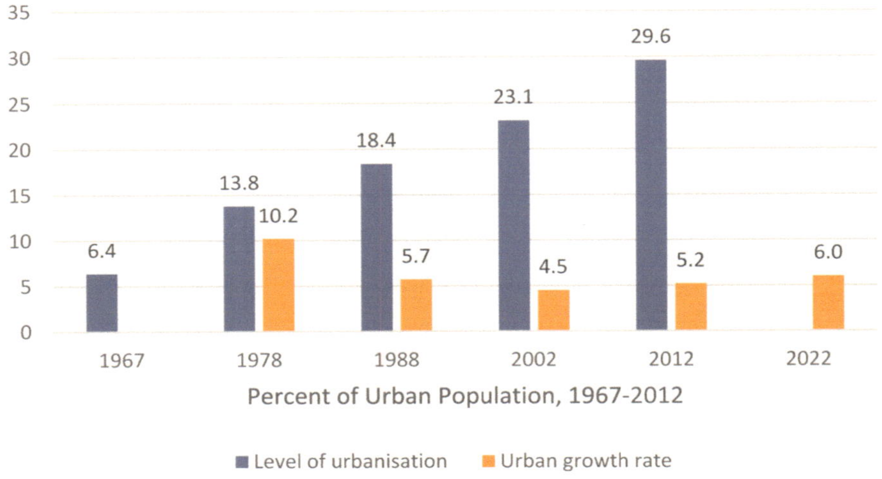


**Figure 1.**
*Percent of urban population, source: Population and housing census, 2012.*

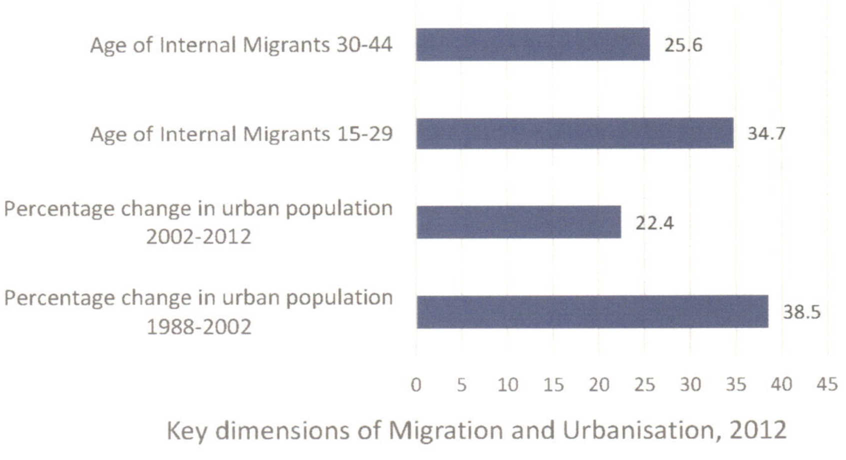


**Figure 2.**
*Key dimensions of migration and urbanization, source: Urban monograph, population and housing census, 2012.*

the main urban center accounted for 31 percent of all internal migrants in 2012 (**Figure 2**).

The high proportion of youth among migrants means that urban areas can increasingly be described as young, poor, high fertility, and low-skilled [27]. Poverty is both an effect and driver of demographic change. Poor rural households had higher household population size, dependency rates, reported illness and injury, low literacy levels, and access to social amenities such as access to water supply, energy sources, and electricity [27].

A combination of urban migration, poverty, youthful population is transforming the urban population structure. The growth in urban youth population has been followed by high urban youth employment, the rise of street vendors, the rise of informal urban housing and settlements; and rising patterns of infectious diseases including new HIV transmissions, tuberculosis (TB), cholera, pulmonary infections; higher rates of Coronavirus (Covid) infections [28].

The potential gains from urbanization include increased commerce, trade, concentration of financial services, community infrastructure, and facilities, and better supply of utilities, housing, and transport. These served as "pull-factors" in the migration to cities. On the other hand, rapid urbanization increases traffic congestion, air pollution, informal housing and slums, sewerage pollution, and strain on existing urban infrastructure such as transport, housing, healthcare, schools, and water systems. Typically, urban areas had high inequality rates where the population living in disadvantaged parts of urban areas suffered from extreme poverty [10, 13, 19, 27].

The growth of the national population also reflects patterns of fertility, age composition, urbanization, and changes in life expectancy [6, 14]. The country's TFR has declined since the first census in 1967, but it still remains high. Population growth accelerated (**Figure 3**) [6] because fertility remained high (**Figure 4**), especially among adolescent and young women, low-income groups, and rural families.

National fertility rates peaked between the late 1960s and the start of the new millennium and this "baby-boom" period has profound implications for Tanzania's population and its economy [14]. The "youth bulge" from this period of growth can be turned into a positive "demographic divided" if proper attention is given to human capital development targeting this population group. Human capital in this instance refers to health, education, and skills needed to transform the economy; as well as access to decent employment [29]. However, the participation of youth in productive employment remains minimal. Although youth were the majority in the population pyramid, they were often uneducated or lacked relevant skills to take advantage of emerging economic opportunities, and were most vulnerable to new infections of HIV. In this case, they remained unharnessed for effective participation in economic transformation. This provides an important nexus between social demography, population studies, social policy, and economic development. This nexus needs to be studied carefully in order to determine the right policies needed to take advantage of population change.

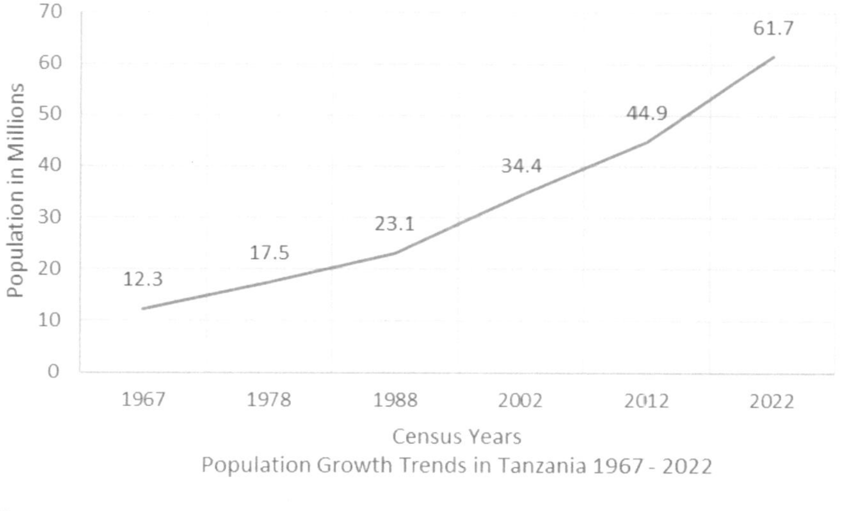


**Figure 3.**
*Population growth trends in Tanzania; source: Preliminary results, population and housing census, 2022.*

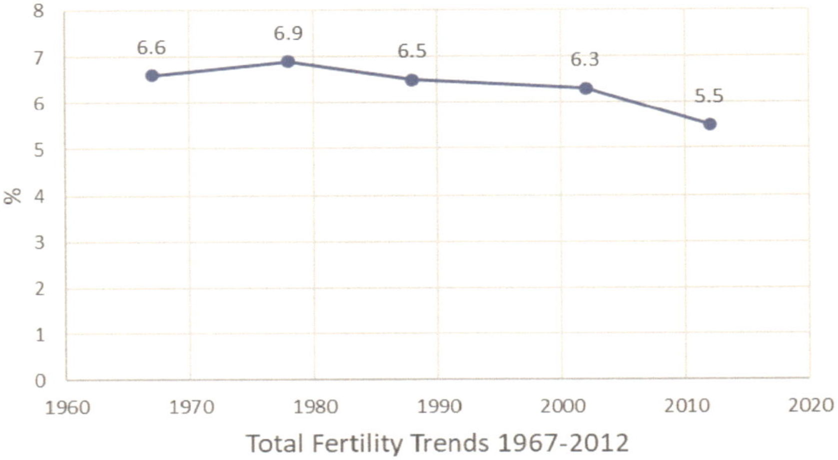


**Figure 4.**
*Total fertility trends; source: Preliminary results, population and housing census, 2022.*

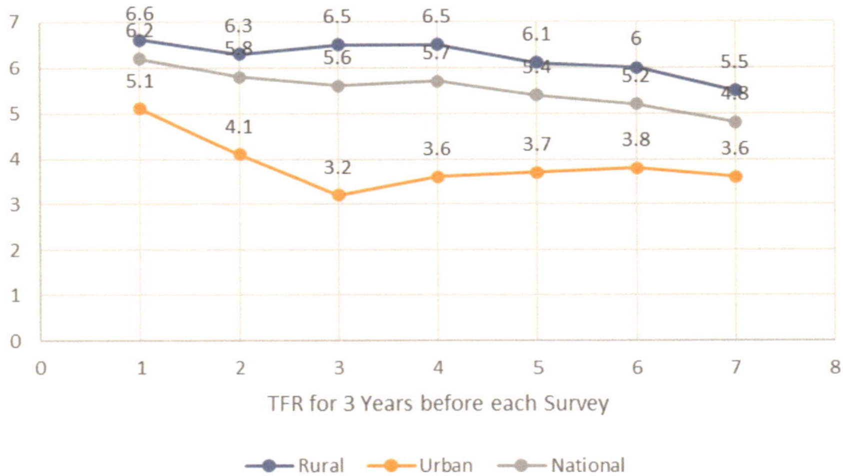


**Figure 5**
*Preliminary results, population and housing census, 2022.*

Even as fertility declines nationally, this decline is not even across population groups. The declines vary depending on several factors including rural location, age, level of education, and income. Empirical evidence shows main demographic groups with fertility rates above the average TFR were young women between 18 and 24; women who lived in rural areas, and among low-income groups [11, 12, 30, 31]. Empirical evidence from surveys and archives shows rural fertility was driving national trends nationally as shown in **Figure 5**.

Although fertility as a whole is declining, it is still relatively high among women with low education and income. Age-specific fertility rate peaked between ages 20 and 29. A main policy focus here was to control TFR and subsequently, PGR would delay the age of first childbirth. Programs to do so seek to extend universal, free, compulsory education from seven to 11 years of the first 4 years of secondary education. This policy has led to limiting the age of the first childbirth for young women [11].

| Age | % |
|---|---|
| 15 | 4.4 |
| 16 | 11.4 |
| 17 | 23 |
| 18 | 38.2 |
| 19 | 56.7 |

*Source: TDHS, 2017.*

**Table 1.**
*Proportion of adolescents and young women who have started birth 2015–2016, Tanzania.*

Early pregnancy remained common among school-going girls, contributing to a high drop-out rate, and widening gender disparities beginning in secondary education [32].

Social demography factors contributed to low teenage median age at first birth. The median age at first birth reflects the age at which half the women in a cohort have already had their first child. This median age was 19.8 years among females aged 25–49.

A further disaggregation of trends among young women under age 19 demonstrated high early fertility (**Table 1**) which affects the TFR, i.e., the average number of children a woman would have by the end of her childbearing years.

There was a drastic rise in the proportion of women who had started childbearing by age 19. The Government undertook concerted efforts to increase the median age at first birth through measures such as extending compulsory education and economic empowerment to adolescent girls and young women (AGYW) [32, 33]. Increasing the median age at first birth would help reduce birth rates. Relevant policies included extending compulsory basic education from 7 to 11 years, addressing early, child-forced, and arranged marriages, strengthening knowledge and awareness on contraceptives and family planning use targeting adolescent and young women, and socio-economic empowerment of adolescent and young women [23, 24, 34, 35]. However, despite these efforts, early childbearing remains largely unchanged: the percentages of women aged 15–19 who had begun childbearing was 26 percent in 2005–2005; it decreased to 23 percent in 2010; but increased again to 27 percent in 2015–2016 [12].

Increasing the spacing of births is another way to reduce TFR. This can be done by improving access to family planning and contraceptive use in the population. It is also contingent on other factors such as knowledge, attitude, and practices favorable to contraceptive use, and family planning; socio-cultural issues that influence the number of desired children, and other structural barriers such as location, socioeconomic status, and level of education [36, 37]. The median birth interval rate was 35 months or 2.9 years since the preceding birth. It increased modestly over the last decade with a median interval lengthening by 1.6 months between 2004 and 2005 and 2015–2016 as shown in **Table 2**.

## 4. Social implications of demographic change

Improvements in social development have fostered modest gains in life expectancy [23, 24, 38, 39]. These gains were specifically driven by improvements in social service

| TDHS Year | No. of Months |
|---|---|
| 91–92 | 33.3 |
| 1996 | 33.7 |
| 1999 | 33.4 |
| 2005–2005 | 33.4 |
| 2010 | 33.9 |
| 2015–2016 | 35 |
| *Source: TDHS, 2017.* | |

**Table 2.**
*Trends in birth interval (median number of months since preceding birth), Tanzania 1991–1992 to 2015–2016.*

delivery especially in primary health services, basic education among girls, and provision of clean, portable drinking water. On the other hand, these gains were offset by slow progress in reducing age dependency rates, reducing inequalities, or raising incomes [40–42].

Poverty is also a key driver of recent demographic change [13]. Rural areas were the largest contributor to TFR, in part because of lower socioeconomic conditions, illiteracy levels, women's equality, empowerment, and opportunities especially for AGYW [43–50]. High fertility in rural communities also stems from low rates of contraceptive use, high preference for large progenies, or early marriage. Women in rural areas express preference for larger families because they need assistance with domestic work and childcare. Indeed, data show how adult women bear a heavy domestic workload (15+ years). In most cases (73.1 percent) adult women are responsible for fetching water [13, 22]. They are occasionally assisted by female children under 15 years (4.7 percent) or male children under 15 (2.8 percent) [13].

Longer distances from home to the water source in rural areas are among the factors of the increased demand for domestic labor, and hence the preference for high fertility. About 22.6 percent of households were located more than 1 kilometer from a water source; 6.5 percent between 2 and 5 kilometers; 1.3 percent between 5 and 8; and 0.8 greater than 8 kilometers [6]. High demand for domestic work was determined by the predominance of farm work in rural dwellings, and disproportionately less access to services such as water supply, electricity, and other energy sources. Rural women typically also keep small livestock within their homestead. Rural women want multiple children, including those late in their reproductive lives, because they expect children to assist in these domestic chores as they age [22]. It was also more difficult for rural women to access modern contraceptive and family planning services. Most (98.8) rural women know about modern contraception, but many who would like to use it lack access (53.2 percent).

Poverty was a contributing factor to fertility and population growth [13, 22]. Multidimensional poverty among poor households served to transform them as drivers of recent demographic change. It can be seen from **Figure 6** below there was a direct relationship between household size and poverty.

Thus, a clear relationship exists between the poverty of households and their fertility. Poverty raises the demand for high fertility while lowering the knowledge and use of modern contraception. Literacy rates especially among women represent a

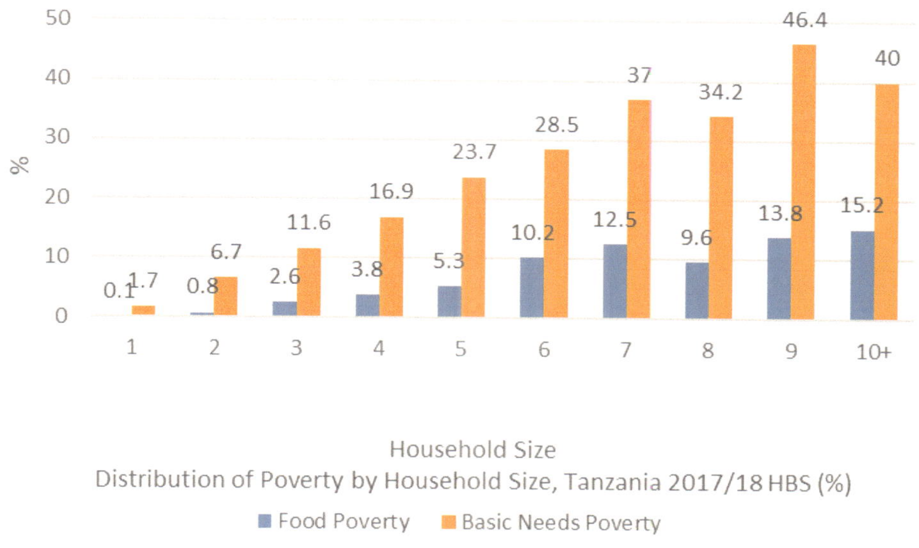


**Figure 6.**
*Relationship between household size and poverty; source: TDHS, 2017.*

barrier to fertility reduction among women from poor households [51]. Poverty is a driver of high fertility. In turn, high fertility exacerbates poverty.

Poverty can be measured in multiple ways. One is food poverty, the proportion of the total population whose food consumption per adult equivalent falls below the food poverty line [52]. A second is absolute poverty, the population below the poverty line. People who live in extreme poverty or sometimes referred to as abject, or absolute poverty. These represent the proportion of the population who cannot afford a single meal with sufficient nutrient levels usually denoted as calorific intake. Calorific intake is taken as a measurement because different foods generate different calories. A basket of foods yielding the minimum required calorific levels per adult equivalence is used to generate the food poverty line [53]. The poverty line depicting the minimum food basket for estimation of calorific intake was calculated from prevailing food prices. The extreme poor are defined as those whose consumption falls below the national food poverty line [14]. It consequently follows that extreme poverty is sensitive to the national price index. A rise in the food price index (i.e., a rise in food prices) would trigger a rise in the proportion of people in extreme poverty. The concept of adult equivalence is also relevant at this point. The required calorific intakes are higher for adults than children [14].

**Figure 7** shows how demographic change in the form of rising population growth can affect household size, with implications on food and income poverty.

A third metric is basic needs poverty, or the proportion of the total population unable to meet basic needs which, according to the Human Development Index (HDI) include education, health, safe drinking water, shelter, and clothing [51, 52, 54, 55]. Other categories considered in this basket include utilities, transport, and communication. The poverty line based on basic needs is the cost for a basket of basic needs and is therefore sensitive to changes in prices.

Social demography pays great attention to the relationship between quantitative and qualitative aspects of the total population. It is not enough to just analyze

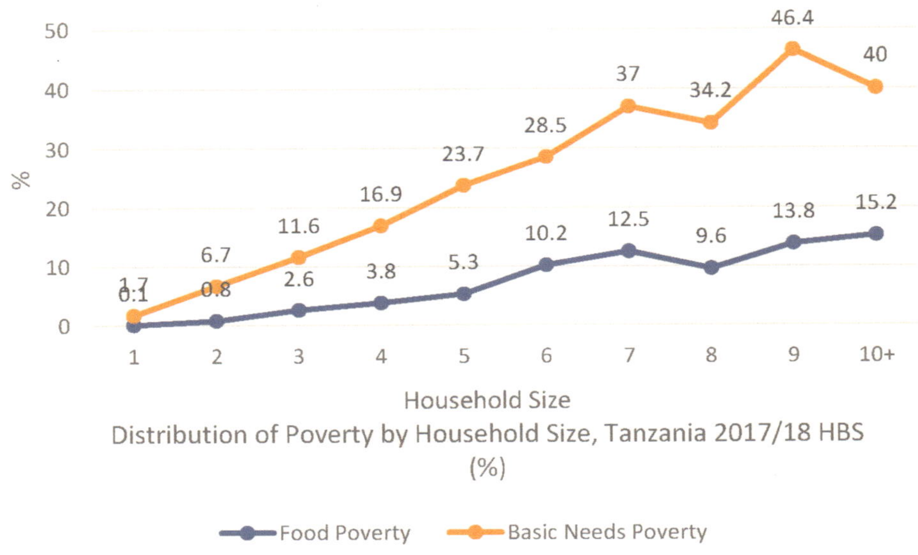


**Figure 7.**
*Rising population growth affect on household size: Source: HBS, 2017–2018.*

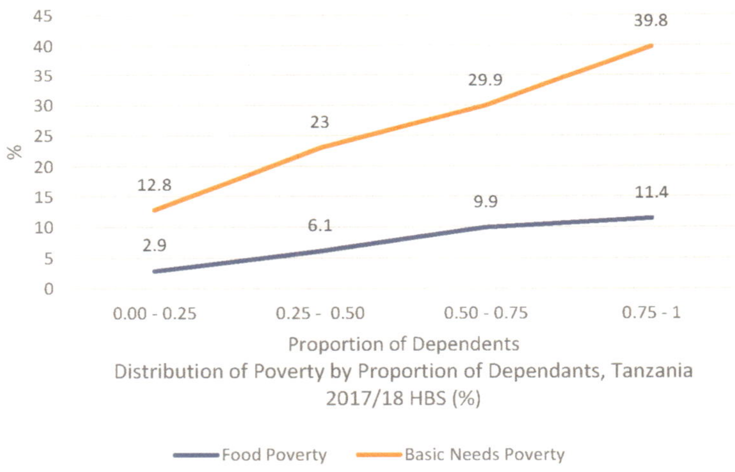


**Figure 8.**
*Relationship between household poverty and number of dependents.*

population growth rates and structure. One must also pay attention to how demography affects the distribution of welfare across the population [56]. How faster population growth affects inequality depends on rural-urban migration, economic growth, unemployment, health, and household structure. **Figure 8** shows a direct relationship between household poverty and number of dependents.

Several demographic factors fuel household dependency. These include life expectancy and high fertility. Poverty depends on the age structure of households. A household is less likely to be poor if it consists of household heads who are 35 years and younger as shown in **Figure 9**.

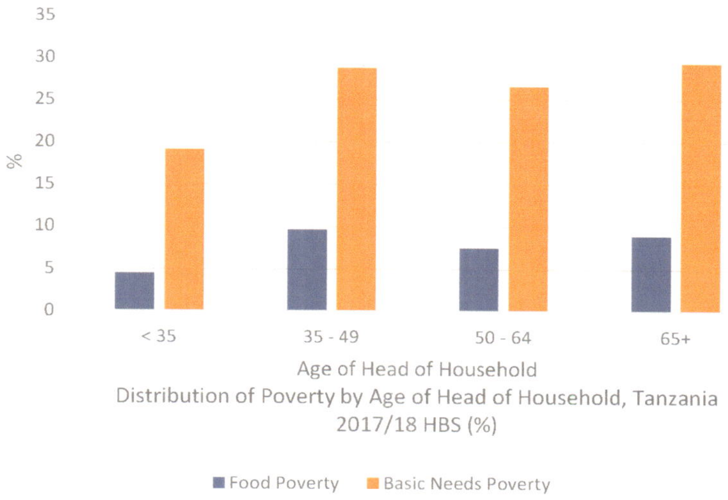


**Figure 9.**
*Poverty and age structure of households.*

Poverty and inequality are also key concepts in demographic analysis. Poverty is measured through headcount ratio, the number of people under a poverty line. Households are the primary unit in poverty analysis. It is noteworthy that poverty lines are determined by enumerating household incomes. However, household incomes are often based on expenditure records as proxies, even as they do not always reflect income. Households may spend income on luxuries and lack food and then they would still be considered poor. Households may also have income or assets but still be considered poor under the HDI. This is the case for pastoralists who own cattle but still fall short of meeting their minimum food intake [57].

Inequality, the other concept, reflects the even distribution of income within the population (6), [16]. It is measured by the Gini-coefficient where zero (0) denotes a situation of perfect equality where every person has the same consumption expenditure, and one (1) where there is total inequality where a few people hoard all the income [13, 49, 58].

## 5. Conclusion

The chapter explored the relationships between demographic and social demographic change in Tanzania. The country's population has continued to grow, fueled by changes in fertility, mortality, and internal migration. These drivers themselves reflect trends in poverty, literacy, and infrastructure development. Poverty, especially, is a crucial factor. Partly because of the demand for domestic labor, rural women aspire to bear more children. This in turn reproduces rural poverty and high levels of unmet need for modern contraception. Overall, the relationship between family size and poverty works in both directions.

Although birth rates are lower in urban areas, rural-to-urban migration fuels a rapid growth of the urban population. Migrants are young and low-skilled, thus giving urban poverty a youthful face. Even though urban areas had the potential to spur economic transformation, low employment is an important brake. Much of the employment remains confined to the informal, low-pay, or illegal sectors, and this compromises the harnessing of a demographic dividend that is expected to follow impending falls in birth rates. The Government was making sensible choices in social policy including expanding education, primary health care, HIV prevention, and provision of antiretrovirals. However, high population growth continues to offset the gains expected from these policy investments. Social demography offers a cogent framework to explore the broad socioeconomic consequences associated with recent demographic changes in Tanzania.

## Author details

Christopher S. Awinia
Open University of Tanzania, Dar-es-Salaam, Tanzania

*Address all correspondence to: christopher.awinia@out.ac.tz; chrisawinia@gmail.com

## References

[1] Mahmud A. Differentiation between Formal Demography and Population Studies: A Discussion on the Nature, Scope and Importance of Social Demography. Kumargaon: Shahjalal University of Science and Technology; 2020

[2] Caldwell JC. Demography and social science. Population Studies Journal. 1996;**50**(3):305-333

[3] Gerandielle WK. What Is the Difference between Demography and Population Studies. New Delhi: PEDDIA; 2022

[4] Muller AS, Abrutyn S, Pescosolido B, Diefendorf S. The social roots of suicide: Theorizing how the external social world matters to suicide and suicide prevention. Frontiers in Psychology Journal. 2021;**12**:621569. DOI: 10.3389/fpsyg.2021.621569

[5] Klimczuk A. Introductory to Demographic Analysis: Selected Concepts, Tools, and Applications. London, UK, London: IntechOpen; 2021

[6] United Republic of Tanzania [URT], Ministry of Finance and Planning [MoFP], National Bureau of Statistics [NBS] Tanzania Mainland, and President's Office-Finance and Planning [PO-FP], Office of the Chief Government Statistician [OCGS], Zanzibar. 2022 Population and Housing Census: Administrative Units Population Distribution Report: Tanzania. Dodoma: URT, MoFP, NBS, PO-FP, OCGS; 2022

[7] Oxford Reference Dictionary of Sociology, Overview: Social Demography [Internet]. 2011. Available from: https://www.oxfordreference.com/display/10.1093/oi/authority.20110803100515871jsessionid=DEFF904240B5884A9B8635D7D6442F49

[8] Tabutin D. Whither demography? Strengths and weaknesses of the discipline over fifty years of change. Population Journal. 2007;**62**(1) INED:15-31

[9] Crimmins EM. Demography: The past 30 years, the present, and the future. Demography Journal. 1993;**30**(4):579-591

[10] Foote KA, Hill KH, Martin LG. Demographic Change in Sub-Saharan Africa: Population Dynamics of Sub-Saharan Africa. Michigan: ProQuest Ebook Central; 1993

[11] Wizara ya Fedha na Mipango, Ofisi ya Taifa ya Takwimu–Tanzania na Ofisi ya Rais-Fedha na Mipango, Ofisi ya Mtakwimu Mkuu wa Serikali Zanzibar. Sensa ya Watu na Makazi ya Mwaka 2022: Matokeo ya Mwanzo. Dodoma, Tanzania: Wizara ya Fedha na Mipango, Ofisi ya Taifa ya Takwimu–Tanzania na Ofisi ya Rais-Fedha na Mipango, Ofisi ya Mtakwimu Mkuu wa Serikali Zanzibar; 2022

[12] Ministry of Health [MoH], National Bureau of Statistics (NBS) Tanzania Mainland, Ministry of Health [MoH], Office of the Chief Government Statistician [OCGS] Zanzibar, and ICF. Tanzania Demographic and Health Survey and Malaria Indicator Survey 2022: Key Indicators Report. Dodoma, and Rockville: MoH, OCGS, NBS; 2023

[13] Ministry of Finance and Planning-Poverty Eradication Division [MoFP-PED], National Bureau of Statistics [NBS] Tanzania Mainland, and World Bank. Tanzania Mainland Household Budget Survey 2017/18. Final Report: MoFP-PED, NBS and World Bank. Dodoma and Washington DC: MoFP-PED, NBS; 2020

[14] Agwanda A, Amani H. Population Growth, Structure, Momentum in. Tanzania: ESRF; 2014 ISBN: 978-9987-610-96-9

[15] Bumpass LL, Taeuber KE, Sweet JA. Studies in Population Social Demography. Massachusetts: Academic Press; 1978

[16] Suharto S. Complementary Sources of Demographic and Social Statistics. New York: Department of Economic and Social Affairs, United Nations Secretariat; 2001

[17] Meshack L. Social Cultural Factors Influencing Fertility of at Least Three Children among Women in Arusha District Council [thesis]. Tanzania: Mzumbe University; 2015

[18] Ofisi ya Waziri Mkuu wa Jamhuri ya Muungano wa Tanzania na Ofisi ya Makamu wa Pili wa Rais, Zanzibar. Sensa ya Watu na Makazi ya Mwaka 2022: Mwongozo wa Kitaifa wa Matumizi ya Matokeo ya Sensa. Dodoma: Ofisi ya Waziri Mkuu wa Jamhuri ya Muungano wa Tanzania na Ofisi ya Makamu wa Pili wa Rais, Zanzibar; 2022

[19] Ministry of Planning, Economy and Empowerment [MoPEE], National Bureau of Statistics [NBS]. Tanzania Census 2002 Analytical Report. Vol. X. Dar-es-Salaam: MoPEE, NBS; 2006

[20] United Republic of Tanzania [URT]. Questionnaire for the 2022 Population and Housing Census. Dodoma: NBS; 2022

[21] President's Office, Planning Commission [PO–PC]. 1988 Population Census Methodology. Dar-es-Salaam: PO-PC; 1988

[22] Mainland, Ministry of Health (MoH) [Zanzibar], National Bureau of Statistics (NBS), Office of the Chief Government Statistician (OCGS), CIF. Tanzania Demographic Health and Malaria Indicator Survey 2022 Key Indicators Report. Rockville Maryland: MoH, NBS, OCGS; 2023

[23] Ministry of Finance and Planning (MoFP) [Tanzania Mainland], President's Office Finance and Planning [Zanzibar], National Bureau of Statistics (NBS), Office of the Chief Government Statistician (OCGS). 2022 Census Preliminary Results: Dodoma. Dodoma: MoFP, NBS, OCGS; 2022 Available from: https://www.nbs.go.tz/nbs/takwimu/Census2022/matokeomwanzooktoba2022.pdf

[24] Economic and Social Research Foundation [ESRF]. Tanzania Human Development Report 2017: Social Policy in the Context of Economic Transformation. Dar-es-Salaam: ESRF; 2018

[25] Boucher FC. What is Doubling Time and How it is Calculated? [Internet]. 2015. Available from: https://populationeducation.org/what-doubling-time-and-how-it-calculated/

[26] National Bureau of Statistics [NBS] Ministry of Finance and Planning, Office of the Chief Government Statistician (OCGS) President's Office Finance, Economy and Planning Zanzibar. Migration and Urbanisation Monograph: NBS and OCGS. NBS, OCGS; 2015

[27] Awinia C. Structural Barriers, Constraints and Urban Youth Employment: The Case of Ilala Municipality. Dar-es-Salaam: Mkuki wa Nyota Publishers; 2014

[28] Awinia CS. Poor structural quality of housing conditions as a reflection of underlying urban poverty and inequalities: The case of Mnyamani and Kisiwani settlements in Dar-es-salaam.

Journal of Building and Land Development; Dar-es-Salaam. 2021;**22**(1): 1-15 ISSN: 0856-0501

[29] National Bureau of Statistics [NBS]. Women and Men in Tanzania: Facts and Figures 2017. Dar-es-Salaam: NBS; 2017 Available from: https://www.nbs.go.tz/nbs/takwimu/WomenAndMen/women_and_men_booklet.pdf

[30] National Bureau of Statistics [NBS] Ministry of Finance and Planning, Office of the Chief Government Statistician (OCGS) President's Office Finance, Economy and Planning Zanzibar. 2012 Population and Housing Census Vol. IV Fertility and Nuptiality. NBS and OCGS; 2015

[31] Ministry of Health, Community Development, Gender, Elderly and Children [MoHCDGEC], National Bureau of Statistics [NBS] Tanzania Mainland, Ministry of Health [MoH], Office of the Chief Government Statistician [OCGS], and CIF. Tanzania Demographic Health and Malaria Indicator Survey (TDHS-MIS). Rockville Maryland: MoHCDGEC, NBS, OCGS, MoH; 2016. pp 85-183

[32] Awinia C. Free basic education and gender disparities in Tanzania: An empirical assessment of challenges and policy options: Huria Journal of the Open University of Tanzania Vo. 26. No. 2: 2019 ISSN: 0856-6739, Available from: https://www.ajol.info/index.php/huria/article/view/198490

[33] Kikula I, Kipokola J, Shivji I, Semboja J, Tarimo B, editors. Researching Poverty in Tanzania: Problems, Policies and Perspectives. Mkuki wa Nyota Publishers; 2005

[34] Bernardi L, Hutter I. The anthropological demography of Europe. Demographic Research Journal. 2007;**17**: 18, 541-566. DOI: 10.4054/DemRes.2007.17.18

[35] Exavery A, Shamte A, Bietsch K, Mosha D, Mbaruku G, Masanja H. Levels and correlates of non-adherence to WHO recommended inter-birth intervals in Rufiji, Tanzania. BMC Pregnancy Childbirth Journal. 2012. DOI: 10.1186/1471-2393-12-152

[36] Amaral EFL. Theories of demography. Population and Society Journal. 2022

[37] Sanga LA, Mtuy T, Philemon RN, Mahande MJ. Inter-pregnancy interval and associated adverse maternal outcomes among women who delivered at Kilimanjaro Christian medical Centre in Tanzania, 2000-2015. PLoS One. San Francisco. 2020;**15**(2):e0228330

[38] United Republic of Tanzania. The Constitution of the United Republic of Tanzania of 1977 Chapter 2 of the Laws. United Republic of Tanzania; Dar-es-Salaam. 2005 Available from: https://www.parliament.go.tz/uploads/documents/publications/en/1475140028-The%20Constitution.pdf

[39] Narayan D, Pritchett L, Kapoor S. Moving out of Poverty: Success from Bottom-Up. Vol. 2. London: Palgrave Macmillan; 2009

[40] Sen A. Development as Freedom. Oxford: Oxford University Press; 1999

[41] World Bank. Poverty Assessment in Tanzania. World Bank; 2018

[42] UNDP. Overcoming Human Poverty. New York: Oxford University Press, UNDP; 1998

[43] Fafchamps M. Rural Poverty, Risk and Development. Edward Elgar Publishing Limited; 2003. pp 146-188

[44] Awinia CS. The sociology of intra-Africa pastoralist migration: The case of Tanzania: Migration and society section. Journal of Frontiers Sociology. 2020;**5**

[45] Awinia CS. Loss of ecological control, pastoralist migration and indigenous. Tanzania Journal of Population and Development. forthcoming ISSN: 0856-0227

[46] Cyril S, Oldroyd JC, Renzaho A. Urbanisation, Urbanicity, and health: A systematic review of the reliability and validity of Urbanicity scales. BMC Public Health Journal. New York. 2013;**13**:513

[47] Ushakov D. Migration and Urbanisation: Local Solutions for Global Economic. Pennsylvania: IGI Global; 2019

[48] National Bureau of Statistics (NBS), World Bank. Tanzania's Productive Social Safety Net: Findings from the Impact Evaluation Baseline Survey: Dar-es-Salaam, 2016. Washington D.C: NBS, World Bank; 2020

[49] Fields GS. Poverty, Inequality and Development. Cambridge: Cambridge University Press; 1980

[50] Aho G, Lariviere S, Martin F. Poverty Analysis Manual: With Application in Benin. Quebec City: Universite Laval; 1998

[51] Kane S, Kirby M. Wealth, Poverty and Welfare. London: Palgrave Macmillan; 2003

[52] National Bureau of Statistics and Oxford Policy Management Ltd. Developing a Poverty Baseline in Dar-es-Salaam: Tanzania. Printpak (Tanzania) Ltd; 2000

[53] Bagachwa MSD, editor. Poverty Alleviation in Tanzania: Recent Research Issues. Dar-es-Salaam: Dar-es-Salaam University Press; 1994

[54] Challenges. In: 2020 Lines T. Making Poverty a History. Pennsylvania: Zed Books Ltd: IGI Global; 2008

[55] Repinki G, Stahl H. Poverty and Poverty Reduction Strategies in the East-African Community (EAC). Arusha: GTZ; 2005

[56] Kotler P, Lee NR. Up and out of Poverty: The Social Marketing Solution Toolkit for Policy Makers. Philadelphia: Wharton School Publishing; 2009

[57] Sachs JD. The End of Poverty: How we Can Make it Happen in our Life Time. Penguin Books; 2005

[58] Taylor M. Christianity, Poverty and Wealth: The Findings of Project 21. Geneva: WCC Publications;

Chapter 12

# Of DNA and Demography

*Emily Klancher Merchant*


## Abstract

Over the past 40 years, the focus of demography has expanded beyond the causes and consequences of population growth (and how to stem it) into the causes and consequences of socioeconomic inequality and health disparities, giving rise to new data sources: large-scale longitudinal cohort studies. More recently, these studies have begun to collect a variety of biomarkers, including DNA and epigenetic measures. This chapter explains the three ways in which demographers have used genomic and epigenetic data (epigenetic dependent variables with socioeconomic independent variables, genomic control variables with biomedical dependent variables, and genomic independent variables with socioeconomic dependent variables) and the key findings from each type of research. It describes the shift from candidate gene studies to genome-wide association studies and explores ongoing challenges with using genome-wide association studies and the polygenic scores they produce in demographic research.


**Keywords:** sociogenomics, genome-wide association study, polygenic score, demography, behavior genetics, epigenetics

## 1. Introduction

Demography has changed dramatically over the past 40 years. Beginning in the late 1970s, the field's emphasis expanded beyond population problems into social demography [1]. Whereas the former focused on the causes and consequences of rapid population growth (primarily in the Global South) and ways to slow growth by reducing fertility, the latter focuses on the causes and consequences of socioeconomic inequality (primarily in the Global North) and ways to promote population health [2, 3]. This new focus has spurred the development of large-scale longitudinal cohort studies, including the Wisconsin Longitudinal Study (WLS), the Panel Study of Income Dynamics, the Health and Retirement Study (HRS), the National Longitudinal Study of Adolescent to Adult Health (Add Health), and the Future of Families and Child Wellbeing Study (formerly the Fragile Families and Child Wellbeing Study) in the United States; a series of nationally representative birth cohort studies in the UK; the English Longitudinal Study of Ageing; and the Dunedin Multidisciplinary Health and Development Study in New Zealand [4–10]. Longitudinal demographic studies began to collect biomarkers from participants around the turn of the twentieth century, giving rise to biodemography [11]. Today, they also make genomic data available to users, facilitating the development of the new field of sociogenomics [12].

This chapter explains how demographers and other social scientists use genomic data and what they have learned from doing so. However, the use of DNA in demography and other social sciences has also come in for critique, as will be described in greater detail in Sections 3.3 and 4. The final section of the chapter explores some of the challenges demographers still face in using genomic data and explains why sociogenomics has not lived up to the expectations set by early adopters, but also expresses optimism for new approaches to integrating genomic and epigenetic data into demography.

## 2. How demographers use genomic data

Demographers typically use genomic data in one (or more) of three ways. First, they use epigenetic measures as dependent variables, examining how social factors contribute to changes or differences in the epigenome. This research uses epigenetics to explore somatic responses to social experiences. Second, demographers use a measure of DNA (the genome itself) as a control variable in an analysis with a biomedical outcome, holding genomic variation constant to better identify the effects of social variables. This research treats the genome as a somatic moderator of social determinants of health and treats social factors as moderators of somatic determinants of health. Third, demographers use a measure of DNA as an independent variable in an analysis with a socioeconomic dependent variable, estimating the effects of genetic variation on various forms of socioeconomic inequality. This research seeks somatic causes of social outcomes. Since the epigenome and the genome are ontologically distinct, I will discuss the first approach (hereafter Type 1 Sociogenomics) separately from the other two (hereafter Type 2 and Type 3 Sociogenomics).

### 2.1 Epigenetic dependent variables (somatic responses to social experience)

Epigenetic measures are biomarkers that are near the genome but not part of an individual's genetic sequence. Unlike the DNA itself, epigenetic measures change over the course of a person's life and are influenced by the physical and social environment. The two primary epigenetic markers demographers have considered so far are methylation and telomere length. In methylation, a methyl group binds to a segment of DNA, turning the relevant genes off so they do not get expressed [13]. Methylation can, therefore, explain differential bodily functioning among people with the same genetic sequences. Telomeres are the protective caps at the ends of chromosomes. They get shorter when DNA replicates, so telomere length is a measure of aging at the cellular level [14].

Type 1 Sociogenomics seeks correlations between socioeconomic independent variables and epigenetic dependent variables. It, therefore, examines potential cellular pathways through which social experiences and social inequality "get under the skin" to cause somatic changes. This approach originates in medical sociology, fundamental tenets of which are that the social world influences our health and that socioeconomic inequalities cause health disparities [15]. Demographers working in Type I Sociogenomics have primarily utilized the Future of Families Study (for example, see [16]).

### 2.2 Genomic independent variables (somatic moderators of social determinants of health, social moderators of somatic determinants of health, and somatic causes of social outcomes)

The genome itself comprises approximately three billion pairs of nucleotides, segmented into 23 pairs of chromosomes. Some of these nucleotides form protein-coding sequences, known as genes. Humans have approximately 20,000 genes, but most of our DNA is not part of any gene. Twenty years after the completion of the Human Genome Project, scientists still do not know how (or if) the majority of our DNA functions. Type 2 and Type 3 Sociogenomics seek genomic causes for biomedical and socioeconomic outcomes to answer the age-old "nature vs. nurture vs. structure" question: to what degree are a variety of biomedical and social outcomes determined by social variables as opposed to our genetic makeup? Over the past 20 years, demographers have moved from a candidate gene approach to a genome-wide approach to discovering associations between DNA and a variety of diseases, behaviors, and social processes.

### *2.2.1 Candidate genes*

When demographers began sampling the DNA of survey respondents in the first decade of the twentieth century, they looked for known variants of specific genes, typically genes that relate to neurotransmitters. Efforts to link variants of these genes to particular social outcomes were known as "candidate gene" studies. Major foci of the candidate gene approach in demography and other social sciences included the MAOA gene, which codes for monoamine oxidase A; 5-HTTLPR, which is the promoter region of the serotonin transporter gene; DRD2, which codes for the dopamine receptor D2; and DRD4, which codes for the dopamine receptor D4. Information about these genes and four others was incorporated into Wave III of Add Health for the sibling subsample, spurring an outpouring of candidate gene research across the social sciences [17].

Early results seemed promising, especially outside of demography. Political scientists found that MAOA appeared to predict credit card debt, and MAOA and 5-HTTLPR both appeared to predict voter turnout [18, 19]. DRD2 appeared to predict partisanship, and DRD4 appeared to predict political ideology [20, 21]. In the first decade of the twenty-first century, scholars in a variety of fields identified correlations between these genes and an astounding range of behaviors, from sugar consumption to susceptibility to victimization [22]. Yet demographers were more circumspect. They pointed out that most of these associations failed to replicate, and their carefully designed studies on outcomes that should have followed logically from the genes' known functions turned up negative or inconclusive results (for example, [23, 24]).

By 2012, demographers and other social scientists had concluded that most of the findings from candidate gene studies were false positives [25]. Candidate gene research had tested small samples for associations between a small number of genes and tens of thousands of phenotypes, without correcting for multiple hypothesis testing [22]. Meanwhile, research in medical and animal genetics had begun to suggest that most traits—physiological as well as behavioral—were massively polygenic, influenced by tens if not hundreds of thousands of nucleotides across the genome (not just in genes) [26]. The effect of any individual gene or nucleotide would, therefore, be minuscule, requiring enormous sample sizes for identification. By this time, it was becoming cheaper and easier to genotype individuals at thousands of points along the genome (not just specific genes), and demographic studies that had already collected the DNA of participants—including HRS, Add Health, and WLS—were able to reanalyze stored samples.

### *2.2.2 Genome-wide association studies and polygenic scores*

In the wake of the candidate gene debacle, demographers and other social scientists followed the lead of medical and psychiatric genetics and embarked upon genome-wide association studies (GWAS). GWAS rely not on variants of specific genes, but on single-nucleotide polymorphisms (SNPs), which represent individual nucleotides at loci across the genome where humans are known to differ from one another. At each locus, each person receives one nucleotide from each parent. At most loci, everyone's genome looks exactly the same, and we each receive the same nucleotide from each of our parents. But at about four or five million loci (~0.1% of the genome), humans differ from one another in substantial proportions. At those loci, an individual may be homozygous, meaning that they receive the same nucleotide from each parent, or heterozygous, meaning that they receive different nucleotides from each parent. For example, at a given locus, it might be that some people have two copies of adenine (AA), but others have two copies of thymine (TT) and others yet have one of each (AT or TA). The nucleotide that is more common in the population is known as the "major allele" and the one that is less common is known as the "minor allele." Each of these loci is known as a SNP [27]. SNP arrays or "SNP chips" genotype individuals at hundreds of thousands or even millions of SNPs across the genome. Stored DNA can be regenotyped as SNP chips get larger and, therefore, become capable of identifying more SNPs.

A GWAS uses a series of regression models (one for each measured SNP) to identify correlations between an outcome of interest and each SNP available in the dataset (measured as 0, 1, or 2 depending on the number of minor alleles) [28]. The outcome of interest may be a medical diagnosis (such as schizophrenia or diabetes), a physiological trait (such as height or body mass index [BMI]), a behavior (such as smoking), or a socioeconomic outcome (such as educational attainment). GWAS summary statistics provide a formula for calculating an individual's polygenic score (PGS, also known as a "polygenic risk score" or "polygenic index") for the outcome in question. The PGS multiplies the regression coefficients for each SNP by the individual's value for each SNP (0, 1, or 2) and sums across all SNPs. It is measured in standard deviations from the mean (0).

GWAS require enormous samples and PGS cannot be calculated for individuals included in the GWAS. This means that a single demographic study, such as HRS or Add Health, cannot run its own GWAS to calculate PGS for its participants. Instead, these studies and others participate in the Social Science Genetic Association Consortium (SSGAC) and other consortia, which organize GWAS across demographic and many other data sources—such as the UK Biobank and 23andMe—to produce summary statistics that each study *can* use to calculate PGS for its participants. Several longitudinal demographic studies currently include a vast array of PGS for disease states (e.g., coronary artery disease, myocardial infarction, diabetes, Alzheimer's disease, schizophrenia), biomarkers (e.g., cholesterol and triglycerides), physical characteristics (e.g., height, body mass index, waist circumference, waist-to-hip ratio, and ages at menarche and menopause), mental characteristics (e.g., cognitive function, intelligence, worry, and positive affect), behaviors (e.g., smoking, drinking, children born, age at first birth, and religious attendance), and socioeconomic outcomes (e.g., educational attainment) for each participant. Each PGS is a single variable that demographers and other social scientists can include in standard quantitative models [29].

## 3. What demographers have learned from genomic data

In general, demographic research with genomic data has validated rather than challenged what demographers previously understood with regard to population health and the causes and consequences of socioeconomic inequality. Even when genetic variation is taken into account, social inequality is self-perpetuating and causes health disparities. This section reviews some of the major findings of each type of sociogenomics.

### 3.1 Epigenetic dependent variables and socioeconomic independent variables (Type 1 Sociogenomics: somatic responses to social experience)

Demographic research using epigenetic dependent variables and socioeconomic independent variables has demonstrated that a variety of adverse social circumstances correlate with adverse epigenetic outcomes. For example, mothers and boys living in disadvantaged environments (in the Future of Families sample) have shorter telomeres (indicating more rapid cellular aging) than mothers and boys living in nondisadvantaged environments [30, 31]. Boys in the Future of Families sample who have lost their fathers (through divorce, incarceration, or death) have shorter telomeres than boys who have not [32]. Children who have experienced family violence and disruption have shorter telomeres than children who have not [33]. Children who experience depression have different methylation patterns than those who do not, indicating differential functioning of the same genes [34]. Adults in the 1958 British Birth Cohort Study who had low socioeconomic status as children have different methylation patterns than those who had high socioeconomic status as children [35]. More recent research has indicated other epigenetic mechanisms linking low childhood socioeconomic status to poor adult health [36]. To further explore these mechanisms, Add Health has begun to add blood-based transcriptional profiles for a nationally representative subsample of the original cohort [37]. Demographers have long known that adverse social circumstances produce adverse health consequences. These studies begin to suggest some of the cellular pathways that may mediate between social causes and somatic consequences.

### 3.2 Genomic control variables and biomedical dependent variables (Type 2 Sociogenomics: somatic moderators of social determinants of health and social moderators of somatic determinants of health)

Type 2 Sociogenomics, like Type 1 Sociogenomics, originates in medical sociology and aims to identify social determinants of health and disease. In this type of research, outcomes are typically disease states or adverse biomarkers or other metrics, and analysts typically use PGS for the outcome in question (or a related outcome) to control for individual genomic propensities for that outcome.

Research in Type 2 Sociogenomics has largely found that previously identified social determinants of health remain salient when PGS for disease states or biomarkers are included in quantitative models. For example, stressful life events still predict depressive symptoms in older adults (in the HRS sample), even when individual PGS for depression are taken into account [38]. Similarly, the high school environment continues to influence later-life cognitive function (in the WLS sample), even when controlling for the PGS for cognitive function [39]. Controlling for the PGS for BMI does not change the inverse correlation between educational attainment and BMI in the Add Health sample [40]. In the same study, depression and self-rated health remained correlated with educational attainment when their PGS were taken into account, but the magnitude of the correlation was attenuated, indicating that some (but not all) of the correlation was driven by genetic factors.

Research in this area has also turned up interesting interactions between the genome and the social world. For example, it has long been known that higher socioeconomic status correlates with lower BMI, but recent research in Type 2 Sociogenomics suggests that higher socioeconomic status actually reduces the genetic influence on BMI [41], as does higher educational attainment [42]. Conversely, perceiving one's neighborhood as disorderly exacerbates the genetic risk of type 2 diabetes for older adults in the HRS sample [43]. For younger adults (in the Add Health sample), having a higher PGS for type 2 diabetes increases disease risk only when living in high-crime neighborhoods because living in a high-crime neighborhood increases the risk of obesity [44].

Type 1 and Type 2 Sociogenomics have made valuable contributions to medical sociology [15]. Further research in these areas, particularly in Type 1 Sociogenomics using new epigenetic markers, promises to better elucidate how specific social determinants of health and disease operate and, in particular, how they influence the workings of the human genome. However, several caveats attach to any research using PGS (Type 2 Sociogenomics). These will be discussed further in Section 4.

### 3.3 Genomic independent variables and socioeconomic dependent variables (Type 3 Sociogenomics: somatic causes of social outcomes)

Type 3 Sociogenomics also uses PGS as independent variables, but the dependent variables it seeks to explain are socioeconomic outcomes. It, therefore, uses PGS for markers of socioeconomic status. The overwhelming focus of research in this area has been the PGS for educational attainment, and that will be the focus of this discussion as well.

Although Type 3 Sociogenomics looks similar to Type 2 Sociogenomics in the sense that both use PGS as independent variables, Type 3 Sociogenomics originates in a different corner of the social sciences: behavior genetics, the subfield of psychology concerned with establishing a genetic basis for human and animal behavior [45]. Throughout the second half of the twentieth century, nonmolecular research on twins and adoptees formed the core of human behavior genetics [46]. These studies focused on estimating the "heritability" of behaviors and social outcomes: the proportion of the variance in outcome that arises from genetic variation as opposed to nongenetic (environmental) variation [47]. However, when it became possible to look for molecular causes of particular behaviors and outcomes, the candidate gene approach failed, as described above. For a moment, it appeared that the field would not survive in the molecular age [29, 46].

In 2013, however, the SSGAC breathed new life into behavior genetics with its first GWAS of educational attainment [48]. With this GWAS, behavior genetics expanded into sociogenomics, bringing on board economists and demographers, particularly those associated with long-running studies that had genotyped their participants: HRS, Add Health, and WLS. Although the SSGAC has led GWAS for a few other behavioral outcomes, its primary focus has been educational attainment, for three reasons. First, educational attainment initially appeared to be a reasonable proxy for intelligence, which had long been the focus of behavior genetics and its predecessor, differential psychology [49]. Second, educational attainment (unlike more direct measures of intelligence) was widely available across the disparate data sources available for inclusion in the GWAS (recall from above that GWAS require enormous samples). Third, demographers and other sociologists had long ago identified education as the primary vehicle for social mobility in the United States [50].

The first GWAS of educational attainment (EA1) had a discovery sample of 101,069 people. In validation samples, the PGS it produced accounted for about 2% of the variance in educational attainment [48]. The second GWAS of educational attainment (EA2) had a discovery sample of 293,723 people. Its PGS accounted for about 3.2% of the variance in educational attainment in replication samples [51]. With the 2017 release of data from the UK Biobank [52], the SSGAC was able to coordinate a GWAS of educational attainment with a discovery sample of 1,131,881 people (EA3) [53]. In replication, the PGS accounted for 12.7% of variance in educational attainment in Add Health and 10.6% in HRS.

Social scientists debated whether an $R^2$ of 12.7% was large or small, but behavior geneticists were triumphant. These GWAS appeared to demonstrate that specific genetic variants played a decisive role in producing differences in educational attainment [54]. Some even argued that an individual's PGS for educational attainment provided a more accurate representation of their intelligence than an IQ test and proposed that it be used to distribute educational opportunities and occupational placements [49]. The start-up Genomic Prediction, founded by physicist Stephen Hsu, biochemist Nathan Treff, and bioinformatician Laurent Tellier, offered couples undergoing in-vitro fertilization the opportunity to screen embryos for low predicted educational attainment [55]. The first baby born of this technology entered the world in 2020 [56].

GWAS of educational attainment and the claims made on their behalf by behavior geneticists drew severe critique from sociologists, historians, and other scholars, who warned that this research threatened to substitute genetic determinism for social science and to give new legitimacy to eugenics [57–59]. Geneticists began to express these concerns as well in response to a 2019 GWAS of same-sex sexual activity led by the Broad Institute [60]. Their fears were validated by the nearly immediate release of an app called "How Gay Are You?" which allowed users to upload their raw genetic data and calculate their PGS for same-sex sexual activity [61]. Today, the company Traitwell offers the same service for the PGS of educational attainment [62].

Demographers were initially optimistic about the GWAS of educational attainment. Research using genetically enhanced demographic surveys (primarily Add Health, HRS, WLS, and the Dunedin Study) found that the PGS for educational attainment predicts a number of markers of socioeconomic success: social-class mobility [63], adult occupational status [64], geographic mobility [65], labor earnings [66], wealth at retirement [67], and of course educational attainment itself [68].

Demographers and other sociologists, however, were more interested in using PGS for educational attainment and other socioeconomic outcomes to control for unobserved (genetic) heterogeneity, thereby producing a clearer picture of how social variables contribute to socioeconomic outcomes [12]. This research has demonstrated that, even when the PGS for educational attainment is taken into account, childhood socioeconomic status remains an important predictor of educational outcomes and adult socioeconomic status. In the HRS sample, respondents whose PGS was in the lowest quartile but whose fathers' income was in the highest quartile graduated from high school at a higher rate than respondents whose PGS was in the highest quartile but whose fathers' income was in the lowest quartile. The same was true of college graduation rates [66]. Data from HRS also showed that correlations between a child's educational attainment and that of their parents are primarily driven by social inheritance rather than genetic inheritance [69]. Data from the UK Biobank showed that children with higher socioeconomic status had greater returns to schooling, net of the PGS for educational attainment [70].

In 2022, researchers associated with SSGAC published a fourth GWAS of educational attainment (EA4) [71]. This study used a discovery sample of 3,037,499 individuals, more than two-thirds of whom came from 23andMe. The resulting PGS accounts for 15.8% of the variance in educational attainment in the Add Health sample and 12.0% of the variance in educational attainment in the HRS sample (sample-size-weighted mean of 13.3%) [71].

By that time, however, these larger $R^2$ figures had come to seem less impressive. A raft of research had demonstrated that an individual's PGS for educational attainment is correlated with socioeconomic advantage at family and neighborhood levels [68, 72], and that a substantial proportion of the predictive power of the PGS for educational attainment is due to its correlation with a person's living environment rather than to biochemical effects in a person's body (direct genetic effects) [73]. Several studies found that the PGS for educational attainment lost upward of half of its predictive power in samples of siblings as opposed to unrelated individuals [63, 74]. Research comparing adopted children to nonadopted children found that the PGS for educational attainment was substantially less predictive of actual educational attainment for adopted children [75] and that parents' PGS for educational attainment predicted the educational attainment of both biological and adopted children (though less well for adopted children than for biological children) [76]. Researchers typically describe the effect of the parents' PGS on the child's education as "genetic nurture" or an "indirect genetic effect," but there is no evidence that the parents' DNA has a direct effect on the environment they provide for their children. Data from the Brisbane Adolescent Twin Study suggest that this effect is entirely accounted for by parents' socioeconomic status [77].

In the most recent GWAS of educational attainment (EA4), within-family analysis demonstrated that only 30.9% of the $R^2$ could be attributed to direct genetic effects [71]. That is, an individual's own SNPs account for only 4.1% (30.9% of the sample-size-weighted mean $R^2$ of 13.3%) of the variance in educational attainment in HRS and Add Health. Moreover, the findings of within-family studies cannot be generalized to between-family differences [78]. Just in the past two years, social and medical geneticists have warned publicly against using PGS (for any outcomes, but especially for educational attainment) to select embryos, as they do not have the effect that companies like Genomic Prediction claim [79]. Genetic differences do seem to have some bearing on educational attainment (and therefore other socioeconomic outcomes), but their effect is small, and we still do not know which genes matter or *how* they matter.

## 4. The drawbacks of GWAS and PGS

Only six years ago, demographers were optimistic that GWAS could produce PGS that would allow them to control for unobserved genetic heterogeneity, increasing the explanatory power of their social models [12]. As the previous section indicates, however, GWAS and PGS for educational attainment have not lived up to the hype that accompanied their introduction. Educational attainment is the most studied social outcome in Type 3 Sociogenomics, but the difficulty of identifying direct genetic effects, even with discovery samples that include millions of people, suggests that GWAS for other socioeconomic outcomes will face similar challenges. This section describes two additional problems with GWAS and PGS that apply to biomedical outcomes (those used in Type 2 Sociogenomics) as well as socioeconomic outcomes (those used in Type 3 Sociogenomics): their lack of portability and their mismeasurement of genetic risk.

### 4.1 The nonportability of PGS

Across biomedical and social genomics, GWAS discovery samples are typically limited to white people with exclusively European genetic ancestry [80]. The rationale for this limitation derives from a racist thought experiment known as "the chopsticks problem": if a GWAS of facility with chopsticks were performed on students from a US university, it would inevitably identify SNPs that are more common among Asian Americans, regardless of whether such SNPs have any bearing on manual dexterity [81]. The issue is what geneticists term "population stratification": DNA and culture both vary geographically. Ideally, in a GWAS discovery sample, the only systematic genetic differences between cases and controls would be in SNPs that cause (or are in linkage [correlated] with SNPs that cause) the outcome in question. However, since the purpose of the GWAS is to identify the SNPS that cause (or are in linkage with SNPs that cause) the outcome in question, there is no way to apply this limitation in advance. Instead, researchers typically use race as a proxy for genetic similarity. They do so in the language of "genetic ancestry" [54] and identify it with genetic markers (either ancestry informative markers or principal component analysis) [82]. However, GWAS typically define ancestry as the continent from which one's recent ancestors originated, thereby conflating ancestry with the socially constructed racial categories used in the United States, even though human genetic variation occurs continuously across continents rather than categorically between them [83]. Boundaries between the so-called ancestry groups are arbitrary and artificial [59].

Owing to the large sample sizes required by GWAS, white/European ancestry subjects have been most readily available, and all of the GWAS of educational attainment have been limited to white/European ancestry samples (as identified by ancestry informative markers or principal components analysis). Three problems remain, however. First, these large white/European ancestry samples are not representative of any actual population. GWAS discovery samples rely heavily on two sources of data. One is the UK Biobank, which is volunteer-based and has consistently experienced low participation rates, and is therefore not representative of the UK population [84]. The other is 23andMe, a direct-to-consumer genetic testing company that collects research samples from customers who have paid for some type of genetic testing [85]. Its customer base comes primarily from the United States, but is far from representative of the US population. These samples become even less representative when combined with each other and with additional samples. Second, limiting GWAS discovery samples to white/European ancestry populations does not fully solve the problem of population stratification because stratification occurs geographically at scales much finer than the continent [86] and socially within geographic locations [87]. Third, the PGS that are created from these GWAS have limited portability, both outside of and within white/European ancestry populations.

In biomedical as well as social genetics, PGS constructed from GWAS that include only white people are much less predictive (if predictive at all) for nonwhite individuals [88]. The PGS constructed from the most recent GWAS of educational attainment (EA4) accounts for only 1.3% of the variance in educational attainment among African Americans in HRS and 2.3% of the variance in educational attainment among African Americans in Add Health, as compared to 12.0% (HRS) and 15.8% (Add Health) for white Americans [71]. The use of biomedical or socioeconomic PGS for clinical or policy purposes, therefore, threatens to exacerbate existing disparities [88]. Several efforts are currently underway to make GWAS for biomedical outcomes more diverse, but these have encountered scientific challenges along with those related to recruiting participants [89].

The lack of portability across racial categories is typically explained in biological terms: perhaps there are different SNPs that account for the outcomes in question in non-European-ancestry populations, or perhaps the SNPs identified in the GWAS are in linkage (correlated) with different SNPs in non-European-ancestry populations than they are in European-ancestry populations. However, it is equally possible that genetic variation has different consequences in different social environments [15]. For example, data from HRS, Add Health, and WLS indicate that the PGS for educational attainment became more predictive for white American women across the twentieth century, as gender discrimination abated [90]. Currently, the nonportability of the PGS for educational attainment beyond white/European subjects means that responsible research using this PGS must be limited to white/European samples (though irresponsible research does occasionally get published, for example, [91]).

Demographers and geneticists have recently found that PGS have limited portability even among white individuals with exclusively European ancestry, indicating substantial genetic diversity within this racially defined group. For example, PGS constructed from GWAS using individuals with ancestry in Northwest Europe do a much worse job of predicting outcomes in individuals with ancestry in other parts of Europe [92]. Research using data from WLS has demonstrated that the PGS for educational attainment does not predict outcomes for Jewish individuals as well as it does for non-Jewish individuals [93]. Research using data from the UK Biobank has shown that PGS also fail to port across other social categories, including age, sex, and socioeconomic status [94]. While researchers can account for the lack of portability outside of white/European ancestry samples by limiting their studies to white individuals with exclusively European ancestry, they cannot account for the lack of portability within white/European ancestry samples because the factors limiting portability are rarely known in advance.

### 4.2 PGS and the mismeasurement of genetic risk

The final problem with the use of GWAS and PGS in demography is that they do not effectively do what demographers need them to do: account for genetic heterogeneity and thereby facilitate the production of better models and more accurate estimates of social parameters [12, 54]. That is, the PGS produced by GWAS of educational attainment and other social outcomes do not accurately capture individual genomic propensity for those outcomes. As this chapter has shown, existing methods generate PGS that are seriously confounded by social and other environmental factors, and whose portability is severely limited in ways that are both known (beyond white/European ancestry samples) and unknown (within white/European ancestry samples). Additionally, GWAS measure only one type of genetic risk: the additive effects of SNPs. They exclude rare variants, structural variants, insertions, and deletions. They also exclude the X and Y chromosomes and mitochondrial DNA [78].

PGS, therefore, exclude genetic information that may be relevant and include social information that is relevant to the outcome in question but not caused by DNA [95]. They, therefore, mismeasure the genetic risk of the outcomes they are supposed to index, even in individuals who resemble the discovery sample. Medical geneticists have already moved away from PGS as indicators of disease risk. Demography, however, seems to be moving in the opposite direction, with long-running studies increasingly genotyping participants and adding PGS to their public data offerings. Proponents have claimed that any social research that does not include a PGS is akin to bank robbery: a waste of public money due to omitted variable bias [54]. But it is becoming increasingly clear that PGS do not solve the problem of unobserved genetic heterogeneity, and that including them in social models may produce worse rather than better parameter estimates. They, therefore, threaten to naturalize social inequality and thereby preserve the status quo. While this is primarily a problem for Type 3 Sociogenomics, any cautions about using PGS also apply to Type 2 Sociogenomics.

## 5. Conclusions

The use of genomic and epigenetic data in demography is quite new—dating only from the first decade of the present century—and rapidly changing. So far, it has validated nongenetic research in social demography, demonstrating that educational attainment is strongly conditioned by childhood socioeconomic status and that socioeconomic inequality in both childhood and adulthood produces health disparities. With the development of new epigenetic measures in particular, it may be possible to get a more detailed picture of exactly how the social world influences health, which may point to new ways to advance population health and health equity.

Yet, while the use of genomic and epigenetic data has provided new evidence for the ways in which *social* variables produce social and biomedical outcomes, it has provided scant new evidence for the ways in which DNA contributes to these outcomes. Candidate gene studies proved a boondoggle, demonstrating that genetic influences on socioeconomic and biomedical outcomes are weaker than previously expected and more widely distributed across the genome. Individual genes rarely have identifiable effects, either medically or socially. GWAS identify SNPs that are *correlated* with particular outcomes, but they do not identify causal pathways. They give credence to the long-standing claim of behavior genetics that DNA influences all human outcomes, but do not provide any specific information about *how*.

Six years ago, demographers were enthusiastic about the prospect that GWAS would produce PGS that could simply be dropped into quantitative models to control for genetic heterogeneity and better clarify social processes. Increasingly, however, it has become clear that PGS are not adequate to this task, though they may have other uses. Research by demographers has been key to identifying the limitations of PGS, particularly the PGS for educational attainment, and to demonstrating the impossibility of separating genetic and environmental causes of socioeconomic and biomedical outcomes. This research has clearly shown that genes matter differently in different social contexts. GWAS may eventually be consigned to the same dustbin as candidate gene studies, or they may prove useful beyond the construction of PGS.

Several new lines of research are beginning to appear on the horizon of sociogenomics. One is further inquiry into the genetics of education and other social outcomes, moving beyond SNPs and into rare variants and structural variants. A second is the study of endophenotypes: biomarkers or subclinical phenomena that show stronger correlations with DNA than the phenotypes demographers have studied to this point (socioeconomic outcomes and diseases states). Finally, RNA and new epigenetic phenomena might provide additional insights into the social determinants of health, particularly as they relate to aging and to the effects of childhood experiences on later life health. Undoubtedly, demographers will continue to use genomic and epigenetic data to advance the project of social demography in creative and productive ways.

## Acknowledgements

This research was funded in part by a Hellman Fellowship from the University of California, Davis, and partially completed while the author was a member of the School of Social Science at the Institute for Advanced Study in Princeton, NJ. It was inspired and shaped by conversations with many demographers, sociologists, and sociogenomicists. Particular thanks are due to Dalton Conley, Sam Trejo, and the members of the Biosociology Lab at Princeton University.

## Author details

Emily Klancher Merchant
University of California, Davis, United States

*Address all correspondence to: ekmerchant@ucdavis.edu

## References

[1] Preston SH. The contours of demography: Estimates anssociation of telomered projections. Demography. 1993;**30**:593-606. DOI: 10.2307/2061808

[2] Merchant EK. A digital history of Anglophone demography and global population control, 1915-1984. Population and Development Review. 2017;**43**:83-117. DOI: 10.1111/padr.12044

[3] Merchant EK, Alexander CS. U.S. demography in transition. Historical Methods: A Journal of Quantitative and Interdisciplinary History. 2022;**55**:168-188. DOI: 10.1080/01615440.2022.2098216

[4] Herd P, Carr D, Roan C. Cohort profile: Wisconsin Longitudinal Study (WLS). International Journal of Epidemiology. 2014;**43**:34-41. DOI: 10.1093/ije/dys194

[5] Johnson DS, McGonagle KA, Freedman VA, Sastry N. Fifty years of the Panel Study of Income Dynamics: Past, present, and future. The ANNALS of the American Academy of Political and Social Science. 2018;**680**:9-28. DOI: 10.1177/0002716218809363

[6] Sonnega A, Faul JD, Ofstedal MB, Langa KM, Phillips JWR, Weir DR. Cohort profile: The Health and Retirement Study (HRS). International Journal of Epidemiology. 2014;**43**:576-585. DOI: 10.1093/ije/dyu067

[7] Harris KM, Halpern CT, Whitsel EA, Hussey JM, Killeya-Jones LA, Tabor J, et al. Cohort profile: The National Longitudinal Study of Adolescent to Adult Health (Add Health). International Journal of Epidemiology. 2019;**48**:1415-1415k. DOI: 10.1093/ije/dyz115

[8] Reichman NE, Teitler JO, Garfinkel I, McLanahan SS. Fragile Families: Sample and design. Children and Youth Services Review. 2001;**23**:303-326. DOI: 10.1016/S0190-7409(01)00141-4

[9] Steptoe A, Breeze E, Banks J, Nazroo J. Cohort profile: the English Longitudinal Study of Ageing. International Journal of Epidemiology. 2013;**42**:1640-1648. DOI: 10.1093/ije/dys168

[10] Poulton R, Moffitt TE, Silva PA. The Dunedin Multidisciplinary Health and Development Study: Overview of the first 40 years, with an eye to the future. Social Psychiatry and Psychiatric Epidemiology. 2015;**50**:679-693. DOI: 10.1007/s00127-015-1048-8

[11] National Research Council. Conducting Biosocial Surveys: Collecting, Storing, Accessing, and Protecting Biospecimens. Washington, DC: National Academies Press; 2010

[12] Conley D, Fletcher J. The Genome Factor: What the Social Genomics Revolution Reveals about Ourselves, Our History, and the Future. Princeton: Princeton University Press; 2017. p. 296

[13] Singal R, Ginder GD. DNA methylation. Blood. 1999;**93**:4059-4070. DOI: 10.1182/blood.V93.12.4059

[14] Blasco MA. Telomere length, stem cells and aging. Nature Chemical Biology. 2007;**3**:640-649. DOI: 10.1038/nchembio.2007.38

[15] Boardman JD, Fletcher JM. Evaluating the continued integration of genetics into medical sociology. Journal of Health and Social Behavior. 2022;**62**:404-418. DOI: 10.1177/00221465211032581

[16] Notterman DA, Mitchell C. Epigenetics and understanding the impact of social determinants of health. Pediatric Clinics. 2015;**62**:P1227-P1240. DOI: 10.1016/j.pcl.2015.05.012

[17] Harris KM, Halpern CT, Smolen A, Haberstick BC. The National Longitudinal Study of Adolescent Health (Add Health) twin data. Twin Research and Human Genetics. 2012;**9**:988-997. DOI: 10.1375/twin.9.6.988

[18] De Neve JE, Fowler JH. Credit card borrowing and the monoamine oxidase A (MAOA) gene. Journal of Economic Behavior and Organization. 2014;**107**:428-439. DOI: 10.1016/j.jebo.2014.03.002

[19] Fowler JH, Dawes CT. Two genes predict voter turnout. The Journal of Politics. 2008;**70**:579-594. DOI: 10.1017/S0022381608080638

[20] Dawes CT, Fowler JH. Partisanship, voting, and the dopamine D2 receptor gene. The Journal of Politics. 2009;**71**:1157-1171. DOI: 10.1017/S002238160909094X

[21] Settle JE, Dawes CT, Christakis NA, Fowler JH. Friendships moderate an association between a dopamine gene variant and political ideology. The Journal of Politics. 2010;**72**:1189-1198. DOI: 10.1017/S0022381610000617

[22] Charney E, English W. Candidate genes and political behavior. The American Political Science Review. 2012;**106**:1-34. DOI: 10.1017/S0003055411000554

[23] Haberstick BC, Lessem JM, Hewitt JK, Smolen A, Hopfer CJ, Halpern CT, et al. MAOA genotype, childhood maltreatment, and their interaction in the etiology of adult antisocial behaviors. Biological Psychiatry. 2014;**75**:25-30. DOI: 10.1016/j.biopsych.2013.03.028

[24] Haberstick BC, Boardman JD, Wagner B, Smolen A, Hewitt JK, Killeya-Jones LA, et al. Depression, stressful life events, and the impact of variation in the serotonin transporter: Findings from the National Longitudinal Study of Adolescent to Adult Health (Add Health). PLoS One. 2016;**11**:e0148373. DOI: 10.1371/journal.pone.0148373

[25] Chabris CF, Hebert BM, Benjamin DJ, Beauchamp J, Cesarini D, van der Loos M, et al. Most reported genetic associations with general intelligence are probably false positives. Psychological Science. 2012;**23**:1314-1323. DOI: 10.1177/0956797611435528

[26] Chabris CF, Lee JJ, Benjamin DJ, Beauchamp JP, Glaeser EL, Borst G, et al. Why it is hard to find genes associated with social science traits: Theoretical and empirical considerations. American Journal of Public Health. 2013;**103**:S152-S166. DOI: 10.2105/AJPH.2013.301327

[27] Brookes AJ. The essence of SNPs. Gene. 1999;**234**:177-186. DOI: 10.1016/S0378-1119(99)00219-X

[28] Bush WS, Moore JH. Genome-wide association studies. PLoS Computational Biology. 2012;**8**:e1002822. DOI: 10.1371/journal.pcbi.1002822

[29] Harden KP. "Reports of my death were greatly exaggerated": Behavior genetics in the postgenomic era. Annual Review of Psychology. 2021;**72**:37-60. DOI: 10.1146/annurev-psych-052220-103822

[30] Massey DS, Wagner B, Donnely L, McLanahan S, Brooks-Gunn J, Garfinkel I, et al. Neighborhood disadvantage and telomere length: Results from the

Fragile Families Study. The Russell Sage Foundation Journal of the Social Sciences. 2018;**4**:28-42. DOI: 10.7758/RSF.2018.4.4.02

[31] Mitchell C, Hobcraft J, McLanahan SS, Siegel SR, Berg A, Brooks-Gunn J, et al. Social disadvantage, genetic sensitivity, and children's telomere length. Proceedings of the National Academy of Sciences. 2014;**111**:5944-5949. DOI: 10.1073/pnas.1404293111

[32] Mitchell C, McLanahan S, Schneper L, Garfinkel I, Brooks-Gunn J, Notterman D. Father loss and child telomere length. Pediatrics. 2017;**140**:e20163245. DOI: 10.1542/peds.2016-3245

[33] Drury SS, Mabile E, Brett ZH, Jones E, Shirtcliff EA, Theall KP. The association of telomere length with family violence and disruption. Pediatrics. 2014;**134**:e128-e137. DOI: 10.1542/peds.2013-3415

[34] De Vito R, Grabski IN, Aguiar D, Schneper LM, Verma A, Fernandez JC, Mitchell C, Bell J, McLanahan S, Notterman DA, Engelhardt BE. Differentially methylated regions and methylation QTLs for teen depression and early puberty in the Fragile Families Child Wellbeing Study. BioRxiv 2021. DOI: 10.1101/2021.05.20.444959

[35] Borghol N, Suderman M, McArdle W, Racine A, Hallett M, Pembrey M, et al. Associations with early-life socio-economic position in adult DNA methylation. International Journal of Epidemiology. 2012;**41**:62-74. DOI: 10.1093/ije/dyr147

[36] Carmeli C, Kautalik Z, Mishra PP, Porcu E, Delpierre C, Delaneau O, et al. Gene regulation contributes to explain the impact of early life socioeconomic disadvantage on adult inflammatory levels in two cohort studies. Scientific Reports. 2021;**11**:3100. DOI: 10.1038/s41598-021-82714-2

[37] Cole SW, Shanahan MJ, Gaydosh L, Harris KM. Population-based RNA profiling in Add Health finds social disparities in inflammatory and antiviral gene regulation emerge by young adulthood. Proceedings of the National Academy of Sciences. 2020;**117**:4601-4608. DOI: 10.1073/pnas.1821367117

[38] Musliner KL, Seifuddin F, Judy JA, Pirooznia M, Goes FS, Zandi PP. Polygenic risk, stressful life events and depressive symptoms in older adults: A polygenic score analysis. Psychological Medicine 2014; 45:1709-1720. DOI: 10.1017/S0033291714002839

[39] Moorman SM, Greenfield EA, Garcia S. School context in adolescence and cognitive functioning 50 years later. Journal of Health and Social Behavior. 2020;**60**:493-508. DOI: 10.1177/0022146519887354

[40] Boardman JD, Domingue BW, Daw J. What can genes tell us about the relationship between education and health? Social Science & Medicine. 2015;**127**:171-180. DOI: 10.1016/j.socscimed.2014.08.001

[41] Liu H, Guo G. Lifetime socioeconomic status, historical context, and genetic inheritance in shaping body mass in middle and late adulthood. American Sociological Review. 2015;**80**:705-737. DOI: 10.1177/0003122415590627

[42] Barcellos SH, Carvalho LS, Turley P. Education can reduce health differences related to genetic risk of obesity. Proceedings of the National Academy of Sciences. 2018;**115**:E9765-E9772. DOI: 10.1073/pnas.1802909115

[43] Robinette JW, Boardman JD, Crimmins EM. Differential vulnerability to neighbourhood disorder: A gene-x-environment interaction study. Journal of Epidemiology and Community Health. 2019;**73**:388-392. DOI: 10.1136/jech-2018-211373

[44] Guo F, Harris KM, Boardman JD, Robinette JW. Does crime trigger genetic risk for type 2 diabetes in young adults? A G x E interaction study using national data. Social Science & Medicine. 2022;**313**:115396. DOI: 10.1016/j.socscimed.2022.115396

[45] Knopik V, Neiderhiser J, DeFries J, Plomin R. Behavioral Genetics. New York: Macmillan; 2017

[46] Panofsky A. Misbehaving Science: Controversy and the Development of Behavior Genetics. Chicago: University of Chicago Press; 2014. p. 320

[47] Keller EF. The Mirage of a Space between Nature and Nurture. Durham: Duke University Press; 2010. p. 120

[48] Rietveld CA et al. GWAS of 126,559 individuals identifies genetic variants associated with educational attainment. Science. 2013;**340**:1467-1471. DOI: 10.1126/science.1235488

[49] Plomin R. Blueprint: How DNA Makes Us Who We Are. Cambridge: MIT Press; 2018. p. 280

[50] Blau P, Duncan OD. The American Occupational Structure. New York: John Wiley and Sons; 1967. p. 520

[51] Okbay A et al. Genome-wide association study identifies 74 loci associated with educational attainment. Nature. 2016;**533**:539-542. DOI: 10.1038/nature17671

[52] Bycroft C, Freeman C, Petkova D, Band G, Elliott LT, Sharp K, et al. The UK Biobank resource with deep phenotyping and genomic data. Nature. 2018;**562**:203-209. DOI: 10.1038/s41586-018-0579-z

[53] Lee JJ et al. Gene discovery and polygenic prediction from a genome-wide association study of educational attainment in 1.1 million individuals. Nature Genetics. 2018;**50**:1112-1121. DOI: 10.1038/s41588-018-0147-3

[54] Harden KP. The Genetic Lottery: Why DNA Matters for Social Equality. Princeton: Princeton University Press; 2021. p. 312

[55] Adler S. G: Unnatural selection. RadioLab. July 25, 2019. Available from: https://www.wnycstudios.org/podcasts/radiolab/articles/g-unnatural-selection [Accessed: December 12, 2022]

[56] Shanks P. The first polygenic risk score baby. Biopolitical Times. September 30 2021. Available from: https://www.geneticsandsociety.org/biopolitical-times/first-polygenic-risk-score-baby [Accessed: December 12, 2022]

[57] Bliss C. Social by Nature: The Promise and Peril of Sociogenomics. Stanford: Stanford University Press; 2018. p. 304

[58] Henn B, Merchant EK, O'Connor A, Rulli T. Why DNA is no key to social equality: On Kathryn Paige Harden's *The Genetic Lottery*. LA Review of Books. September 21, 2021. Available from: https://lareviewofbooks.org/article/why-dna-is-no-key-to-social-equality-on-kathryn-paige-hardens-the-genetic-lottery/ [Accessed: December 12, 2022]

[59] Coop G, Przeworski M. Lottery, luck, or legacy. A review of The Genetic Lottery: Why DNA Matters for Social

Equality. Evolution. 2022;**76**:846-853. DOI: 10.1111/evo.14449

[60] Ganna AA et al. Large-scale GWAS reveals insights into the genetic architecture of same-sex sexual behavior. Science. 2019;**365**:eaat7693. DOI: 10.1126/science.aat7693

[61] Maxmen A. Controversial "gay gene" app provokes fears of a genetic Wild West. Nature. 2019;**574**:609-610. DOI: 10.1038/d41586-019-03282-0

[62] Explore your educational possibilities. Available from: https://www.traitwell.com/app/EA. [Accessed: December 12, 2022]

[63] Belsky DW, Domingue BW, Wedow R, Arseneault L, Boardman JD, Caspi A, et al. Genetic analysis of social-class mobility in five longitudinal studies. Proceedings of the National Academy of Sciences. 2018;**115**:E7275-E7284. DOI: 10.1073/pnas.1801238115

[64] Belsky DW, Moffitt TE, Corcoran DL, Domingue B, Harrington H, Hogan S, et al. The genetics of success: How single-nucleotide polymorphisms associated with educational attainment relate to life-course development. Psychological Science. 2016;**27**:957-972. DOI: 10.1177/0956797616643070

[65] Abdellaoui A, Hugh-Jones D, Yengo L, Kemper KE, Nivard MG, Veul L, et al. Genetic correlates of social stratification in Great Britain. Nature Human Behaviour. 2019;**3**:1332-1342. DOI: 10.1038/s41562-019-0757-5

[66] Papageorge NW, Thom K. Genes, education, and labor market outcomes: Evidence from the Health and Retirement Study. Journal of the European Economic Association. 2020;**18**:1351-1399. DOI: 10.1093/jeea/jvz072

[67] Barth D, Papageorge NW, Thom K. Genetic endowments and wealth inequality. Journal of Political Economy. 2020;**128**:1474-1522. DOI: 10.1086/705415

[68] Domingue BW, Belsky DW, Conley D, Harris KM, Boardman JD. Polygenic influence on educational attainment: New evidence from the National Longitudinal Study of Adolescent to Adult Health. AERA Open. 2015;**1**:1-13. DOI: 10.1177/2332858415599972

[69] Conley D, Domingue BW, Cesarini D, Dawes C, Rietveld CA, Boardman JD. Is the effect of parental education on offspring biased or moderated by genotype? Sociological Science. 2015;**2**:82-105. DOI: 10.15195/v2.a6

[70] Barcellos SH, Carvalho L, Turley P. The effect of education on the relationship between genetics, early-life disadvantages, and later-life SES. NBER Working Paper. 2021:28750. DOI: 10.3386/w28750

[71] Okbay A et al. Polygenic prediction of educational attainment within and between families from genome-wide association analyses in 3 million individuals. Nature Genetics. 2022;**54**:437-449. DOI: 10.1038/s41588-022-01016-z

[72] Trejo S, Belsky DW, Boardman JD, Freese J, Harris KM, Herd P, et al. Schools as moderators of genetic associations with life course attainments: Evidence from the WLS and Add Health. Sociological Science. 2018;**5**:513-540. DOI: 10.15195/v5.a22

[73] Young AI, Benonisdottir S, Przeworski M, Kong A. Deconstructing the sources of genotype-phenotype

associations in humans. Science. 2019;**365**:1396-1400. DOI: 10.1126/science.aax3710

[74] Howe LJ et al. Within-sibship genome-wide association analyses decrease bias in estimates of direct genetic effects. Nature Genetics. 2022;**54**:581-592. DOI: 10.1038/s41588-022-01062-7

[75] Cheesman R, Hunjan A, Coleman J, Ahmadzadeh Y, Plomin R, McAdams T, et al. Comparison of adopted and nonadopted individuals reveals gene-environment interplay for education in the UK Biobank. Psychological Science. 2020;**31**:582-591. DOI: 10.1177/0956797620904450

[76] Domingue BW, Fletcher J. Separating measured genetic and environmental effects: Evidence linking parental genotype and adopted child outcomes. Behavior Genetics. 2020;**50**:301-309. DOI: 10.1007/s10519-020-10000-4

[77] Bates TC, Maher BS, Colodro-Conde L, Medland SE, McAloney K, Wright MJ, et al. Social competence in parents increases children's educational attainment: Replicable genetically-mediated effects of parenting revealed by non-transmitted DNA. Twin Research and Human Genetics. 2019;**22**:1-3. DOI: 10.1017/thg.2018.75

[78] Burt C. Challenging the utility of polygenic scores for social science: Environmental confounding, downward causation, and unknown biology. Behavioral and Brain Sciences. Forthcoming. 2001. DOI: 10.1017/S0140525X22001145

[79] Turley P, Meyer MN, Wang N, Cesarini D, Hammonds E, Martin AR, et al. Problems with using polygenic scores to select embryos. The New England Journal of Medicine. 2021;**385**:78-86. DOI: 10.1056/NEJMsr2105065

[80] Popejoy AB, Fullerton SM. Genomics is failing on diversity. Nature. 2016;**538**:161-164. DOI: 10.1038/538161a

[81] Hamer D, Sirota L. Beware the chopsticks gene. Molecular Psychiatry. 2000;**5**:11-13. DOI: 10.1038/sj.mp.4000662

[82] Tian C, Gregersen PK, Seldin MF. Accounting for ancestry: Population substructure and genome-wide association studies. Human Molecular Genetics. 2008;**17**:R143-R150. DOI: 10.1093/hmg/ddn268

[83] Fujimura JH, Bolnick DA, Rajagopalan R, Kaufman JS, Lewontin RC, Duster T, et al. Clines without classes: How to make sense of human variation. Sociological Theory. 2014;**32**:208-227. DOI: 10.1177/0735275114551611

[84] Keyes KM, Westrich D. UK Biobank, big data, and the consequences of non-representativeness. The Lancet. 2019;**393**:1297. DOI: 10.1016/S0140-6736(18)33067-8

[85] Harris A, Wyatt S, Kelly SE. The gift of spit (and the obligation to return it): How consumers of online genetic testing services participate in research. Information, Communication & Society. 2013;**16**:236-257. DOI: 10.1080/1369118X.2012.701656

[86] Abdellaoui A, Dolan CV, Verweij KJH, Nivard MG. Gene-environment correlations across geographic regions affect genome-wide association studies. Nature Genetics. 2022;**54**:1345-1354. DOI: 10.1038/s41588-022-01158-0

[87] Merchant EK. The social stratification of population as a source

of downward causation. Behavioral and Brain Sciences. 2023

[88] Martin AR, Kanai M, Kamatani Y, Okada Y, Neale BM, Daly MJ. Clinical use of current polygenic risk scores may exacerbate health disparities. Nature Genetics. 2019;**51**:584-591. DOI: 10.1038/s41588-019-0379-x

[89] Ruan Y et al. Improving polygenic prediction in ancestrally diverse populations. Nature Genetics. 2022;**54**:573-580. DOI: 10.1038/s41588-022-01054-7

[90] Herd P, Freese J, Sicinski K, Domingue BW, Harris KM, Wei C, et al. Genes, gender inequality, and educational attainment. American Sociological Review. 2019;**84**:1069-1098. DOI: 10.1177/0003122419886550

[91] Piffer D. Evidence for recent polygenic selection on educational attainment and intelligence inferred from GWAS hits: A replication of previous findings using recent data. Psychiatry. 2019;**1**:55-75. DOI: 10.3390/psych1010005

[92] Privé F, Aschard H, Carmi S, Folkersen L, Hoggart C, O'Reilly PF, et al. Portability of 245 polygenic scores when derived from the UK Biobank and applied to 9 ancestry groups from the same cohort. American Journal of Human Genetics. 2022;**109**:12-23. DOI: 10.1016/j.ajhg.2021.11.008

[93] Freese J, Domingue B, Sicinski K, Trejo S, Herd P. Problems with a causal interpretation of polygenic score differences between Jewish and non-Jewish respondents in the Wisconsin Longitudinal Study. SocArXiv. 2019. DOI: 10.31235/osf.io/eh9tq

[94] Mostafavi H, Harpak A, Agarwal I, Conley D, Pritchard JK, Przeworski M. Variable prediction accuracy of polygenic scores within an ancestry group. eLife. 2020;**9**:e48376. DOI: 10.7554/eLife.48376

[95] Cecile A, Janssens JW. Validity of polygenic risk scores: Are we measuring what we think we are? Human Molecular Genetics. 2019;**28**:R143-R150. DOI: 10.1093/hmg/ddz205

Chapter 13

# Demographic Data in the Built Environment and Human Health Studies

*Huaqing Wang and Louis G. Tassinary*


## Abstract

Demographic data is widely used in both built environment and population health studies. Traditional data sources include national, state, and local surveys as well as archived data from longitudinal studies and newly emerging sources such as digitally accessible administrative data and real-time data from mobile devices. The value of these diverse data sets hinges on their accuracy, completeness, reliability, relevance, and timeliness. This chapter reviews the literature published in this field, provides a selective overview of the extant published research based on such data, and offers suggestions for the continuing access and use of such datasets.


**Keywords:** epidemiology, social context, community, neighborhood, city

## 1. Introduction

The built environment encompasses aspects of the inhabited constructed world that affect such fundamental human activities and needs as play, rest, work, mobility, shelter, etc. These constructed environments typically consist of homes, buildings, streets, open and green spaces, neighborhoods and communities, grocery stores, healthcare facilities, schools, and other artifacts. Research to date has consistently found that aspects of the built environment affect a person's health in different ways. For example, sedentary habits are reinforced for individuals with limited access to sidewalks or bike paths, and a higher prevalence of obesity is positively related to the proximity of fast-food restaurants to primary dwellings. In addition, urban density generally increases the likelihood of significant air and noise pollution, which in some studies is related to the prevalence of respiratory disease and hearing. Exposure to loud noise can also cause high blood pressure, heart disease, sleep disturbances, and stress. And both laboratory experiments and field-based quasi-experiments have repeatedly shown that exposure to greenspace helps reduce stress or restore attention.

Scholars from the distinct yet converging fields of landscape architecture, city planning, environmental science, psychology, public health, preventive medicine, and geography each provide unique perspectives on the complex multi-level relationships between the built environment and human health. Environmental psychologists typically conduct research in lab and field settings to explore psychophysiological individual reactions to natural and constructed environments, whereas epidemiologists usually examine such phenomena through aggregate cross-sectional or longitudinal observational studies. Researchers in landscape architecture, city planning, and geography focus primarily on the spatial distribution of certain city elements and human health associations through the conduct of field surveys and experiments in actual human settlements.

Regardless of either the discipline or method, nearly all such research requires some form of social demographic data. Social and demographic factors such as age, gender, race, income, or education all affect human health and therefore need to be controlled or accounted for in any scientific investigation. Some studies control such variation through research design, for example, by an explicit focus on older adults' mental well-being and how it is affected by neighborhood characteristics [1] or an exploration of children's obesity and the influence of their community environment [2]. Alternatively, social demographic variables often moderate the built environment and human health relationships. In these cases, the social demographic variables are controlled through statistical models. For example, the health benefits of exposure to urban greenspace have repeatedly been found to be stronger among lower-income and lower-educated populations [3]. Due to the role of such effects, it is necessary to include social demographic factors in all studies on the built environment and human health relationships.

This chapter offers an overview of the social demographic data that is widely used in the built environment and human health field, through a scoping review of the literature. We will introduce (i) what types of social demographic data have been used; (ii) how to currently obtain these data; (iii) the accuracy, completeness, reliability, relevance, and timeliness of such data; and (iv) offer suggestions for the future use of such datasets in the built environment and population health studies.

## 2. Methods

A scoping review methodology was selected to best accommodate the wide diversity of studies that have addressed built environment and human health relationships. We searched the literature using Scopus®. We employed "built environment," "health," and "social" as search terms, stopping the search as of January 3, 2023. Subject areas that were not expected to cover the literature examining built environment and health topics (e.g., physics, math, chemistry, etc.) were excluded.

The retrieved literature was screened by reviewing titles and abstracts in terms of relevance to the research question. The four inclusion criteria were that each publication must be an original research article, use a quantitative analysis method, examine built environmental factors, and explore human health outcomes and unhealthy behaviors. The remaining relevant documents were subsequently considered for full-text review and assessed for eligibility. Ineligible documents either did not have a full text available, were not in English, did not concern human health, or did not include variables or analyses relevant to the built environment.

Social demographic variables, the analytical unit of a study, the country in which the studies were conducted, and the types of built environment factors and health-related variables investigated were all codified and reviewed.

## 3. Overview of the studies on the built environment and human health

The initial search yielded 1398 documents that were screened for relevance. Of these, 927 were excluded, resulting in 471 documents being considered for a full-text review. Of these, 132 were excluded because they were neither in English, original research, analyzed quantitatively, nor included either built environment or human health variables. A total of 339 documents were then reviewed. As shown in **Figure 1**, there has been a marked increase in the number of original articles per year on this topic.

Of the 339 studies, there are 11 articles exploring the topic in two or more countries. The largest proportion of single-country studies was in high-income countries, as defined by the World Bank [4]. Specifically (**Figure 2**), the United States alone published 40.85% of the original research articles. Followed by Australia (34%), Canada (29%), China (21%), and the United Kingdom (20%). 81.25% of the articles were conducted in high-income countries. Only 1.5% of the articles were conducted in low-income countries, including India, Bangladesh, Ghana, Kenya, and Nigeria.

Based on our review, three factors emerged as the most commonly examined in the literature: namely, the effects of promoting physical activity, promoting a healthy food environment, and enhancing contact with nature. Ninety-three percent of the

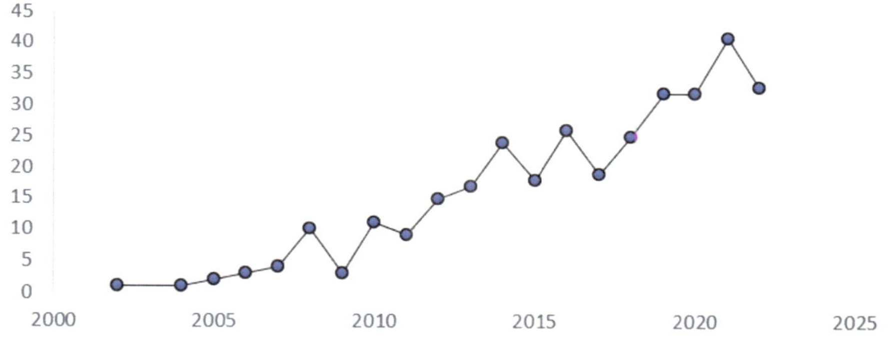


**Figure 1.**
*Number of original research articles published between 2002 and 2022.*

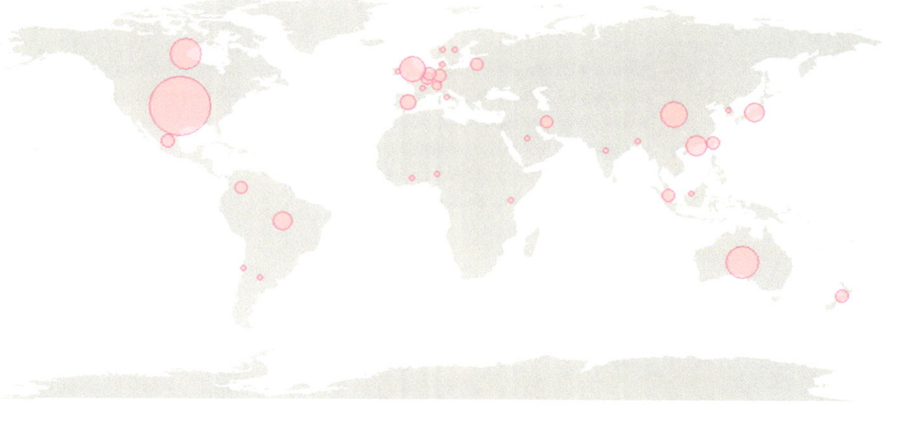

**Figure 2.**
*Map of study countries.*

studies used data at the individual level, and some combined with data from the neighborhood level. Only 22 (6%) out of the 339 studies used data at census block groups, census tracts, communities, districts, cities, counties, zip code levels, etc., and adopted an ecological study design. The most widely used built environment variables include walkability of the neighborhood, vacancy rate, land use mix, street connectivity, availability of community facilities, residential density, greenspace and recreational resources, transportation facilities or destinations (i.e., bus, metro, or subway station density), and food environment (both convenience and grocery store density). These variables were derived either from surveys or measured by using Geographic Information System (GIS).

A variety of health outcomes have been reported in the literature. Nearly 15%(n = 50) of the studies explored two or more health outcomes. For example, simultaneously focusing on walking, weight status, and obesity; physician-diagnosed chronic disease and self-rate general health; or physical and mental health. For the studies that focused on single health outcomes, 54.0% (n = 156) investigated physical activity, sedentary behavior, weight, and obesity-related outcomes, whereas slightly more than 15% (n = 44) focused on mental health, cognitive health, and dementia. Other studies explored chronic disease mortality and/or morbidity including hypertension, diabetes, heart disease, asthma, etc. Four studies focus on healthcare system utilization, and 10 studies examined the self-reported quality of life.

## 4. Role of social demographic variables

Social demographic factors have been included in almost all (336/339) of the studies reviewed. They have been used mostly as control variables in quantitative statistical analyses, yet a few studies went further and explored the moderating role of social-economic factors on the built environment and human health relationships [5]. The most widely used variables include age, gender, education, income, race/ethnicity, marital status, employment, etc. The data-collecting methods and sample sizes limit the ability of any single study to control all these social demographic variables, yet almost all the articles reviewed attempted to control at least some of these social demographic factors (**Figure 3**).

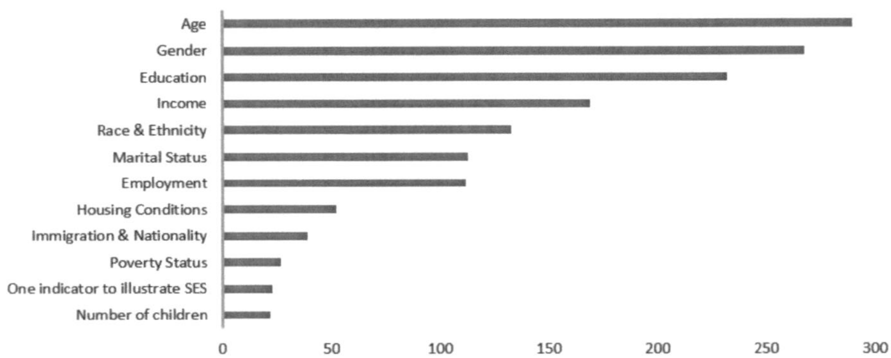


**Figure 3.**
*Frequency of commonly used social demographic variables in the reviewed built environment and human health relationship studies.*

The reason for such inclusion is that the built environment and human health relationship are complex and can be influenced by social demographic variables. Failure to incorporate these demographic factors is generally believed to distort our understanding of how various aspects of the built-in environment affect human health. Age plays a role in that older adults may be more sensitive to environmental factors such as air pollution and extreme temperatures and may have different mobility needs than younger adults [6]. Gender is influential in that men and women may have different patterns of physical activity and access to certain built environment resources, such as public transportation or parks [7, 8]. Race and ethnicity are important because minority groups may experience disparities in access to healthy food options, safe neighborhoods, and green spaces [9–12]. Lower-income individuals may have limited access to resources such as safe housing, healthy food options, and healthcare services, which can impact their health outcomes [13, 14]. Individuals with higher levels of education may have a greater awareness of health behaviors and resources and may be more likely to engage in healthy behaviors [15, 16]. Married individuals may have greater social support and access to resources than single individuals, which can impact their health outcomes [17–19].

Therefore, when social demographic variables are included in studies of the built environment and human health, researchers can better understand how different groups are affected by their environment and identify strategies for promoting health equity. Walkable neighborhoods can promote physical activity and improve health outcomes. However, when social demographic variables are included in the analysis, the relationship varies. The relationship was stronger for women than for men, and the association varied by race and ethnicity [20, 21]. Male cardiovascular disease and respiratory disease mortality rates decreased with increasing green space, but no significant associations were found for women [22]. Perceived walkability was directly linked to the happiness of people aged 36–45 and, to a lesser extent, those aged 18–35 years of age [23]. Studies regarding access to healthy food and obesity relationships reported social demographic variables such as income and race can influence access to healthy food [13, 24]. The association between supermarket access and obesity varied by income level, with the relationship being stronger for lower-income individuals [25, 26]. The relationship between green spaces and mental health was weaker for higher socioeconomic groups [27]. Greenspace exposure had no correlation with birth weight, until when maternal education was considered; an increase in birth weight was detected among the lowest education level group [28].

It is important to recognize that the inclusion of social demographic variables when investigating the relationship between the built environment and health varies depending on the specific health outcome being studied, the demographic group being considered, the built environment factors being examined, and even the place where the studies are conducted. A study focusing specifically on birth outcomes did not include gender as a variable, as all the participants are women biologically [29]. A study examining the environment and changes in physical activity of high school students did not control age, given high school students are generally within the same age group [30]. Studies on children and adolescents often include the education level of parents as a controlling factor instead of the grade level of the participants, and there is generally no need to control marital status [31–34]. Some studies from Australia used the Index of Relative Socio-Economic Advantage and Disadvantage to control social economic status as this index is readily available and widely used in Australia [35–37].

Given the importance of examining social demographic variables in the built environment and human health studies, it is also vital to effectively obtain social demographic data for research. There are five major sources in the literature. The first one is accessing data from national, state, and local surveys. The second one is to obtain administrative data. The third is to utilize data from previous longitudinal studies. The fourth way is to survey by using questionnaires, either organized via paper-based, online, telephone-based, or face-to-face questionnaires. The new trend is data collected from health-related applications on mobile devices. Some studies obtained data from two or more of these sources [38].

## 5. Access data from the national, state, and local surveys

Socio-demographic data is widely available from many national, state, and local surveys. Government institutions from developed countries usually collect health and related social demographic data periodically and often offer freely accessible data to the public. The data collected by such institutes are generally considered to be of high quality and reliable. These countries usually established rigorous standards and procedures to ensure the accuracy, completeness, and reliability of their data, including the use of standardized data collection methods and quality control procedures. Many developing countries, however, either do not conduct such surveys, or the survey results are of poor quality, making them either unavailable or unreliable for academic research purposes [39–41].

In the United States, one of the widely used built environment and human health databases is the Behavioral Risk Factor Surveillance System (BRFSS). It is a national telephone survey system used by the Centers for Disease Control and Prevention (CDC) to collect data on health behaviors, chronic health conditions, and the use of preventive services among the adult population. A variety of studies have utilized such data in the built environment and human health field [42–45]. The BRFSS collects data from a random sample of noninstitutionalized adults in each state and the District of Columbia. The survey is conducted monthly and has been in operation since 1984. Some of the topics covered by the BRFSS include tobacco use, physical activity, diet, chronic disease, access to health care, and preventive health practices.

BRFSS also collects social demographic data as part of its survey. The demographic data collected by the BRFSS includes age, gender, race/ethnicity, education level, employment status, income, and marital status, among others. The demographic information collected is used to provide a descriptive profile of the respondents and to help identify and address health disparities in the population. By collecting information on social and demographic characteristics, the BRFSS can help to understand how health behaviors and outcomes are related to individual characteristics and can inform the development of targeted public health interventions. The database can be accessed through CDC's official website (https://www.cdc.gov/brfss/). This data is matched and combined with the built environment data, usually based on zip codes when used in research.

The National Center for Health Statistics (NCHS) is a division of the Centers for Disease Control and Prevention (CDC) and is the nation's principal health statistics agency. A study examining associations between environmental quality and preterm birth in the United States utilized data from NCHS on 24,483,348 participants [29]. NCHS provides a wide range of health data and information, including (a) vital statistics: data on births, deaths, marriages, and divorces. (b) National Health Interview

*DOI: http://dx.doi.org/10.5772/intechopen.1002670*

Survey (NHIS): a large, ongoing survey that collects information on the health of the U.S. population. (c) National Health and Nutrition Examination Survey (NHANES): a nationally representative survey of the U.S. population that provides data on health and nutritional status, including information on diet, physical activity, and exposure to environmental contaminants. Similar surveys exist in other countries. South Korea, for example, also conducts a national-level survey (i.e., Korea National Health and Nutrition Examination Survey [KNHNES]) [46]. (d) Mortality data: data on causes of death in the United States. (e) Health care utilization: data on the use of health care services, including hospital stays, physician visits, and prescription drug use. A study focusing on greenspace and historical redlining used such data to explore their impact on emergency department utilization [47]. (f) Health behavior and risk factors: data on behaviors and risk factors that impact health, including smoking, alcohol use, and physical activity. (g) Chronic conditions: data on the prevalence and impact of chronic conditions, such as heart disease, diabetes, and cancer.

NCHS data is publicly available and can be accessed through the NCHS website (https://www.cdc.gov/nchs/). Many of the data sets collected by the National Center for Health Statistics (NCHS) include social demographic information such as age, race/ethnicity, education, income, and other demographic characteristics. For example, the National Health Interview Survey (NHIS) and the National Health and Nutrition Examination Survey (NHANES) both collect data on social demographics as part of their surveys. Similarly, vital statistics data on births, deaths, marriages, and divorces include demographic information such as age, race/ethnicity, and other characteristics of the individuals involved.

Another major resource is data available through the American Community Survey (ACS). The ACS is a nationwide survey conducted by the U.S. Census Bureau to collect data on the social, economic, and housing characteristics of the U.S. population. The ACS is designed to provide data on small geographic areas, including neighborhoods and communities, and is conducted continuously throughout the year. The survey collects data on a range of topics, including age, race/ethnicity, income, education, employment, housing, and others. The ACS is one of the largest surveys conducted by the U.S. government and provides important information on the social and economic characteristics of the U.S. population. The ACS data is available to the public and can be accessed through the U.S. Census Bureau's website (www.census.gov). To be useful, however, ACS data needs to be combined with built environment data and health data at the same spatial location and scale. For example, a study focusing on neighborhood-built environments, obesity risks, and racial composition combined data from ACS as well as the Southeastern Pennsylvania Household Health Survey [48].

Some states and localities conduct surveys that collect data on specific health and environmental issues. The California Health Interview Survey (CHIS) is a well-known example. CHIS is a large, statewide health survey conducted by the UCLA Center for Health Policy Research. The survey is designed to collect data on the health and well-being of California residents and is one of the largest state health surveys in the nation. The survey collects data on a range of topics, including health behaviors, chronic conditions, access to health care, health insurance coverage, and more. The survey also collects social demographic information such as age, race/ethnicity, education, income, and others. CHIS data is used by researchers to study the determinants of health and health disparities. For example, a study examining the influence of urban tree canopy on health utilized the data from CHIS [49]. The CHIS data is publicly available and can be accessed through the UCLA Center for Health Policy

Research's website (https://www.uclahealthpolicy.org/). This website provides data sets, documentation, and tools for accessing and analyzing the data, including the CHIS Data Online tool, which allows users to create custom data tables and visualizations. The data is available for a variety of geographic levels, including state, county, and subcounty areas, and can be used to study health and healthcare issues at the state and local levels.

## 6. Administrative data

Six percent (n = 21) of the examined studies utilized administrative data, yet a growing number of studies are using such data in recent years in health-related studies [50]. Administrative data, including data from Medicaid, Medicare, and electronic health records (EHRs), can provide a wealth of information on the health status, utilization, and costs of specific populations. Administrative data is generated from the day-to-day operations of healthcare organizations, such as hospitals and clinics, and is used to manage patient care, billing, and reimbursement. One advantage of administrative data is that it is often comprehensive, covering a large number of individuals and including a wide range of health information. A study examining built environmental factors and body mass index trajectories among youth used EHRs from 2001 to 2012 from 163,820 youth aged 3–18 years from 1288 communities [51]. Medicaid and Medicare data can provide information on the health status, utilization, and costs of older adults and individuals with disabilities, while the data can provide detailed information on patient diagnoses, medications, and other health-related information. This allows researchers to examine particular health measures, like changes in left ventricular ejection fraction, that are otherwise difficult to capture without such data sets [52].

Administrative data often include social demographic information such as age, race/ethnicity, gender, and other demographic characteristics. It is important to note, however, that the completeness and accuracy of the demographic information in administrative data can vary and may be subject to data quality issues concerning reliability and validity. As the data is generated from the day-to-day operations of healthcare organizations, errors can occur during the data collection and recording process and may occasionally fail to capture all relevant information. Administrative data may be generated using different data standards and definitions, which can impact its comparability across different data sources and over time. Compared to the official survey data collected by government agencies mentioned above, administrative data requires more effort from the researcher to ensure data integrity.

Additionally, privacy and security concerns must be carefully considered when using administrative data for research. The data must be protected following privacy and security regulations, such as the Health Insurance Portability and Accountability Act (HIPAA). This is a US federal law that sets standards for the privacy and security of protected health information (PHI) in the healthcare industry. It requires healthcare providers, health plans, and healthcare clearinghouses to maintain the privacy and security of individuals' PHI and to provide individuals with certain rights concerning their PHI. HIPAA also establishes penalties for noncompliance and provides for enforcement of its requirements by the Department of Health and Human Services. This use of this data will likely require data use agreements, data security measures, and other measures to protect the confidentiality and security of the data. Overall, when used appropriately, administrative data is a valuable source of information for researchers.

The Centers for Medicare & Medicaid Services (CMS), a federal agency within the US Department of Health and Human Services (HHS), is the primary source of Medicare and Medicaid data. CMS collects, maintains, and provides access to a variety of data on Medicare and Medicaid beneficiaries, providers, and payments. The website (see https://www.cms.gov/) provides access to a range of data sets, including the Medicare Provider Utilization and Payment Data, the Medicaid Statistical Information System, and the National Health Expenditure Accounts. Researchers can also submit a Freedom of Information Act (FOIA) request or a data use agreement request to obtain specific Medicare or Medicaid data sets.

There are a variety of sources that researchers can contact directly to obtain electronic health records. They are (a) Healthcare providers: hospitals, clinics, and individual practitioners, that maintain and use EHRs to manage patient information. Data is available but typically only accessible by certain professionals, such as physicians. In such situations, active collaborations with staff physicians are an option. A study exploring the role of neighborhood characteristics and the racial disparities in childhood obesity obtained EHRs of 44,810 children seen at 14 Massachusetts pediatric practices in 2011–2012 [53]. (b) Health information exchanges (HIEs): HIEs are organizations that collect and securely exchange health information between healthcare providers. HIEs can provide access to EHR data for research and other purposes, subject to certain conditions and requirements. (c) Government agencies such as the National Institutes of Health (NIH) and the Agency for Healthcare Research and Quality (AHRQ), maintain and provide access to EHR data for research and other purposes. (d) Commercial vendors, such as Epic Systems, Cerner, and Allscripts, offer EHR systems for healthcare providers and organizations and may also provide access to EHR data for research and other purposes.

## 7. Secondary data from previous longitudinal studies

Using data from previous longitudinal studies for a cross-sectional built environment and human health study can be a valuable approach, as it can provide a historical perspective on the relationship between the built environment and human health. Previous longitudinal health studies may or may not include social demographic variables. The type and amount of data collected in a study can vary depending on the specific research questions and methods used. Typically, however, social demographic variables can be important factors, and many longitudinal health studies routinely collect such data.

Relying on secondary data, however, can present challenges. For example, the data may not be representative of current conditions, the measurement of the built environment and health outcomes may have changed over time, and the data may fail to dovetail with the specific research questions and methods. It is, therefore, important to carefully review the data and consider its limitations when conducting the analysis. When selecting the relevant data, factors such as the time period of the study, the geographic location, the type of health outcomes measured, and the type of built environment data collected must be examined, as well as if it is even possible to spatially and temporally link the health and social demographic data with the built environment data. It is also important to determine what variables are included and whether they are suitable for the specific research questions and methods being used in the current study. In some cases, additional data sources or secondary data analysis may be necessary to obtain the required social demographic variables.

There are several sources where a researcher can check websites or contact directly to inquire about obtaining data from previous longitudinal studies. Sometimes, such data are not free, and extramural funding is needed to purchase access. The sources are (a) Research institutions and universities often conduct and archive data from longitudinal studies. For example, one study focusing on the weight status of low-income elementary school children obtained data from the third author from her NIH-funded grant [54]. In a study from China, the researchers used survey data collected by the Public Health College of Fudan University [55]. (b) Government agencies, such as the NIH and the CDC, often conduct and archive data from longitudinal studies. A study examining childhood obesity obtained data from the NIH environmental influences on child health outcomes (ECHO) program [56]. (c) Professional organizations and societies, such as the American Public Health Association (APHA) and the American Medical Association (AMA), may conduct and archive data from longitudinal studies. (d) There are several publicly available databases, such as the National Longitudinal Study of Adolescent to Adult Health (Add Health: https://addhealth.cpc.unc.edu/), that provides access to data from longitudinal studies.

## 8. Firsthand data collected through questionnaires by researchers

Questionnaires can be designed to collect data from all kinds of aspects. It can be used to gather information on the exposure of individuals to various built environment factors, such as access to green spaces, exposure to air pollution, or availability of sidewalks for active transportation [57]. It can also be used to gather information on physical activity and sedentary behavior, including frequency, intensity, and duration, and the built environment factors that influence these behaviors [58]. Researchers can also gather information on the perceptions and attitudes of individuals toward their neighborhood and the built environment, including perceived safety, walkability, and social cohesion [59, 60]. Studies could use questionnaires to collect information on various health outcomes, including physical and mental health, health behaviors, and health-related quality of life [61, 62]. Also, questionnaires can be used to gather demographic information, such as age, gender, education, and income, which can be used to control potential confounding variables in the analysis.

In this review, approximately 40% (n = 138) of the published original research articles collected firsthand social demographic data through a custom-designed questionnaire. These studies are typically conducted at the individual level and are usually able to collect all the social demographic factors that the researchers are interested in. Due to the reason that the questionnaire focuses on a single study, the sample size is usually relatively small compared to the above-mentioned national or state surveys. A study focusing on spatial accessibility to physical activity facilities and food outlets and overweight among French youth randomly selected 3293 students from eastern France middle schools [63]. Questionnaires are especially useful when the available secondary data is insufficient or its quality is questionable.

For developing countries where the above-mentioned secondary data is unavailable or unreliable, collecting data via questionnaire is the major method to conduct built environment and human health studies. In most cases, such questionnaires usually focus on one geographic local area. For example, a study from China exploring social capital, built environment, and mental health used data collected from 591 participants in Nanjing City [64]. Yet occasionally, it also allows researchers to conduct across-country studies where the same set of questionnaires has been used across multiple different districts, communities, or even countries, allowing the comparison between geographic areas [65]. For instance, A study examining the impact of neighborhood environments on sedentary time collected data across 10 countries [66]. The questionnaire can also be easily modified if, during the study, the researcher determines it is necessary to change the questionnaire. Questionnaires are relatively easy to administer and can reach a sufficient number of participants in a short period of time, making it a convenient method for collecting data. In addition, questionnaires are often relatively inexpensive to administer; in some cases, questionnaires can be designed and distributed purely online; if there are no incentives for the participants, then it is virtually free.

Custom questionnaires allow researchers to dig deeper into the social demographic characteristics of a particular group of participants, going beyond the routinely collected variables such as age, gender, race, education, income, and employment. For example, studies focusing on school students could collect information regarding which grade the participants are at [67]. Other research examining immigrants' health could collect factors such as country of birth and how long they have been in the original country and destination country, as the built environment in different countries could vary significantly [68].

One limitation to using questionnaires in the built environment and human health studies is that the health measures are based on self-reported signs and symptoms [69] and thus are subject to the vagaries of memory and an accurate understanding of the questions. With respect to studying sensitive topics, however, questionnaires may be preferred because they do not require physical examination or intervention. Below is a questionnaire constructed to illustrate this manner of data collection. These questions are just an example and can be adapted to meet the specific needs of a study. It is important to note that the response options must be culturally sensitive and

| Data Types | Example Questions | Example Response Options |
|---|---|---|
| Age | What is your current age? | 18–24, 25–34, 35–44, 45–54, 55–64, 65, or older |
| Gender | What is your gender? | Male, Female, Other |
| Education | What is the highest level of education you have completed? | Less than high school, High school/GED, Some college, College degree, Graduate degree |
| Employment | What is your current employment status? | Employed full-time, Employed part-time, Unemployed, Retired, Other |
| Income | What is your annual household income? | Less than \$20,000, \$20,000–\$39,999, \$40,000–\$59,999, \$60,000–\$79,999, \$80,000 or more |
| Ethnicity | What is your ethnicity/race? | White, Black or African American, Asian, Native American or Alaska Native, Native Hawaiian or Pacific Islander, Other |
| Marital status | What is your marital status? | Single, Married, Divorced, Widowed, Separated |
| Number of children | How many children do you have? | None, 1, 2, 3, 4, or more |
| Residential location | What is your current residential location? | Urban, Suburban, Rural |

**Table 1.**
*Example questions and response options for collecting social demographic data.*

appropriate for the target population, and it may be necessary to include additional demographic variables that are relevant to your study. For instance, it is important to collect race/ethnicity data in the United States, yet it is much less worthwhile to collect such data in big cities in China due to the ethnic health disparity between Han and non-Han is believed to depend more on the regions where people live than on actual ethnic differences (**Table 1**) [70].

## 9. Emerging trend: data collected from health-related applications on mobile devices

Smartphones, smartwatches, and fitness bands often come with accelerometers and GPS facilities which track data regarding physical activity, as well as geographic locations. With the growing utilization of smartphone fitness apps, many researchers now collect such data for the built environment and human health studies. The amount of data that can be collected in his manner is often quite large and is generated in real-time. A study from China published in 2021 examining built environment and physical activity obtained such data for more than 3 million users [71]. Another study from Canada explored neighborhood characteristics and running, and purchased user data from Strava Metro, which allows the researchers to analyze a total of 242,265 segments [72]. Strava anonymized and aggregated user activities in a spatial file made up of line segments representing routes. Segments contain count information for Strava users and running activities using bins of five to protect individual privacy. Strava categorizes users by gender and age groups which offer a minimum level of demographic information.

Such methods often provide large amounts of physical activity data with relatively accurate location information, which researchers can match with built environment measures. Anonymized aggregated data, however, typically obscures the fine-grained social demographic information necessary to examine the moderating effects of age, gender, income, etc., on the built environment and human health relationships. In addition, data collected through mobile apps may not be representative of the general population; rather, it might be more likely to represent a physically active or health awareness population.

While with care in mind, researchers can obtain a rich source of information about individual behavior, preferences, and experiences in the built environment from mobile devices. With the right apps, data can be collected on the physical activity levels of users, such as the number of steps taken, distance traveled, and calories burned. This data can be used to study the relationship between physical activity and the built environment, such as the availability of parks and sidewalks. They can also facilitate the collection of data on travel behavior, such as mode of transportation, travel time, and the routes taken. This data can be used to study the impact of the built environment on travel behavior, affording the exploration of transit accessibility and pedestrian-friendly design. They facilitate the collection of data on health outcomes, such as sleep quality, stress levels, and mood. This data can be used to study the relationship between the built environment and health outcomes, such as the impact of green space on stress reduction. They can also help in the collection of data on user preferences and experiences, such as ratings of parks and public spaces. This data can be used to study the impact of the built environment on user experience and to inform decisions about the design and maintenance of public spaces.

## 10. The way forward

In the realm of the built environment and human health research, the inclusion of social demographic variables and the utilization of reliable and valid data sources hold paramount importance. When collecting social demographic data, it is beneficial to consider (1) accuracy – ensuring correct and precise data; (2) completeness – including all relevant information in the dataset; (3) reliability – consistency and stability of the data over time and sources; (4) relevance – aligning the data with research objectives and questions; (5) timeliness – using up-to-date and current data; and (6) magnitude – the scale and abundance of the data. **Table 2** offers a detailed description of these characteristics of social demographic data collected from the major sources.

Moving forward, a key future direction lies in expanding and refining data collection methods. This involves the integration of emerging technologies, such as wearable devices, mobile applications, and sensor networks, to capture real-time and objective data on individuals' behaviors, exposures, and environmental attributes. Furthermore, the integration of multiple data sources might be a potentially valuable way to enrich the breadth and depth of social demographic variables. For example, by combining traditional survey-based approaches with health data collected from mobile devices, geospatial data, and digital footprints, researchers can create comprehensive databases that capture diverse aspects of individuals' lives.

Government and health data-collecting agencies could foster the integration of data from different sources to create comprehensive datasets. Emphasize interoperability to facilitate seamless data sharing and exchange between different platforms and systems, enabling researchers to leverage multiple data sources effectively. This integration fosters a more holistic understanding of the social, economic, and environmental contexts in which individuals interact with their built environment, enabling researchers to uncover nuanced associations and identify potential mechanisms through which social demographics influence health outcomes.

New advanced analytics and methodologies could be developed and utilized, such as machine learning, spatial analysis, and data mining, to extract meaningful insights from complex social demographic datasets. Embrace innovative methodologies that can handle large-scale and diverse data sources effectively. Researchers could also engage in validation studies to assess the reliability of new data sources and methodologies, comparing them against well-established measures. By establishing strong foundations of data reliability and validity, the field can build a solid evidence base to inform policymaking, urban planning, and public health interventions.

| Data Source | Accuracy | Completeness | Reliability | Relevance | Timeliness | Magnitude |
|---|---|---|---|---|---|---|
| National, state, and local surveys | *** | *** | *** | *** | ** | *** |
| Administrative data | ** | * | ** | * | ** | ** |
| Previous longitudinal studies | *** | ** | *** | ** | * | * |
| Questionnaires | *** | *** | *** | *** | ** | * |
| Apps on mobile devices | * | * | * | *** | *** | *** |

**Table 2.**
*Summary of data characters from different sources.*

## 11. Conclusion

In conclusion, this chapter has provided a comprehensive overview of the demographic data used in built environment and population health studies. From traditional data sources like national surveys to emerging data sources such as administrative databases and mobile devices, the chapter highlights the importance of data quality and its impact on decision-making. The chapter has also discussed the trends in demographic data usage and variable selection and offers suggestions for accessing and using different datasets in the built environment and population health studies. Understanding the relative strengths and limitations of accessible and burgeoning diverse data sets is crucial to making informed decisions and affording valid field research. This chapter hopefully serves as a useful resource for researchers and practitioners seeking to use demographic data to deepen our understanding of the important and complex relationships between the built environment and population health.

## Author details

Huaqing Wang[1*] and Louis G. Tassinary[2]

1 Utah State University, Logan, Utah, USA

2 Texas A&M University, College Station, Texas, USA

*Address all correspondence to: huaqing.wang@usu.edu

## References

[1] Pun VC, Manjourides J, Suh HH. Close proximity to roadway and urbanicity associated with mental ill-health in older adults. Science of the Total Environment. 2019;**658**:854-860

[2] Spence JC, Cutumisu N, Edwards J, et al. Influence of neighbourhood design and access to facilities on overweight among preschool children. International Journal of Pediatric Obesity. 2008;**3**:109-116

[3] Wang H, Tassinary LG. Effects of greenspace morphology on mortality at the neighbourhood level: A cross-sectional ecological study. Lancet Planet Health. 2019;**3**:e460-e468

[4] New World Bank country classifications by income level: 2021-2022. Available from: https://blogs.worldbank.org/opendata/new-world-bank-country-classifications-income-level-2021-2022. 2021 [Accessed 20 February 2023]

[5] Sun P, Lu W, Song Y, Gu Z. Influences of built environment with hilly terrain on physical activity in Dalian, China: An analysis of mediation by perceptions and moderation by social environment. International Journal of Environmental Research and Public Health. 4 Dec 2019;**16**(24):4900. DOI: 10.3390/ijerph16244900

[6] Hong Y-C. Aging society and environmental health challenges. Environmental Health Perspectives. 2013;**121**:a68-a69

[7] Azevedo MR, Araújo CLP, Reichert FF, et al. Gender differences in leisure-time physical activity. International Journal of Public Health. 2007;**52**:8

[8] Cohen DA, Williamson S, Han B. Gender differences in physical activity associated with urban Neighborhood parks: Findings from the National Study of Neighborhood parks. Womens Health Issues. 2021;**31**:236-244

[9] Block JP, Scribner RA, DeSalvo KB. Fast food, race/ethnicity, and income: A geographic analysis. American Journal of Preventive Medicine. 2004;**27**:211-217

[10] Price JH, Khubchandani J, McKinney M, et al. Racial/ethnic disparities in chronic diseases of youths and access to health Care in the United States. BioMed Research International. 2013;**2013**:787616

[11] Richardson LD, Norris M. Access to health and health care: How race and ethnicity matter. Mount Sinai Journal of Medicine. 2010;**77**:166-177

[12] Li M, Zhong R, Zhu S, Ramsay LC, Li F, Coyte PC. Access to community living infrastructure and its impact on the establishment of community-based day care centres for seniors in rural China. International Journal of Environmental Research and Public Health. 6 Jun 2018;**15**(6):1184. DOI: 10.3390/ijerph15061184

[13] Ziso D, Chun OK, Puglisi MJ. Increasing access to healthy foods through improving food environment: A review of mixed methods intervention studies with residents of low-income communities. Nutrients. 2022;**14**:2278

[14] Kushel MB, Gupta R, Gee L, et al. Housing instability and food insecurity as barriers to health care among low-income Americans. Journal of General Internal Medicine. 2006;**21**:71-77

[15] Fletcher JM, Frisvold DE. Higher education and health investments: Does more schooling affect preventive health care use? Journal of Human Capital. 2009;**3**:144-176

[16] Ross CE, Wu C. The links between education and health. American Sociological Review. 1995;**60**:719-745

[17] Joung IMA, van der Meer JBW, Mackenbach JP. Marital status and health care utilization. International Journal of Epidemiology. 1995;**24**:569-575

[18] Verbrugge LM. Marital status and health. Journal of Marriage and the Family. 1979;**41**:267-285

[19] August KJ, Sorkin DH. Marital status and gender differences in managing a chronic illness: The function of health-related social control. Social Science & Medicine 1982. 2010;**71**:1831-1838

[20] Choi A, Blanco L, Hays RD. Race and ethnicity differences in walking and associations with neighborhood perceptions among older adults in California. Journal of Applied Gerontology: The Official Journal of the Southern Gerontological Society. 2022;**41**:2499-2510

[21] Althoff T, Sosič R, Hicks JL, et al. Large-scale physical activity data reveal worldwide activity inequality. Nature. 2017;**547**:336-339

[22] Richardson EA, Mitchell R. Gender differences in relationships between urban green space and health in the United Kingdom. Social Science & Medicine. 2010;**71**:568-575

[23] Leyden KM, Hogan MJ, D'Arcy L, Bunting B, Bierema S. Walkable neighborhoods: Linkages between place, health, and happiness in younger and older adults. Journal of the American Planning Association. 11 Apr 2023:1-4

[24] Hill JL, Chau C, Luebbering CR, Kolivras KK, Zoellner J. Does availability of physical activity and food outlets differ by race and income? Findings from an enumeration study in a health disparate region. International Journal of Behavioral Nutrition and Physical Activity. 6 Sep 2012;**9**:105. DOI: 10.1186/1479-5868-9-105

[25] Moore LV, Die Roux AV. Associations of neighborhood characteristics with the location and type of food stores. American Journal of Public Health. 2006;**96**:325-331

[26] Drewnowski A, Aggarwal A, Hurvitz PM, et al. Obesity and supermarket access: Proximity or Price? American Journal of Public Health. 2012;**102**:e74-e80

[27] Maas J, Verheij RA, Groenewegen PP, et al. Green space, urbanity, and health: How strong is the relation? Journal of Epidemiology and Community Health. 2006;**60**:587-592

[28] Dadvand P, de Nazelle A, Figueras F, et al. Green space, health inequality and pregnancy. Environment International. 2012;**40**:110-115

[29] Rappazzo KM, Messer LC, Jagai JS, Gray CL, Grabich SC, Lobdell DT. The associations between environmental quality and preterm birth in the United States, 2000-2005: A cross-sectional analysis. Environmental Health. 9 Jun 2015;**14**:50. DOI: 10.1186/s12940-015-0038-3

[30] Molina-García J, Queralt A, Castillo I, et al. Changes in physical activity domains during the transition out of high school: Psychosocial and environmental correlates. Journal

of Physical Activity & Health. 2015;**12**:1414-1420

[31] Wong BY-M, Ho S-Y, Lo W-S, et al. Longitudinal relations of perceived availability of neighborhood sport facilities with physical activity in adolescents: An analysis of potential moderators. Journal of Physical Activity & Health. 2014;**11**:581-587

[32] Carlson JA, Sallis JF, Kerr J, et al. Built environment characteristics and parent active transportation are associated with active travel to school in youth age 12-15. British Journal of Sports Medicine. 2014;**48**:1634-1639

[33] Vanhelst J, Béghin L, Salleron J, et al. A favorable built environment is associated with better physical fitness in European adolescents. Preventive Medicine. 2013;**57**:844-849

[34] Bringolf-Isler B, Grize L, Mäder U, et al. Built environment, parents' perception, and children's vigorous outdoor play. Preventive Medicine. 2010;**50**:251-256

[35] Mazumdar S, Learnihan V, Cochrane T, Phung H, O'Connor B, Davey R. Is walk score associated with hospital admissions from chronic diseases? Evidence from a cross-sectional study in a high socioeconomic status Australian city-state. BMJ Open. 8 Dec 2016;**6**(12):e012548. DOI: 10.1136/bmjopen-2016-012548

[36] Abe T, Carver A, Sugiyama T. Associations of neighborhood built and social environments with frailty among mid-to-older aged Australian adults. Geriatrics & Gerontology International. 2021;**21**:893-899

[37] Collyer C, Bell MF, Christian HE. Associations between the built environment and emotional, social and physical indicators of early child development across high and low socioeconomic neighbourhoods. International Journal of Hygiene and Environmental Health. Jun 2022;**243**:113974. DOI: 10.1016/j.ijheh.2022.113974

[38] Jaime PC, Duran AC, Sarti FM, et al. Investigating environmental determinants of diet, physical activity, and overweight among adults in Sao Paulo, Brazil. Journal of Urban Health. 2011;**88**:567-581

[39] Poor data hurts African countries' ability to make good policy decisions. Quartz. Available from: https://qz.com/africa/762729/poor-data-is-hurting-african-countries-ability-to-make-good-policy-decisions/. 2016 [Accessed 20 February 2023]

[40] Runde D. The data revolution in developing countries has a long way to go. Forbes; 2017. Available from: https://www.forbes.com/sites/danielrunde/2017/02/25/the-datarevolution-in-developing-countrieshas-a-long-way-to-go/. [Accessed 20 February 2023]

[41] In low-income countries fundamental data issues remain for COVID-19 response. TReNDS. Available from: https://www.sdsntrends.org/blog/covid19andlowincome-countries?locale=en. 2020 [Accessed 20 February 2023]

[42] Xu Y, Wang F. Built environment and obesity by urbanicity in the U.S. Health & Place. 2015;**34**:19-29

[43] Briggs AC, Black AW, Lucas FL, Siewers AE, Fairfield KM. Association between the food and physical activity environment, obesity, and cardiovascular health across Maine counties. BMC Public Health.

3 Apr 2019;**19**(1):374. DOI: 10.1186/s12889-019-6684-6

[44] Cunningham SA, Patel SA, Beckles GL, et al. County-level contextual factors associated with diabetes incidence in the United States. Annals of Epidemiology. 2018;**28**: 20-25.e2

[45] West ST, Shores KA, Mudd LM. Association of available parkland, physical activity, and overweight in America's largest cities. Journal of Public Health Management and Practice. 2012;**18**:423-430

[46] Choi Y, Yoon H. Do the Walkability and Urban Leisure Amenities of Neighborhoods Affect the Body Mass Index of Individuals? Based on a Case Study in Seoul, South Korea. International Journal of Environmental Research and Public Health. 20 Mar 2020;**17**(6):2060. DOI: 10.3390/ijerph17062060

[47] Wang H, Li D. Emergency department visits for mental disorders and the built environment: Residential greenspace and historical redlining. Landscape and Urban Planning. 2023;**230**:104568

[48] Li K, Wen M, Henry KA. Residential racial composition and black-white obesity risks: Differential effects of neighborhood social and built environment. International Journal of Environmental Research and Public Health. 2014;**11**:626-642

[49] Ulmer JM, Wolf KL, Backman DR, et al. Multiple health benefits of urban tree canopy: The mounting evidence for a green prescription. Health & Place. 2016;**42**:54-62

[50] Ulrich EH, So G, Zappitelli M, Chanchlani R. A review on the application and limitations of administrative health care data for the study of acute kidney injury epidemiology and outcomes in children. Frontiers in Pediatrics. 27 Oct 2021;**9**:742888. DOI: 10.3389/fped.2021.742888

[51] Poulsen MN, Glass TA, Pollak J, Bandeen-Roche K, Hirsch AG, Bailey-Davis L, et al. Associations of multidimensional socioeconomic and built environment factors with body mass index trajectories among youth in geographically heterogeneous communities. Preventive Medical Reports. 29 Jun 2019;**15**:100939. DOI: 10.1016/j.pmedr.2019.100939

[52] Zhang Y, Tayarani M, Al'Aref SJ, et al. Using electronic health records for population health sciences: A case study to evaluate the associations between changes in left ventricular ejection fraction and the built environment. JAMIA Open. 2020;**3**:386-394

[53] Sharifi M, Sequist TD, Rifas-Shiman SL, et al. The role of neighborhood characteristics and the built environment in understanding racial/ethnic disparities in childhood obesity. Preventive Medicine. 2016;**91**:103-109

[54] Miles R, Wang Y, Johnson SB. Neighborhood built and social environments and change in weight status over the summer in low-income elementary school children. International Journal of Environmental Research and Public Health. 31 May 2018;**15**(6):1124. DOI: 10.3390/ijerph15061124

[55] Zheng Z, Liu W, Lu Y, Sun N, Chu Y, Chen H. The influence mechanism of community-built environment on the health of older adults: from the perspective of low-income groups.

BMC Geriatrics. 16 Jul 2022;**22**(1):590. DOI: 10.1186/s12877-022-03278-y

[56] Tylavsky FA, Ferrara A, Catellier DJ, et al. Understanding childhood obesity in the US: The NIH environmental influences on child health outcomes (ECHO) program. International Journal of Obesity. 2020;**44**:617-627

[57] Pierce JR Jr, Denison AV, Arif AA, et al. Living near a trail is associated with increased odds of walking among patients using community clinics. Journal of Community Health. 2006;**31**:289-302

[58] Wu ZJ, Song Y, Wang HL, Zhang F, Li FH, Wang ZY. Influence of the built environment of Nanjing's Urban Community on the leisure physical activity of the elderly: An empirical study. BMC Public Health. 6 Nov 2019;**19**(1):1459. DOI: 10.1186/s12889-019-7643-y

[59] Su M, Tan Y-Y, Liu Q-M, et al. Association between perceived urban built environment attributes and leisure-time physical activity among adults in Hangzhou, China. Preventive Medicine. 2014;**66**:60-64

[60] Ali O, Di Nardo F, Harrison A, et al. The link between perceived characteristics of neighbourhood green spaces and adults' physical activity in UK cities: Analysis of the EURO-URHIS 2 study. European Journal of Public Health. 2017;**27**:761-765

[61] Araya R, Montgomery A, Rojas G, et al. Common mental disorders and the built environment in Santiago, Chile. The British Journal of Psychiatry. 2007;**190**:394-401

[62] Camargo DM, Ramírez PC, Fermino RC. Individual and environmental correlates to quality of life in park users in Colombia. International Journal of Environmental Research and Public Health. 19 Oct 2017;**14**(10):1250. DOI: 10.3390/ijerph14101250

[63] Casey R, Chaix B, Weber C, et al. Spatial accessibility to physical activity facilities and to food outlets and overweight in French youth. International Journal of Obesity. 2012;**36**:914-919

[64] Tang S, Lee HF, Feng J. Social capital, built environment and mental health: A comparison between the local elderly people and the 'laopiao' in urban China. Ageing and Society. 2022;**42**:179-203

[65] Ding D, Adams MA, Sallis JF, Norman GJ, Hovell MF, Chambers CD, et al. Perceived neighborhood environment and physical activity in 11 countries: Do associations differ by country? International Journal of Behavioral Nutrition and Physical Activity. 2013 May 14;**10**:57. DOI: 10.1186/1479-5868-10-57

[66] Owen N, Sugiyama T, Koohsari MJ, et al. Associations of neighborhood environmental attributes with adults' objectively-assessed sedentary time: IPEN adult multi-country study. Preventive Medicine. 2018;**115**:126-133

[67] Hobin E, Leatherdale S, Manske S, et al. A multilevel examination of factors of the school environment and time spent in moderate to vigorous physical activity among a sample of secondary school students in grades 9-12 in Ontario, Canada. International Journal of Public Health. 2012;**57**:699-709

[68] Ohanyan H, Portengen L, Kaplani O, Huss A, Hoek G, Beulens JWJ, et al. Associations between the urban exposome and type 2 diabetes: Results from penalised regression by least absolute shrinkage and selection operator and random forest models.

Environment International. Dec 2022;**170**:107592. DOI: 10.1016/j.envint.2022.107592

[69] Curl A, Ward Thompson C, Aspinall P. The effectiveness of 'shared space' residential street interventions on self-reported activity levels and quality of life for older people. Landscape and Urban Planning. 2015;**139**:117-125

[70] Liu J, Zhang Y. Health status and health disparity in China: A demographic and socioeconomic perspective. China Population and Development Studies. 2019;**2**:301-322

[71] Chen L, Zhang Z, Long Y. Association between leisure-time physical activity and the built environment in China: Empirical evidence from an accelerometer and GPS-based fitness app. PLoS One. 31 Dec 2021;**16**(12):e0260570. DOI: 10.1371/journal.pone.0260570

[72] Harden SR, Schuurman N, Keller P, Lear SA. Neighborhood characteristics associated with running in metro Vancouver: A preliminary analysis. International Journal of Environmental Research and Public Health. 2 Nov 2022;**19**(21):14328. DOI: 10.3390/ijerph192114328

Chapter 14

# Text as Data in Demography: Russian-Language Experience

*Irina Kalabikhina, Natalia Loukachevitch, Eugeny Banin and Anton Kolotusha*

## Abstract

We propose to consider our experience in data use of Russian-language texts of social networks, electronic media, and search engines in demographic analysis. Experiments on the automatic classification of opinions have been carried out. Conversational RuBERT has been used in most cases. The following main scientific results on text data will be described: (1) short-term forecasts of fertility dynamics according to Google trend data, (2) automatic measurement of the demographic temperature of various demographic groups (pronatalists and antinatalists) in social networks, (3) sentiment analysis of reproductive behavior, sentiment analysis of vital behavior in pandemic, sentiment analysis of attitudes toward demographic and epidemiological policy according to social network data, (4) analysis of the arguments of social network users, and (5) analysis of media publications on demographic policy. A description of the created open databases of all these studies will be provided. All of the studies described will contain reflections on the advantages and difficulties of using texts as data in demographic analysis.

**Keywords:** text as data, demographic values, demographic behaviour, Russian-language, digital data, conversational RuBERT, sentiment analysis, demographic temperature, stance and arguments, natural language processing, demographic policy, Google trend data, social network

## 1. Introduction and brief literature review

Only recently have texts begun to be used as data in social sciences. With the growing access to high-speed Internet and the creation of search engines and social networks, researchers can receive a large number of comments on issues in social sciences, including behavior, trends, phenomena, and politics.

In social sciences, the practical application of texts in research covers a variety of topics ranging from questions of authorship, stock prices estimation, Central Bank communication impact, nowcasting, policy uncertainty, media slant, market definition and innovation impact, topics in research, politics, and law [1]; and different aspects of consumer behavior [2–4].

In demographic studies, issues of interest include many aspects of demographic behavior, demographic trends and the assessment of demographic, epidemiological, and other types of population policy. For all these topics, the use of text as data (information on search platforms, social networks, and mass media) can prove useful. Research in the field of digital demography is a new promising trend. Researchers across the world are just beginning to apply an algorithm for extracting, structuring, processing, and combining socio-demographic data about populations.

One simple way to use the new data is to identify the frequency of search queries on different demographic topics. Google data can be used to calculate the volume and geography of abortions in the United States and other countries [5] to forecast fertility trends ahead of the official data of statistical agencies [6, 7], estimate migration trends between couple of countries with virtually no time delay [8] (Russia-Germany case), and monitor the spread of diseases. For instance, Google Flu Trends project, aimed to predict epidemics of diseases from 2009 to 2014, based on weekly and monthly Google search queries data in the United Kingdom [9], and spread of the COVID-19 pandemic in different countries and regions was studied. The short-term forecast of fertility on Russian data [7] is based on using the SARIMA/ARIMA predictive model on the time series of Google query data since 2004 with a monthly data collection step that showed high accuracy with a 2-year forecast horizon. The search engines, for example, Google and Yandex[1], have developed their own algorithms to popularize and simplify work using simple queries. The digital traces of other platforms can be used to study population trends together with various frequency data (the cellular operator data, among others). A couple of good examples can be shown with Russian data. The migration of the population of the Russian Arctic was investigated on the profiles of users of the social network VKontakte[2] at the municipal level, in combination of the ticket services data [10]. The difference between Russian regions in relation to the sensitivity of regional media to the events of the legislative process in the field of maternity (family) capital was studied using public.ru platform [11]; an open dataset of the sentiment of the texts of 0.5 million media publications on the use of the maternity (family) capital [12]. Track record data from the resumes of the LinkedIn professional social network participants were used [13] to determine the volume of migration influx of educated personnel and students to the United States and Asian countries.

The second direction in using big unstructured data research in demographic analysis involves the collection of texts of social and professional networks and media as data through sentiment analysis. Artificial intelligence algorithms allow users to explore the emotional background of texts in terms of selected demographic topics. A demographic topic is identified in a social network ("becoming a parent", "abortion", "illness", "vaccination", etc.) or in the media and the ratio of positive, negative, and neutral statements is assessed. One can add other assessments/opinions (e.g., irony [14]). So, an analysis based on information from Twitter with a variety of computational linguistic methods allows users to find out the feelings of people about to have a child, how they plan to have children [15]. The sentiment analysis on demographic issues includes abortion [16–21], in particular, the legalization of abortion [22], various aspects of parenthood [14, 15], health issues [5, 21, 23, 24], drivers of demographic processes (e.g., natural disasters [25]), the demographic structure and trend of telemedicine [26], and the COVID-19 pandemic and other infections [27–32].

1 Website: https://trends.google.ru/, https://wordstat.yandex.ru/.

2 Website: https://vk.com/.

Topics closely related to demographics were also studied by sentiment analysis: these include sexual harassment or violence [33–35], attitudes towards genetic testing [36], processes of racial segregation [37]. Based on Facebook data, the features of assimilation of Mexican immigrants to the United States were investigated [38]. In Ref. [39], using the example of migration analysis in Poland, it was demonstrated how big data from the Facebook social network can help effectively to investigate narrow population groups that would normally be inaccessible to demographers.

The development of databases [40] and softs [e.g., [41]] in the field of sentiment analysis of texts in Russian has pushed the emergence of works using sentiment analysis, including the social sciences [42]. In a few demographic studies based on Russian-language data and sentiment analysis, the authors studied the positions on the vaccination of children [43] (the dataset is composed of posts from social networks VKontakte, divided into two cases: "for" and "against") as well as health issues [44] (DigitalFreud profile data, VKontakte user data, phone application data).

Deep thematic analysis of texts is associated with the automation of arguments on different issues such as the analysis of opinions, including not only stance but also the supporting arguments behind that stance. For example, we can not only observe the share of positive and negative assessments about birth, having many children, abortion, the childfree phenomenon, unregistered marriage, etc. but also get a structured share of positive and negative arguments, that is, why do people choice positive or negative reaction.

Modern methods of natural language processing do not provide a universal tool for the automatic determination of argumentation in texts. Researchers essentially "manually" analyze the data, answering the question of why a particular topic is perceived negatively or positively by people. Or they re-conduct a time-consuming sentiment analysis already on topics-arguments.

The analysis of arguments from social media comments has gained popularity in environmental research in recent years due to the growing discussion of new topics such as COVID-19: vaccination [45–47], quarantine [48]. In addition, the comments are used to monitor and make operational decisions on COVID-19 and its consequences [49, 50]. But most researchers in the analysis of social media content concentrate mainly on assessing the emotional background of posts and comments [51–53], without attempting to extract the argumentation of users' positions. If we compare the number of studies on the thematic analysis of stances and the thematic analysis of arguments, the latter clearly lose out to the former (see, e.g., the analysis of stances on abortion [5, 16–19, 21, 54] and analysis of arguments on abortion [16]). In particular, for opinions about abortion, the authors received eight most common arguments for abortion and five arguments against abortion [16]. There are fewer argument analysis works since this requires the additional theoretical processing of argument structures for using text processing methods. That is why it is important to learn how to identify the presence of argumentation and somehow automatically classify the arguments found.

In this chapter, we present the results of over 3-years of work on sentiment analysis of Russian-language texts in social networks, as they pertain to demographic issues. We conduct a consistent sentiment analysis of comments in the social network VKontakte of selected demographically oriented groups, the so-called "pro-natalist" and "anti-natalist" groups with different reproductive attitudes. Our approach consists of three steps: (1) the automated measurement of the dynamic of the emotional phone of groups in social networks during long period of time in the framework of demographic and family policy in Russia, (2) the sentiment analysis of reproductive attitudes and opinions on pro-natalist demographic policy according to social network users from the same groups (demographic temperature of the second type), and (3) the search of general algorithm of the sentiment analysis of the arguments of positive or negative opinions on reproductive issues and police according to social network users from the same groups.

## 2. Data and methodology

Our methodological approach is based on the sequential study of selected demographically oriented groups in a social network.

The research was based on an array of data containing comments from users of the VKontakte social network, pre-selected according to the principle of relevance to issues of reproductive behavior. This data is publicly available [55, 56]. The selected demographically oriented groups in a social network include pro-natalists (supporters of childbearing) and anti-natalists (supporters of refuse of childbearing, child-free groups).

The data collection was carried out in several stages. First, using the built-in API (application programming interface), user groups dedicated to the topic of reproductive behavior, both pro- and anti-natalist orientation, were selected. The search for groups was carried out by keywords ("mom", "child", "parents", "childfree", etc.). Then the selected groups were cleared of irrelevant ones, in particular advertising or inactive groups. Thus, as a result, out of over 1000 groups selected at the first stage, about 350 groups remained after cleaning. It was revealed that there are significantly more pro-natalist groups, and they are usually represented by a significantly larger number of participants, whereas anti-natalist groups are more active, that is, they contain a greater number of posts and discussions. The final sample included 341 pro-natalist and 8 anti-natalist groups.

The number of groups was chosen based on the amount of text (using a threshold of more than 100 thousand of comments). Supporters of the childless lifestyle (keywords "childfree" and their variations) published significantly more posts and comments than representatives of other groups. In the reproductive dataset, only resonant comments (at least 5 likes) from relevant thematic (related to issues of childhood, motherhood, pregnancy) and representative in size (at least 500 subscribers) groups are taken into account. The search depth was 5000 posts.

At the final stage, texts (user comments) were extracted from these groups, which were brought to a unified format within the framework of standard algorithms for preprocessing text information: translation to lowercase, removal of stop words, numbers and punctuation marks, lemmatization (reduction to the initial form) and stemming (removal of endings). A structured array (corpus) of texts has been formed. Thematic clusters were identified based on Latent Dirichlet allocation (LDA). Further, the collected textual information was additionally filtered by the presence of keywords related to reproductive topics in order to exclude most irrelevant comments.

Additionally, irrelevant comments were deleted during expert annotation both on thematic analysis stage and argument automation stage. For the reproductive data subset with reproductive and pro-natalist policy topics on thematic analysis see Ref. [57].

Moreover, we constructed a database of health-related behavior using VKontakte users' comments discussing COVID-19 news texts [58]. We use this dataset to strengthen some conclusions on sentiment analysis of Russian-language text of social networks on demographic topics [59]. Altogether, about 11,000 reproductive-related comments and about 10,000 health-related comments were annotated by stance and arguments.

We replicated this three-step methodology using the same data for all steps. First, we examine the general emotional background of the pro-natalist and anti-natalist groups with different reproductive attitudes with demographic trends and developments in the field of population policy. This is the so-called demographic temperature of the first type.

The demographic temperature is the author's term by which we understand the emotional background or the predominance of positive or negative statements on topics related to family values, the birth of children, and other topics in the field of reproductive behavior. Demographic temperature is measured as the difference (or ratio) between the number of positive and negative statements over a certain period [60].

The demographic temperature of the first type is the difference (or ratio) between the number of *any* positive and negative statements of users of selected demographic groups with different reproductive attitudes. We propose that most of the comments of our users of these groups are devoted to reproductive and pro-natalist policy topics. Monitoring of the demographic temperature of the first type in different groups when superimposed on the calendar of phenomenon gives us an understanding of hypothetically impact of the phenomenon (economic crises, population policy, and so on) on the emotional background in different demographic groups.

Then we conduct a sentiment analysis of the social network comments of these selected demographic groups on demographic topics. This is the demographic temperature of the second type.

The demographic temperature of the second type is the difference (or ratio) between the number of *reproductive* positive and negative statements of users of our groups. Theoretically, we can implement the sentiment analysis using the reproductive statements of any users of social networks. However, we choose the same reproductive groups to reduce the challenge of representation (we gather the reproductive sentiments in the reproductive groups) and to get the statements from selected marginal groups of people with opposite reproductive attitudes. Using data from different groups of the VKontakte social network avoids data homogeneity which is one of the weak points of the sentiment analysis [61].

Finally, we analyze the arguments of the positive and negative statements of our users at the previous stage of the analysis. The last step is the development of the algorithm of the argument thematic analysis through natural language processing methods to monitor both the emotional background of social groups and their arguments of the positive or negative demographic temperature of stances. The main idea of this step is argument's thematic analysis automation.

As a subject of research in this chapter, we consider reproductive behavior and the public's opinion on the measures of demographic policy in the field of fertility. We conduct a complex investigation of social user opinions reproductive attitudes and population policy: the emotional background measurement of demographic groups, the thematic analysis of social network users' comments about demographic behavior and demographic policy, and argument analysis, which potentially helps us grasp motivation behind social network users' comments.

In addition, we constructed the dataset on health-related behavior based on VKontakte users' comments discussing COVID-19 news texts [58]. The sensitive thematic analysis on health-related behavior was made with the same method of sentiment analysis as in the case of the reproductive dataset but on the base of the alternative dataset. We use the research direction with the health-related behavior dataset in this chapter to strengthen some conclusions on sentiment analysis of Russian-language text of social networks on demographic topics.

A more detailed disclosure of the methods of solving our demographic problems is presented in appendix.

## 3. Results

### 3.1 Automated measurement of demographic temperature (temperature of the first type)

Our study was a pioneering attempt to analyze the sentiment of Russian-language comments on social networks to determine the demographic temperature (ratio of positive and negative comments) in certain reproductive-related behavior groups of social network users was made. Using the available data in two types of groups since 2012, an asynchronous structural shift in comments of the corpuses of pro-natalist and anti-natalist thematic groups has been revealed [[60], Fig. 11, 12]. We contrast two thematic groups, which differ in their reproductive and family attitudes. This technique allowed us to identify asymmetric trends in changes in the sentiment of anti-natalists and pro-natalists from 2012 to 2020 before and after the introduction of family policy with an emphasis on traditional family values in 2014.

The pro-natalists are more positive in general during the total period. The average demographic temperature for the period is slightly negative, which is 0.951. (A value of "1" indicates a neutral demographic temperature, below "1" is a negative temperature, and above "1" is a positive one). The anti-natalists have a lower average demographic temperature over the period, which is 0.691 [[60], Fig. 15, 16]. Both pro-natalists and anti-natalists have been reducing the demographic temperature from 2014 to the present. Anti-natalists did it in 2014, and pro-natalists decreased later, in 2017, 3 years after the family policy started. We have found that the demographic temperature in the pro-natalist groups closely repeats the key events in demographic policy (indexation and extension of maternity capital, family, and demographic policy initiatives).

The method-related result of this stage is that comments under posts are more suitable and relevant for analyzing the sentiment of statements than the texts of posts.

### 3.2 Sentiment analysis of reproductive attitudes and opinions about demographic policy (temperature of the second type)

Using the data from the social network VKontakte, the opinions of network users about the birth of children were examined. A dataset has been compiled with a markup of opinions in three classes of positions in relation to six topics related to the birth of children and pro-natalist politics. Experiments on the automatic classification of opinions were carried out.

The predominance of positive assessments of childlessness, individualism and abortion permits, and the predominance of negative assessments of having many children, maternity capital, and parental leave has been revealed.

The created dataset enables drawing meaningful conclusions on the attitude of VKontakte users to issues of reproductive behavior. The easiest topic to determine relevance is "Abortions", since in the vast majority of cases the topic is determined by the word "abortion" itself or the words formed from it. In this case, the topic with high quality is also determined by keywords. The prevalence of markups "for" on the topic "Abortion" (51.6%) is associated with the position of social network users regarding what women should have right to abortion; with the population's attitude towards abortion as an acceptable means of birth control. The abortion rate significantly has currently decreased in Russia, but the attitude towards this method of birth control shows not so much readiness for action, as much as recognition of reproductive rights.

It is revealed that the phenomenon of conscious childlessness is actively represented on the web, and having many children remains a poorly spread behavior model. The predominance of negative opinions about having many children (44.9%) is due to the growing heterogeneity of the population in the number of children born. The increase in the share of large families among families with minor children during the period of demographic policy (from 7 to 9%, according to the 2010 census and 2015 micro-census) does not change the fact that the type of reproductive behavior, oriented towards having many children, remains rare.

On the topic "childlessness" one can see the prevalence of positive assessments (60.0%), since supporters of this pattern are quite emotional, the topic is apparently active during the period of growth of representatives of this model. In addition, we must remember about selection – we work with text groups of antinatalists and pronatalists. Among antinatalists, the topic of childlessness is expressed predominantly positively, but among pronatalists, this topic is less popular. This can also explain the prevalence of positive assessments in the topic "individualism" (62.8%), which interpreted as self-development, directing resources to one's own pleasure. This topic often appears in the context of justification positive position on childlessness, our hypothesis about this justification was confirmed.

The predominance of the negative statements about parental leaves (35.9%) is explained by the fact that maternity leave, and carer's leave children are perceived negatively by employers and colleagues; and the fact that women themselves often complain about the increased workload during this period, about the change of lifestyle during such holidays, and about the lack of free time. Opinions about childcare benefits (45.5%) are also rather negative since their size appears small for the recipients. And also supporters of childfree do not want their taxes to go towards family benefits.

The reproductive dataset's statistics by topics and positions are shown in **Table 1**.

As far as the health-related behavior dataset the best results achieved in evaluation were 0.70 for stance detection and 0.74 for argument identification. These results were obtained with the approach which applied the RuBERT classifier to determine the relevance of the texts using the NLI-method: to form an input example, a second sentence with the aspect ("masks", "quarantine", or "vaccination") was added to each original sentence from the dataset [64]. For the stance classification task, the texts were pre-processed and then translated into English using the pre-trained seq2seq-model (https://huggingface.co/Helsinki-NLP/opus-mt-ru-en). This made it possible to use a specialized BERT COVID model trained on texts discussing COVID (https://huggingface.co/digitalepidemiologylab/covid-twitter-bert-v2).

The method-related result of this stage is that the best results were obtained using the BERT neural network model in the NLI (Natural language Inference) formulation. Our results are similar to other authors. In Ref. [27], three groups of methods for determining the author's position in relation to COVID aspects are compared: based on the LSTM and CNN networks, as well as based on the BERT model [65]. The best results with a large margin are given by models based on BERT.

| Topic | "Relevant" | "For" | "Against" | "Other" |
|---|---|---|---|---|
| Having many children | 341 | 75 (22.0%)* | 153 (44.9%) | 113 (33.1%) |
| Childlessness | 1422 | 853 (60.0%) | 134 (9.4%) | 435 (30.6%) |
| Individualism | 739 | 464 (62.8%) | 119 (16.1%) | 156 (21.1%) |
| Abortion | 1374 | 709 (51.6%) | 161 (11.7%) | 504 (36.7%) |
| Maternity capital (Childcare benefits) | 813 | 184 (22.6%) | 370 (45.5%) | 259 (31.9%) |
| Parental leaves | 992 | 201 (20.3%) | 356 (35.9%) | 435 (43.9%) |
| Total | 5681** | 2486 (43.8%) | 1293 (22.7%) | 1902 (33.5%) |

*Notes: (1) the share of markups (*) with the corresponding token from the total number of relevant markups for a given topic in the line is indicated in parentheses, (2) the total number of markups (**) in the table is greater than the total number of comments analyzed since some comments contained opinions on several topics. Source: compiled by the authors (see more Refs. [62, 63]).*

**Table 1.**
*Distribution of markups on topics related to the birth of children.*

### 3.3 Analysis of the arguments of social network users: the search of general classification and automatic algorithm of monitoring of demographic issues

An algorithm for identifying arguments and automatically distinguishing certain types of arguments (based on the assessment of personal and public arguments) has been built using the Conversational RuBERT neural network model. The method used for automatic extraction and classification of the "VKontakte" social network users' opinions has proven that we can accurately classify users' comments submitted as the model's input for the presence of argumentation and an argument's type within the "personal-public" dichotomy to identify personal and social attitudes, values, stories, and opinions to study reproductive behavior. For the task of detecting the presence of arguments, the comments of VKontakte users were classified into two classes: Class "1" if at least two out of three annotators agreed that the comment contained an argument, and Class "0" if only one annotator or none of them indicated the presence of an argument.

As a result, six experiments were carried out, differing in the dataset and the classification option. In the first three experiments, classification was carried out only by the presence of an argument, but different types of data were used.

In Experiment 1, the reproductive data was used, consisting of comments from VKontakte users on reproductive behavior and the evaluation of demographic policy measures. The training, test, and validation sample comprised a total of 5410 comments. Standard pre-processing techniques were applied, including removing capital letters, punctuation, stop words, and empty comments.

In Experiment 2, COVID-19-related comments from VKontakte users, such as vaccination, mask-wearing, and quarantine restrictions, were added to the reproductive data. The new comments were included only in the training set, and the additional data consisted of 6716 comments, forming the training sample for the COVID-19 data.

In Experiment 3, training was conducted in two stages: pre-training on the COVID-19 data and fine-tuning and evaluation of the model on the reproductive data.

The results of training models with the indication of quality metrics are shown in **Table 2**.

| | F-score – Class "0" (there is no argument) | F-score – Class "1" (there is argument) | Accuracy |
|---|---|---|---|
| Experiment 1: reproductive data | 0.81 | 0.61 | 0.75 |
| Experiment 2: reproductive and health-related data | 0.82 | 0.49 | 0.73 |
| Experiment 3: pre-training on health-related data, fine-tuning on reproductive data | 0.79 | 0.48 | 0.70 |

*Source: compiled by the authors (see more Ref. [66]).*

**Table 2.**
*Classification is based on the presence of an argument (class "0" – no argument, class "1" – Presence of an argument).*

The results in **Table 2** indicate that the addition of COVID-19 data did not improve the results of argument extraction in the reproductive collection. The model trained on the reproductive data alone performed better in this task.

In subsequent experiments, the type of argument was taken into account. In the fourth experiment, the focus was on the search for personal arguments (class "1"), while public comments and comments without arguments were generally taken into account equally in class "0". Similarly, in the fifth experiment, the focus was on public arguments (class "1"). In the last experiment, all three classes were evaluated separately ("0" – absence of an argument, "1" – public argument, "2" – personal argument). The results are presented in **Table 3**.

The ratio of comments by class averaged 40:60 for comments with arguments versus those without arguments. The classification by the presence of an argument was the most accurate in terms of the ratio of quality metrics in the first experiment, where only reproductive data were used. From this, we can conclude that models trained on the data of the same subject show better results. The classification by argument type was more accurate when using two rather than three classes. In our static measurement, the share of personal arguments was around 40%. Public arguments prevailed in comments on VKontakte during the period under review in the demographic groups under consideration.

| | F-score – Class "0" (no argument) | F-score – Class "1" (public argument) | F-score – class "2" (personal argument) | Accuracy |
|---|---|---|---|---|
| Experiment 4: two classes with the emphasis on personal arguments | 0.86 | 0.71 | — | 0.81 |
| Experiment 5: two classes with the emphasis on public arguments | 0.70 | 0.81 | — | 0.77 |
| Experiment 6: three classes | 0.78 | 0.52 | 0.34 | 0.67 |

*Source: compiled by the authors (see more Ref. [66]).*

**Table 3.**
*Classification model according to the type of argument ("personal" – Based on personal experience, "public" – Based on public perceptions).*

Based on the results of this work, we have made sure that we can extract and analyze the data of reasoned opinions of users of the largest Russian social network in automatic mode. All experiments have shown high accuracy of the methods used. In addition, the general approach based on the "personal-public" dichotomy is suitable for any type of demographic behavior, making it universal.

In future, models trained in this way can be used to monitor public attitudes on reproductive behavior and many others. The monitoring of the "personal-public" dichotomy in the future research will test our hypothesis on the growth of the share of personal arguments as a signal for policy-makers. The speed of automated analysis of such data will enable quick monitoring and responding appropriately to changes.

## 4. Conclusion and discussion

We developed and tested a method for measuring the demographic temperature of the first type (the mood of specific demographic groups in social networks) and the second type (the extraction of opinions on demographic topics in social networks). We have identified differences in the demographic behavior of social network users in different socio-demographic groups and their opinions about parenthood and childbearing on the VKontakte social network. The search for a general structure of demographic arguments was conducted based on the "personal-public" dichotomy.

*There are limitations* in the use of such data in demographic analysis, which are discussed by researchers. These are all kinds of biases, issues with representativeness and fragmentation, a tendency to make negative statements in comments, data access-related difficulties, the presence of bots, the risk of false information and changes in the algorithms of the data platforms themselves, the difficulty of interpreting data due to the use of initially unstructured texts, the discrepancy of scientific terms and the language of social networks, the double meaning of some words, and also due to the limited information on the characteristics of users.

The limitations of our research are similar to those mentioned above. The sentiment thematic analysis is sensitive to the following:

- Representativeness and fragmentation of data. The characteristics of the users of the social network VKontakte may not coincide in socio-demographic characteristics with the population of the country. As far as it relates to reproductive dataset, the bias is not so strong. The users of VKontalte are close to the age-sex structure of reproductive age. Nevertheless, we can lose some socio-demographic groups.

- The risk of disconnection between the scope and name of the groups and the demographic values of its commentators. We checked the connection between the scope of the reproductive-related groups of pro-natalists and anti-natalists, their socio-demographic profile, and demographic values of various groups' participators. The connection has been found. Our groups are relevant for the comparative analysis of groups with opposite demographic values [67].

- The tendency to negative statements in the comments, which is a specific characteristic of social networks.

- Limited access to data, presence of bots, risk of false information [68, 69], and changes in the algorithms of the data platforms themselves.

*DOI: http://dx.doi.org/10.5772/intechopen.1003274*

- The complexity of data interpretation due to the use of initially unstructured texts, the discrepancy between scientific terms and the language of social networks, the double meaning of some words, and the limited visible characteristics of users [10, 70, 71].

- The cross-cultural analysis can be limited by the circumstance that usually models are initially trained mostly in English texts and could not be easily extrapolated in the case of Russia. Studying the existing software systems for Russian text analysis reveals their low accuracy compared to English [40].

Overcoming the limitations of textual data lies in the field of stratification and other methods of correcting text data biases [72]; using different data sources [73]; supervised machine learning; development of algorithms for collecting; and processing digital data for the possibility of discussing and repeating the research path for comparative purposes [37].

Sentiment analysis and extraction of opinions (stance and arguments) is an actively developing field of research that analyzes opinions, moods, assessments, attitudes, arguments, and emotions of people based on written or spoken language [74, 75]. Such studies are conducted based on a corpus of comments under videos on the YouTube platform [76] and under news posts published on social media [77]. However, researchers Castellano Parra, Meso Ayerdi and Pena Fernandez, when analyzing the comments under news posts on social portals, as well as comments on the social network pages of certain Spanish newspapers, came to the conclusion that both the level of engagement (the number of comments per one reader) and the proportion of reasoned comments on social networks are higher than in the comments on news portals [78]. In our research, we use text data from social networks to extract opinions on demographic issues also because it contains much larger data than if we conducted our research analyzing comments on news portals.

*The prospects* for using texts as data in demographic research are significant. The further direction of research may be related to expanding a methodology to a wider range of demographic behaviors, including matrimonial (marriage), migration, and health. The search for universal general types of arguments should continue. Their combination may eventually give a more complete picture of automated arguments on demographic issues, for example, in assessing private or public services in the field of healthcare, maternity care, partner search, infrastructure projects for families with children, and social support for certain demographic groups. The statements can be made about the quality of the service itself (the result of treatment) and about the quality of environment (the attitude of the doctor, the availability of equipment, cleanliness, timing, etc.). We also expect that our experience can be extended to other linguistic and cultural spaces at least within the countries where the demographic transition has been completed. We believe that it is possible because we have a comparable level of public Internet coverage, and we are at a similar stage of the natalistic transition and the second demographic transition. Cultural differences and institutes are inevitable in every country and constitute the essence of comparative analysis, which is possible when using the same methodology and methods in different language corpora. Cross-cultural analysis of demographic behavior using big data in Russia and other countries can also be an interesting subject for further research.

Another path of development is applying large language models (LLM), which are currently considered to be one of the most powerful instruments for analyzing text data. Despite the fact that this instrument is rather new, one can already witness a number of successful applications in different fields, including social sciences. We expect that, in the future, large language models will be able to provide opportunities for deeper and more profound analysis of demographic data.

The prospects of working with texts as data in demographic analysis are impressive in the speed and frequency of obtaining information, and the ability to reveal information in the field of inaccessible issues within the framework of official statistics, the ability to combine different data within one research question.

## 5. Research support

The manuscript was prepared with the financial support of the Scientific and Educational School of Lomonosov Moscow State University "Brain, Cognitive Systems, Artificial Intelligence" (the sentiment analysis of reproductive attitudes and public opinion on demographic policy, dataset on reproductive behavior) and the Faculty of Economics of Moscow State University within the framework of research on the topic "Reproduction of the population in a socio-economic development" (the demographic temperature of the first type, dataset on pro-natalist and anti-natalist groups).

The work of Natalia Loukachevitch on annotating and experimenting with the health-related dataset (the vital behavior during the pandemic COVID-19) is supported by Russian Science Foundation (project 21-71-3003).

## Appendix

### Appendix.1 method for emotional background of demographic groups measurement: demographic temperature of the first type

We aimed to develop an algorithm that would quickly measure the emotional background, that is the demographic temperature in contrasting demographic groups according to reproductive attitudes on the basis of big data over a long period of time. A thematic model was applied to the generated array of texts to implement the task of reverse thematic modeling. That is, for each set of words and texts, based on the probabilistic distributions of the frequencies of words and topics, the most appropriate topic corresponding to these sets was determined. This allowed us to form thematic clusters. For each thematic cluster, the task of analyzing the statements was carried out. TensorFlow[3] and tflearn[4] libraries were used for sentiment analysis. The neural network for sentiment analysis has three-level architecture: the first level corresponds to the dimension of the commentary corpus dictionary, the second-level consists of 125 neurons (fully connected layer, ReLU activation function[5]), the third-level consists of 25 neurons (fully connected layer, ReLU activation function), the output-level is binary ("0" – negative, "1" – positive, activation function – softmax[6]). Specification of the learning algorithm[7]:

[3] Official website of the project tensorflow.org.

[4] Official website of the project tflearn.org.

[5] Function description by link https://en.wikipedia.org/wiki/Rectifier_ (neural_networks).

[6] Function description by link https://ru.wikipedia.org/wiki/Softmax.

[7] Description by link http://tflearn.org/layers/estimator/.

*Rg = tflearn.regression (*neural network layer*.*
*, optimizer = "sgd".*
*, loss = "categorical_crossentro").*

The sum of the output level signals is equal to one, that is, the output is two numbers characterizing the probability that comment is negative or positive. Neural network training is based on the principle of error backpropagation. Neural network training was carried out on a marked-up database of short messages from Twitter [79]. Neural network training was performed in the Google Colab environment using a graphics accelerator (GPU, *graphics processing unit*). See Ref. Kalabikhina et al. [60] for other model parameters and more details.

## Appendix.2 method for a thematic analysis of social network users' opinions on demographic behavior and demographic policy: the demographic temperature of the second type

The research directions for the analysis of rare reproductive patterns and the attitude to the main measures of demographic policy were determined by experts. The analysis of stances of reproductive dataset took place on six topics: having many children, childlessness, individualism (argument topic for childlessness), abortion, maternity capital, parental leave. The first three topics concern the reproductive attitudes, the last three topics concern the opinion on demographic policy on fertility side (see more Refs. [62, 63]).

The sentences from the collected sample were marked up by six annotators. The annotators' group included professional linguists and demographers. Since several issues could be discussed in each sentence, the annotator marked each sentence by all topics and by six following labels:

"irrelevant" (it means that the text does not contain stance on the topic);

"for" (positive stance, which means that the speaker expresses his support for the topic);

"against" (negative stance, the topic of discussion is not endorsed by the speaker);

"neutral" (this label is used for factual sentences without any visible attitudes from the author);

contradictory stance (for such a label, evident positive and negative attitudes should be seen in a message);

"unclear" (the presence of a stance is seen, but the context of the sentence does enable determining it).

We consider three main classes: "for", "against", and "others" ("neutral", contradictory stance, "unclear").

The created dataset was divided into three sets: training, validation, and test ones. The neural network model BERT [65] was used as the main method, in the version of Conversational RuBERT, for the creation of which the Russian-language model RuBERT [41], which was further trained on Russian-language dialogs and texts of social networks. Three variants of the BERT model training were used: classification of the target utterance, as well as the so-called NLI (Natural Language Inference) and QA (question-answering) approaches. In the NLI and QA approaches [80], the model received pairs (text, assumption). For the classification of the relevance of NLI and the classification of the QA position, this assumption was the aspect itself ("Abortions", "Payments", etc.), for the classification of the NLI position, the assumption also included the position itself ("Negative to abortion", "Neutral to payments", etc.). To assess the quality of classification, the following measures are used: accuracy of classification (Accuracy) and F-measure.

As we mentioned earlier, the sensitive thematic analysis on health-related behavior is based on VKontakte users' comments discussing COVID-2019 news with the same method of sentiment analysis on the base of alternative dataset [58]. The sentences were labeled in relation to the following claims: (1) "Vaccination is beneficial for society."; (2) "The introduction and observance of quarantine is beneficial for society."; (3) "Wearing masks is beneficial for society" (see more [59]).

The annotation process included two stages: labelling by stance and labelling by premises. At the first stage of stance annotation, each sentence was labeled by several experts (three on average) [81]. An annotator should indicate the stance it expresses towards each of the above-mentioned aspects (or indicate that the sentence is not relevant to the aspect). The annotators' group included professional linguists and psychologists. We consider four stance labels, namely: "irrelevant", "for", "against", "other" (like in reproductive case).

In the second stage of annotation, the dataset was also annotated by arguments for all three claims [59]. The following four classes (labels) were used: "irrelevant" (text does not contain stance and, consequently, premise on the topic), "for" (the stance is supported with an argument in favor of the topic), "against" (the argument explains the author's negative outlook on the topic), "no argument" (no explanation is given for the topic). A sentence was considered as a premise if the annotator could use it to convince an opponent about the given claim, such as "Masks help prevent the spread of disease". The task of premise annotation should be separated from stance detection and sentiment analysis tasks. For example, the following statement does not contain a premise in relation to masks, although there is an author's stance "for": "It is high time to involve the city of 'brides' in the production of protective masks". It is also necessary to distinguish between sentiment polarity (positive and/or negative) and argumentation. In the following sentence, there is a negative polarity towards quarantine, a positive polarity towards Trump, but no rational premises "for" or "against" quarantine are given: "And the fact that Trump did not introduce a suffocating quarantine is well done!"

The created dataset was also divided into three sets: training, validation, and test ones and was utilized for RuArg-2022 shared task which attracted 16 participants[8].

It is important to stress that the described argument's thematic analysis of the reproductive-related and health-related comments was made by the same approach as the stance's thematic analysis. We annotated "for", "against", and "other" marks of relevant comments (comments with arguments) in the health-related dataset. The context of these arguments does not understandable for us in this case. Another way is that we annotated "for", "against", and "other" marks of an argument-type topic ("individualism") in the reproductive-related dataset. The numerical link between anti-natalist attitudes ("childfree") and argument-type topic ("individualism") does not visible for us in that case.

## Appendix.3 argument analysis's method: search of the automatic general algorithm for demographic studies

The previous paragraph describes our methods to study of the reproductive (and health) behavior of Russians based on the opinions of users of the largest social

8 https://www.dialog-21.ru/en/dialogue-evaluation/competitions/dialogue-evaluation-2022/ruarg-2022/.

network in Russia, VKontakte, using natural language processing methods (supervised machine learning). Our next step is to identify the arguments in the statements of VKontakte users on reproductive behavior (or any demographic behavior).

We have proposed a dichotomous "personal-public" approach for such a broad classification of arguments. The arguments where the author of the statement appeals to his own experience, personal preferences or attitudes are considered personal. Public statements were considered to be statements aimed at the authors' reflections on how the family should be arranged in society as a whole. This type of division was chosen because the ratio of personal and public arguments plays an important role in understanding the "acuteness" of public sentiment and the need for policy-makers to respond to an alarm signal if the proportion of personal arguments increases significantly. Thus, in addition to identifying arguments, the second level of classification was automatically carried out according to the principle of attributing an argument to "personal" or "public" (see for more details see Ref. [Kalabikhina et al. [66, 67]]).

In demography, a dichotomous "personal-public" is not the new view. Well-known the example of using such dichotomous in the framework of fertility survey: "What is the ideal number of children in your opinion?" (the public site); "How many children do you plan to have based on your capabilities?" (the personal site). The examples of comments with arguments in the categories "personal" and "public" in our study of arguments: "I have three children. They make a mess better than without children. There is no meaning to life without children" (the personal site); "In countries with a ban on abortion, the crime rate goes off scale" (the public site).

The total volume of the final sample for with stage of our investigation was 5412 comments. The classification method was chosen as the main one according to two criteria: the presence and type of argument. These comments were marked up by experts according to the following principle: if there is argumentation or not[9]; if an argument is present, then it is determined whether it is personal or public. In different experiments, different classification options were used: only by the presence of an argument, by the presence of arguments of both types (personal and public), or by the presence of a specific type of argument.

The analysis of the annotated data was carried out using the Python programming language in the PyTorch environment and the Transformers and Scikit Learn libraries. The Conversational RuBERT model was used for experiments[10]. See Ref. [Kalabikhina et al. [66, 67]] for other model parameters and more details.

[9] Note that we have also tested the method of finding arguments based on personal pronouns in statements. This method gave a worse result compared to the markup.

[10] DeepPavlov archive on Hugging Face to access the model: https://huggingface.co/DeepPavlov/rubert-base-cased-conversational.

## Author details

Irina Kalabikhina[1*], Natalia Loukachevitch[1], Eugeny Banin[2] and Anton Kolotusha[1]

1 Lomonosov Moscow State University, Russia

2 Bauman Moscow State Technical University, Russia

*Address all correspondence to: ikalabikhina@yandex.ru

## References

[1] Gentzkow M, Kelly B, Taddy M. Text as data. Journal of Economic Literature. 2019;**57**(3):535-574

[2] Kalpak KK, Arti DK, Dinesh S, Piyush S. A typology of viral ad sharers using sentiment analysis. Journal of Retailing and Consumer Services. 2020;**53**:101739

[3] Dinesh KS, Fernandes S. Impact of e-WOM on consumer purchase behaviour through twitter sentiment analysis using Vader and machine learning. AIP Conference Proceedings. 2023;**2523**(1):30012

[4] Karn AL, Karna RK, Kondamudi BR, et al. Customer centric hybrid recommendation system for E-commerce applications by integrating hybrid sentiment analysis. Electronic Commerce Research. 2023;**23**:279-314

[5] Reis BY, Brownstein JS. Measuring the impact of health policies using internet search patterns: The case of abortion. BMC Public Health. 2010;**10**:1-5

[6] Billari F, D'Amuri F, Marcucci J. Forecasting births using Google. In: Carma 2016: 1st International Conference on Advanced Research Methods in Analytics. Valencia: Editorial Universitat Politècnica de València; 2016. p. 119

[7] Kalabikhina IE, Abduselimova IA, Arkhangelsky VN, Banin EP, Klimenko GA, Kolotusha AV, et al. Short-term forecasting of demographic trends based on Google trends data. Applied Computer Science. 2020;**15**(6):91-118. (In Russian)

[8] Bronitsky G, Vakulenko E. Using Google trends for external migration prediction. Demographic Review. 2022;**9**(3):75-92. DOI: 10.17323/demreview.v9i3.16471 (in Russian)

[9] Ginsberg J, Mohebbi MH, Patel RS, Brammer L, Smolinski MS, Brilliant L. Detecting influenza epidemics using search engine query data. Nature. 2009;**457**(7232):1012-1014

[10] Smirnov A. Digital traces of the population as a data source on migration flows in the Russian Arctic. Demographic Review. 2022a;**9**(2):42-64

[11] Kalabikhina I, Kazbekova Z, Klimenko G, Kolotusha A. Demographic regional rankings by media activity on maternal (family) capital. Applied Econometrics. 2022b;**67**:46-73

[12] Kalabikhina IE, Klimenko GA, Banin EP, Vorobyeva EK, Lameeva AD. Database of digital media publications on maternal (family) capital in Russia in 2006-2019. Population and Economics. 2021d;**5**(4):1-29

[13] State B, Rodriguez M, Helbing D, Zagheni E. Migration of professionals to the US. In: Social Informatics: 6th International Conference, SocInfo 2014, Barcelona, Spain, November 11-13, 2014. Proceedings. Cham: Springer International Publishing; 2014. pp. 531-543

[14] Mencarini L, Hernández-Farías DI, Lai M, Patti V, Sulis E, Vignoli D. Happy parents' tweets. Demographic Research. 2019;**40**:693-724

[15] Vignoli D, Farías DIH, Mencarini L, Lai M, Patti V, Sulis E, et al. Happy parents' Tweet? An Exploration of 3 Milion Italian Twitter Data. In: 2017 International Population Conference. Cape Town, South Africa: IUSSP; 2017

[16] Hasan KS, Ng V. Stance classification of ideological debates: Data, models, features, and constraints. In: Proceedings of the Sixth International Joint Conference on Natural Language Processing. IJCNLP. Nagoya, Japan: Asian Federation of Natural Language Processing. 2013. pp. 1348-1356

[17] Ntontis E, Hopkins N. Framing a 'social problem': Emotion in anti-abortion activists' depiction of the abortion debate. British Journal of Social Psychology. 2018;**57**(3):666-683

[18] Roldán-Robles PR, Umaquinga-Criollo AC, García-Santillán JA, Herrera-Granda ID, García-Santillán ID. A conceptual architecture for content analysis about abortion using the twitter platform. Revista Ibérica de Sistemas e Tecnologias de Informaçao. 2019;**E22**:363-374

[19] Sharma E, Saha K, Ernala SK, Ghoshal S, De Choudhury M. Analyzing ideological discourse on social media: A case study of the abortion debate. In: Proceedings of the 2017 International Conference of the Computational Social Science Society of the Americas. New York, NY, United States: Association for Computing Machinery; 2017. pp. 1-8

[20] Graells-Garrido E, Baeza-Yates R, Lalmas M. How representative is an abortion debate on twitter? In: Proceedings of the 10th ACM Conference on Web Science. New York, NY, United States: Association for Computing Machinery; 2019. pp. 133-134

[21] LaRoche KJ, Jozkowski KN, Crawford BL, Haus KR. Attitudes of US adults toward using telemedicine to prescribe medication abortion during COVID-19: A mixed methods study. Contraception. 2021;**104**(1):104-110

[22] Misra A, Oraby S, Tandon S, Ts S, Anand P, Walker M. Summarizing dialogic arguments from social media. arXiv preprint arXiv:1711.00092. 2017

[23] Shah Z, Martin P, Coiera E, Mandl KD, Dunn AG. Modeling spatiotemporal factors associated with sentiment on twitter: Synthesis and suggestions for improving the identification of localized deviations. Journal of Medical Internet Research. 2019;**21**(5):e12881

[24] Liu S, Li J, Liu J. Leveraging transfer learning to analyze opinions, attitudes, and behavioural intentions toward COVID-19 vaccines: Social media content and temporal analysis. Journal of Medical Internet Research. 2021;**23**(8):302-351

[25] Mandel B, Culotta A, Boulahanis J, Stark D, Lewis B, Rodrigue J. A demographic analysis of online sentiment during hurricane Irene. In: Proceedings of the Second Workshop on Language in Social Media. 2012. pp. 27-36

[26] Talpada H, Halgamuge MN, Tran Q, Vinh N. An analysis on use of deep learning and lexical-semantic based sentiment analysis method on twitter data to understand the demographic trend of telemedicine. In: 2019 11th International Conference on Knowledge and Systems Engineering (KSE), Da Nang, Vietnam: IEEE; 2019. pp. 1-9

[27] Glandt K et al. Stance detection in COVID-19 tweets. In: Proceedings of the 59th Annual Meeting of the Association for Computational Linguistics and the 11th International Joint 46 Conference on Natural Language Processing. Vol. 1: Long Papers. Stroudsburg, PA, USA: Association for Computational Linguistics; 2021. pp. 1596-1611

[28] Liu S, Liu J. Public attitudes toward COVID-19 vaccines on English-language

twitter: A sentiment analysis. Vaccine. 2021;**39**(39):5499-5505

[29] Miao L, Last M, Litvak M. Twitter data augmentation for monitoring public opinion on COVID-19 intervention measures. In: Proceedings of the 1st Workshop on NLP for COVID-19 (Part 2) at EMNLP 2020. Association for Computational Linguistics; 2020

[30] Abosedra S, Laopodis NT, Fakih A. Dynamics and asymmetries between consumer sentiment and consumption in pre-and during-COVID-19 time: Evidence from the US. The Journal of Economic Asymmetries. 2021;**24**:e00227

[31] Huerta DT, Hawkins JB, Brownstein JS, Hswen Y. Exploring discussions of health and risk and public sentiment in Massachusetts during COVID-19 pandemic mandate implementation: A twitter analysis. SSM-Population Health. 2021;**15**:100851

[32] Alamoodi AH, Zaidan BB, Zaidan AA, Albahri OS, Mohammed KI, Malik RQ, et al. Sentiment analysis and its applications in fighting COVID-19 and infectious diseases: A systematic review. Expert Systems with Applications. 2021;**167**:114155

[33] Andalibi N, Haimson OL, De Choudhury M, Forte A. Understanding social media disclosures of sexual abuse through the lenses of support seeking and anonymity. In: Proceedings of the 2016 CHI Conference on Human Factors in Computing Systems. New York, NY, United States: Association for Computing Machinery; 2016. pp. 3906-3918

[34] Al-Rawi A, Grepin K, Li X, Morgan R, Wenham C, Smith J. Investigating public discourses around gender and COVID-19: A social media analysis of twitter data. Journal of Healthcare Informatics Research. 2021;**5**(3):249-269

[35] Xue J, Macropol K, Jia Y, Zhu T, Gelles RJ. Harnessing big data for social justice: An exploration of violence against women-related conversations on Twitter. Human Behavior and Emerging Technologies. 2019;**1**(3):269-279

[36] Mittos A, Zannettou S, Blackburn J, Cristofaro ED. Analyzing genetic testing discourse on the web through the lens of twitter, reddit, and 4chan. ACM Transactions on the Web (TWEB). 2020;**14**(4):1-38

[37] Cesare N, Lee H, McCormick T, Spiro E, Zagheni E. Promises and pitfalls of using digital traces for demographic research. Demography. 2018;**55**(5):1979-1999

[38] Stewart I, Flores RD, Riffe T, Weber I, Zagheni E. Rock, rap, or reggaeton?: Assessing Mexican immigrants' cultural assimilation using Facebook data. In: The World Wide Web Conference. New York, NY, United States: Association for Computing Machinery; 2019. pp. 3258-3264

[39] Pötzschke S, Braun M. Migrant sampling using Facebook advertisements: A case study of polish migrants in four European countries. Social Science Computer Review. 2016;**35**(5):633-653

[40] Dvoynikova AA, Karpov AA. Analytical review of approaches to Russian text sentiment recognition. Information and Control Systems. 2020;**4**:20-30. (In Russian)

[41] Kuratov Y, Arkhipov M. Adaptation of deep bidirectional multilingual transformers for Russian language. arXiv preprint arXiv:1905.07213. 2019

[42] Smetanin S. The applications of sentiment analysis for Russian language texts: Current challenges and future perspectives. IEEE Access. 2020;**8**:110693-110719

[43] Vychegzhanin SV, Kotelnikov EV. Stance detection based on ensembles of classifiers. Programming and Computer Software. 2019;**45**(5):228-240

[44] Panicheva P, Mararitsa L, Sorokin S, et al. Predicting subjective well-being in a high-risk sample of Russian mental health app users. EPJ Data Science. 2022;**11**:21

[45] Melton CA, Olusanya OA, Ammar N, Shaban-Nejad A. Public sentiment analysis and topic modeling regarding COVID-19 vaccines on the reddit social media platform: A call to action for strengthening vaccine confidence. Journal of Infection and Public Health. 2021;**14**(10):1505-1512

[46] Wawrzuta D, Jaworski M, Gotlib J, Panczyk M. What arguments against COVID-19 vaccines run on facebook in Poland: Content analysis of comments. Vaccine. 2021;**9**(5):481-492

[47] Wawrzuta D, Klejdysz J, Jaworski M, Gotlib J, Panczyk M. Attitudes toward COVID-19 vaccination on social media: A cross-platform analysis. Vaccine. 2022;**10**(8):1190

[48] Karami A, Anderson M. Social media and COVID-19: Characterizing anti-quarantine comments on twitter. Proceedings of the Association for Information Science and Technology. 2020;**57**(1):349-353

[49] Han X, Wang J, Zhang M, Wang X. Using social media to mine and analyze public opinion related to COVID-19 in China. International Journal of Environmental Research and Public Health. 2020;**17**(8):2788

[50] Oyebode O, Ndulue C, Adib A, Mulchandani D, Suruliraj B, Orji FA, et al. Health, psychosocial, and social issues emanating from the COVID-19 pandemic based on social media comments: Text mining and thematic analysis approach. JMIR Medical Informatics. 2021;**9**(4):227-234

[51] Donchenko D, Ovchar N, Sadovnikova N, Parygin D, Shabalina O, Ather D. Analysis of comments of users of social networks to assess the level of social tension. Procedia Computer Science. 2017;**119**:359-367

[52] Sidorov N, Slastnikov S. Some features of sentiment analysis for Russian language posts and comments from social networks. Journal of Physics: Conference Series. IOP Publishing. 2021;**1740**(1):12-36

[53] Smetanin S, Komarov M. Share of toxic comments among different topics: The case of Russian social networks. In: 2021 IEEE 23rd Conference on Business Informatics (CBI). Vol. 2. Bolzano, Italy: IEEE; 2021. pp. 65-70

[54] Hopkins N, Zeedyk S, Raitt F. Visualising abortion: Emotion discourse and fetal imagery in a contemporary abortion debate. Social Science & Medicine. 2005;**61**(2):393-403

[55] Kalabikhina IE, Banin EP. Database "pro-family (pro-natalist) communities in the social network VKontakte". Population and Economics. 2020;**4**:98

[56] Kalabikhina IE, Banin EP. Database "childfree (anti-natalist) communities in the social network VKontakte". Population and Economics. 2021;**5**(2):92-96

[57] Kalabikhina IE, Loukachevitch NV, Banin EP, Alibaeva KV, Rebrey SM. Automatic extraction of opinions of

users of social networks on reproductive behaviour issues [dataset]. Zenodo. 2021b. DOI: 10.5281/zenodo.5561126

[58] Chkhartishvili A, Gubanov D, Kozitsin I. Covid-19 information consumption and dissemination: A study of online social network VKontakte. In: 2021 14th International Conference Management of Large-Scale System Development (MLSD). Moscow, Russian Federation: IEEE; 2021. pp. 1-5

[59] Kotelnikov E, Loukachevitch N, Nikishina I, Panchenko A. RuArg-2022: Argument mining evaluation. Computational Linguistics and Intellectual Technologies: Proceedings of the International Conference “Dialogue 2022”. Moscow: Dialogue; 2022

[60] Kalabikhina IE, Banin EP, Abduselimova IA, Klimenko GA, Kolotusha AV. The measurement of demographic temperature using the sentiment analysis of data from the social network VKontakte. Mathematics. 2021c;**9**(9):987

[61] Taj MN, Girisha GS. Insights of strength and weakness of evolving methodologies of sentiment analysis. Global Transitions Proceedings. 2021;**2**(2):157-162

[62] Kalabikhina IE, Loukachevitch NV, Banin EP, Alibaeva KV, Rebrey SM. Automatic extraction of opinions of users of social networks on reproductive behaviour. Software Systems: Theory and Applications. 2021a;**12**(51):33-63. (In Russian)

[63] Kalabikhina IE, Loukachevitch NV, Banin EP, Alibaeva KV. Automatic analysis of reproductive values of VKontakte network users. Intelligent Systems. Theory and Applications. 2022a;**26**(1):90-96. (In Russian)

[64] Alibaeva K, Loukachevitch N. Analyzing COVID-related stance and arguments using BERT-based natural language inference. Computational Linguistics and Intellectual Technologies. Computational Linguistics and Intellectual Technologies: Proceedings of the International Conference “Dialogue 2022”. Moscow: Dialogue; 2022

[65] Devlin J, Chang MW, Lee K, Toutanova K. Bert: Pre-training of deep bidirectional transformers for language understanding. arXiv preprint arXiv:1810.04805. 2018

[66] Kalabikhina I, Zubova E, Loukachevitch N, Kazbekova Z, Kolotusha A, Banin E, et al. Arguments on reproductive behaviour of users of social network by natural language processing method. Population and Economics. 2023a;7(2):40-59

[67] Kalabikhina IE, Kazbekova ZG, Banin EP, Klimenko GA. Demographic values and socio-demographic profile of VKontakte users: Is there a connection? In: Moscow University Bulletin. Series 6: Economy. 3. 2023b. pp. 157-180. (In Russian)

[68] Golder SA, Macy MW. Digital footprints: Opportunities and challenges for online social research. Annual Review of Sociology. 2014;**40**:129-152

[69] Lazer D, Radford J. Data ex machina: Introduction to big data. Annual Review of Sociology. 2017;**43**:19-39

[70] Loukachevitch N. Automatic Sentiment Analysis of Texts: The Case of Russian. In: Gritsenko D, Wijermars M, Kopotev M, editors. The Palgrave Handbook of Digital Russia Studies. Cham: Palgrave Macmillan; DOI: 10.1007/978-3-030-42855-6_28

[71] Rusnachenko N, Loukachevitch NV. Extracting sentiment attitudes from analytical texts. In: Computational Linguistics and Intelligent Technologies: Proceedings of the International Conference "Dialogue 2018". May 30–June 2, 2018. Moscow: Lomonosov Moscow State University; 2018. pp. 459-468

[72] Hughes C, Zagheni E, Abel G, Wi'sniowski A, Sorichetta A, Weber I, et al. Inferring Migrations: Traditional Methods and New Approaches Based on Mobile Phone, Social Media, and Other Big Data. Luxembourg: Publications Office of the European Union; 2016

[73] Alburez-Gutierrez D, Zagheni E, Aref S, Gil-Clavel S, Grow A, Negraia DV. Demography in the Digital Era: New Data Sources for Population Research. SocArXiv; 2019. DOI: 10.31235/osf.io/24jp7

[74] Liu B. Sentiment analysis and opinion mining. Synthesis Lectures on Human Language Technologies. 2012;**5**(1):1-167

[75] Pozzi FA, Fersini E, Messina E, Liu B. Challenges of sentiment analysis in social networks: An overview. Sentiment Analysis in Social Networks. 2017:1-11. DOI: 10.1016/B978-0-12-804412-4.00001-2

[76] Sagredos C, Nikolova E. 'Slut I hate you': A critical discourse analysis of gendered conflict on YouTube. Journal of Language Aggression and Conflict. 2022;**10**(1):169-196

[77] Ehret K, Taboada M. Are online news comments like face-to-face conversation?: A multi-dimensional analysis of an emerging register. Register Studies. 2020;**2**(1):1-36

[78] Castellano Parra O, Meso Ayerdi K, Pena Fernandez S. Behind the Comments Section: The Ethics of Digital Native News Discussions. 2020

[79] Loukachevitch N, Rubtsova Y. Entity-oriented sentiment analysis of tweets: Results and problems. In: Text, Speech, and Dialogue: 18th International Conference, TSD 2015, Pilsen, Czech Republic, September 14-17, 2015, Proceedings 18. Pilsen, Czech Republic: Springer International Publishing; 2015. pp. 551-559

[80] Sun C, Huang L, Qiu X. Utilizing BERT for aspect-based sentiment analysis via constructing auxiliary sentence. arXiv preprint arXiv:1903.09588. 2019

[81] Nugamanov E, Loukachevitch N, Dobrov B. Extracting sentiments towards COVID-19 aspects. In: Supplementary 23rd International Conference on Data Analytics and Management in Data Intensive Domains. DAMDID/RCDL 2021; 2021. pp. 299-312

Chapter 15

# Small Area Estimation for Demographic Analysis

*Aja M. Sutton and Zack W. Almquist*


## Abstract

In this chapter we will introduce recent developments in the application of small area estimation (SAE) such as combining new statistical methods, e.g., multilevel regression and poststratification (MRP) and neighborhood spatial smoothing models (e.g., a modified Besag-York-Mollié, or BYM2), and consider recent applications for demographic processes such as mortality or migration estimation at local levels. We will discuss recent methodological developments and important applications of SAE such as the United Nations COVID-19 national and subnational mortality estimates. Last, we will provide a clear example of SAE using United States ZIP code-level data for core demographic questions relating to mortality and migration.


**Keywords:** small area estimation, forecasting, demographic data, geographic data, areal units

## 1. Introduction

Demography is a discipline dependent on the accurate enumeration of population-level processes. The foundational unit of measurement for analyzing many demographic processes is the count of individuals; it allows demographers to derive all other statistical descriptions of population dynamics. Therefore, it is crucial to have reliable population counts of the outcome of interest whether they relate to mortality (e.g., number in the population who died), fertility (e.g., number of births in the population), morbidity (e.g., number who contracted a disease), population-level social attitudes (e.g., measurable responses to a sociological survey), migration (e.g., counts of movement between locations), or otherwise. Unless there is near-perfect enumeration through a census, it is often difficult to establish the count of an outcome in a population. Classic survey methods and modern statistics offer a way to directly estimate these counts. However, when a survey has inadequate sample size, it may not be possible to make reliable direct estimates of the outcome of interest (e.g., counts of people 5–10 years old in Nigeria). Instead, it is often possible to make indirect estimates through methods that are often referred to as small area estimation (SAE). Here, a small area may either refer geographic areas/regions (e.g., counties, states, provinces, census tracts, etc.) or demographic groups (i.e., the various combinations

 IntechOpen

of demographic characteristics present in survey data used to categorize individual participants, including sex, age, race/ethnicity, employment status, etc.) [1]. Small area estimation methods use additional contextual information to produce statistically robust estimates of under- or unobserved subpopulations or geographic units. Classic spatial models used for public health mapping and small area estimation include the Fay-Herriot model [2], the Besag-York-Mollié model [3], and the modified Besag-York-Mollié model (referred to as the BYM2 model) [4]. While SAE may use such spatial models in producing estimates, recent advancements in computational power mean that in many cases these models are only just beginning to be considered as potentially viable additions to more common SAE methods like multilevel regression and poststratification.

## 2. Small area estimation in demographic research

The building blocks of demographic research are census and survey data. As discussed, sometimes these data are unreliable, incomplete, or not measured in a timely manner. Increasingly, demographers are using SAE methods to attempt to produce more reliable indirect estimates as part of their analytic processes. This is especially true in high- and middle-income countries where data sparseness may exist in some geographic regions or demographic domains, but data quality and presence are otherwise high. While direct methods of SAE may incorporate estimation needs into survey designs, it is frequently also the case that post-hoc SAE is necessary using data not gathered explicitly for the purpose of generating estimates of the outcome of interest. In this case, indirect estimates may be produced using SAE methods applied to either census or survey data.

### 2.1 Small area estimation and census data

Many census authorities and national statistics offices have begun to use SAE for minor applications focused on tracking population trends during inter-census periods among subpopulations that are difficult to enumerate or underrepresented in inter-census data. For example, the United States Census Bureau has several small projects aimed at incorporating both geographic and temporal SAE methods to generate estimates in response to data user demands for increasingly finer-grain geographic areas like census tracts when complete domain data and/or adequate sample size are not available [5]. The American Community Survey (ACS) is perhaps the most well-known United States-based project that uses SAE methods; every month the ACS samples select households in all counties and produces model-based direct estimates of many outcomes of interest. A significant product of the ACS is indirect estimates of the number of school-aged children living in poverty at the county and school district levels which are published in yearly and five-year aggregates, as are all other ACS estimates. At such a fine-grain geographic level it may be difficult and invasive to directly enumerate the number of children experiencing poverty, but SAE methods allow the researcher to leverage sub-population level demographic data from sampled households to produce indirect estimates in a reasonably unobtrusive yet reliable manner. Similar work has been undertaken to produce indirect estimates for public health surveillance, including estimating disease prevalence such as with cancer cases [6], and health insurance coverage [7].

## 2.2 Small area estimation and non-census survey data

Just as with census authority work, a survey design or model may be produced to best represent attitudes by demographic characteristics and geographic context of any number of questions from opinion survey responses. In this context, SAE methods may then be used by organizations or groups interested in attitudes or opinions such as in academic contexts (e.g., sociologists, anthropologists, etc.), or business (e.g., market research). While classic use cases regarding public opinion polls are referenced below, some interesting and unique examples of these include estimating forest land ownership for the United States Department of Agriculture National Forest Service [8] and Australian electoral district-level attitudes toward same-sex marriage [9]. However, with these examples there is a presumption of high-quality data and limited "missingness" in terms of even fine-grain geographic coverage. In countries that may have fewer or limited resources for adequate enumeration efforts through a formal census (often low-income countries), additional information may be generated from observed population data using SAE. For example, the UNICEF Under 5 Year Mortality Estimates are a series of regularly produced estimates of small area mortality rates that use national census and survey data, and complex SAE methods for countries of particular concern regarding child survival rates [10]. In this way, SAE offers estimation methods of varying complexity and with varying thresholds of statistical expertise required for implementation but is also a suite of methods that can be applied flexibly to various population enumeration needs given data availability and adequate consideration. However, one SAE method that can be implemented with an accessible threshold level of expertise and is increasingly popular in high- and middle-income contexts is multilevel regression and poststratification.

# 3. Multilevel regression and poststratification: a basic introduction

Multilevel regression and poststratification (MRP) is a model-based statistical method that uses national/high-level administrative survey or census data[1] to adjust for non-representativeness in subnational surveys using national survey or census estimates, and/or to provide small area estimation (SAE) in areas where subnational survey data are sparse or nonexistent. MRP is computationally inexpensive and able to yield quick, consistent, and accurate estimates. Consequently, it is used for resource allocation and policy planning in settings such as public health administration. Prevailing methods of MRP for SAE borrow strength from other administrative areal data through partial pooling. While this approach is powerful, it does not account for any potential existing "neighborhood" spatial structure in the data. Including spatial specifications in MRP can be a valuable way to better handle spatial relationships and generate more accurate area-level estimates.

---

[1] For the sake of clarity, here "survey data" refers to the unrepresentative data used to build the model, and "census data" are the data representing the known population used to adjust the unrepresentative data and from which population count estimates of the modeled outcome are made. However, it is possible to use large, representative data from the known population such as the American Community Survey 5-year estimates in the United States.

### 3.1 Traditional multilevel-regression and poststratification

The traditional MRP method described initially by Gelman and Little [11], and later expanded upon to consider applications for public opinion polls and surveys (e.g., [11, 12]; see also: [13–15]), is able to estimate the joint posterior distributions of the outcome of interest according to the survey population structure, and using Bayesian methods[2] to generate marginal estimates for unobserved subpopulations. It then adjusts these distributions using census or large-scale weighted population survey data to reflect the known population structure. If desired, it is then possible to use the mean posterior estimate (i.e., Bayesian methods) for each subpopulation in addition to the known area-level subpopulation counts from the same census data to predict the number of individuals in each area exhibiting the outcome of interest (the outcome is often assumed to have a binomial distribution, but this is not strictly required).

### 3.2 Data requirements for model fitting and poststratification

While a relatively straightforward procedure (described more thoroughly below), MRP has strict data requirements. Typically, the multilevel regression model built must only use as covariates the variables present in both the survey data used to train the model, and also the census data used to poststratify the marginal posterior probabilities. These complementary variables must be organized and coded in the exact same way (e.g., if "age" is used as a covariate, then each dataset must either represent age as a continuous variable, or bin age groups in the same manner). The individual-level survey data should contain at minimum two demographic characteristics per observed participant, in addition to good data availability for the outcome of interest to be modeled. For example, in addition to the respondent's reported value for the outcome of interest, the sex and age; or sex and race/ethnicity; or sex, age and race/ethnicity must be known for each participant, and these characteristics must also be present in the census data. More concretely, if a model is built with the survey data using sex, age and race/ethnicity as the model covariates on which to later poststratify with the census data, then the census data must contain the known number of individuals belonging to each combination of covariate characteristics even if that number is zero (e.g., the number of people in the state of California who are identified as Black, male and aged 18–24; or the number of people in King County, Washington, USA, who are identified as White, female, and aged 25–34, etc., and every possible combination of these demographic characteristics). To this end, there must be a poststratification table that contains only the variables from the census data used to weight the joint posterior estimates and derive an estimated population count of the outcome. Furthermore, to adjust the estimates using the census data contained in the original poststratification table, it is necessary to calculate the inclusion weights of each poststratification level (e.g., the number of individuals in the poststratification level in ZIP code X divided by the total number of individuals in all poststratification levels in ZIP code X; these levels are clarified below).

---

[2] In this case, we have used Integrated Nested Laplace Approximation (INLA), and so more correctly, our example figures are generated using a method that approximates Bayesian processes.

### 3.3 Traditional MRP versus MRP using spatial specifications

For the multilevel model aspect of the MRP method, covariates are typically either modeled as fixed effects or random effects and may include interaction terms between fixed effects. The model is also where the traditional MRP method differs from MRP using spatial specifications. Traditional MRP methods may specify a hierarchical model of the probability of some outcome (which can then be extrapolated to estimate the count of individuals exhibiting the outcome in the population) as follows. Imagine we are estimating an outcome within the adult population (18 years and older) of a state, such as California, USA, and we have access to individual-level information about the outcome of interest within the California population; specifically the survey respondents' ages and their county of residence. Define $N_{ij}$ as the population in age strata $j = 1, \dots 7$ (where 1 = 18–24 years, 2 = 25–34 years, 3 = 35–44 years, 4 = 45–54 years, 5 = 55–64 years, 6 = 65–74 years, and 7 = 75 years and over) within each county $i = 1, \dots 58$ (there are 58 counties in this state). The total population in each county in the state of California is $N_i = \sum_{j=1}^{J} N_{ij}$, whereas the total population in the state of California is $N = \sum_{i=1}^{I} \sum_{j=1}^{J} N_{ij}$. Let $y_{ij}$ be the number of people who exhibited the outcome out of the total $N_{ij}$ people in county $i$ and age strata $J$, with $p_{ij}$ the probability of the outcome. We specify the hierarchical model,

$$y_{ij}|p_{ij} \sim Binomial\left(N_{ij}, p_{ij}\right), \tag{1}$$

$$\log it\left(p_{ij}\right) = \alpha + \beta_j + e_i, \tag{2}$$

$$\underline{\beta} = [\beta_1, \cdots \beta_J] \sim RW2\left(\sigma_\beta^2\right), \tag{3}$$

$$e_i \sim iid\, N\left(0, \sigma_e^2\right), \tag{4}$$

and $\alpha$ the intercept (to include an intercept, the RW2 model requires a sum-to-zero constraint for identifiability). Here, RW2 is a random walk of the second order on age (perhaps an optimistic assumption with so few age categories, but a good example of a structured random effect one might use in these contexts). In this form, it is possible to specify the geographic area covariate as a random effect for partial local pooling within the context of each of the areas between different categories within a demographic variable (e.g., partial pooling within ZIP code X within different categories of race/ethnicity), but this formulation does not account for spatial structure (i.e., the model does not specify a "neighborhood" spatial structure, and there is no sharing between geographic areas contingent on proximity).

It is possible to use spatial terms in the model if the survey data contain any spatial information also identifiable in the census data (e.g., if the geographic area level of interest is the county level in the context of the United States, these would be United States Census Bureau county FIPS codes which represent each individual county and for which a spatial polygon/shapefile may be easily obtained). While covariates in the model in the traditional MRP method are specified as being independent and identically distributed (IID), the flexible nature of multilevel models can be leveraged such that a spatial random effect may be included in the model (after [16]).

### *3.3.1 Spatial specifications and poststratification data needs*

A common spatial model used to specify the spatial random effect is the modified Besag-York-Mollié (BYM2) model [4]. This model uses a spatial grid, or spatial adjacency matrix, generated using the survey data and associated spatial polygons to take advantage of identifiable "neighborhood" structures of the data. Consequently, it also requires all poststratification data to be known for each geographic area of interest (e.g., if the level of geographic interest in the county level in the state of California, then the number of people described by each demographic characteristic combination used in the model in each county in California must be known).[3] These are perhaps most simply thought of as poststratification levels (i.e., each possible combination of demographics for each geographic area, such as each county). In this way, while some covariates may be specified as IID, the spatial covariate included in the model is specified as using the modified Besag-York-Mollié (BYM2) model. When this is done, the data smoothing, and pooling is limited such that only information between immediate or "first-order" neighbors[4] is shared (**Figure 1**).

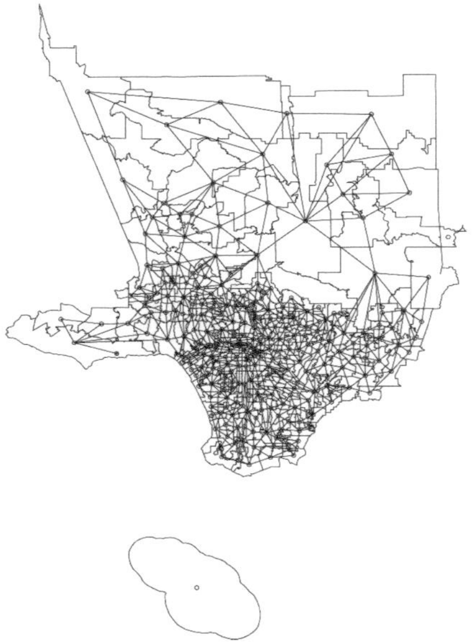

**Figure 1.**
*Spatial adjacency queen-style "Neighborhood" structure. This simple map represents the United States Census Bureau ZIP Code Tabulation Areas (ZCTAs) roughly approximating Los Angeles County, California, USA. Each ZCTA has a point representing its approximate center, and a queen-style adjacency term has been specified to identify first-order neighbors (represented by the network of lines linking these points, called centroids). Note that the rough shape of Santa Catalina Island at the bottom of the figure has no neighbors identified due to it not sharing a border with any other ZCTA. There are methods of handling these instances such as with islands, but this is beyond the scope of this discussion. Image generated in 'R' [16] using 'tidyverse'-based [17] packages including 'tidycensus' [18]; additionally, 'R-INLA' [19], and also geographic data sourced from the United States Census Bureau Tiger/Line Shapefiles.*

---

[3] While any geographic level that is present may be used, such as census tract or state, the present discussion will refer to the county level for simplicity.

[4] As determined by the first-order neighborhood structure/grid. First-order neighbor areas share a common geographic boundary, such as immediately neighboring counties.

This is unlike the traditional MRP method that smooths and pools across the entirety of the data of interest even if the model includes a covariate that might seem spatial but is instead handled as an IID random effect (i.e., though a county is a geographic term, in traditional MRP it would not be handled using a spatial model, but instead specified as IID).

### 3.4 Implementing spatial specifications for multi-level regression and poststratification

In terms of implementation of spatial specifications for MRP, Gao, Kennedy and Simpson [20] proposed a modification to the MRP model, where the spatial random effects in area $i$, level $j$ are produced by including the the BYM2 model. Take again the example of Californian counties and age data for adult residents of these. Once again, we define $N_{ij}$ as the population in age strata $j = 1, \ldots 7$ (recall that 1 = 18–24 years, 2 = 25–34 years, 3 = 35–44 years, 4 = 45–54 years, 5 = 55–64 years, 6 = 65–74 years, and 7 = 75 years and over) within each county $i = 1, \ldots 58$ (there are 58 counties in this state). The total population in each county in the state of California is $N_i = \sum_{j=1}^{J} N_{ij}$, whereas the total population in the state of California is $N = \sum_{i=1}^{I} \sum_{j=1}^{J} N_{ij}$. Let $y_{ij}$ be the number of people who exhibited the outcome out of the total $N_{ij}$ people in county $i$ and age strata $J$, with $p_{ij}$ the probability of the outcome. We specify the hierarchical model,

$$y_{ij}|p_{ij} \sim BetaBinomial\left(N_{ij}, p_{ij}, d\right), \tag{5}$$

$$\log it\left(p_{ij}\right) = \alpha + \beta_j + \gamma_i, with \tag{6}$$

$$\underline{\beta} = [\beta_1, \cdots \beta_J] \sim RW2\left(\sigma_\beta^2\right), \tag{7}$$

$$\underline{\gamma} = [\gamma_1, \cdots \gamma_I] \sim BYM2\left(\sigma_\gamma^2, \phi\right), \tag{8}$$

$d$ the overdispersion parameter for the Betabinomial distribution, and $\alpha$ the intercept (as before with the non-spatial model, to include an intercept the RW2 and BYM2 models require a sum-to-zero constraint for identifiability). This spatial random effect may be placed on any reasonable covariate while still leveraging area spatial adjacency; it may, for instance, be reasonable to assume that specific age categories in neighboring areas are most likely to share similarities, and so specifying a BYM2 random effect on age may ameliorate the model.

#### *3.4.1 Overview of the multilevel regression and poststratification process*

When the preferred predictive multilevel model of the outcome of interest has been selected,[5] the model is fit using Bayesian statistical software to the survey data. The model fit is then used to predict the outcome for each spatial level (e.g., each county) contingent on the population structure represented by the poststratification

[5] Typical procedures for building a reasonable model of the outcome of interest may be applied here, including visual interaction checks and model selection processes, but these are beyond the scope of the present discussion.

data.[6] During this process, through the power of the smoothing and pooling specifications used in the model, joint posterior distributions are also predicted for poststratification levels that are not present in the survey data. Then, one thousand draws are made from the resulting prediction object such that a table of the joint posterior distribution for each poststratification level is produced. For each level in each county, each joint posterior estimate is then multiplied by the inclusion weight previously calculated using the poststratification data from the census to create a distribution of weighted posterior estimates. At this point, the median[7] of each of these distributions is taken to produce the median weighted probability for each poststratification level in

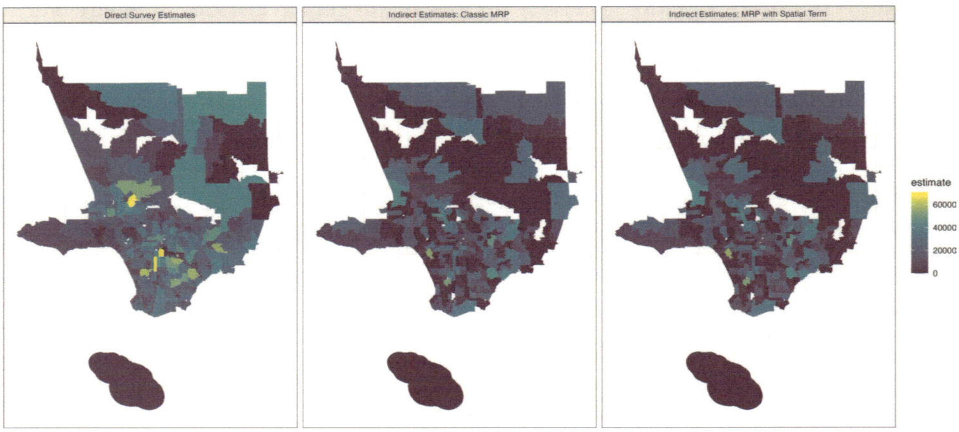


**Figure 2.**
*Comparison of number of vaccinated individuals: Direct survey estimates and indirect estimates (classic MRP and MRP with a spatial term) for ZCTAs in Los Angeles County, California, September 2020.The direct survey estimates (left) represent the most common approach to generating population estimates of an outcome (in this case, the number of individuals vaccinated in Los Angeles County, California in September 2020 according to survey results from Carnegie Mellon University's Delphi Group [21]). The direct estimates are slightly higher in certain areas, whereas the indirect estimates appear to be virtually identical in this format. However, when the aggregate estimates are considered (**Table 1**), it is evident that in this case using MRP with a spatial term subtly improves the estimates. Figure created using 'ggplot2' [22] and 'viridis' [23] packages in 'R'.*

| Method | Estimate (95% confidence interval) | Difference from direct estimate |
|---|---|---|
| Direct estimates: survey weights | 6807511 (6046260, 7568759) | Baseline |
| Indirect estimates: classic MRP | 6738749 (6119071, 7358432) | 18.6% less than baseline |
| Indirect estimates: MRP with spatial term | 6740796 (6118052, 7363537) | 18.2% less than baseline |

**Table 1.**
*Comparison of direct estimates and MRP estimates: aggregated estimates of the number of vaccinated individuals in ZCTAs approximating Los Angeles County, September 2020.*

[6] The present discussion is informed by building a MRP process with spatial specifications using Integrated Nested Laplace Approximation in R (R-INLA) because of INLA's flexibility in handling spatial models, but similar processes may be undertaken using STAN.

[7] While the mean is often taken for this and subsequent steps in the literature referenced above, perhaps a more Bayesian approach is to take the median.

each county. Thus, the first application for MRP is complete: the non-representative survey data have been adjusted using the census data.

If small area estimates are desired for each geographic area (e.g., each county), the median weighted probability for each poststratification level in each county is then multiplied by the number of known individuals in each county's matching poststratification level using the poststratification table. These poststratification level-specific outcome estimates are finally grouped by county and summed to create a population-level estimate of the outcome for each county but may be also informative if subpopulation estimates are desired. It is important to note that MRP with a spatial term is not limited to the county level. **Figure 2** compares direct estimates of the number of individuals who were vaccinated in the Los Angeles County, California area in September 2020, at the ZIP code (U.S. Census Bureau ZCTA, or ZCTAs) level using traditional survey methods with indirect estimates generated using classic MRP and MRP with a spatial term. While the indirect estimates appear to be virtually identical in this format, and slightly below the direct estimates, when considering aggregated population results in **Table 1** it is evident that the spatial term has somewhat improved the estimates, which are closer in total and in variance to the direct estimates. This indicates that using a spatial term for MRP may be an effective way of producing a reliable indirect estimate in the absence of traditional survey weighted direct estimates.

**Table 1** Caption: Direct estimates represent the standard against which to compare the performance of the indirect estimate results. While both indirect estimates from the classic MRP method and the MRP method that uses a spatial term have predicted lower counts of the number of vaccinated individuals in the Los Angeles County, California area in September 2020, it is evident that using MRP with a spatial term has in this instance somewhat improved insofar as the estimate and confidence interval is closer to the direct estimates. While these are small gains, there may be potentially greater gains in analyses where the outcome has even greater spatial dependence.

### *3.4.2 Spatial data needs and methodological limitations*

At this point, it is worth noting that spatial specifications for MRP are only useful if there is spatial structure to the outcome of interest (i.e., the outcome has spatial dependence). Furthermore, it is important to be cautious with the MRP method; whether a spatial term is used, MRP will provide a predicted estimate for every area and every combined demographic category based on the model prediction. It is up to the analyst to determine whether these estimates are reliable or artifacts of predictive modeling using smoothing parameters. Similarly, data availability and richness is important; the spatial model described here requires first-order neighbors, while many missing geographic areas amounting to poor data availability, or else spatial data with little spatial proximity between neighbors (i.e., limited first-order neighbors) will produce unreliable models and potentially incorrect estimates. Consequently, this required data quality and richness is why MRP is often only used in high-income country contexts. If these requirements are ignored, it is possible smoothing parameters may potentially "over-smooth" and create estimates for unobserved areas that are unreliable. Perhaps a reasonable threshold for spatial data missingness is roughly 10%; for example, if we were conducting an analysis of ZCTAs in the whole of the state of California, approximately a maximum of about 10% of the ZCTAs should have missing/unobserved values if we were interested in using spatial specifications, lest the model potentially over-fit the data and produce spurious results.

## 4. Multilevel regression and poststratification: in application and future developments

Small area estimation procedures have been used to estimate migration patterns (e.g., [24]), homeless population counts (e.g., [25, 26]), and disaster response (e.g., [27]). These applications have had a direct impact on policy and general demographic knowledge. More recently, in collaboration with the World Health Organization [28] Msemburi et al. [29] used SAE methods to understand the impact of COVID-19 in hard to measure parts of the world, including low- and middle-income countries, like India, where health and mortality reporting may not be centralized nor records readily available. They found that between 2020 and 2021, there was a global all-cause excess mortality of 14.9 million people due to the COVID-19 pandemic, with 84% of these deaths in Europe, South-East Asia, and the Americas.

One applied example of MRP using a spatial term for the estimation of difficult-to-measure phenomena is its potential for producing estimates of mortality among under-counted populations, including people experiencing homelessness. In the Seattle, Washington, USA area, deaths among people presumed to have been experiencing homelessness are increasing [30]. While the King County Medical Examiner has collected data pertaining to deaths of individuals presumed to be homeless since 2003, including approximate location of the death and demographic records, these represent only reported and observed deaths. Therefore, the true mortality rate for this vulnerable population is unknown. There may be two ways to estimate the all-cause mortality rate among people experiencing homelessness in Seattle. One way would be to assume the distribution of mortality is similar between the population experiencing homelessness and the total population; people experiencing homelessness are accounted for in the total population mortality. Thus, it would be reasonable to use the records of individual deaths to calculate the percentage of people experiencing homelessness in each demographic stratum in each census tract (i.e., age, sex and race/ethnicity) to fit the model, and use the total population mortality to produce estimates of the percentage of the total population within each demographic stratum in each

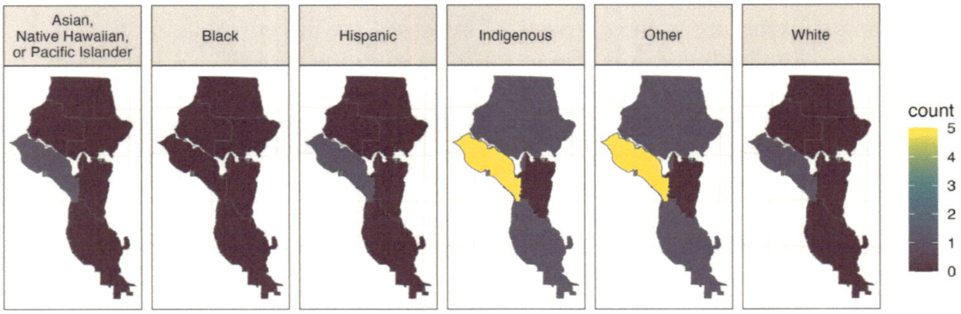


**Figure 3.**
*Estimated mortality among people experiencing homelessness in Seattle, Washington, USA 2021, poststratified by race/ethnicity and City Council district, using MRP with a spatial term. Indirect estimates of race/ethnicity-specific mortality (counts) among people experiencing homelessness in Seattle, Washington, USA, in 2021 were produced using a binomial logistic regression model of the probability of mortality, with a fixed effect on race/ethnicity category, and a BYM2 spatial smoothing term on city council district (area). Data used for the model included Seattle-King County Public Health records of deaths among individuals presumed to have been experiencing homelessness, as well as data pertaining to observed living persons that included race/ethnicity. Poststratification was achieved using data from the Continuum of Care Point-in-Time counts for Seattle/King County. Figure created using 'ggplot2' [22] and 'viridis' [23] packages in 'R'.*

census tract to poststratify. Another way would be to estimate the percentage of all-cause mortality from the point-in-time (PIT) one-night counts of unhoused people from the Department of Housing and Urban Development [31] to obtain a percentage estimate of mortality for people experiencing homelessness.

**Figure 3** provides a conceptual example of the methods described above. King County Medical Examiner's Office records for individuals who had died and were presumed to be experiencing homelessness in 2021 [31], as well as Seattle-King County Public Health records for live individuals experiencing homelessness in 2021 [32] were used to produce a binomial logistic regression model of death using only race/ethnicity as a fixed effect, and a BYM2 spatial smoothing term on the city council district (area) in which the individual died or was observed alive. When the city council district was unknown, individuals were randomly assigned to a city council district using population proportions derived from data provided by REACH Evergreen Treatment Services, the largest provider of homelessness stabilization and support services for Seattle-King County Public Health. Poststratification was done based on race/ethnicity in each city council district using data from the United States Department of Housing and Urban Development's Continuum of Care Point-in-Time counts for Seattle/King County for 2021 [33], and randomly imputing the distribution of each individual by city council district by weighting each area using the proportions from the REACH Evergreen Treatment Services data described above. It was not possible to include both race/ethnicity and age in the MRP process due to a lack of stratum-specific data available. However, it is evident from this figure that there is variation across Seattle city council districts in terms of total mortality as well as race/ethnicity-specific mortality. More demographic strata in the model fitting data, and poststratification data would doubtlessly provide clearer resolution on these trends. Future directions for small area estimation include the use of novel data sources (e.g., geolocated social media posts), extending MRP with spatial terms using in- and out-migration data, and incorporating time components to take advantage of long-term trends among covariates for outcomes of interest.

## 5. Conclusion

In this chapter we have reviewed the major importance of small area estimation in demographic and population health fields. Specifically, it is important for demographers and other population scientists to be able to estimate the counts of individuals in arbitrary geographic polygons (e.g., neighborhoods or cities). This is of particular interest for researchers in the Western world interested in non-administrative areas, and those interested in estimating outcomes without high quality census in areas of Africa and parts of Southeast Asia, such as India. Here, we have reviewed the state-of-the-art methods for SAE such as MRP and other statistical smoothing techniques. We have concluded with applications to migration, homelessness and COVID-19.

## Acknowledgements

Partial support for this research came from University of Washington Population Health Initiative Grant, a Eunice Kennedy Shriver National Institute of Child Health and Human Development research infrastructure grant, P2C HD042828, and Shanahan Endowment Fellowship, and a Eunice Kennedy Shriver National Institute of

Child Health and Human Development training grant, T32 HD101442, to the Center for Studies in Demography & Ecology at the University of Washington. An NSF CAREER Award #2142964 and ARO Award #W911NF-19-1-0407. The content is solely the responsibility of the authors and does not necessarily represent the official views of the NIH, NSF, or ARO.

## Author details

Aja M. Sutton and Zack W. Almquist*
University of Washington, Seattle, USA

*Address all correspondence to: zalmquist@uw.edu

## References

[1] Jiang J, Rao JS. Robust small area estimation: An overview. Annual Review of Statistics and Its Application. 2020; **7**(1):337-360. DOI: 10.1146/annurev-statistics-031219-041212

[2] Fay RE, Herriot RA. Estimates of income for small places: An application of James-Stein procedures to Census data. Journal of the American Statistical Association. 1979;**74**(366):269-277

[3] Besag J, York J, Mollié A. Bayesian image restoration with applications in spatial statistics (with discussion). Annals of the Institute of Statistical Mathematics. 1991;**43**:1-59. DOI: 10.1007/BF00116466

[4] Riebler A, Sørbye SH, Simpson D, Rue H. An intuitive Bayesian spatial model for disease mapping that accounts for scaling. Statistical Methods in Medical Research. 2016;**25**(4):1145-1165. DOI: 10.1177/0962280216660421

[5] United States Census Bureau. Small Area Estimation. 2022. Available from: https://www.census.gov/topics/research/stat-research/expertise/small-area-est.html

[6] National Cancer Institute. Small Area Estimates for Cancer-Related Measures. 2022. Available from: https://sae.cancer.gov/.

[7] United States Census Bureau. Health Insurance. 2022. Available from: https://www.census.gov/topics/health/health-insurance.html

[8] Harris V, Caputo J, Finley A, Butler BJ, Bowlick F, Catanzaro P. Small-area estimation for the USDA Forest Service, National Woodland Owner Survey: Creating a fine-scale land cover and ownership layer to support county-level population estimates. Frontiers in Forests and Global Change. 2021;**4**:1-11. DOI: 10.3389/ffgc.2021.745840

[9] Jackman S, Ratcliff S, Mansillo L. Small Area Estimates of Public Opinion: Model-Assisted Post-stratification of Data from Voter Advice Applications [Unpublished Manuscript]. 2019. Available from: https://www.cambridge.org/core/membership/services/aop-file-manager/file/5c2f6ebb7cf9ee1118d11c0a

[10] UNICEF. Under-five Mortality. UNICEF DATA; 2023. Available from: https://data.unicef.org/topic/child-survival/under-five-mortality/

[11] Gelman A, Little TC. Poststratification into many categories using hierarchical logistic regression. Survey Methodology. 1997;**23**(2):127-135

[12] Gelman A, Lax J, Phillips J, Gabry J, Trangucci R. Using Multilevel Regression and Poststratification to Estimate Dynamic Public Opinion. 2016. p. 2

[13] Kastellec JP, Lax JR, Phillips JH. Estimating State Public Opinion With Multi-Level Regression and Poststratification Using R

[14] Park DK, Gelman A, Bafumi J. Bayesian multilevel estimation with poststratification: State-level estimates from national polls. Political Analysis. 2004;**12**(4):375-385

[15] Lax JR, Phillips JH. Gay rights in the states: Public opinion and policy responsiveness. American Political Science Review. 2009;**103**(3):367-386

[16] Lax JR, Phillips JH. How should we estimate public opinion in the states?

American Journal of Political Science. 2009;**53**(1):107-121

[17] R Core Team. R: A Language and Environment for Statistical Computing. Vienna, Austria: R Foundation for Statistical Computing; 2022. Available from: https://www.R-project.org/

[18] Wickham H, Averick M, Bryan J, Chang W, McGowan LD, François R, et al. Welcome to the tidyverse. Journal of Open Source Software. 2019;**4**(43): 1686. DOI: 10.21105/joss.01686

[19] Walker K, Herman M. tidycensus: Load US Census Boundary and Attribute Data as 'tidyverse' and 'sf'-Ready Data Frames. R Package Version 1.3.0.9000. 2022. Available from: https://walker-data.com/tidycensus/

[20] Rue H, Martino S, Chopin N. Approximate Bayesian inference for latent Gaussian models using integrated nested Laplace approximations (with discussion). Journal of the Royal Statistical Society, Series B. 2009;**71**(2): 319-392. Available from: www.r-inla.org

[21] Gao Y, Kennedy L, Simpson D. Treatment effect estimation with multilevel regression and Poststratification. 2021. arXiv preprint arXiv:2102.10003

[22] Salomon JA, Reinhart A, Bilinski A, Chua EJ, La Motte-Kerr W, Rönn MM, et al. The US COVID-19 trends and impact survey: Continuous real-time measurement of COVID-19 symptoms, risks, protective behaviors, testing, and vaccination. Proceedings of the National Academy of Sciences. 2021;**118**(51): e2111454118. DOI: 10.1073/pnas.2111454118

[23] Wickham H. ggplot2: Elegant Graphics for Data Analysis. New York: Springer-Verlag; 2016. Available from: https://ggplot2.tidyverse.org

[24] Garnier S, Ross N, Rudis R, Camargo PA, Sciaini M, Scherer C. Viridis—Colorblind-friendly color maps for R. 2021 10.5281/zenodo.

[25] Hauer M, Byars J. IRS county-to-county migration data, 1990–2010. Demographic Research. 2019;**40**: 1153-1166

[26] Almquist ZW, Helwig NE, You Y. Connecting continuum of care point-in-time homeless counts to United States census areal units. Mathematical Population Studies. 2020;**27**(1):46-58

[27] Almquist ZW. Large-scale spatial network models: An application to modeling information diffusion through the homeless population of San Francisco. Environment and Planning B: Urban Analytics and City Science. 2020; **47**(3):523-540

[28] Maas P, Almquist Z, Giraudy E, Schneider JW. Using social media to measure demographic responses to natural disaster: Insights from a large-scale Facebook survey following the 2019 Australia Bushfires. 2020. arXiv preprint arXiv:2008.03665

[29] World Health Organization. 14.9 million excess deaths associated with the COVID-19 pandemic in 2020 and 2021 [News release]. 2022. Available from: https://www.who.int/news/item/05-05-2022-14.9-million-excess-deaths-were-associated-with-the-covid-19-pandemic-in-2020-and-2021.

[30] Msemburi W, Karlinsky A, Knutson V, Aleshin-Guendel S, Chatterji S, Wakefield J. The WHO estimates of excess mortality associated with the COVID-19 pandemic. Nature

(London). 2022;**613**(7942):130-137. DOI: 10.1038/s41586-022-05522-2

[31] King County Medical Examiner's Office. Homeless Deaths Investigated by the King County Medical Examiner's Office [Dashboard]. 2022. Available from: https://kingcounty.gov/depts/health/examiner/services/reports-data/homeless.aspx

[32] Seattle-King County Public Health. Integrating Data to Better Measure Homelessness. 2023. Available from: https://kingcounty.gov/~/media/depts/community-human-services/department/documents/KC_DCHS_Cross_Systems_Homelessness_Analysis_Brief_12_16_2021_FINAL.ashx?la=en

[33] Department of Housing and Urban Development Exchange. Point-in-Time Count and Housing Inventory Count. 2023. Available from: https://www.hudexchange.info/programs/hdx/pit-hic/

Chapter 16

# Using National Transfer Accounts to Face Aging

*Gemma Abio, Concepció Patxot and Guadalupe Souto*

## Abstract

Aging is one of the great challenges in modern societies after their demographic transition. Changes in population age structure affect socioeconomic organization and force a reconsideration of social structures consolidated under a pyramidal age composition, which is slowly vanishing. To study the impact of aging, National Transfer Accounts (NTA) and its natural extension, National Time Transfer Accounts (NTTA), are valuable data sources. They provide national cross-section age profiles of the main economic (market and nonmarket) variables, informing about how resources are produced, shared, and consumed by individuals of different ages co-living at the same moment. This chapter presents selected applications of NTA data to show its potential to study the generational economy, including both the demographic dividend—how aging affects economic growth—and the effects of aging on the welfare system. Overall, the NTA has proved to be a precious data source to enrich the analysis of the effects of aging on our societies.

**Keywords:** aging, demographic dividend, generational economy, intergenerational transfers, national transfer accounts, welfare state

## 1. Introduction

The change in population age composition is a rising challenges in contemporary societies. Over the past century, steady declines in mortality, followed by a decline in birth rates, have caused most countries to transition toward societies with a much greater percentage of elderly. According to United Nations projections (see [1]), in 2050, one in every six people in the world will be over 65 years of age, and the proportion will rise to one in four by 2100, compared to one in 11 in 2019. Europe, and particularly South European countries, are among the most affected by this change in population age structure. In 2019, one in five Europeans was over 65 years old, and it is expected to be one in four in 2050, and one in three by 2100.

The change in the population age structure implies the need to adapt social structures and institutions that exist today but are only consistent with a pyramidal age composition. To understand this, it is useful to think carefully about how the human lifecycle is organized, from an economic perspective. It can be divided into three broad periods, the exact limits of which can be discussed. In the first stage, which can generally be referred to as "childhood", individuals need to consume, but they do not have the ability to generate the necessary resources to finance it. Then, during the so-called "active age", individuals have the capacity to generate income and resources and, obviously, they continue to consume. Finally, during the "retirement" age, people again lose the ability to produce, while they continue to need resources to finance their consumption. In short, people do need to consume throughout our lives but only have the ability to directly finance such consumption while they are able to work. That is, there is a "deficit" during childhood and retirement, and a possible "surplus" during the working age. Hence, societies need mechanisms that allow the intertemporal redistribution of income from the working age to the other two lifecycle periods. There are three basic mechanisms of resource allocation. First, individuals can reallocate income intertemporally through markets: we can save during our working years and use these savings when we retire. The parallel reasoning does not work for children, though, as they (or their parents) might not have the ability to take out a loan at birth to be repaid during their working life. Thus, the main mechanism of intertemporal reallocation is not the market, either for children or for the elderly, but two other institutions: the family and the state, respectively. However, the intervention of families and the public sector implies that the redistribution of resources is not necessarily intertemporal (between different moments in the lifecycle of the same person) but intergenerational (between different age groups).

The role of markets, families, and the public sector in the intertemporal and intergenerational redistribution of resources changed radically over the past century in advanced countries, mainly due to two trends. On the one hand, economic development led to an extension of marketization. This process is closely related to the abovementioned demographic transition. In traditional societies, the family looked after the economic needs of all its members, redistributing resources from working adults to children and the elderly through the so-called intergenerational pact. On the other hand, in addition to the growing development of the capital market, the so-called welfare state was set up and became consolidated, through which the public sector comes into play as a redistributor of resources. Like families, the public sector focuses on redistribution between different generations by implementing social spending programs mainly aimed at economically dependent age groups but financed with taxes and contributions from working individuals.

In this chapter, we aim to analyze how National Transfer Accounts (NTA) estimates contribute to analyzing and understanding what has been called the generational economy: how individuals of different ages, co-living at the same moment in a given society, interact to produce, share, and consume resources. The next section is devoted to shortly describing the methodology, while Section 3 presents its natural extension, the National Time Transfer Accounts (NTTA), to incorporate nonmarket activities and obtain the full picture of resource production and consumption in society. Section 4 presents selected recent applications of NTA in order to show its potential to analyze the role of the generational economy and consequently to offer a broader view of the effects of aging on welfare. Final remarks are presented in Section 5.

## 2. National transfer accounts

National Transfer Accounts (NTA) is a methodology designed to provide an accounting framework of economic flows to and from the residents of a country, classified by age, in a given year. As such, they give information about the economic lifecycle and age reallocations, offering a cross-sectional picture of the intergenerational transfers within an economy. The aggregate values of NTA are consistent with those in National Accounts (NA), but they provide additional information, such as showing how resources in a given year are allocated across ages. The construction of NTA was initiated at the start of this century as part of a collaborative international network, and the first results for 23 countries were published in 2011 in [2]. Nowadays, the NTA project involves more than 90 countries around the world, and its corresponding methodological manual has been published by the United Nations Population Division [3].

The idea behind NTA methodology is easy to understand: individuals need to consume across their whole lifecycle, but they can only produce resources to finance that consumption during a limited period (typically, the working age). This means that a system for transferring resources across ages is needed. NTA disentangles how resources move between different age groups by means of family transfers, government intervention, and capital markets. The starting point is the transformation of the NA identity for a given year as:

$$YL + YA + TG^{+} + TF^{+} = C + S + TG^{-} + TF^{-} \qquad (1)$$

which implies that total income resources must equal total income uses. The left-hand side includes the resources, where YL is labor income, YA asset income, and $TG^{+}$ and $TF^{+}$ represent public and private transfers received by individuals. The right-hand side collects, in turn, income uses: C is consumption, S stands for savings, and $TG^{-}$ and $TF^{-}$ are transfers from individuals to the public sector—and to other individuals—respectively. Private transfers, mainly made by the family, are not measured in NA. In fact, NTA is the first standardized attempt to measure them in a comprehensive way. Rearranging this equation, the following expression is obtained:

$$C - YL = (YA - S) + (TG^{+} - TG^{-}) + (TF^{+} - TF^{-}) \qquad (2)$$

In NTA methodology, the difference between consumption and labor income is known as the lifecycle deficit (LCD) which, in fact, can be positive (a deficit) or negative (a surplus, that is, consumption is lower than labor income). This difference between consumption and labor income has to be financed with reallocations through the three ways illustrated on the right-hand side of Eq. (2): asset-based reallocations (ABR)—measured as the difference between asset income and savings (YA-S), net public transfers (TG) or net family transfers (TF)—in both cases calculated as the difference between inflows (+) and outflows (−), that is:

$$LCD = ABR + TG + TF \qquad (3)$$

It should be stressed that Eq. (3) holds both for the whole economy and for each specific age group for which NTA is obtained. During nonproductive ages (essentially childhood and retirement), the LCD is expected to be positive (a deficit), while during most of the working age, it should be negative (a surplus). When positive, the LCD needs to be financed via the three mechanisms on the right-hand side of Eq. (3).

For example, children would be expected to finance their LCD primarily via family transfers (TF) and public transfers (TG), such as education and health services, ABR being almost nonexistent.

In the case of the elderly, they receive, especially in developed countries, a high amount of TG (mainly pensions and health) and probably use ABR (dissaving, asset income), while TF would be limited, even negative (transfers from the old to younger family members), if the other two mechanisms are sufficiently developed. When the LCD is negative, labor income is higher than consumption, so individuals can save, although they typically pay more in taxes than they receive in public transfers. Eq. (3) highlights an interesting characteristic of the so-called generational economy: the standard of living of the society is heavily dependent on the success of the working-age population in generating sufficient resources to finance the LCD of the two economically dependent age groups (children and the elderly). This means that the population age structure is a critical factor in the analysis.

For illustration purposes, **Figure 1** shows NTA estimations for six selected countries. In particular, it shows the per capita age profiles of consumption (C) and labor income (YL) as stated in the left-hand side of the previous Eq. (2), as well as the LCD (the difference between them). All the profiles are estimated in terms of the average per capita labor income for ages 30–49, the standard normalization method employed in NTA in order to ease international comparisons. **Figure 1** allows verification of the expected inverted U-shape of labor income during working ages, with small differences between countries in the age pattern, the age of maximum wage, and also at the exit ages of the labor market. As for consumption, the pattern is also similar across countries, presenting some divergences for old ages, when some countries present an increase in per capita consumption (the United States, the United Kingdom from age 50; France and Sweden from age 75), while it remains quite stable in others (Spain and China).

NTA estimates require complex estimation procedures that combine NA aggregates, household surveys, and other external sources. NA aggregates need to be reclassified in the relevant categories shown in previous equations, subject to the availability of microdata, allowing variables to be imputed by age. Micro data come from household surveys including data on consumption and/or income, taxes, and transfers. External information on transfers and public consumption is employed to improve or complement the information given by household surveys. This procedure is standardized in order to make estimates comparable, while it is conditional on the data existing in each country. In some cases, it has been possible to obtain estimates using harmonized international surveys. In the case of Europe, several projects have obtained (AGENTA, WELTRANSIM) or are obtaining (WELLCARE, SUSTAINWELL) estimates combining the European Union Statistics on Income and Living Conditions (EU-SILC) and the Household Budget Survey (HBS) and other harmonized surveys for European countries.[1]

[1] The AGENTA Project obtained the first set of standard NTA estimates using EU surveys (available at http://dataexplorer.wittgensteincentre.org/nta/). WELTRANSIM Project (https://www.weltransim.eu/) built disaggregated NTA by education level and family type in four European countries. SUSTAINWELL project, starting soon, will extend these efforts to more European countries, building more standard estimates and going deeper at micro level, while WELLCARE (www.ub.edu/wellcare) is extending NTA to measure in more detail all the elements defining the economy of care.

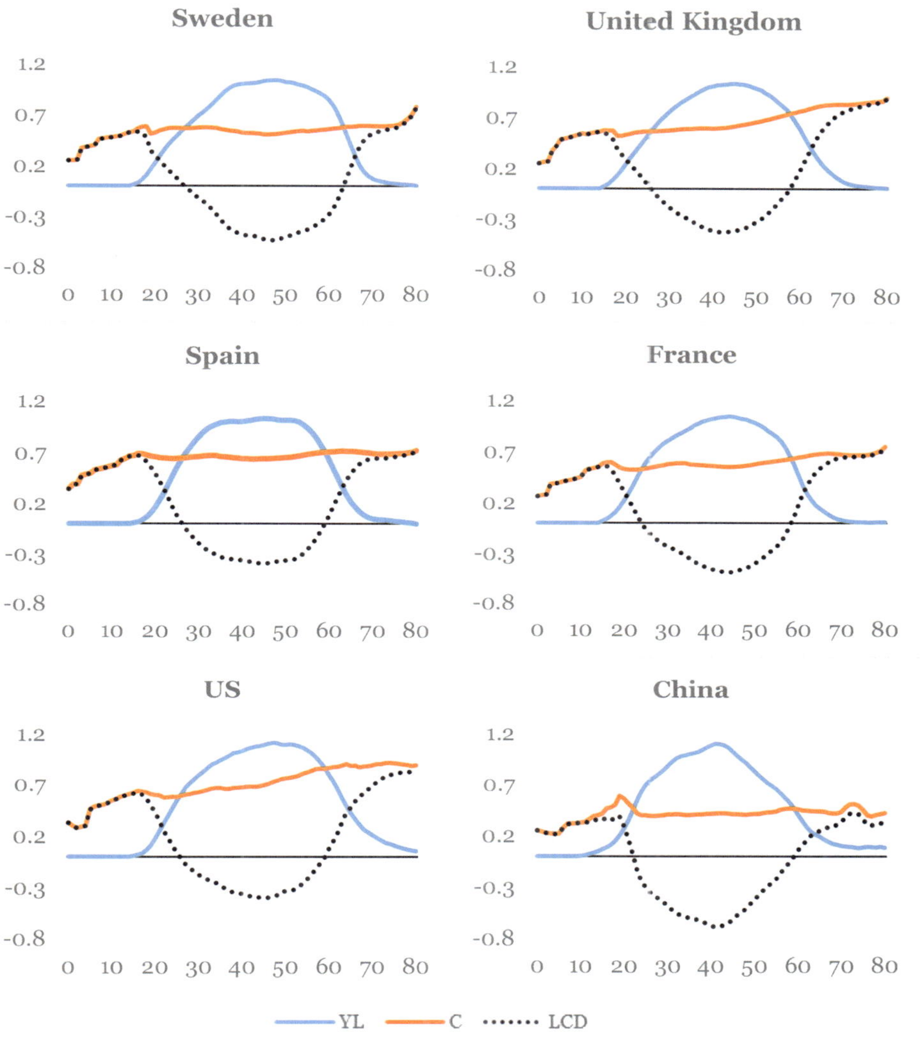


**Figure 1.**
*Per capita age profiles of consumption (C), labor income (YL), and lifecycle deficit (LCD) in selected countries (in terms of the national average labor income for ages 30–49). Source: Authors' elaboration with data extracted from AGENTA project (http://dataexplorer.wittgensteincentre.org/nta/) for European countries and NTA project (www.ntaccounts.org) for US and China. Estimations for AGENTA countries referred to year 2010, to 2003 for the US and 2002 for China.*

## 3. Incorporating nonmarket activities: the national time transfer accounts

It is well-known that the macroeconomic aggregates do not consider those activities that are not exchanged through the market. Neither does traditional NTA, as it is consistent with NA. However, human well-being rely, in large part, on these kinds of activities, such as housework and care for/by other family members, to cite two of the most remarkable. For that reason, a thorough analysis of the generational economy requires the consideration of all kinds of production and consumption activities and how resources are shared by the individuals living at the same moment.

Moreover, incorporating nonmarket activities is a necessary condition for a proper analysis of the generational economy from a gender perspective as, typically, women are more specialized in nonmarket activities, while men are more specialized in market production.

The so-called National Time Transfers Accounts (NTTA) is the natural extension of NTA to measure and value the resources produced, consumed, and shared in society aside from the markets (see [4] for an excellent review of the method). NTTA uses the information collected in time-use surveys to estimate age profiles of production and consumption of nonmarket activities, typically differentiating housework and care. Unlike market production, home production cannot be saved. Hence, consumption must equal production at a given moment of time, in aggregate terms. Differences arise at each age group, leading to transfers. The real interest in measuring nonmarket activities lies in knowing the total production in a society, and how it is shared by the different community members. Once the age profiles (in this case, production, consumption, and transfers) have been estimated in terms of time, in a second step, they need to be monetized and finally aggregated to the standard NTA in order to capture the whole picture of the generational economy.

Counting Women's' Work project (CWW) summarizes estimations of NTTA in different countries around the world, allowing for interesting comparisons. For example, in India, total nonmarket production is estimated as 45% of the national GDP, while only 21% in Turkey (**Figure 2**). Nonmarket activities are also important in developed countries, such as United States (31%) and Spain (24%).

Regarding the distribution by gender, NTTA estimations confirm that women perform the majority of nonmarket activities around the world, while market production is led by men (**Figure 3**). Developed countries show higher participation of men in nonmarket activities, although still far from an equal share.

**Figure 4** details the age profiles of time devoted by men and women to nonmarket activities in four European countries, estimated in AGENTA project using harmonized

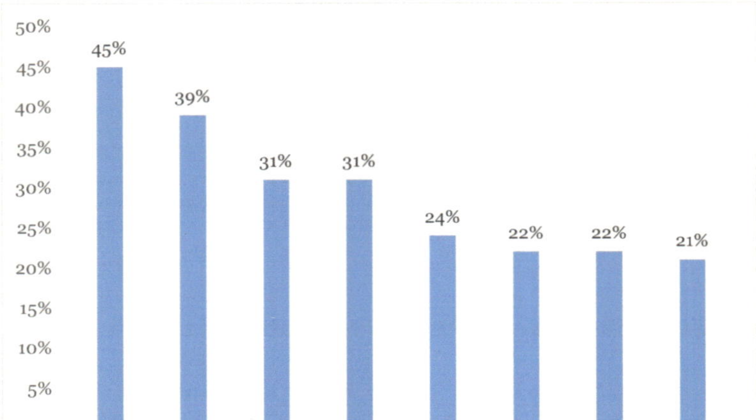


**Figure 2.**
*Estimation of the contribution of nonmarket economy to GDP in different countries. Source: Authors' elaboration with data from CWW, based on NTTA estimates for each country (https://www.countingwomenswork.org/).*

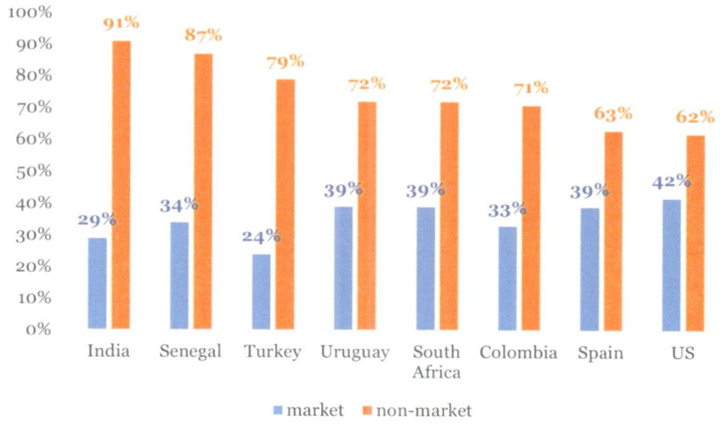


**Figure 3.**
*Estimation of women's contribution to market and nonmarket production in different countries. Source: Authors' elaboration with data from CWW, based on NTTA estimates for each country (https://www.countingwomenswork.org/).*

time use surveys collected in HETUS 2000.[2] We have selected four countries, representative of the four well-known welfare state models: Sweden for the Nordic system; United Kingdom for the Anglo-Saxon; France for the Conservative, and Spain for the Mediterranean.[3] In all four countries, the gender gap in time devoted to household production is remarkable, but interesting features can be identified. Sweden shows the lowest difference in total time devoted to home production between men and women, while Spain presents the highest, with the UK and France somewhere in between. This gender difference is higher during working ages, and particularly coinciding with early parenthood ages, while it tends to decrease later and follow a different path: after age 50 in Sweden, 60 in France and Austria, and 65 in Spain, although it remains clearly higher in this last country. Gender differences for working ages are likely related to female participation in the labor market (the highest in Sweden, the lowest in Spain), which in turn is linked to the welfare state organization. Nordic welfare state is based on policies promoting female employment, while Mediterranean countries had much weaker family policies by the beginning of the 21st century (the period of the data employed in the estimations). **Figure 4** also shows that, from age 50–55, when childrearing practically disappears, housework production increases for both men and women and it starts to decrease again at very old ages (70–75+). It is worth mentioning that time devoted to home production by women is always the highest in Spain, while exactly the opposite happens for men (the lowest at any age in this country).

Several studies using more recent data show some convergence of the gender profiles, although a gender gap still remains in the majority of countries. For example, in [7], the 2010 wave of the Spanish Time Use Survey is employed use the 2010 wave of the Spanish national TUS to obtain closer age profiles for men and women than those estimated previously in AGENTA, although the gender gap is still high compared to other countries.

---

[2] Data available in AGENTA dataexplorer (http://dataexplorer.wittgensteincentre.org/nta/). The estimations are based on data from HETUS (wave 1). See [5] for a description of the methodology and the results.

[3] See [6] for an analysis of how to use NTA to study the organization of the welfare state and its socioeconomic implications.

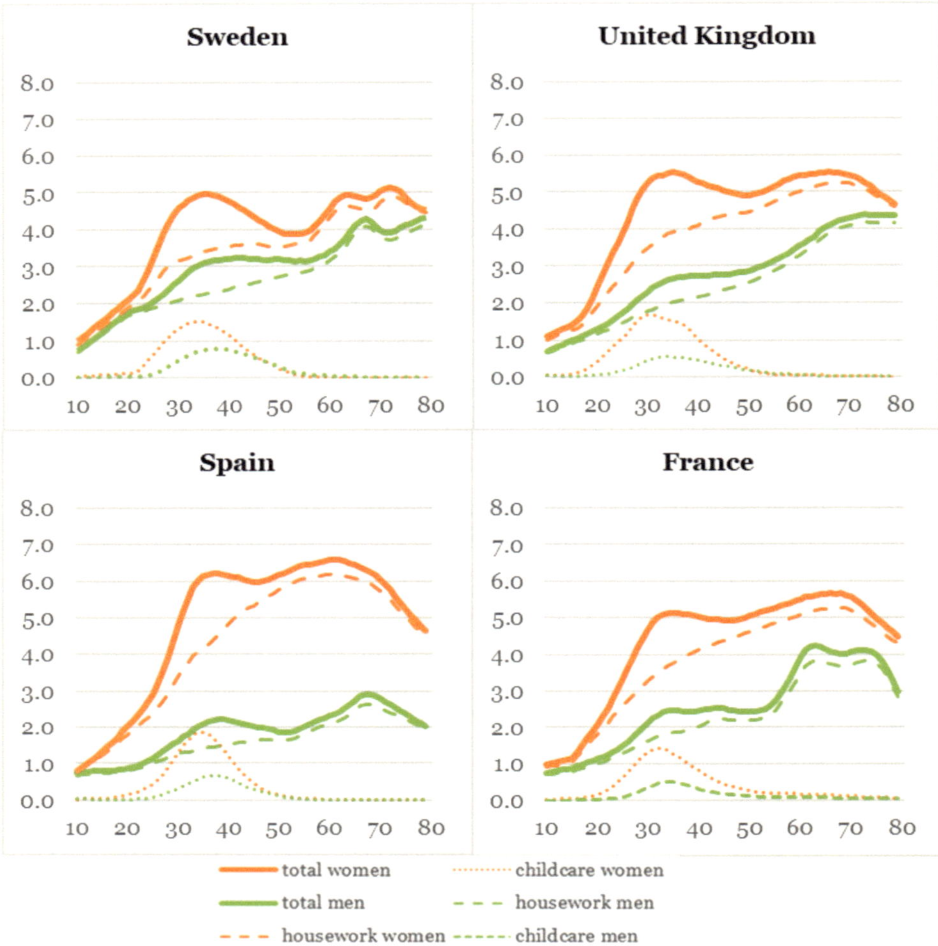


**Figure 4.**
*Per capita age profiles of time devoted to nonmarket activities by gender in four European countries (in hours per day). Note: Total profiles of nonmarket activities collect childcare, housework, and interhousehold production (nonmarket services provided to outside the own household). Source: Authors' elaboration with data from AGENTA project, available at: http://www.agenta-project.eu/en/dataexplorer.htm. Estimations refer to year 1999 (France), 2001 (Sweden, the UK), and 2002 (Spain).*

The difference between nonmarket production and consumption is called nonmarket LCD, symmetrically to the LCD obtained from the traditional NTA. **Figure 5** shows the age profiles of monetized nonmarket LCD in the same four countries shown above, again differentiated by gender. For ages 0–10, the LCD matches consumption, as there is no production. The first remarkable feature is the difference in the level of profiles, caused by the monetization method: as wages are much lower in Spain than the other countries considered, although Spanish women dedicate more hours to home production, the total value of their outcome is significantly lower. Therefore, in central working ages, the nonmarket surplus for Spanish women is the lowest, and it barely exists for men. Second, it is clearly observed that the surplus period for men is much shorter, and it coincides with the childrearing period. After age 45–50, it becomes a deficit for the rest of their lifecycle, while women start with

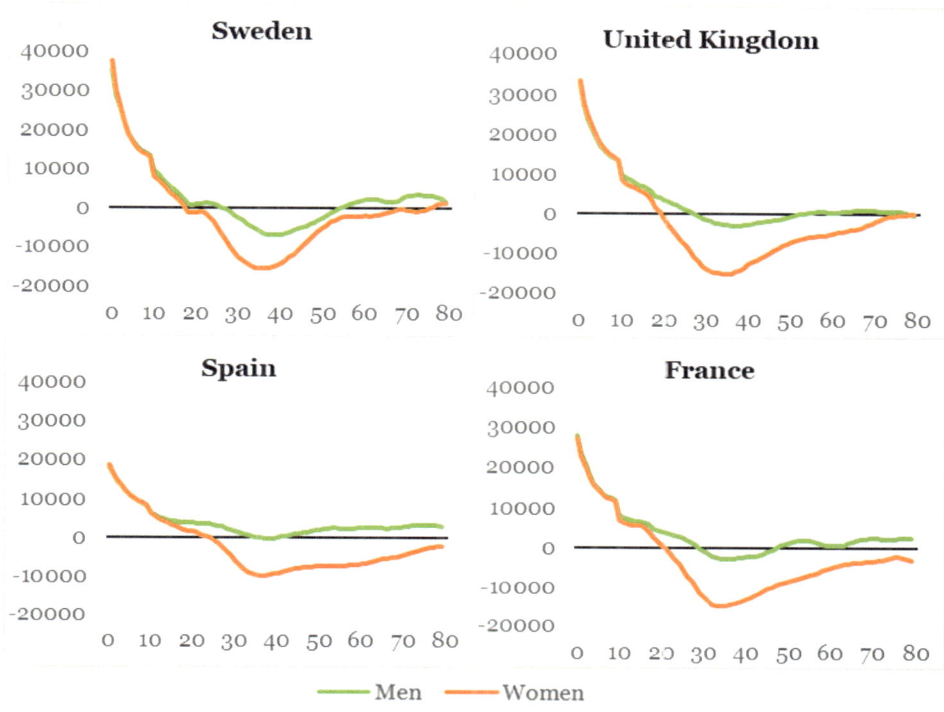


**Figure 5.**
*Per capita age profiles of nonmarket lifecycle deficit by gender in four European countries (in € per year). Source: Authors' elaboration with data from AGENTA project (available at: http://www.agenta-project.eu/en/dataexplorer.htm).*

their surplus at younger ages (20–25), and it remains for the rest of their lives (only in Sweden does it finish at very old ages).

Traditional NTA disaggregated by gender typically shows a less favorable lifecycle deficit profile for women, especially during working ages, reflecting both their lower participation and the gender wage gap in the labor market. Incorporating NTTA into traditional NTA would help to properly understand how society is actually organized as regards production, consumption, and sharing of resources. Some studies combining NTTA with NTA profiles include [8] for Germany, [9] for Italy, [10] for Hungary (although in this case results are not disaggregated by gender), and more recently [11] for 15 European countries. For illustration purposes, **Figure 6** shows the estimations of market and total LCD for Spain in 2010, using AGENTA data for NTA and results in [7] for NTTA. As expected, the differences in lifecycle deficit between men and women shrink when monetized NTTA profiles are aggregated to the traditional NTA (solid lines). It is worth mentioning that, as previously obtained in [7], Spanish women spend more time working than men at any age, although they participate less in the labor market. However, as the monetary value assigned to domestic production is low, women present a lower total surplus over working ages.[4] From age 65, however,

[4] In [11] the opposite result for Spain is obtained: a higher total contribution for women. This is due to the fact that they use a different valuation method to monetize NTTA profiles, in particular the average net wage of the economy instead of the replacement method. Moreover, they argue that these results can be regarded as a lower bound of alternative valuations of unpaid work in relation to paid work.

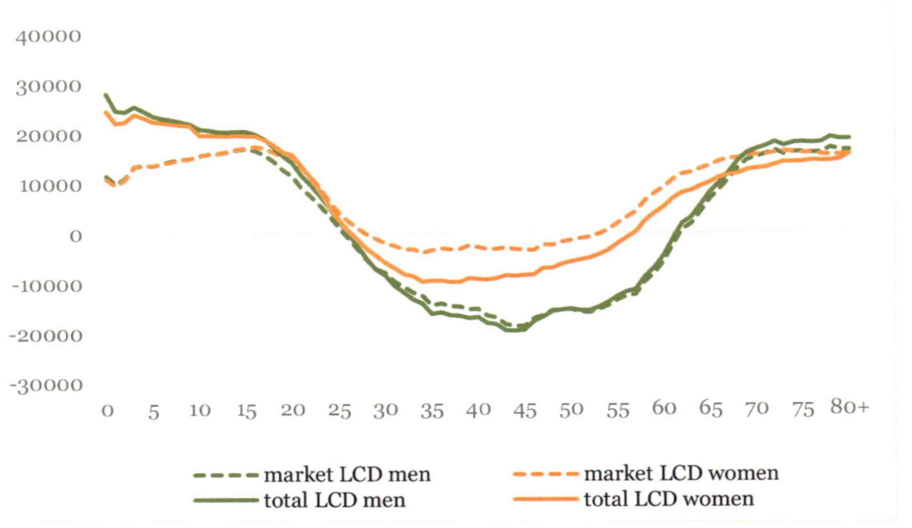


**Figure 6.**
*Per capita age profiles of market and total lifecycle deficit (LCD) in Spain (2010) (in € per year). Source: Authors' elaboration with data from [7] for nonmarket, and AGENTA project (available at: http://www.agenta-project.eu/en/dataexplorer.htm) for market. In both cases, data refer to 2010.*

as labor income disappears and only market production remains, the total deficit becomes higher for men.

## 4. Some applications of NTA data

### 4.1 The effects of the demographic transition on economic development: measuring the demographic dividend

In this section, we include applications related to the use of NTA data to evaluate the impact of the demographic transition on economic development. That process started in Western countries, which are already experiencing the aging process, followed by middle and low-income countries.[5] After several attempts to analyze the interplay between demographics and economic growth, population age structure was explicitly introduced in the analysis by Bloom and Williamson [13]. They coined the term "demographic gift" to refer to the positive effect on economic development in the early stages of the demographic transition, when the working-age population relatively increases with respect to those on the extremes of the lifecycle (children and the elderly). The term was later renamed the demographic dividend (see [14]), defined as the growth rate of the support ratio (working age divided by total population). All countries, through the demographic transition to aging societies, have (had) a demographic dividend period (understood as positive growth of their support ratio).

[5] An outstanding example of the cross- fertilization between economics and demographics literature is Galor's Unified Growth Theory in [12], which extends endogenous growth models to introduce a changing demographic structure.

In the analysis of the demographic dividend, NTA becomes a valuable source of data, as it allows demographic indicators to be enriched with economic content. In particular, NTA is used to transform the pure demographic support ratio into an economic support ratio, computed by dividing the number of effective producers (instead of the working-age population) by the number of effective consumers (instead of the total population). Effective producers are computed by multiplying the working population by the per capita age profile of labor income, while effective consumers are the product of the total population and the per capita age profile of consumption. Among the papers using NTA in the analysis of the demographic dividend, it is worth mentioning the seminal one by Mason [15], followed by others such as [16–18]. Estimations show that most high-income countries have already finished their demographic dividend period and are right now in a postdividend stage (see [18]), with decreasing economic support ratios. In particular, this is the case of European countries, as shown in **Figure 7**, reproduced from [19].

In Ref. [20], Mason and Lee took a step forward by introducing a possible second demographic dividend, which would follow the first under certain circumstances. The idea behind the second demographic dividend is simple: in aging societies, as people live longer, they have incentives to save more and accumulate assets during their working ages. This would eventually lead to an economy more capital intensive and possibly to higher productivity. However, this second demographic dividend is not automatic, and it will highly depend on agents' behavior and public policies (for instance, individuals may not incentivized to save for their old age if they trust in the government and/or their families to care about them). Again, NTA is a precious source of data for estimations of the second demographic dividend (see [18] for the most recent results in this line).

An additional element to consider is the fact that the demographic transition has coincided in time with another relevant event affecting population composition: the education expansion. Indeed, the population has not only changed in terms of age structure but also in its level of education, as the educational attainment of

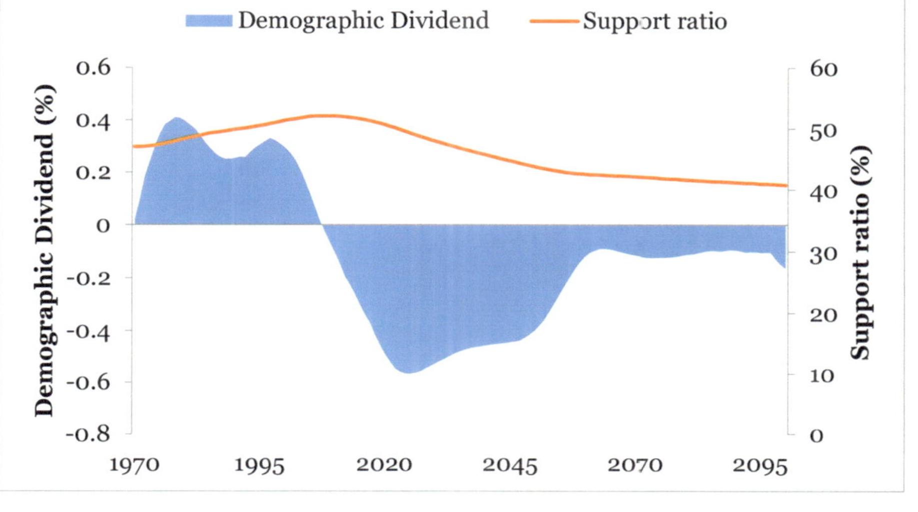


**Figure 7.**
*Support ratio and demographic dividend in Europe, 1970–2100. Source: Reproduced from [19].*

the younger generations has been growing steadily (although not homogenously) around the world. Although some research has been devoted to analyzing the role of education in economic development (see [21] for a review), only a few studies have considered the change both in age structure and in level of education. Again, the information provided by NTA is especially valuable for this kind of analysis if the age profiles are differentiated by educational attainment. In Ref. [22], authors used NTA disaggregated by level of education in Spain and Mexico, two countries with different path in the demographic transition, to disentangle the age and education effects on the demographic dividend. They performed a simulation exercise using the population projections by level of education in [23]. Their results (**Figure 8**) show that the education effect has always been higher than the age effect in the demographic dividend. Moreover, it could continue to be positive (although decreasing) throughout the twenty-first century, while the age effect became negative for Spain before 2020 (a little later in Mexico). In Spain, the effects of the sharp demographic transition caused by the baby boom (from 1957 to 1977) and the subsequent baby bust are clearly visible, leading to a strong decrease in the age effect from 2015 to 2040 (coinciding with the retirement of those numerous generations).

In Ref. [22], the authors employ a mechanical projection method combining NTA profiles and other economic information with population projections. There are a variety of projection strategies that allow the different dimensions of the complex interaction among economics and demographics to be captured to a different extent. In a later work [24], an Overlapping Generations (OLG) model is used, calibrated with NTA data, individuals being heterogeneous according to their level of education, to isolate age and education effects in the demographic dividend in Spain historically (1850–2000). In this case, the OLG model structure allowed the endogenous evolution of capital intensity and productivity (all aspects of the second demographic dividend) to be captured. They found that age transition explains

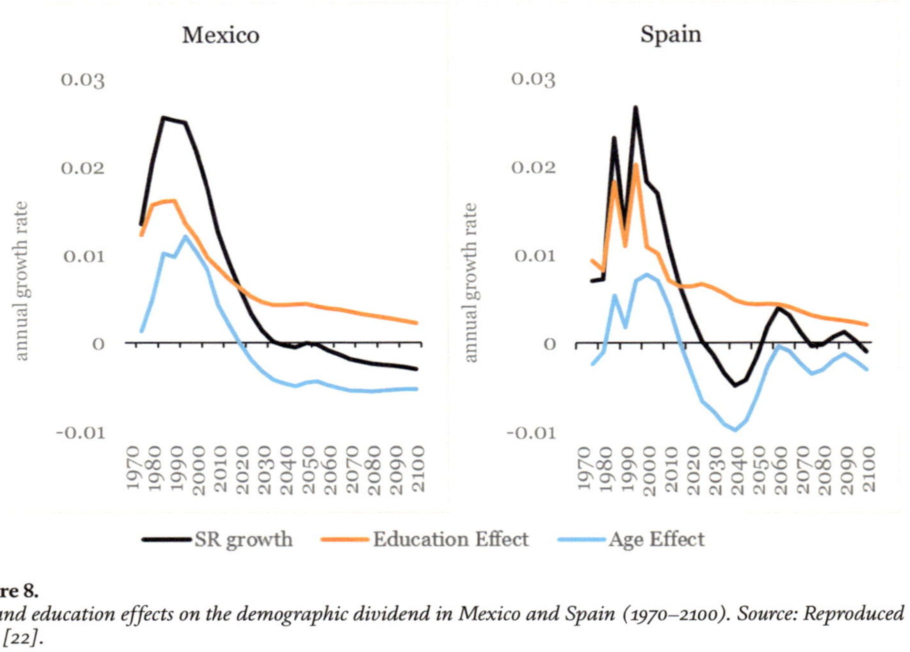


**Figure 8.**
*Age and education effects on the demographic dividend in Mexico and Spain (1970–2100). Source: Reproduced from [22].*

around 17% of the per capita growth ratio in the period, while education expansion accounts for nearly 10%.[6]

Finally, more recently, NTA estimates and population projections were used in [25] to investigate how aging would restructure global GDP as a result of the continuation of the demographic transition. Overall, NTA has proved to be a valuable data source to enrich the analysis of the effects of aging on economic development.

### 4.2 Analyzing the welfare state: who is actually protected?

This section summarizes how NTA has been used to analyze the role and development of the welfare state. This institution is, undoubtedly, one of the main social achievements of the past century. It aims to ensure a minimum quality of life for all citizens, regardless of any other condition. Although it was created with a clear vocation of redistributing resources from the rich to the poor, nowadays, the most important social transfers actually act as intergenerational redistribution devices. This is the case of the three main pillars of the welfare state (education, health, and pensions), which redistribute resources from working-age people (who bear the highest taxes) to economically dependent ages: children (mainly through public education) and, especially, the elderly, who are the main recipients of public pensions and health services. As a whole, the welfare state is organized as a pay-as-you-go (PAYGO) system, in which the available resources at any given time (obtained from social contributions and taxes mainly raised from the working-age population) are distributed among the recipients of social transfers (mainly on the two lifecycle tails). For this reason, the population age structure is crucial to keep it running. Demographic change, together with the PAYGO financial rule, inevitably implies intergenerational redistribution. This is more explicit in the public pension system (organized as a PAYGO system in most countries), while it is also present by definition in the education and health system (which are also financed through an implicit PAYGO scheme).

NTA provides valuable information to observe how the welfare state effectively works by redistributing resources across generations at a given moment. The age profiles of taxes and public transfers paid/received at each age in each country inform about both the relative size of the welfare state and its specific composition (which social transfers are more important). Although, as expected, NTA data show that the level of development of the welfare state is not homogenous across countries, a common feature is almost universal: the welfare state tends to protect the elderly much more than children. This is clearly observed in **Figure 9**, built with NTA data of per capita public transfers received by the elderly (65+) and the young (0–24) in 15 different countries, with regard to their level of consumption. **Figure 9** shows important differences across countries in the protection of the elderly and children, it always being much higher for the former than the latter. In Finland, the country with the highest transfers to the young, the government funds 46% of children's consumption, while in the UK it hardly reaches 20%. For the elderly, the differences are much larger, going from 99% of public financing of elderly consumption in Sweden to just 28% in the US.

6 In this case, the OLG model structure allowed the endogenous evolution of capital intensity and hence the second demographic dividend to be captured. There are a variety of projection strategies that allow the different dimensions of the complex interaction among economics and demographics to be captured in different ways.

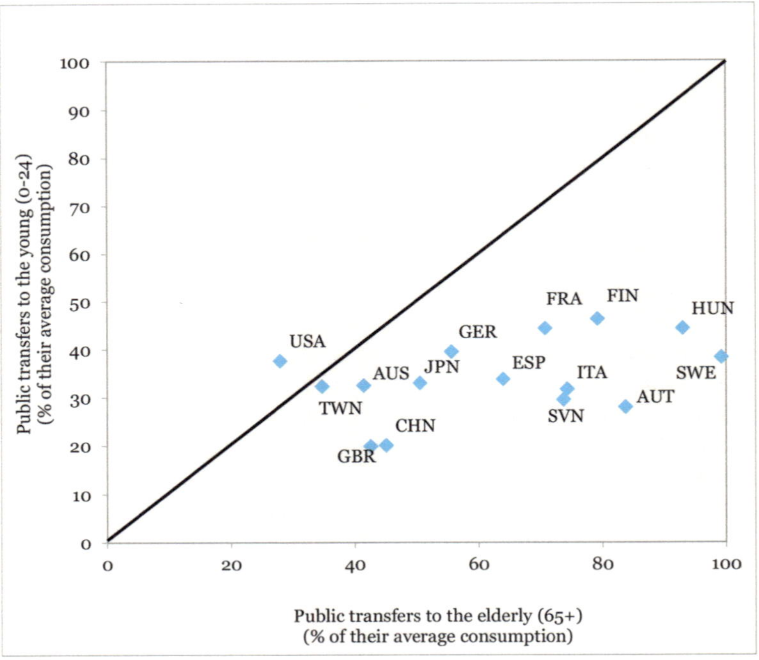


**Figure 9.**
*Public transfers received by children (ages 0–24) and the elderly (ages 65+) as a percentage of their average consumption. Source: Authors' elaboration with data from NTA project (www.ntaccounts.org). Data correspond to years 2003 (Sweden-SWE), 2004 (Japan-JPN), 2005 (Hungary-HUN), 2006 (Finland-FIN), 2007 (United Kingdom-GBR and China CHN), 2008 (Germany-GER, Italy-ITA and Spain-ESP), 2010 (Australia-AUS, Austria-AUT, Slovenia-SVN and Taiwan-TWN) and 2011 (France—FRA and the US—USA).*

Overall, **Figure 9** informs that, to some extent, the public sector has replaced the traditional role of families in caring for their elders, socializing ("from all to all") this duty in most European countries. However, the welfare state has not evolved in the same line as regards childrearing, which has mainly remained as a family duty, aside from this socialization process.

This fact has been analyzed using standard NTA (see, for example, [26, 27]). Recently, in [28], NTA data have been used to go a step forward, analyzing the interplay between the welfare state and private transfers as redistribution devices at both inter and intragenerational levels. The authors chose four European countries representing the four different welfare state regimes: Austria (Conservative), Finland (Nordic), Spain (Mediterranean), and the UK (Anglo-Saxon). By employing a microsimulation model, authors can project the cross-sectional NTA age profiles disaggregated by gender, educational level, and family structure, simulating the lifetime net transfers received by individuals from both the government and the private sphere (mainly the family). Their analysis confirms the expected results by gender and educational level, showing interesting differences according to the welfare state regime. For instance, a gender gap in labor income is present across countries independently of the level of education. When differentiating by parenthood status, the gender gap remains but is always larger for parents. Moreover, fathers tend to earn more labor income than childless men, while the opposite happens to women. Austria (conservative welfare state regime) shows the highest difference in labor income between mothers and nonmothers, while Finland (social-democratic) presents the lowest, probably due to public policies promoting full employment.

More interestingly, the microsimulation exercise performed in [28] computes an estimation of the total (public and private) transfers to be received by the generation born in 2010 according to their level of education and parenthood status over their whole lifecycle. Results are summarized in **Figure 10**. Private transfers received are positive for any country and educational level, being larger for the childless: they receive resources from their parents when they are children, but later, they do not have to rear their own children. Public transfers, however, show differences. First, they are positive for low and medium levels of education but negative for the highly educated (revealing that this group pays more taxes than benefits received, contributing to the distributional role of the welfare state). More interestingly, the net

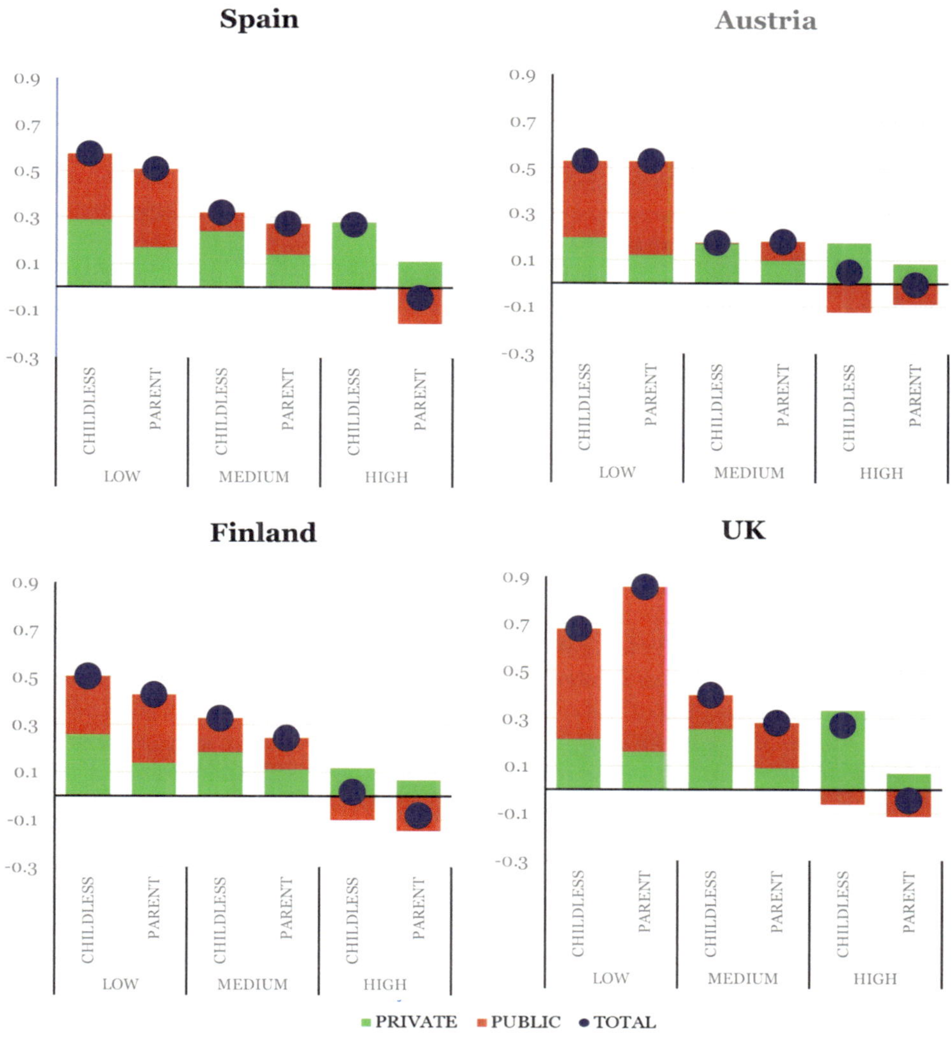


**Figure 10.**
*Lifetime net transfers as a share of lifetime labor income for representative individuals born in 2010 (by educational level and parenthood status). Source: Reproduced from [28].*

contribution of highly educated parents is higher than that of the childless, except in Austria. Second, public transfers received tend to be higher for parents but, with the sole exception of the low educated in the UK, they are not enough to equal the total amount received by childless people. Austria shows a similar amount of total transfers for low and medium-educated parents and nonparents, but this is not the case for the highly educated, for the medium and high levels of education in the UK, or for Finland and Spain in any educational attainment.

## 5. Final remarks

This chapter outlines the National Transfer Accounts (NTA) method and gives an updated account of some of the main applications developed so far. NTA breaks down National Accounts by age. More specifically, it identifies the age pattern of Life Cycle Deficit (LCD)—defined as the difference between consumption and labor income at any age—and it measures how the surplus at working age is transferred to dependent ages through the three available resource allocation devices (assets market and public and private transfers). A key feature of the methodology is to offer, for the first time, an explicit account of the private transfers given and received through the family. Moreover, National Time Transfer Accounts (NTTA) complete the picture by estimating production, consumption, and transfers of home production (in terms of time) also occurring in the private sphere.

NTA estimates offer valuable information to analyze the interaction between economics and demographic change and the political process that led to the development of the welfare state. NTA data are increasingly used in this direction, while some applications have been developed within the project. In this work, we have focused on two main applications. In Section 4.1, we gave an account of different attempts to investigate the interplay between demographic and economic development. First, NTA estimates allow us to measure the extent to which, at the earlier stages of the demographic transition, a demographic dividend occurs while the working population grows faster than the total population. Second, NTA data help to investigate the extent to which this first dividend can be followed by a second demographic dividend as long as positive effects arise from the education transition and/or from capital intensification.

Section 4.2 focuses on the lessons that NTA data offer on the income redistribution produced by the welfare state at inter and intragenerational levels. NTA and NTTA provide a better understanding of the roots of the gender differences observed in production and, consequently, in the LCD. They can also be employed to measure the extent to which parents might end up subsidizing childless individuals if public transfers do not compensate for the lower private transfers received by parents over their lifecycle.

Overall, the contribution of NTA to enrich the analysis of the economic effects of aging is undeniable. Today, most high-income countries have completed their demographic transition. They can only expect positive effects of aging on economic growth through improvements in worker productivity, coming from capital accumulation and/or further improvements in educational attainment. Interestingly, their experience could greatly help developing countries, which started their demographic transition much later. They can still benefit from the demographic dividend to shape better policies and foster the second demographic dividend. For these countries, the availability of rigorous analysis about how public policies can help to make the most of the demographic dividend period is crucial.

## Acknowledgements

Financial support was received by the WELLCARE project (a project of the Horizon 2020 Joint Program Initiative More Years, Better Lives, grant numbers PCI2021-121913 and PCI2021-121975); and the Spanish Ministry of Science, Innovation, and Universities, Spain (grant number PID2020-114040RB-I00).

The authors thank their co-authors Marian Fink, Thomas Hovarth, Tanja Istenic, Ivan Mejía-Guevara, Elisenda Rentería, and Martin Spielauer, for agreeing to reproduce some of our common research results in several figures in this chapter. Likewise, the authors are especially grateful to Ron Lee and Andy Mason, the NTA project founder members, who have always supported and encouraged our work in this project. They have also agreed their results on estimations of the demographic dividend in Europe to be reproduced in this chapter (**Figure 7**).

## Author details

Gemma Abio[1], Concepció Patxot[1*] and Guadalupe Souto[2]

1 Department of Economics, Universitat de Barcelona, Barcelona, Spain

2 Department of Applied Economics, Universitat Autonoma Barcelona, Barcelona, Spain

*Address all correspondence to: cio.patxot@ub.edu

## References

[1] United Nations. World Population Prospects 2022. UN Population Division. 2022. Available from: https://population.un.org/dataportal/home [Accessed: January 9, 2023].

[2] Mason A, Lee R, editors. Population Aging and the Generational Economy: A Global Perspective. Chentelham: Edward Elgar; 2011. DOI: 10.4337/9780857930583

[3] United Nations. National Transfer Accounts Manual: Measuring and Analysing the Generational Economy. New York: Population Division, Department of Economic and Social Affairs, United Nations; 2013

[4] Donehower G. Methodology of the National Time Transfers Accounts. In: Urdinola P, Tovar J, editors. Time Use and Transfers in the Americas. Cham, Switzerland: Springer; 2019. pp. 5-40. DOI: 10.1007/978-3-030-11806-8

[5] Vargha L, Seme A, Gál R, Hamer B, Sambt, J. Manual of NTTA methodology and guidelines to the AGENTA NTTA data explorer. AGENTA project, deliverable D.2.3: 2016. Available from: http://www.agenta-project.eu/Jacomo/upload/publications/d-2.3-submitted.pdf [Accessed: December 10, 2022]

[6] Istenič T, Vargha L, Sambt J. Is there a connection between welfare regimes and inter-age reallocation systems? The Journal of the Economics of Ageing. 2019;**14**:art. 100202. DOI: 10.1016/j.jeoa.2019.100202

[7] Rentería E, Scandurra R, Souto G, Patxot C. Intergenerational money and time transfers by gender in Spain: Who are the actual dependents? Demographic Research. 2016;**34**:689-704. DOI: /10.1080/13545701.2011.582822

[8] Kluge FA. The economic lifecycle by gender–results combining monetary and time use estimates. Comparative Population Studies. 2014;**39**(4):707-726. DOI: 10.12765/CPoS-2014-13en

[9] Zannella M. Reallocation of resources between generations and genders in the market and non-market economy. The case of Italy. The Journal of the Economics of Ageing. 2015;**5**:33-44. DOI: 10.1016/j.jeoa.2014.09.003

[10] Gál RI, Szabó E, Vargha L. The age-profile of invisible transfers: The true size of asymmetry in inter-age reallocations. The Journal of the Economics of Ageing. 2015;**5**:98-104. DOI: 10.1016/j.jeoa.2014.09.010

[11] Hammer B, Spitzer S, Vargha L, Istenič T. The gender dimension of intergenerational transfers in Europe. The Journal of the Economics of Ageing. 2020;**2020**(15):100234. DOI: 10.1016/j.jeoa.2019.100234

[12] Galor O. From stagnation to growth: Unified growth theory. In: Aghion P, Durlauf S, editors. Handbook of Economic Growth. Vol. 1. Amsterdam: Elsevier; 2005. pp. 171-293. DOI: 10.1016/S1574-0684(05)01004-X

[13] Bloom DE, Williamson JG. Demographic transitions and economic miracles in emerging Asia. World Bank Economic Review. 1998;**12**(3):419-456. DOI: 10.1093/wber/12.3.419

[14] Bloom DE, Canning D, Sevilla J. The Demographic Dividend: A New Perspective on the Economic Consequences of Population Change. Santa Monica, CA: RAND; 2003. DOI: 10.7249/MR1274

[15] Mason A. Demographic transition and demographic dividends in developed

and developing countries. In: United Nations Expert Group Meeting on Social and Economic Implications of Changing Population Age Structure. New York: United Nations Population Division. Mexico; 2005 UN/POP/PD/2005/2. Available from: https://www.un.org/development/desa/pd/sites/www.un.org.development.desa.pd/files/unpd_egm_200508_09_mason.pdf [Accessed: October 10, 2022]

[16] Lee R, Mason A. Fertility, human capital, and economic growth over the demographic transition. European Journal of Population. 2010;**2010**(26):159-182. DOI: 10.1007/s10680-009-9186-x

[17] Mason A, Lee R, Jiang JX. Demographic dividends, human capital, and saving. The Journal of the Economics of Ageing. 2016;**7**:106-122. DOI: 10.1016/j.jeoa.2016.02.004

[18] Mason A, Lee R, Abrigo M, Lee S-H. Support ratios and demographic dividends: Estimates for the world. In: Population Division, Department of Economic and Social Affairs, Technical Paper 2017/1. New York: United Nations Publications; 2017

[19] Lee R, Mason A. The Demographic Dividend, an Opportunity for the Development of the Economy and the Welfare State. Barcelona: The Social Observatory, La Caixa Foundation; 2021. Available from: https://elobservatoriosocial.fundacionlacaixa.org/en/-/el-dividendo-demografico-una-oportunidad-para-el-desarrollo-de-la-economia-y-del-estado-del-bienestar [Accessed: November 25, 2022]

[20] Mason A, Lee R. Reform and support systems for the elderly in developing countries: Capturing the second demographic dividend. Genus. 2006;**52**(2):11-35. DOI: 10.2307/29789308

[21] Johnes G, Johnes J, editors. International Handbook of the Economics of Education. Cheltenham: Edward Elgar; 2004. p. 872. DOI: 10.1080/00131940802368562

[22] Rentería E, Souto G, Mejía-Guevara I, Patxot C. The effect of education on the demographic dividend. Population and Development Review. 2016;**42**(4):651-671. DOI: 10.1111/padr.12017

[23] Lutz W, Butz WP, KC S. World population and human capital in the twenty-first century. In: Wittgenstein Centre Data Explorer. Oxford: Oxford University Press; 2014 Version 1.2

[24] Sánchez-Romero M, Abio G, Patxot C, Souto G. Contribution of demography to economic growth. SERIEs. 2018;**9**(1):27-64. DOI: 10.1007/s13209-017-0164-y

[25] Mason A, Lee R, members of the NTA network. Six ways population change is affecting the global economy. Population and Development Review. 2022;**48**(1):51-73. DOI: 10.1111/padr.12469

[26] Patxot C, Rentería E, Sanchez-Romero M, Souto G. Measuring the balance of government intervention on forward and backward family transfers using NTA estimates: The modified Lee arrows. International Tax and Public Finance. 2012;**19**:442-461. DOI: 10.1007/s10797-012-9220-5

[27] Gál R, Vanhuysse P, Vargha L. Pro-elderly welfare states within child-oriented societies. Journal of European Public Policy. 2018;**25**:944-958. DOI: 10.1080/13501763.2017.1401112

[28] Spielauer M, Horvath T, Fink M, Abio G, Souto G, Patxot C, et al. Measuring the lifecycle impact of welfare state policies in the face of ageing. Economic Analysis and Policy. 2022;**75**: 1-25. DOI: 10.1016/j.eap.2022.05.002